Accounting
for Non-Accounting Students

Accounting
for Non-Accounting Students

FIFTH EDITION

J R Dyson

*The School of Management,
Heriot-Watt University, Edinburgh*

FINANCIAL TIMES
Prentice Hall

An imprint of **Pearson Education**

Harlow, England · London · New York · Reading, Massachusetts · San Francisco · Toronto · Don Mills, Ontario · Sydney
Tokyo · Singapore · Hong Kong · Seoul · Taipei · Cape Town · Madrid · Mexico City · Amsterdam · Munich · Paris · Milan

Pearson Education Limited

Edinburgh Gate
Harlow
Essex CM20 2JE
England

and Associated Companies around the world

Visit us on the World Wide Web at
www.pearsoneduc.com

First edition published in Great Britain under the Pitman Publishing imprint in 1987
Second edition 1991
Third edition 1994
Fourth edition published under the Financial Times Pitman Publishing imprint in 1997
Fifth edition published in 2001

© Pearson Professional Limited 1987, 1991, 1994, 1997
© Pearson Education Limited 2001

The right of John R. Dyson to be identified as author
of this work has been asserted by him in accordance with
the Copyright, Designs and Patents Act 1988.

ISBN 0 273 64683 4

British Library Cataloguing-in-Publication Data
A CIP catalogue record for this book can be obtained from the British Library.

Library of Congress Cataloging-in-Publication Data
A catalog record for this book can be obtained from the Library of Congress.

10 9 8 7 6 5 4 3 2 1
06   05   04   03   02   01

Typeset by 30.
Printed and bound by
Ashford Colour Press Ltd., Gosport

Contents

costs · Production overhead · A comprehensive example · Non-production
overhead · Predetermined absorption rates · Conclusion · Key points · Check
your learning · Group discussion questions · Practice questions

Preface

This is a book for non-accountants. It is intended primarily for students who are required to study accounting as part of a non-accounting degree or professional studies course. It should also be of value to those working in commerce, government or industry who find that their work involves them in dealing with accounting information. It is hoped that the book will help to explain why there is need for such information.

Non-accounting students (such as engineers, personnel managers, purchasing officers, and sales managers) are sometimes unable to understand why they are required to study accounting. This is often found to be the case when they have to take an examination in the subject, especially when they are then presented with a paper of some considerable technical rigour.

Accounting books written specifically for the non-accountant are also often extremely demanding. The subject needs to be covered in such a way that non-accounting students do not become confused by too much technical information. They do not require the same detailed analysis that is only of relevance to the professional accountant. Some accounting books specially written for the non-accountant go to the opposite extreme. They outline the subject so superficially that they are of no real practical help either to examination candidates or to those non-specialists requiring some guidance on practical accounting problems.

The aim of this book is to serve as a good introduction to the study of accounting. The subject is not covered superficially. In certain areas the book goes into considerable detail, but only where it is necessary for a real understanding of the subject. It is appreciated that non-accountants are unlikely to be involved in the *detailed* preparation of accounting information, such as, the compilation of a company's annual accounts. However, if such accounts are to provide the maximum possible benefit to their users, it is desirable that users should have a good knowledge of how they are prepared and how to extract the maximum possible information from them.

This concept is analogous to that of driving a car. It is perfectly possible to drive a car without knowing anything about how it works, although it is useful to know *something* about the engine in order to get the best possible performance from the car. None the less, it is not necessary to know as much about the car as a motor mechanic; all that is required is just sufficient knowledge to be able to drive the car so that it operates at its maximum efficiency. Similarly, it is not absolutely necessary to know how to prepare accounts to be able to use them, but they will mean a great deal more if the user knows something about their construction.

Accounting is now a compulsory subject for many non-accounting students on certificate, diploma and degree courses in colleges and universities. While the syllabuses for such courses have sometimes to be approved by external bodies, their detailed contents are often left to the individual lecturer to determine. This book was written with that type of course very much in mind.

The book is divided into three parts. Part 1 introduces the student to the subject of accounting and the profession of accountancy. Part 2 deals mainly with financial accounting and reporting, while Part 3 is concerned with management accounting.

Many further and higher education institutions have now adopted a modular structure for the delivery of their courses. The book will be useful, therefore, on those modules offered to non-accountants that include elements of both financial accounting and management accounting. However, it will also avoid students having to purchase two textbooks if financial accounting and management accounting are taken in separate modules. Equally, if some chapters in the various parts of the book are not relevant for some syllabuses, module leaders will find that it is quite easy to omit those chapters that do not relate to their particular modules.

The fifth edition

My thanks are due to those lecturers and students who once again have been kind enough to suggest improvements for the new edition. I have tried to take all their recommendations into account. Unfortunately, some of their ideas could not be accommodated because they were either too specialised for non-accounting students or they would add too much to the size of the book. Indeed, one of the objectives of this new edition was to stop it growing! This proved to be enormously difficult, and it has had to be achieved mainly by transferring most of the answers to the 'end of chapter questions' into the *Lecturer's Guide*.

The new edition has been revised and brought up to date and a considerable number of changes have been made. The more significant ones are as follows.

1 The structure of the book has been simplified by reducing the number of parts from six to three. The 20 original chapters have been largely retained, although there has been a slight change in the order of some of them. There is one completely new chapter, two chapters have been merged, one has been extended, and some have been retitled. The details are shown in Table 1.

2 The answers to 'Check your learning' questions at the end of each chapter have been transferred to Appendix 3. The discussion questions are now referred to 'Group discussion questions' and follow on immediately from the 'Check your learning' questions. The 'other' questions and the 'additional' questions have been merged into 'Practice questions'; a few questions have been taken out of the book altogether. The practice ques-

Table 1 Changes to text introduced by fifth edition

New chapter number	New chapter title	Amendments	Old chapter number	Old chapter title
1	The accounting world	Extra material	1	The accounting world
2	Accounting rules	Extra material	2	Accounting rules
3	Recording data	Extra material	3	Recording data
4	Trading entity accounts	Extra material	4	Basic financial accounts
5	Accounting for adjustments	Minor	5	Accounting for adjustments
6	Company accounts	Minor	7	Company accounts
7	Other accounts	Substantial	This is a new chapter that includes part of the old Chapter 6 Manufacturing accounts	
8	Cash flow statements	Substantial	8	Cash flow statements
9	Interpretations of accounts	Minor	9	Interpretation of accounting data
10	Disclosure of information	Minor	10	Disclosure of information
11	The annual report	Minor	11	The annual report
12	Contemporary issues in financial reporting	Rewritten	12	Contemporary issues in financial reporting
13	The framework of management accounting	Rewritten	13	Cost accounting procedures
14	Cost accounting	Substantial	14 and 15	Direct costs; Absorption costing
15	Planning and control: budgeting	Extra material	17	Budgetary planning systems
16	Planning and control: standard costing	Extra material	18	Standard costing systems
17	Decision-making: contribution analysis	Substantial	16	Marginal costing
18	Decision-making: specific decisions	New chapter		
19	Decision-making: capital investment	Extra material	19	Capital expenditure and investment
20	Contemporary issues in management accounting	Rewritten	20	Contemporary issues in management accounting

tions have been graded, the slightly easier ones being listed before the more difficult ones. Suggested answers to the group discussion questions and most of the answers to the practice questions may now be found in the *Lecturer's Guide*. A selected number of answers for the practice questions may still be found at the back of this book in Appendix 4. Additional practice questions are available on the Internet.

3 The number of case studies has been reduced from five to four, although some additional case studies will be included on the Internet if there is a demand for them.

More specialist texts are, of course, available if a particular syllabus requires students to go into more detail than is covered in this book, and some guidance on suitable reading is given in Appendix 1 (Further reading). Even so, unless particular modules are covered by national requirements, I would urge some caution. It is as well to consider whether most non-accountants really need to know much more about accounting than is covered in this book.

How to use the book

Lecturers will have their own way of introducing the various subjects. It is to be hoped, however, that they will still use the various exhibits in the book to demonstrate particular accounting procedures. It is believed that lecturers spend far too much time (and money) photocopying questions for use in lectures. The students then spend *their* time in lectures trying to take down what the lecturer is writing on the blackboard or overhead projector without really listening to what is being said.

If this book is used as it is intended, it is not necessary for lecturers to photocopy additional exhibits and answers. The book contains sufficient Exhibits (and some additional Figures and Tables) for most modules or courses, and every exhibit is followed by a detailed solution. Thus there is no need for students to copy answers that have been written on the blackboard or overhead projector; they should be able to listen to the lecturer as each point is demonstrated step by step.

Most chapters are also followed by a number of tutorial exercises. Some detailed solutions for these questions are contained in Appendix 4. The remaining solutions may be found in the *Lecturer's Guide*. That *Guide* is available at no cost to lecturers adopting this book, on application to the publishers.

A word to students

If you are using this book as part of a formal course, your lecturer will provide you with a work scheme that will outline just how much of the book you are expected to cover each week. In addition to the work done in your lecture, you will probably have to read each chapter two or three times. As you read a chapter, work through each Exhibit, and then have a go at doing it without reference to the solution.

You are also recommended to attempt as many of the questions that follow each chapter as you can; avoid looking at the solutions until you are absolutely certain that you do not know how to answer the question. The more questions that you attempt, the more confident you will be that you really do understand the subject matter. However, you must not spend all your time studying accounting, so make sure that you put enough time into your other modules.

Many students study accounting without having the benefit of attending lectures. If you fall into this category, it is suggested that you adopt the following study plan:

1 Organise your private study so that you have covered every topic in your syllabus by the time of your examination.
2 Read each chapter slowly, being careful to work through each Exhibit. Do not worry if you do not immediately understand each point; read on to the end of the chapter.

3 Read the chapter again, this time making sure that you understand each point. Try doing each Exhibit without looking at the solution.
4 Attempt as many questions at the end of the chapter as you can, but do not look at the solutions until you have finished or you are certain that you cannot do the question.
5 If you have time, reread the chapter.

One word of caution. Accounting is not simply a matter of elementary arithmetic. The solution to many accounting problems often calls for a considerable amount of personal judgement; hence there is bound to be some degree of subjectivity attached to each solution.

The problems demonstrated in this book are not readily solved in the real world and the suggested answers ought to be subject to a great deal of argument and discussion. It follows that non-accountants ought to be severely critical of any accounting information that is supplied to them, although it is difficult to be constructive in your criticism unless you have some knowledge of the subject matter. This book aims to provide you with that knowledge.

A Companion Web Site accompanies
Accounting for Non-Accounting Students
5th edition by J R Dyson

Visit the Companion Web Site at
http://www.booksites.net/dyson
to find valuable teaching and learning material including:

For Students
- Study material designed to help you improve your results
- Multiple Choice Questions to help test your learning
- Links to relevant sites on the World Wide Web
- Extra question material (with answers available to Lecturers)

For Lecturers
- A secure, password-protected site with teaching material
- Complete downloadable *Lecturer's Guide*
- Downloadable OHP masters for use in lectures
- Answers to extra question material in the student area

Also: This regularly maintained and updated site will have a syllabus manager, search functions and email results functions.

Acknowledgements

This book could not have been written and revised without the help of a considerable number of people. Many of them have contributed directly to the ideas that have gone into the writing of it, while in other cases I may have absorbed their views without always being fully conscious of doing so.

I am indebted to far too many people to name them all individually, but I would like to place on record my thanks to all of my colleagues at Heriot-Watt University and my former colleagues at Napier University. Without their ready assistance and tolerant benevolence, this book would be all the poorer. I would also like to thank all those lecturers and students elsewhere who have made various suggestions for improving the fifth edition.

My thanks are also due to the Editors of *Accountancy*, *Accountancy Age*, *Financial Times*, *Management Accounting*, *The Scotsman* and *Scotland on Sunday* for permission to reproduce copyright material. This material may not be reproduced, copied or transmitted unless written permission is obtained from the original owner or publisher. I hope that the inclusion of some actual news stories enlivens the introduction to each chapter. I also hope that it will encourage students to read regularly the financial pages of some high-quality newspapers and journals!

PART 1

Introduction to accounting

1 The accounting world

Why some accountants don't like to reveal their profession

By Michelle Perry

One in three finance directors do not admit to being an accountant at parties because of the profession's reputation as boring and dull.

However, in a boost to the profession's image, 48% of more than 200 FDs interviewed for this week's *Accountancy Age*/Reed Personnel Big Question said they were not embarrassed to refer to themselves as accountants.

Some 32% said they did not admit to being an accountant either because of the baggage associated with the word 'accountant' or because their listeners usually want their financial problems solved.

Richard Cooper, finance director of John Rannoch Foods, said: 'I'm an accountant, so I don't get invited to parties.' Another FD said: '[I'm] bombarded with questions.'

A further 20% said they sometimes told people their real profession depending on the circumstances.

'Honest. Often I say I'm afraid I'm an accountant, but I'm not that boring!' said one FD.

But another FD is more candid. He tells people he is an accountant 'because that's what I am, and its ridiculous to pretend you are anything else'. Others prefer to avoid the subject entirely. 'Definitely at the wrong party if I'm talking about it!' said Stephen Ashton Smith, FD of Maby Hire.

Accountancy Age, 11 May 2000. Reprinted with permission.

Accountants: are they dull and boring?

This chapter is an introduction to the world of accounting. It begins with an explanation of the nature and purpose of accounting. This is followed by a section outlining the reasons why it is important for non-accountants to study the subject. The next section describes briefly the main branches of accounting. A further section summarizes the basic structure of the accountancy profession. The final section describes the major types of organizations that may be found in the United Kingdom.

Learning
objectives **By the end of this chapter, you should be able to:**

- **define the nature and purpose of accounting;**
- **explain why non-accountants need to know something about accounting;**
- **identify five important branches of accounting;**
- **list six accountancy bodies that operate within the United Kingdom;**
- **outline the main types of public and private entities.**

The nature and purpose of accounting

The word *account* in everyday language is often used as a substitute for an *explanation* or a *report* of certain actions or events. If you are an employee, for example, you may have to explain to your employer just how you have been spending your time, or if you are a manager, you may have to report to the owner on how the business is doing. In order to explain or to report, you will, of course, have to remember what you were doing or what happened. As it is not always easy to remember, you may need to keep some written record. In effect, such records can be said to form the basis of a rudimentary accounting (or reporting) system.

In a primitive sense, man has always been involved in some form of accounting. It may have gone no further than a farmer (say) measuring his worth simply by counting the number of cows or sheep that he owned. However, the growth of a monetary system enabled a more sophisticated method to be developed. It then became possible to calculate the increase or decrease in individual wealth over a period of time, and to assess whether (say) a farmer with ten cows and fifty sheep was wealthier than one who had sixty pigs. Table 1.1 illustrates just how difficult it would be to assess the wealth of a farmer in a non-monetary system.

Even with the growth of a monetary system, it took a very long time for formal documentary systems to become commonplace, although it is possible

Table 1.1 Accounting for a farmer's wealth

His possessions	A year ago	Now	Change
Cows	●●●●●●●●●●	●●●●●●●●●●●●●●●	+5
Hens [● = 10]	●●●●●●●●●●●	●●●●●●●●	−30
Pigs	●●●●●●	●●●●	−2
Sheep [● = 10]	●●●●●	●●●●●●●	+20
Land [● = 1 acre]	●●●●	●●●●	no change
Cottage	●	●	no change
Carts	●●●	●	−2
Ploughs	●	●●	+1

to trace the origins of modern book-keeping at least as far back as the twelfth century. We know that from about that time, traders began to adopt a system of recording information that we now refer to as double-entry book-keeping. By the end of the fifteenth century, *double-entry book-keeping* was widely used in Venice and the surrounding areas; indeed, the first-known book on the subject was published in 1494 by an Italian mathematician called Pacioli. Modern book-keeping systems are still based on principles established in the fifteenth century, although they have had to be adapted to suit modern conditions.

Why has a recording system devised in medieval times lasted for so long? There are two main reasons:

1 it provides an accurate record of what has happened to a business over a specified period of time;
2 information extracted from the system can help the owner or the manager operate the business much more effectively.

In essence, the system provides the answers to three basic questions which owners want to know. These questions are depicted in Figure 1.1, and they can be summarized as follows:

1 What profit has the business made?
2 How much does the business owe?
3 How much is owed to it?

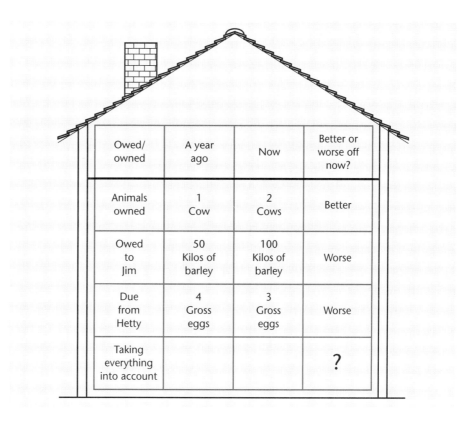

Owed/ owned	A year ago	Now	Better or worse off now?
Animals owned	1 Cow	2 Cows	Better
Owed to Jim	50 Kilos of barley	100 Kilos of barley	Worse
Due from Hetty	4 Gross eggs	3 Gross eggs	Worse
Taking everything into account			?

Figure 1.1
An owner's vital questions

The medieval system dealt largely with simple agricultural and trading *entities* (an 'entity' is simply the jargon accountants use to describe any type of organization). Modern systems have to reflect complex industrial operations and sophisticated financial arrangements. Furthermore, a business may be so big or so complex nowadays that the owners have to employ managers to run it for them. Indeed, the senior managers themselves may be largely dependent upon their junior colleagues telling them what is happening. A traditional book-keeping system did not have to deal with situations where owners were separated from managers. It was designed largely to supply summarized information only to the owner-managers of a business who knew in detail from their own experience what was going on. The system was not intended to cope with frequent day-to-day reporting to managers remote from production or trading operations.

As a result, Pacioli's system has had to be adapted for modern business practice so that it can satisfy the demand for information from two main sources:

1 from owners, who want to know from time to time how the business is doing;
2 from the managers, who need information in order to help plan and control it.

We shall be meeting the terms 'plan' and 'control' frequently in this book. Both terms can have several different meanings, but we shall adopt the following definitions:

> **To plan:** to determine what and how something should be done.
> **To control:** to ensure that the planned results are achieved.

Owners and managers do not necessarily require the same information, and so this has meant that accounting has developed into two main specialisms:

1 *financial accounting*, which is concerned with the supply of information to the *owners* of an entity;
2 *management accounting*, which is concerned with the supply of information to the *managers* of an entity.

We shall be spending a great deal of time in subsequent chapters dealing with both financial and management accounting.

While it is useful to classify accounting into these two broad categories, Figure 1.2 shows that accountants are now involved in supplying information to a wide range of other interested parties, such as customers, employees, governments and their agencies, investors, lenders, the public and suppliers and other trade creditors.

In this book, we are going to be mainly concerned with the supply of information to owners and managers. We begin by examining why non-accountants need to study accounting.

2 *To help you do a better job.* Larger organizations almost certainly have some form of detailed internal information supply. You may be involved in both supplying and receiving it. Its purpose is to help you and other managers do your respective jobs much more efficiently and effectively. It is supposed to help you plan your department's activities, to monitor and to control them, and to provide additional information about decisions you have to take about your department's affairs. This will often be translated and reported to you in financial terms (although you will also receive some non-financial information). It will not mean anything and you will not be able to use it if you do not understand it. Furthermore, you certainly will not have been able to contribute to the development of the information system so that it is of particular benefit to you.

We believe that these arguments fully justify the time that you will be giving to the study of accounting. By the time that you have worked your way through this book, we hope you will find, despite your initial fears, that accounting can be both interesting and useful!

Accounting has now developed into a considerable number of specialisms and, as you are likely to come across at least some of them in your career, it might be helpful if we provide a brief description of the main ones for you. We do so in the next section.

Branches of accounting

The work that accountants now undertake ranges far beyond that of simply summarizing information in order to calculate how much profit a business has made, how much it owes, and how much is owed to it. Although this work is still very important, accountants have gradually got involved in other types of work. Of course, other information specialists (such as market researchers and operational analysts) have also been drawn into the preparation of management information, and at one time, some observers expected accounting to be taken over by these newer and more scientifically-based disciplines. However, this has not happened. There are three main reasons: (a) financial information supply to external users still has a dominant influence on internal management information; (b) other information specialists have been reluctant to become involved in detailed accounting matters; and (c) accountants have been quick to absorb new methods and techniques into their work.

The main branches of accounting are shown in Figure 1.3. A brief description of them is given below.

Accountancy and accounting

Accountancy is a profession whose members are engaged in the collection of financial data, the summary of that data, and then the presentation of the

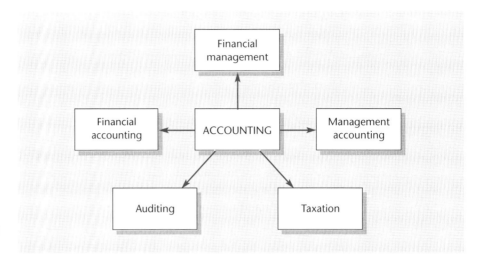

**Figure 1.3
Main branches of
accounting**

information in a form which helps recipients take effective decisions. Many writers use 'accountancy' and 'accounting' as synonymous terms, but in this book we shall use the term *accountancy* to describe the profession, and the term *accounting* to refer to the subject.

Auditing

Auditing forms a most important branch of accountancy. Once accounts have been prepared, they may have to be checked in order to ensure that they do not present a distorted picture. The checking of accounts and the reporting on them is known as *auditing*. Not all businesses have their accounts audited, but for some organizations (such as large limited-liability companies) it is a legal requirement.

Auditors are usually trained accountants who specialize in checking accounts rather than preparing them. If they are appointed from outside the organization, they are usually referred to as *external auditors*. A limited company's auditors are appointed by the shareholders, and not by the management. The auditors' job is to protect the interests of the shareholders; they answer to them, and not to anyone in the company. By contrast, *internal auditors* are employees of the company. They are appointed by, and answer to, the company's management.

Internal auditors perform routine tasks and undertake detailed checking of the company's accounting procedures, whereas external auditors are likely to go in for much more selective testing. None the less, they usually work very closely together, although the distinction made between them still remains important.

It might occur to you that because internal auditors are employees of the company they must have much less independence than external auditors. In practice, however, even external auditors have limited independence. This is because the directors of a company usually recommend the appointment of a particular firm of auditors to the shareholders. It is rare for shareholders to object to the directors' recommendation, and so if the directors are in dispute with the auditors they can always hint that they are thinking of appointing another firm. The auditors can always appeal directly to the shareholders, but they are not usually successful.

Book-keeping

Book-keeping is a mechanical task involving the collection of basic financial data. The data are first entered in special records known as *books of account*, and then extracted and summarized in the form of a *profit and loss account* and a *balance sheet*. This process normally takes place once a year, but it may occur more frequently. We shall be going into some detail in later chapters about profit and loss accounts and balance sheets. For the moment, all you need to remember is the following:

1 a profit and loss account shows whether the business has made a profit or loss during the year, i.e. it measures how well the business has done;
2 a balance sheet lists what the entity owns (its assets), and what it owes (its liabilities) as at the end of the year.

The book-keeping procedures usually end when the basic data have been entered in the books of account and the accuracy of each entry has been tested. At that stage, the accounting function takes over. Accounting tends to be used as a generic term covering almost anything to do with the collection and use of basic financial data. It should, however, be more properly applied to the use to which the data are put once they have been extracted from the books of account. Book-keeping is a routine operation, while accounting requires the ability to examine a problem using both financial *and* non-financial data.

Cost book-keeping, costing, and cost accounting

Cost book-keeping is the process that involves the recording of cost data in books of account. It is, therefore, similar to *book-keeping* except that data are recorded in very much greater detail. Cost accounting makes use of those data once they have been extracted from the cost books in providing information for managerial planning and control. Accountants are now discouraged from using the term 'costing' unless it is qualified in some way, i.e. by referring to some branch of costing (such as standard costing), but even so you will still find the term 'costing' in general use.

The difference between a book-keeping/accounting system and a cost book-keeping/cost accounting system is largely one of degree. A cost accounting system contains a great deal more data, and thus once the data are summarized, there is much more information available to the management of the company.

In this book, the term 'cost accounting' is generally used to cover all of these activities. Cost accounting now forms one of the main sub-branches of *management accounting*.

Financial accounting

Financial accounting is the more specific term applied to the preparation and subsequent publication of highly summarized financial information. The information supplied is usually for the benefit of the owners of an entity, but it can also be used by management for planning and control purposes. It will also be of interest to other parties, e.g. employees and creditors.

Financial management

Financial management is a relatively new branch of accounting that has grown rapidly over the last 30 years. Financial managers are responsible for setting financial objectives, making plans based on those objectives, obtaining the finance needed to achieve the plans, and generally safeguarding all the financial resources of the entity. Financial managers are much more heavily involved in the *management* of the entity than is generally the case with either financial or management accountants. It should also be noted that the financial manager draws on a much wider range of disciplines (such as economics and mathematics) and relies more extensively on non-financial data than does the more traditional accountant.

Management accounting

Management accounting incorporates cost accounting data and adapts them for specific decisions which management may be called upon to make. A management accounting system incorporates *all* types of financial and non-financial information from a wide range of sources.

Taxation

Taxation is a highly complex technical branch of accounting. Accountants involved in tax work are responsible for computing the amount of tax payable by both business entities and individuals. It is not necessary for either companies or individuals to pay more tax than is lawfully due, and so it is quite in order for them to minimize the amount of tax payable. If tax experts attempt to reduce their clients' tax bills strictly in accordance with the law, this is known as 'tax avoidance'. *Tax avoidance* is a perfectly legitimate exercise, but *tax evasion* (the non-declaration of sources of income on which tax might be due) is a very serious offence. In practice, the borderline between tax avoidance and tax evasion can sometimes be a fairly narrow one.

Other aspects

The main branches of accounting described above cannot always be put into such neat categories. Accountants in practice (that is, those who work from an office and offer their services to the public, like a solicitor) usually specialize in auditing, financial accounting or taxation. Most accountants working in commerce, industry or the public sector will be employed as management accountants, although some may deal specifically with auditing, financial accounting, or taxation matters.

One other highly specialist branch of accounting that you may sometimes read about is that connected with *insolvency*, i.e. with bankruptcy or liquidation. *Bankruptcy* is a formal legal procedure. The term is applied to individuals when their financial affairs are so serious that they have to be given some form of legal protection from their creditors. The term *liquidation* is usually applied to a company when it also gets into serious financial difficulties and its affairs have to be 'wound up' (that is, arranged for it to go out of existence in an orderly fashion).

Companies do not necessarily go immediately into liquidation if they get into financial difficulties. An attempt will usually be made either to rescue them or to protect certain types of creditors. In these situations, accountants sometimes act as *administrators*. Their appointment freezes creditors' rights. This prevents the company from being put into liquidation during a period when the administrators are attempting to manage the company. By contrast, *receivers* may be appointed on behalf of loan creditors. The creditors' loans may be secured on certain property, and the receivers will try to obtain the income from that property, or they may even attempt to sell it.

We hope that you never come into contact with insolvency practitioners, and so we will move on to have a look at another topic, namely the structure of the accountancy profession.

The accountancy profession

Within the United Kingdom there is nothing to stop anyone calling himself or herself an accountant, and setting up in business offering accountancy services. However, some accounting work is restricted (such as the auditing of large limited-liability companies) unless the accountant holds a recognized qualification. Indeed, some accountants are sometimes described as being *qualified accountants*. This term is usually applied to someone who is a member of one of the major accountancy bodies (although many 'non-qualified' accountants would strongly dispute that they were not 'qualified' to offer a highly professional service). There are six major accountancy bodies operating in the United Kingdom and they are as follows:

1 Institute of Chartered Accountants in England and Wales (ICAEW);
2 Institute of Chartered Accountants in Ireland (ICAI);

3   Institute of Chartered Accountants of Scotland (ICAS);
4   Association of Chartered Certified Accountants (ACCA);
5   Chartered Institute of Management Accountants (CIMA);
6   Chartered Institute of Public Finance and Accountancy (CIPFA).

The organization of the accountancy profession is also shown in Figure 1.4.

The Irish Institute (ICAI) is included in the above list because it has a strong influence in Northern Ireland.

As can be seen from the list, although all of the six major professional accountancy bodies now have a Royal Charter, it is still customary to refer only to members of ICAEW, ICAI, and ICAS as *chartered accountants*. Chartered accountants have usually had to undergo a period of training in a practising office, i.e. one that offers accounting services to the public, like a solicitor. Much practice work is involved in auditing and taxation but, after qualifying, many chartered accountants go to work in commerce or industry. ACCA members may also obtain their training in practice, but relevant experience elsewhere counts towards their qualification. CIMA members usually train and work in industry, while CIPFA members specialize almost exclusively in central and local government.

Apart from the six major bodies, there are a number of important (although far less well-known) smaller accountancy associations and societies, e.g. the

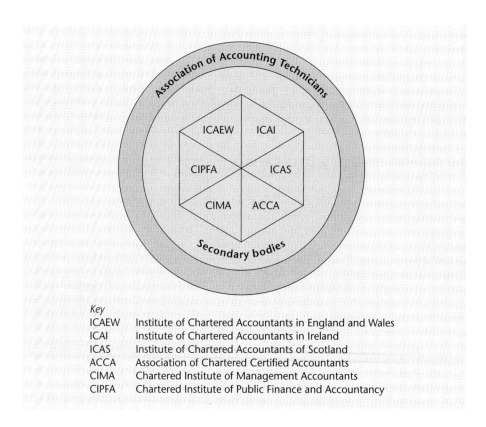

Figure 1.4 Organization of the accountancy profession in the United Kingdom

Key
ICAEW   Institute of Chartered Accountants in England and Wales
ICAI   Institute of Chartered Accountants in Ireland
ICAS   Institute of Chartered Accountants of Scotland
ACCA   Association of Chartered Certified Accountants
CIMA   Chartered Institute of Management Accountants
CIPFA   Chartered Institute of Public Finance and Accountancy

Association of Authorised Public Accountants, the Institute of Company Accountants, and the Institute of Cost and Executive Accountants. Such bodies offer some form of accountancy qualification but they have not yet managed to achieve the status or prestige that is attached to being a member of one of the six major bodies. They are referred to as *secondary bodies.*

There is also another very important accountancy body, known as the Association of Accounting Technicians. The Association was formed in 1980 as a professional organization especially for those accountants who *assist* qualified accountants in preparing accounting information. In order to become an accounting technician, it is necessary to take (or be exempt from) the Association's examinations. These are not easy, although they tend to be less technically demanding and more practical than those of the six major bodies.

You can see that the accountancy profession is extremely diverse, and if you meet people who call themselves accountants, you may not be able to tell exactly what that means. None the less, whatever their qualifications, all accountants will have one thing in common: their job is to help *you* do your job more effectively. Accountants offer a service. They can do a lot to help you, but you do not necessarily have to do what they say. Even so, you should listen to their advice. However, as accountants are largely specialists in financial matters, you also should obtain advice from other sources, then make up your own mind what you should do. If things go wrong, never ever blame the accountant (or the computer!). As a manager, it is *your* decision, right or wrong.

You may be thinking 'This is all very well, but I am not really in a position to disregard the accountant's advice.' Exactly! That is what this book is about. By the end of it you will be in an excellent position to judge the quality of the advice given. We shall be examining in later chapters what you need, but before we end this chapter we must outline the basic structure of the UK economy and the main types of entities with which we shall be dealing.

Public and private entities

The main aim of this section is to introduce you to the two main types of entities with which we shall be primarily concerned in this book: *sole traders* and *companies*. Before we can do this, however, we need to explain a little bit about the structure of the national economy of the United Kingdom.

In order to simplify our analysis, we will assume that the UK economy can be classified into two broad groupings: the *profit-making sector* and the *not-for-profit sector*. Within each of these sectors it is then possible to distinguish a number of different types of organizations (or entities, as we have referred to them earlier). The basic structure that we shall be following in this section is illustrated in Figure 1.5. We begin by examining the profit-making sector.

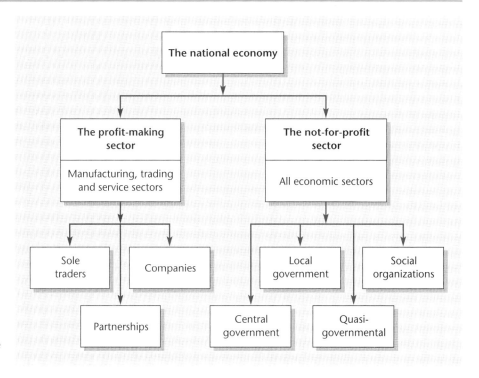

**Figure 1.5
Public and private
entities**

The profit-making sector

The profit-making sector is extremely diverse, but it is possible to recognize three major subdivisions. These are (a) the manufacturing sector; (b) the trading sector; and (c) the service sector.

The manufacturing sector is involved in purchasing raw materials and component parts, converting (or incorporating) them into finished goods, and then selling them to customers. Examples of manufacturing enterprises include the chemicals, glass, iron and steel, and textile industries.

The trading sector purchases finished goods and then sells them to their customers without any further major conversion work normally work being done on them. Trading enterprises are found in the retailing and wholesaling sectors, such as shops, supermarkets and builders' merchants.

The service sector provides advice or assistance to customers or clients, such as hairdressing, legal, and travel services. Unlike the manufacturing and trading sectors, the service sector does not usually deal in physical or tangible goods. However, there are some exceptions: the hotel and restaurant trade, for example, is normally classed as part of the service sector even though it provides major tangible services such as the provision of accommodation, food and drink.

The accounting systems required of manufacturing, trading, and service sector entities are all slightly different, although they are based on similar principles and procedures. Manufacturing entity accounts are the most complex, trading entity are fairly straight forward, while service entity accounts are usually very simple.

Until about 10 years ago, accounting texts tended to concentrate on the manufacturing and trading sectors. This emphasis reflected the origins of nineteenth-century accounting requirements, when the manufacturing and trading sectors were of major significance. More recently, the manufacturing sector has declined in importance and the service sector has become much more significant.

In this text we shall still be spending a great deal of time examining manufacturing and trading entity accounts. We do so for three main reasons: (1) the manufacturing sector still forms a significant part of the national economy; (2) the manufacturing and trading sectors enable us to demonstrate a wide range of accounting techniques and procedures; and (3) to broaden your knowledge, since you may move around the various sectors during your career.

Although there are differences in the nature of the product or the service that they offer, entities within the manufacturing, trading, and service sectors may be organized on similar lines. Three main types can be recognized; these are (1) *sole trader* entities; (2) *partnership* entities; and (3) *companies*. The basic distinction between such entities reflects who owns them, how they are financed and their legal status.

Sole traders

The term 'sole trader' is rather misleading for two reasons: first, 'sole' does not necessarily mean that only one person is involved in the entity; and, second, 'trader' may also encompass manufacturing and service entities.

The term really reflects the *ownership* of the entity; the main requirement is that only one individual should own the entity. Although not essential requirements, the owner would normally be the main source of finance and he would be expected to play a reasonably active part in its management.

Sole traders usually work on a very informal basis and some private matters relating to the owner are often indistinguishable from those of the business. Sole trader accounts are fairly straightforward and there is no specific legislation that covers the accounting arrangements. We shall be using sole trader accounts in Chapters 3, 4 and 5 in order to demonstrate some basic accounting techniques.

Partnerships

A partnership entity is very similar to a sole trader entity except that there must be at least *two owners* of the business. Partnerships sometimes grow out of a sole trader entity, perhaps because more money needs to be put into the business or because the sole trader needs some help in managing it. It is also quite common for a new business to start out as partnerships, for example when some friends get together to start a home-decorating service or to form a car-repair business.

The partners should agree among themselves how much money they will each put into the business, what jobs they will do, how many hours they will work, and how the profits and losses will be shared. In the absence of any agreement (whether formal or informal), partnerships in the United Kingdom are covered by the Partnership Act 1890.

As partnership accounts are very similar in principle to those of sole traders, we shall not be dealing with them in any detail in this book.

Companies

A company is another different type of business organization. There are many different forms of companies but generally the law regards all companies as having a separate existence from that of their owners. In this book, we are going to be primarily concerned with *limited liability companies*. The term 'limited liability' means that the owners of such companies are only required to finance the business up to an agreed amount; once they have contributed that amount, they cannot be called upon to contribute any more, even if the company gets into financial difficulties.

As there is a risk that limited liability companies may not be able to pay off their debts, Parliament has had to give some legal protection to those parties who may become involved with them. The details are contained within the Companies Act 1985. For the moment, we will not say anything more about limited liability companies because we shall be dealing with them in some detail in Chapters 6, 10 and 11.

The not-for-profit sector

By 'not-for-profit' we mean those entities whose primary purpose is to provide a service to the public rather than to make a profit from their operations. We will consider this sector under four main headings: (1) central government; (2) local government; (3) quasi-governmental bodies; and (4) social organizations.

Within the three governmental groups, there is a wide variety of different types of entities. We do not need to consider them in any detail since governmental accounting is extremely specialized and it would require a book of its own. Similarly, we shall not be dealing with the accounts of social organizations in any great depth because their accounting procedures are similar to profit-making entities.

Central government

Central government is responsible for services such as macro-economic policy, education, defence, foreign affairs, health, and social security. These responsibilities are directly controlled by Cabinet ministers who answer to Parliament at Westminster for their actions. In 1999, some of these central government responsibilities were 'devolved', i.e. they became the direct responsibility of elected bodies in Scotland, Wales and Northern Ireland.

Local government

For well over a century, central government has also devolved many of its responsibilities to 'local' authorities, i.e. smaller units of authority that have some geographical and community coherence. Councillors are elected by the local community to be responsible for those services that central government has delegated, for example the local administration of education, housing, the police and social services.

Quasi-governmental bodies	Central government also operates indirectly through quasi-governmental bodies, such as the British Broadcasting Corporation (BBC), the Post Office, colleges and universities. Such bodies are nominally independent of central government, although their main funds are normally provided by central government and their senior managers may be appointed by government ministers.
Social organizations	The social organizations' category covers a wide range of cultural, educational, recreational and social bodies. Some are formally constituted and professionally managed, such as national and international charities, while others are local organizations run by volunteers on a part-time basis, e.g. bridge and rugby clubs.

Conclusion

The main aim of this chapter has been to introduce the non-accountant to the world of accounting. We have emphasized that the main purpose of accounting is to provide financial information to anyone who wants it.

Of course, information must be useful if it is to have any purpose but, as a non-accountant, you may feel reluctant to question any accounting information that lands on your desk. You may also not understand why the accountant is always asking you what you might think are irrelevant questions, and so you respond with any old nonsense. You then perhaps feel a bit guilty and a little frustrated; you would like to know more, but you dare not ask. We hope that by the time you have worked your way through this book, you will have the confidence to ask and, furthermore, that you will understand the answer. Good luck!

Now that the world of accounting has been outlined, we can turn to more detailed subject matter. The first task is to learn the basic rules of accounting. These are covered in the next chapter, but it might be as well if you first read through this chapter again before you move on to the next. It might also be a good idea to attempt some of the questions that end this chapter.

Key points

1 To account for something means to explain about it, or report on it.

2 Owners of an entity want to know (a) how well it is doing; (b) what it owes; and (c) how much it is owed to it.

3 Accounting is important for non-accountants because (a) they must make sure their own entity complies with any legal requirements; and (b) an accounting system can provide them with information that will help them do their jobs more effectively and efficiently.

4 The main branches of accounting are: auditing, financial accounting, financial management, management accounting, and taxation.

5 Other terms used in accountancy include book-keeping (a function of financial accounting), and cost book-keeping, costing, and cost accounting (sub-branches of management accounting).

6 There are six main accountancy bodies: the Institute of Chartered Accountants in England and Wales, the Institute of Chartered Accountants in Ireland, the Institute of Chartered Accountants of Scotland, the Association of Chartered Certified Accountants, the Chartered Institute of Management Accountants and the Chartered Institute of Public Finance and Accountancy.

7 There are two economic sectors within the UK economy: the profit making sector and the not-for-profit sector. Within the profit-making sector, business operations can be classified as being either manufacturing, trading, or servicing, and they may be organized as sole trader entities, as partnerships, or as companies.

8 The not-for-profit sector includes central government and local government operations, quasi-governmental bodies, and social organizations. Governmental operations are extremely complex and the accounting requirements are highly specialized. Social organizations are also diverse and they include various associations, charities, clubs, societies, and sundry voluntary organizations. Their accounting requirements are usually similar to those found in the profit-making sector.

Check your learning

1 Insert the missing words in each of the following sentences:
   (a) The word _____ in everyday language means an explanation or a report.
   (b) The owner of a business wants to know how much _____ it has made.

2 What are the two main branches of accounting?

3 State whether each of the following assertions is either true or false:
   (a) Auditors are responsible for preparing accounts   True/False
   (b) Management accounts are required by law   True/False

4 Which of the following activities is not an accounting function?
   (a) auditing   (b) book-keeping   (c) management consultancy   (d) taxation

5 How many major professional accountancy bodies are there in the British Isles?
   (a) three   (b) six   (c) nine   (d) ten or more

6 Fill in the blanks:
   (a) _____ trader (b) Partnership _____ 1890 (c) limited liability _____

[*The answers to these questions may be found at the back of the book.*]

Group discussion questions

1.1 'Accountants stifle managerial initiative and enterprise.' Discuss.

1.2 Do you think that auditors should be responsible for detecting fraud?

1.3 The following statement was made by a student: 'I cannot understand why accountants have such a high status and why they yield such power.' How would you respond to such an assertion?

Practice questions

[*Note: The questions marked with an asterisk have answers at the back of the book.*]

1.4* Why should a non-accountant study accounting?

1.5* Describe two main purposes of accounting.

1.6* What statutory obligations require the preparation of management accounts in any kind of entity?

1.7 State briefly the main reasons why a company may employ a team of accountants.

1.8* What statutory obligations support the publication of financial accounts in respect of limited liability companies?

1.9 Why does a limited liability company have to engage a firm of external auditors, and for what purpose?

1.10 Assume that you are a personnel officer in a manufacturing company, and that one of your employees is a young engineering manager called Joseph Sykes. Joseph has been chosen to attend the local university's Business School to study for a diploma in management. Joseph is reluctant to attend the course because he will have to study accounting; as an engineer, he thinks that it will be a waste of time for him to study such a subject.

Required:
Draft an internal memorandum addressed to Joseph explaining why it would be of benefit to him to study accounting.

1.11 Clare Wong spends a lot of her time working for a large local charity. The charity has grown enormously in recent years, and the trustees have been advised to overhaul their accounting procedures. This would involve its workers (most of whom are voluntary) in more book-keeping, and there is a great deal of resistance to this move. The staff have said that they are there to help the needy and not to get involved in book-keeping.

Required:
As the financial consultant to the charity, prepare some notes that you could use in speaking to the voluntary workers in order to try to persuade them to accept the new proposals.

2 Accounting rules

Aetna to restate its accounts

By Adrian Michaels in New York

Aetna, the largest US health insurer, is to restate its accounts for 1998 and the first three-quarters of last year after a Securities and Exchange Commission review of its accounting practices.

In a sign of the SEC's increasing interest on what companies classify as operating income, Aetna has agreed to re-account for the $122m sale in 1997 of its Human Affairs International unit to Magellan Health Services.

Part of that deal involved future payments to Aetna to reflect growth in membership of HAI. Aetna booked those payments as operating income but the sale itself as a capital gain.

After a six-month review of Aetna's accounts, the SEC said the membership agreement, which lasts for five years, would not have arisen without the sale, so the whole should be recorded as a capital gain.

Robert Williams, accountancy and taxation analyst at Lehman Brothers, said the error appeared to have been an honest mistake.

The insurer, which is audited by KPMG, said the restatements would not affect total net income for 1998 but would reduce 1999 net income by about $10m, or 7 cents a share, for each of the first and second quarters. For the third quarter, net income will rise about $30m, or 20 cents a share.

Financial Times, 2 February 2000. Reprinted with permission.

When is a sale not a sale?

W e suggested in Chapter 1 that accountancy is a profession engaged in the supply of financial information to a number of interested parties. In practice, the amount of information that is available is so enormous that it is necessary to place some limit on the type of data dealt with.

Modern accounting systems have evolved over a long period of time. They have not developed from any sort of theoretical model, but have grown out of practical necessity. As a result, a number of basic procedures have developed. These procedures may perhaps best be described as the *basic rules of accounting*. Some authors refer to them under a variety of other names, such as assumptions, axioms, concepts, conventions, postulates, principles, or procedures.

Learning objectives

By the end of this chapter, you should be able to:

- identify 14 accounting rules;
- classify them into three broad groupings;
- describe each accounting rule;
- explain why each is important;
- outline the main features of a conceptual framework.

In preparing and presenting information, accountants have considerable freedom over which rules to adopt and how they should be interpreted. Since 1971, the accountancy profession has tried to restrict the room for manoeuvre by issuing a series of accounting guides. The guides issued prior to 1990 are known as Statements of Standard Accounting Practice (SSAPs). Those issued since then are called Financial Reporting Standards (FRSs). When preparing accounting statements, qualified accountants are supposed to follow the letter and not just the spirit of the recommendations contained in SSAPs and FRSs. However, it is impracticable to lay down totally rigid rules for each and every situation, and so accountants are still able to employ a great deal of individual discretion.

It would be possible, of course, to ignore all of the generally recognized accounting rules and to prepare accounts in an entirely novel way. This would be like trying to play football under different rules from the ones laid down by the Football Association. If the accepted rules were disregarded, any match played under entirely new rules would result in a game that would be almost incomprehensible to most of the spectators.

A similar situation would apply in accounting if the conventional rules were abandoned. The rules include the amount and type of information to be collected, and the length of the accounting period. These are practical rules, like those in football covering the size of the pitch and the length of the match. Other accounting rules are more of an ethical nature; for example, all the rules should be applied consistently, and information should not be presented in a deliberately distorted fashion. These rules may again be compared with those in football that cover misconduct, where the ball must not be handled, or an opponent should not be kicked.

The basic accounting rules will be outlined in subsequent sections. For convenience, they have been classified as follows:

1 boundary rules;
2 measurement rules;
3 ethical rules.

A diagrammatic summary of the main accounting rules that we are going to examine is shown in Figure 2.1. The classification shown there is largely arbitrary; it has been chosen to help you examine more clearly some of the most

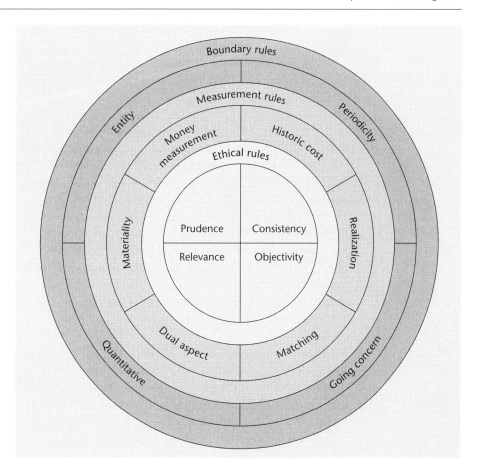

Figure 2.1
The basic
accounting rules

important accounting rules. There are something like 150 identifiable accounting rules, but we are only going to look at the 14 that are of particular relevance to non-accountants.

Boundary rules

In small entities, the owners can probably obtain all the information that they want to know by finding out for themselves. In larger entities, this is often impracticable, and so a more formal way of reporting back to the owners has to be devised. However, it would be difficult to inform the owners about literally *everything* that had happened to the entity. A start has to be made, therefore, by determining what should and should not be reported. Hence, accountants have devised a number of what we will call *boundary rules*. The boundary rules attempt to place a limit on the amount and type of data collected and stored within the entity.

There are four main boundary rules, and they will be examined in the following subsections.

Entity

There is so much information available about any entity that accountants start by drawing a boundary around it.

The accountant tries to restrict the data collected to that of the entity itself. This is sometimes very difficult, especially in small entities where there is often no clear distinction between the public affairs of the entity and the private affairs of the owner. In a profit-making business, for example, the owners sometimes charge their household expenditure to the business, and they might also use their private bank account to pay for goods and services meant for the business. In such situations, accountants have to decide where the business ends and the private affairs of the owners begin. They have then to establish exactly what the business owes the owner and the owner owes the business. The accountants will, however, only be interested in recording in the books of the business the effect of these various transactions on the *business*; they are not interested in the effect that those transactions have on the owners' private affairs. Indeed, it would be an entirely different exercise if the accountants were to deal with owners' private affairs. This would mean that they were accounting for different entities altogether, i.e. private entities instead of public ones, although there may be a great deal of overlap between the two types.

Periodicity

Most entities have an unlimited life. They are usually started in the expectation that they will operate for an indeterminate period of time, but it is clearly unhelpful for the owner to have to wait years before any report is prepared on how it is doing. The owner would almost certainly wish to receive regular reports at frequent short intervals.

If an entity has an unlimited life, any report must be prepared at the end of what must inevitably be an arbitrary period of time. In practice, financial accounting statements are usually prepared annually. Such a time period has developed largely as a matter of custom. It does, however, reflect the natural agricultural cycle in Western Europe, and there does seem to be a natural human tendency to compare what has happened this year with what happened last year. None the less, where entities have an unlimited life (as is usually the case with manufacturing organizations), the preparation of annual accounts presents considerable problems in relating specific events to appropriate accounting periods. We shall be having a look at these problems in Chapter 5.

Apart from custom, there is no reason why an accounting period could not be shorter or longer than twelve months. Management accounts are usually prepared for very short periods, but sometimes this also applies to financial accounts. In the fashion industry, for example, where the product designs may change very quickly, managers may want (say) quarterly reports. By contrast, the construction industry, faced with very long-term contract work, may find it more appropriate to have (say) a five-year reporting period. In fact, irrespective of the length of the main accounting period (i.e. whether it is quarterly or five-yearly), managers usually need regular reports covering a very short period. Cash reports, for example, could be prepared on a weekly, or even on a daily basis.

It must also not be forgotten that some entities (e.g. limited liability companies) are required by law to produce annual accounts, and as tax demands are also based on a calendar year it would not be possible for most entities to ignore the conventional twelve-month period. In any case, given the unlimited life of most entities, you will appreciate that *any* period must be somewhat arbitrary, no matter how carefully a particular entity has tried to relate its accounting period to the nature of its business.

Going concern

The periodicity rule requires a regular period of account to be established, regardless either of the life of the entity or of the arbitrary nature of such a period. The going concern rule arises out of the periodicity rule. This rule requires an assumption that an entity will continue in existence for the foreseeable future unless some strong evidence exists to suggest that this is not going to be the case. It is important to make absolutely certain that this assumption is correct, because a different set of accounting rules need to be adopted if an entity's immediate future is altogether uncertain.

Quantitative

Accountants usually restrict the data that are collected to those that are easily quantifiable. For example, it is possible to count the number of people that an entity employs, but it is difficult to calculate the *skill* of the employees. Such a concept is almost impossible to quantify, and it is, therefore, not included in a conventional accounting system.

Measurement rules

The boundary rules determine *what* data should be included in an accounting system, whereas the measurement rules explain *how* that data should be recorded. There are six main measurement rules, and we outline them briefly in the following subsections.

Money measurement

It would be very cumbersome to record information simply in terms of quantifiable amounts. It would also be impossible to make any fair comparisons between various types of assets (such as livestock and farm machinery), or different types of transactions (such as the sale of eggs and the purchase of corn). In order to make meaningful comparison, we need to convert the data into a common recognizable measure.

As we suggested in Chapter 1, the monetary unit serves such a purpose. It is a useful way of converting accounting data into a common unit, and since most quantifiable information is capable of being translated into monetary terms, there is usually no difficulty in adopting the monetary measurement rule.

Historic cost

The historic cost rule is an extension of the money measurement rule. It requires transactions to be recorded at their *original* (i.e. their historic) cost. Subsequent changes in prices or values, therefore, are usually ignored. Increased costs may arise because of a combination of an improved product, or through changes in the purchasing power of the monetary unit, i.e. through inflation.

As we shall see in Chapter 12, inflation tends to overstate the level of accounting profit as it is traditionally calculated. Over the last 30 years, there have been several attempts in the United Kingdom to change the method of accounting in order to allow for the effects of inflation. There has been so much disagreement on what should replace what is called *historic cost accounting* (HCA) that no other method has been acceptable. Throughout most of this book, we shall be adopting the historic cost rule.

Realization

One of the problems of putting the periodicity rule into practice is that it is often difficult to relate a specific transaction to a particular period. For example, assume that a business arranges to sell some goods in 2001, it delivers them in 2002, and it is paid for them in 2003. In which year were the goods *sold*: 2001, 2002, or 2003? In conventional accounting, it would be most unusual to include them in the sales for 2001, because the business has still got a legal title to them. They could be included in the accounts for 2003 when the goods have been paid for. Indeed, this method of accounting is not uncommon. It is known as *cash flow accounting* (CFA). In CFA, transactions are only entered in the books of account when a cash exchange has taken place. By contrast, in HCA, it is customary to enter most transactions in the books of account when the legal title to the goods has been transferred from one party to another and when there is an *obligation* for the recipient to pay for them. This means that, in the above example, under HCA the goods would normally be considered to have been sold in 2002.

The realization rule covers this point. It requires transactions relating to the sale of goods to be entered in the accounts for that period in which the legal title for them has been transferred from one party to another. In the jargon of accounting, they are then said to be *realized*. It is important to appreciate that for goods and services to be treated as realized, they do not need to have been paid for: the cash for them may be received during a later period (or for that matter, may have been received in an earlier period).

The realization rule is normally regarded as applying to sales, but *purchases* (meaning goods that are intended for resale) may be treated similarly. Thus, they would not be included in an entity's accounts until it had a legal title to them (i.e. until in law it would be regarded as owning them).

The realization rule can produce some rather misleading results. For example, a company may treat goods as having been sold in 2002. In 2003 it finds that the purchaser cannot pay for them. What can it do? Its accounts for 2002 have already been approved and it is too late to change them, but obviously the sales for that year were overstated (and so too, almost certainly, was the profit). The customer defaults in 2003, and so how can the *bad debt* (as it is known) be dealt with in *that* year? We shall be explaining how in Chapter 5.

Matching

The realization rule relates mainly to the purchase and sale of goods, in other words to what are known as *trading items*. However, a similar rule known as the *matching rule* applies to other incomes (such as dividends and rents received) and expenditure (such as electricity and wages).

A misleading impression would be given if the cash received during a particular period was simply compared with the cash paid out during the same period. The exact period in which the cash is either received or paid may bear no relationship to the period in which the business was transacted. Thus, accountants normally adjust cash received and cash paid on what is known as an *accruals and prepayments* basis. An accrual is an amount that is *owed* by the entity at the end of an accounting period in respect of services received during that period. A prepayment is an amount that is *owing* to the entity at the end of the accounting period as a result of it paying in advance for services to be rendered in respect of a future period.

The conversion of cash received and cash paid out on an accruals and prepayments basis at the end of an accounting period often involves a considerable amount of arithmetical adjustment. Account has to be taken for accruals and prepayments at the end of the previous period (i.e *opening* accruals and prepayments), as well as for accruals and prepayments at the end of the current period (i.e. *closing* accruals and prepayments). We shall be dealing with accruals and prepayments in more detail in Chapter 5.

An accruals and prepayments system of accounting enables the incomes of one period to be matched much more fairly against the costs of the same period. The comparison is not distorted by the accidental timing of cash receipts and cash payments. However, as the matching rule requires the accountant to estimate the level of both accruals and prepayments as at the end of each accounting period, a degree of subjectivity is automatically built into the estimate.

Dual aspect

The dual aspect rule is a useful practical rule, although it really only reflects what is obvious. It is built round the fact that every time something is given, someone (or something) else receives it. In other words, every time a transaction take place, there is always a twofold effect. For example, if the amount of cash in a business goes up, someone must have given it; or if the business buys some goods, then someone else must be selling them.

We explained in Chapter 1 that this twofold effect was recognized many centuries ago. It gave rise to the system of recording information known as *double-entry book-keeping*. This system of book-keeping is still widely used. Although the concept is somewhat obvious, it has proved extremely useful, so much so that even modern computerized recording systems are based on it. From long experience, it has been found that the system is a most convenient way of recording all sorts of useful information about the entity, and of ensuring some form of control over its affairs.

There is no real need to adopt the dual aspect rule in recording information: it is entirely a practical rule that has proved itself over many centuries. Voluntary organizations (such as a drama club, or a stamp collecting society) may not think that it is worthwhile to adopt the dual aspect rule, but you are strongly recommended to incorporate it into your book-keeping system in any entity with which you are concerned. If you do, you will find that it gives you more control over the entity's affairs besides providing you with a great deal more information.

Double-entry book-keeping will be examined in more detail in the next chapter.

Materiality

Strict application of the various accounting rules may not always be practical. It could involve a considerable amount of work that may be out of all proportion to the information that is eventually obtained. The materiality rule permits other rules to be ignored if the effects are not considered to be *material*, that is, if they are not significant.

Hence, the materiality rule avoids the necessity to follow other accounting rules to the point of absurdity. For example, it would normally be considered unnecessary to value the closing stock of small amounts of stationery, or to maintain detailed records of inexpensive items of office equipment. However, it should be borne in mind that what is immaterial for a large organization may not be so for a small one.

If you decide that a certain item is immaterial, then it does not matter how you deal with it in the accounts, because it cannot possibly have any significant effect on the results. When dealing with insignificant items, therefore, the materiality rule permits the other accounting rules to be ignored.

Ethical rules

There is an old story in accounting about the company chairman who asked his chief accountant how much profit the company had made. The chief accountant replied by asking how much profit the chairman would like to make. Accountants recognize that there is some truth in this story, since it is quite possible for different accountants to use the same basic data in preparing accounting statements yet still arrive at different levels of profit!

You might think that by faithfully following all of the accounting rules, *all* accountants should be able to calculate exactly the same amount of profit. Unfortunately this is not the case since, as we have seen, most of the main accounting rules are capable of wide interpretation. The matching rule, for example, requires an estimate to be made of amounts owing and owed at the end of an accounting period, while the materiality rule allows the accountant to decide just what is material. Both rules involve an element of subjective judgement, and so no two accountants are likely to agree precisely on how they should be applied.

In order to limit the room for individual manoeuvre, a number of other rules have evolved. These rules are somewhat ethical in nature; and, indeed, some authors refer to them as accounting *principles* (thereby suggesting that there is a moral dimension to them). Other authors, however, refer to *all* of the basic accounting rules as principles, but it really does not matter what you call them as long as you are aware of them. Basically, the ethical rules require accountants to follow not just the letter but the spirit of the other rules.

There are four main ethical accounting rules, and we will review them individually in the following sub-sections.

Prudence

The prudence rule (which is sometimes known as *conservatism*) arises out of the need to make a number of estimates in preparing periodic accounts. Managers and owners are often naturally over-optimistic about future events. As a result, there is a tendency to be too confident about the future, and not to be altogether realistic about the entity's prospects. There may, for example, be undue optimism over the creditworthiness of a particular customer. Insufficient allowance may therefore be made for the possibility of a bad debt. This might have the effect of overstating profit in one period and understating it in a future period. We shall come across this problem again in Chapter 5.

The prudence rule is sometimes expressed in the form of a simple maxim:

If in doubt, overstate losses and understate profits.

Consistency

As we have seen, the preparation of traditional accounting statements requires a considerable amount of individual judgement to be made in the application of the basic accounting rules. To compensate for this flexibility, the consistency rule states that, once specific accounting policies have been adopted, they should be followed in all subsequent accounting periods.

It would be considered quite unethical to change rules just because they were unfashionable, or because alternative ones gave better results. Of course, if the circumstances of the entity change radically it may be necessary to adopt different policies, but this should only be done in exceptional circumstances. If different policies are adopted, then the effect of any change should be clearly highlighted and any comparative figure adjusted accordingly.

The application of this rule gives confidence to the users of accounting statements, because if the accounts have been prepared on a consistent basis they can be assured that they are comparable with previous sets of accounts.

Objectivity

Accounts should be prepared with the minimum amount of bias. This is not an easy task, since individual judgement is required in interpreting the rules and adapting them to suit particular circumstances. Owners may want, for example, to adopt policies which would result in higher profit figures, or in disguising poor results.

If optional policy decisions are possible within the existing rules, it is advisable to fall back on the prudence rule. Indeed, it tends to be an overriding one. If there is any doubt about which rule to adopt (or how it should be interpreted), the prudence rule tends to take precedence.

It must be recognized, however, that if the prudence rules is always adopted as the easy way out of a difficult problem, someone preparing a set of accounts could be accused of lacking objectivity. In other words, you must not use this rule to avoid making difficult decisions. Indeed, it is just as unfair to be as excessively cautious as it is to be widely optimistic. Extremism of any kind suggests a lack of objectivity, so you should avoid being either over-cautious or over-optimistic.

Relevance

The amount of information that could be supplied to any interested party is practically unlimited. If too much information is disclosed, it becomes very difficult to absorb, and so it should only be included if it is it going to help the user.

The selection of relevant information requires much experience and judgement, as well as a great understanding of the user's requirements. The information needs to be designed in such a way that it meets the *objectives* of the specific user group. If too much information is given, the users might think that it is an attempt to mislead them, and as a result, all of the information may be totally rejected.

In this context, accountants try to present accounts in such a way that they represent 'a true and fair view'. The Companies Act 1985, for example, requires company accounts to reflect this particular criterion, and it is advisable to apply it to all entities. Unfortunately, the 1985 Act does not define what is meant by 'true and fair', but it is assumed that accounts will be true and fair if an entity has followed the rules laid down in appropriate accounting and financial reporting standards.

Financial reporting standards are formulated by an Accounting Standards Board (ASB) and professionally qualified accountants are required to follow its recommendations. As we mentioned earlier, these are contained in Financial Reporting Standards (FRSs) and any remaining Standard Statements of Accounting Practice (SSAPs) issued by the former Accounting Standards Committee (ASC). FRSs are not statutory requirements although, as will be seen in Chapter 10, some recognition in law is given to them. Experience suggests that the ASB has much greater power to enforce its recommendations than had the old ASC.

By the time that the ASC had been disbanded in 1990, it had issued 25 SSAPs, three of which had been withdrawn. By early 2000, the ASB had issued 16 FRSs and just 13 of the old SSAPs remained operable.

Such standards are considered to represent the most authoritative view of how certain matters should be dealt within the 'financial statements of a reporting entity that are intended to give a true and fair view of its state of affairs at the balance sheet date and of its profit or loss (or income and expenditure) for the financial period ending on that date' (as the ASB's 'Foreword to accounting standards' puts it). This is perhaps rather a strange way of requiring compliance with the standards, because it suggests that some accounts are not meant to give a true and fair view!

The standards cover such diverse subjects as the accounting policies adopted by an entity, and the treatment of depreciation, taxation and stock valuations. Professionally qualified accountants are supposed to follow the recommendations contained within the standards but they still leave room for considerable individual interpretation. Consequently, no real disciplinary action has been taken against any accountant for not following either the letter or the spirit of the standards.

Summary

It would be convenient at this stage if we summarized the basic accounting rules outlined in the previous section so that it will be easy for you to refer back when studying later chapters. In summary they are as follows:

Boundary rules

1 *Entity*. Accounting data must be restricted to the entity itself. The data should exclude the private affairs of those individuals who either own or manage the entity, except in so far as they impact directly on it.
2 *Periodicity*. Accounts should be prepared at the end of a defined period of time, and this period should be adopted as the regular period of account.
3 *Going concern*. The accounts should be prepared on the assumption that the entity will continue in existence for the foreseeable future.
4 *Quantitative*. Only data that are capable of being easily quantified should be included in an accounting system.

Measurement rules

1 *Money measurement*. Data must be translated into monetary terms before they are included in an accounting system.
2 *Historic cost*. Financial data should be recorded in the books of account at their historic cost, that is, at their original purchase cost or at their original selling price.
3 *Realization*. Transactions that reflect financial data should be entered in the books of account when the legal title to them has been transferred from one party to another party, irrespective of when a cash settlement takes place.
4 *Matching*. Cash received and cash paid during a particular accounting period should be adjusted in order to reflect the economic activity that has actually taken place during that period.
5 *Dual aspect*. All transactions should be recorded in such a way that they capture the giving and the receiving effect of each transaction.
6 *Materiality*. The basic accounting rules must not be rigidly applied to insignificant items.

Ethical rules

1 *Prudence*. If there is some doubt over the treatment of a particular transaction, income should be underestimated and expenditure overestimated, so that profits are more likely to be understated and losses overstated.

2 *Consistency*. Accounting rules and policies should not be amended unless there is a fundamental change in circumstances that necessitates a reconsideration of the original rules and policies.

3 *Objectivity*. Personal prejudice must be avoided in the interpretation of the basic accounting rules.

4 *Relevance*. Accounting statements should not include information that prevents users from obtaining a true and fair view of the information being communicated to them.

Before we finish this chapter, we ought to have a brief look at some accounting theory. No! Don't close the book just yet. It won't be as bad as you think!

A conceptual framework

As we explained at the beginning of this chapter, the basic accounting rules have evolved over a period of time; nobody worked them out on paper before they were applied in practice. This means that when some new accounting problem arises, we do not always know how to deal with it. Some accountants (especially university lecturers), argue, therefore, that what is needed is a *conceptual framework*. In other words, we ought to devise a theoretical model of accounting, and then any new accounting problem could be solved merely by running it through the model.

It sounds very sensible, but it is not easy to devise such a model. Several attempts have been made, and none of them has been successful. Basically, there are two approaches that can be adopted:

1 We can list all the accounting rules that have ever been used, and then extract the ones that are the most widely used. There are two main problems in adopting this approach:
   (a) To be meaningful, we would have to conduct an extremely wide survey of existing practice. As yet, the sheer scale required by this exercise has defeated most researchers.
   (b) Such an exercise would simply freeze existing practice: it would not improve it.

2 Alternatively, we could determine
   (a) who uses accounting statements;
   (b) what they want them for (i.e. we would need to establish *user objectives*); and
   (c) what rules we need to adopt to meet those objectives.

Again, the scale of the exercise has defeated most researchers. Furthermore, even if some agreement could be reached on the users of accounting statements and their objectives, it is not easy to select appropriate rules that would be generally acceptable.

The ASB's job would be much easier if it could deal with the various accounting problems by formulating some theoretical model, i.e. the equivalent of a small-scale physical model frequently used in science and engineering experiments. The ASB has been attempting to build a *theoretical model* (a physical model is clearly impossible) by laying down the *principles* that it thinks should be followed when preparing financial statements. Such a task has proved highly controversial and has taken a long time to formulate. None the less, in December 1999 it issued its definitive version under the title of *Statement of Principles for Financial Reporting*.

The Statement is not an accounting standard and it does not have any such status. Rather, it sets out the basic principles that the ASB believes should underpin the preparation of what it calls 'general purpose financial statements', such as annual financial statements, financial statements in interim reports, preliminary announcements and summary financial statements.

The Statement is some 30 pages long and so we can only give you a flavour of what it contains. There are eight chapters and a brief summary of them is as follows.

Chapter 1 lays down the objectives of financial statements, i.e. 'to provide information that is useful to those for whom they are prepared'. However, consideration needs to be given to those parties who use the information, what information they need and what role financial statements play in that process.

Chapter 2 identifies those entities that ought to publish financial statements. These include those entities that are cohesive economic units and where there is a legitimate demand for the information contained within such statements.

Chapter 3 describes the qualitative characteristics of financial information. As it complements much of the material in *this* chapter, it would be useful if we outline its main contents in a little more detail. The Statement argues that in order to make financial information useful it should consist of the following qualities:

1 *Materiality*. Information should be provided to users if their economic decisions would be affected either by its omission or by misstating it.
2 *Relevance*. Information should be capable of (a) influencing the economic decisions of users; and (b) being provided in time to influence the decisions. You will recall that earlier we regarded 'relevance' as being an 'ethical' rule.
3 *Reliability*. Information should (a) reflect the substance of events and transactions; (b) be free from deliberate bias and material error; and (c) incorporate a degree of caution when containing uncertain circumstances.
4 *Comparability*. Information should be presented in such a way that it is possible to ascertain similarities and spot differences over time and between entities.

5 *Comprehensibility*. The Statement does not object to information being provided even if some users would not understand it. Generally, it expects users to have a 'reasonable knowledge of business and economic activities and accounting and a willingness to study with reasonable diligence the information provided'. Now you know why you are studying accounting!

Chapter 4 identifies the main elements that should go to make up the financial statements such as assets (what the entity owns) and liabilities (what the entity owes). It refers to these elements as 'building blocks'. In subsequent chapters of this book, we will be dealing with the 'building blocks' of accounting.

Chapter 5 considers when events and transactions should be recognised in financial statements. We dealt with this particular aspect in the earlier part of this chapter when outlining the 'measurement' rules. *Chapter 6* complements Chapter 5 and considers how assets and liabilities should be measured. Again, we have covered much of this topic in our 'measurement rule' section earlier in this chapter. *Chapter 7* considers the characteristics of 'good' presentation so that financial statements are communicated clearly and effectively.

Chapter 8 is a highly specialized chapter involving the inclusion of information in financial statements that reflects an entity's interest in other entities. We shall only be dealing briefly with this topic in Chapter 11 of our book.

You will appreciate from the above summary that the Statement is couched in very general terms. It does not provide a precise set of rules for the preparation of financial statements and it certainly is not prescriptive. Thus it is not like the instructions that you get if you purchase board games like *Cluedo* or *Monopoly*. Rather, the ASB has put forward some basic concepts which it thinks should underpin the preparation of financial statements. Hence, you now need how to know how to apply those concepts when you have to prepare a set of financial statements. The remaining chapters in this part of the book aim to provide you with the guidance you need.

You may have found it disappointing (especially if you are an engineer or a scientist) that by the end of this section we have not been able to provide you with a precise conceptual framework equivalent to a laboratory model for the presentation of financial statements. Unfortunately, there are so many variable factors in the social sciences that this is almost an impossible task.

Thus to a non-accountant, the ASB's *Statement of Principles* may appear totally unsatisfactory. None the less, it is a considerable landmark in the history of accounting. There has been much opposition to the ideas being pursued by the ASB and the Board has not felt itself to be in a position to make its principles mandatory. It is likely to be very many years before that position is reached and it is even more doubtful whether a more detailed framework can ever be formulated.

Conclusion

In this chapter we have identified 14 basic accounting rules that accountants usually adopt in the preparation of accounting statements. We have described four of these rules as boundary rules, six as measurement rules and four as ethical rules. We have argued that the boundary rules limit the amount and type of information that is traditionally collected and stored in an accounting system. The measurement rules provide some guidance on how that information should be recorded, and the ethical rules lay down a code of conduct on how all the other rules should be interpreted.

The exact number, classification and description of these various accounting rules is subject to much debate amongst accountants. Most entities can, in fact, adopt what rules they like, although it would be most unusual if they did not accept the going concern, matching, prudence and consistency rules.

In the next chapter, we shall examine the dual aspect rule in a little more detail. This rule is at the heart of double-entry book-keeping and most modern accounting systems are based upon it.

Key points

1 In preparing accounting statements, accountants adopt a number of rules that have evolved over a number of centuries.

2 There are four main boundary rules: entity, periodicity, going concern, and quantitative.

3 Measurement rules include: money measurement, historic cost, realization, matching, dual aspect, and materiality.

4 Ethical rules include: prudence, consistency, objectivity, and relevance.

5 No satisfactory conceptual framework of accounting has yet been developed by the accountancy profession. The ASB, in December 1999, put forward a *Statement of Principles for Financial Reporting*, but this Statement is neither highly prescriptive nor mandatory.

Check your learning

1 State whether each of the following comments is true or false:
   (a) Accounting is based on a theoretical framework.   True/False
   (b) All of the basic accounting rules are codified in law.   True/False
   (c) Accountants can adapt accounting rules to suit particular
       circumstances.   True/False

2 Fill in the missing blanks in the following statement:
   If in doubt, _____ losses and _____ profits.

3 Indicate the category of the following six accounting rules:

	Boundary	Measurement	Ethical
(a) going concern	☐	☐	☐
(b) matching	☐	☐	☐
(c) money measurement	☐	☐	☐
(d) objectivity	☐	☐	☐
(e) periodicity	☐	☐	☐
(f) prudence	☐	☐	☐

[*The answers to these questions may be found at the back of the book.*]

Group discussion questions

2.1 Do you think that, when a set of financial accounts is being prepared, the prudence rule should override the objectivity rule?

2.2 'The law should lay down precise formats, contents, and methods for the preparation of limited liability company accounts.' Discuss.

2.3 The Accounting Standards Board now bases its Financial Reporting Standards on what might be regarded as a 'conceptual framework'. How far do you think that this approach is likely to be successful?

Practice questions

[*Note: The questions marked with an asterisk have answers at the back of the book.*]

In questions 2.4, 2.5 and 2.6 you are required to state which accounting rule the accountant would most probably adopt in dealing with the various problems.

2.4* Electricity consumed in period 1 and paid for in period 2.
Equipment originally purchased for £20 000 which would now cost £30 000.
The company's good industrial relations record.
A five-year construction contract.
A customer who might go bankrupt owing the company £5000.
The company's vehicles, which would only have a small scrap value if the company goes into liquidation.

2.5* A demand by the company's chairman to include every detailed transaction in the presentation of the annual accounts.
A sole-trader business which has paid the proprietor's income tax based on the business profits for the year.
A proposed change in the methods of valuing stock.
The valuation of a litre of petrol in one vehicle at the end of accounting period 1.
A vehicle which could be sold for more than its purchase price.
Goods which were sold to a customer in period 1, but for which the cash was only received in period 2.

2.6* The proprietor who has supplied the business capital out of his own private bank account.

The sales manager who is always very optimistic about the creditworthiness of prospective customers.

The managing director who does not want annual accounts prepared as the company operates a continuous 24-hour-a-day, 365-days-a-year process.

At the end of period 1, it is difficult to be certain whether the company will have to pay legal fees of £1000 or £3000.

The proprietor who argues that the accountant has got a motor vehicle entered twice in the books of account.

Some goods were purchased and entered into stock at the end of period 1, but they were not paid for until period 2.

2.7 The following is a list of problems which an accountant may well meet in practice:

The transfer fee of a footballer.

Goods are sold in one period, but the cash for them is received in a later period.

The proprietor's personal dwelling house has been used as security for a loan which the bank has granted to the company.

What profit to take in the third year of a five-year construction contract.

Small stocks of stationery held at the accounting year end.

Expenditure incurred in working on the improvement of a new drug.

Required:
State:
(1) which accounting rule the accountant would most probably adopt in dealing with each of the above problems; and
(2) the reasons for your choice.

2.8 The Companies Act 1985 lists five prescribed accounting principles, while SSAP 2 (Disclosure of accounting policies) refers to four fundamental accounting concepts.

Required:
Write a report for your managing director comparing and contrasting the five accounting principles laid down in the Companies Act 1985 with the four fundamental accounting concepts outlined in SSAP 2. (*Note*: Before preparing your report, you will need to consult both the Act and the Standard.)

2.9 The adoption of the realization and matching rules in preparing financial accounts requires a great deal of subjective judgement.

Required:
Write an essay examining whether it would be fairer, easier, and more meaningful to prepare financial accounts on a cash flow basis.

3 Recording data

Opera criticised over cash crisis

By Robert Dawson Scott and Conal Urquhart

SCOTTISH Opera almost went bust because its accounting practices were so bad that managers were not aware of the state of their finances, according to a report published yesterday.

Because the company had no financial controller the extent of its problems went unnoticed until the opera was on the verge of bankruptcy.

It was saved by a £2.1 million injection of public money last year when it became clear that its Scottish Arts Council (SAC) grant would not meet its debts. It is still expected to be £1.5 million in debt next year because of over-spending.

The SAC and the Scottish executive were critical of the financial mismanagement of Scottish Opera which is now merged with Scottish Ballet.

An extravagant production of Verdi's *Macbeth* lay at the heart of the opera's financial problems. The opera cost £600,000 and combined with other financial problems to produce a spiral of debt. Without financial help Scottish Opera would have owed £3.3 million.

The SAC was ordered by the executive to analyse how it monitored the finances of the companies that it funded to ensure no repeat of Scottish Opera's slide into debt.

The report found that in the accounts of the Scottish arts companies, the Royal Scottish National Orchestra, the Scottish Chamber Orchestra, Scottish Opera and Scottish Ballet, the figures did not reflect their true financial situation. There was 'a lack of consistency and co-ordination between the long-term financial model, the budgets to which the companies were operating, the cash flow forecasts and the artistic plans'.

Arts companies have an unusual system of financial management with much investment, including productions, not included in accounts until it is shown to the public and has a chance to generate revenue.

The Scotsman, 12 February 2000. Reprinted with permission.

Poor accounting practices can lead to trouble

In the last chapter, a number of basic accounting rules were outlined, including the dual aspect rule. In this chapter, the dual aspect rule will be examined in much more detail.

Most modern book-keeping systems adopt the dual aspect rule, irrespective of whether they are handwritten or computer-based. While it is unlikely that as a non-accountant you will be involved in the recording of accounting data, you may well be presented with information based on such data. In presenting it to you, it is sometimes assumed that you have some knowledge of double-entry book-keeping.

This chapter has been specially designed to introduce the non-accountant to the subject of double-entry book-keeping. The chapter contains a number of book-keeping examples and, while it might seem unnecessary for you to work through them, you are recommended to do so for two main reasons:

1 it will help you to become familiar with accounting terminology;
2 a knowledge of the methods used in preparing accounting information will help you to assess its *usefulness* in doing your job much more effectively.

We had better warn you that this will not be an easy chapter for you to work through. And we mean *work*, rather than just read through. Most sections contain an exhibit which illustrates a particular book-keeping procedure. These exhibits must be studied most carefully.

To help you get the most out of this chapter, you are recommended to adopt the following procedure:

1 read the descriptive material in each section very carefully;
2 make sure that you understand the requirements of each exhibit;
3 examine the answer to each exhibit, paying particular attention to the following points:
    (a) the way in which it has been presented, i.e. its format;
    (b) how the data in the exhibit have been converted in response to the requirements of the question;
4 once you have worked through the answer, try to do the question on your own without reference to the solution;
5 if you go wrong, or you find that you do not know how to do the question, reread the earlier parts of the chapter and then have another go at it.

We begin our study of the dual aspect rule by explaining what is meant by the 'accounting equation'.

By the end of this chapter, you should be able to:

- **explain what is meant by the accounting equation;**
- **describe what is meant bt the terms 'debit' and 'credit';**
- **write up some simple ledger accounts;**
- **extract a trial balance;**
- **identify six accounting errors not revealed in a trial balance.**

The accounting equation

As we explained in Chapters 1 and 2, the system that accountants use to record financial data is known as *double-entry book-keeping*. Double-entry book-keeping is based on the dual aspect rule, i.e. a recognition that every transaction has a twofold effect. Thus if I loan you £100, a two-fold effect arises because (1) I give you some money; and (2) you receive it. The transaction, however, has also a twofold effect on *both of us*. This point may be a little clearer if we summarize the position as follows:

- *The effect on you:* (1) your cash goes up by £100; and (2) what you owe me also goes up by £100.
- *The effect on me:* (2) my cash goes down by £100; and (2) what I am owed by you goes up by £100.

In practice, an accountant would probably only deal with one or other of the entities, i.e. either 'you' or 'me'. This is what accountants mean about a 'twofold effect' and a double-entry book-keeping system captures this effect.

Before we describe how this system works in practice, it is necessary to introduce you to three essential accounting terms. These are as follows:

1 *Assets*: Assets are possessions or resources *owned* by an entity. They include physical or tangible possessions such as property, plant, machinery, stock, and cash and bank balances. They also include intangible assets, i.e. non-physical possessions such as copyright and patent rights, as well as debts owed to the entity, i.e. trade and other debtors.

2 *Capital*: 'Capital' is the term used to describe the amount which the owners have invested in an entity. In effect, their 'capital' is the amount owed by the entity to its owners.

3 *Liabilities*: Liabilities are the opposite of assets. They are the amounts owed *by* an entity to outside parties. They include loans, bank overdrafts, creditors, i.e. amounts owing to parties for the supply of goods and services to the entity that have not yet been settled in cash.

There is a close relationship between assets, capital and liabilities and it is frequently presented in the form of what is called the 'accounting equation'. It is as follows.

Assets = Capital and Liabilities

In other words, what the entity owns in terms of possessions has been financed by a combination of funds provided by the owners and amounts borrowed.

We will illustrate the use of the accounting equation with a simple example. Let us assume that you have decided to go into business. You do so by transferring £1000 in cash from your own private bank account. Invoking the entity rule, we are not interested in your private affairs, but we do want to keep track of how the business deals with your £1000.

You have invested £1000 in the business. This is its capital. However, it now possesses £1000 in cash. The cash is an asset. Hence the £1000 asset equals the £1000 of capital. In other words we can express the relationship between the assets and the capital in equation form as follows:

Assets		Capital	
Cash	£1000	Capital	£1000

(= between the two boxes)

The equation captures the twofold effect of the transaction: the assets of the business have been increased by the capital that has been contributed by the owner.

Now suppose that you then decide to transfer £500 of the cash to a business bank account. The effect on the equation is as follows:

Assets		Capital	
	£		£
Bank	500	Capital	1000
Cash	500		
	1000		1000

(= between the two boxes)

All that has happened is that there has been a change on the *assets* side of the equation.

Suppose now that you borrow £500 in cash from one of your friends to provide further financial help to the business. The assets will be increased by an inflow of £500 in cash, but £500 will be owed to your friend. The £500 owed is a liability and your friend has become a creditor of the business. The business has total assets of £1500 (£500 at the bank and £1000 in cash). Its capital is £1000 and it has a liability of £500. The equation then reads as follows.

Assets			Capital			Liabilities	
	£			£			£
Bank	500	=	Capital	1000	+	Creditor	500
Cash	1000			———			———
	———			1000			500
	1500						

If £800 of goods are purchased in cash for subsequent resale to the entity's customers, the equation would read:

Assets			Capital			Liabilities	
	£			£			£
Stocks	800	=	Capital	1000	+	Creditor	500
Bank	500						
Cash	200			———			———
	———			1000			500
	1500						

All that has happened here is that there has been a change on the assets side of the equation when £800 of the cash (an asset) was used to purchase £800 of goods for resale (i.e. stocks), another asset.

The equation is becoming somewhat complicated but it does enable us to see the effect that *any* transaction has on it. The vital point to remember about the accounting equation may be summarized as follows:

If an adjustment is made to one side of the equation, you *must* make an identical adjustment *either* to the other side of the equation *or* to the same side.

This maxim reflects the basic rule of double-entry book-keeping:

Every transaction must be recorded twice.

We will explain how this is done in the next section.

Double-entry book-keeping

Relevance and importance

Before we examine the mechanics of double-entry book-keeping, it would be as well if we answer two questions which you might be asking yourself.

Question 1: *'Why should we want to record everything twice?'*
There are two main reasons. First, it enables detailed information to be provided about all the assets *owned* and all the liabilities *owed* by the entity (including the capital contributed by the owners). Second, the system acts as a

control mechanism since there is a duplicate record for every transaction that has taken place.

Question 2: *'Why should a non-accountant bother with double-entry book-keeping?'* The honest answer is that it is not absolutely essential. Indeed, there are many accounting lecturers who regard it as a complete waste of time for non-accounting students to study double-entry book-keeping. We do not agree with this view. We think that there are three important reasons why it is advantageous for you to study this subject. They are as follows.

1   *You will be able to speak the accountants' language.* By studying double-entry book-keeping, you will learn the jargon and terminology (i.e. the language) used by accountants. Hence when they provide you with data and information, you will be able to translate it and assess its importance to you much more successfully.
2   *You will be able to understand the basic foundations of accounting reports.* Accounting is a service industry. Accountants are employed to help you do your job more successfully. However, accounting information is difficult to understand fully if you are not familiar with its basic origins. Hence you may feel very vulnerable if you are taking decisions based on information that does not mean very much to you.
3   *You will be able to argue and debate with accountants on equal terms.* Accounting information is based on a considerable number of questionable assumptions which may not be valid in particular circumstances. By being familiar with the language and nuances of fundamental accounting procedures, you will be able to have a much more meaningful and relevant debate with your accountants about the type of information that is useful to you in your job.

We hope that these reasons have convinced you of the importance of having a basic knowledge of double-entry book-keeping. Now please read on.

Mechanics

The accounting equation reflects the twofold effect of every transaction and a double-entry book-keeping system records that effect. This means that just as every transaction results in two adjustments being made to the accounting equation, two 'entries' are made in 'the books of account'.

All transactions are classified into appropriate groupings and each grouping is stored separately in what are known as *accounts*. An account is simply a history or a record of a particular type of transaction. The accounts are usually kept in bound books known as *ledgers*, although most entities now use a computerized system. Both computerized and non-computerized recording systems adopt the same basic accounting principles, so that a study of a manually based system of double-entry book-keeping is still relevant.

The effect of entering a particular transaction once in one ledger account and again in another ledger account is to cause the balance on each of the two accounts either to go up or to go down (in just the same way as happens to the accounting equation). Consequently, a particular transaction could either *increase* or *decrease* the total amount held in an account. In other words, an account either *receives* an additional amount or it *gives* (i.e. releases) an existing amount. It is this receiving and giving effect that has given rise to two terms from Latin that are commonly used in accounting. These terms are as follows:

> **Debit**: meaning to receive, or value received.
> **Credit**: meaning to give, or value given.

Accountants judge the twofold effect of all transactions on particular accounts from a receiving and giving point of view and each transaction is recorded on that basis. Thus, when a transaction takes place, it is necessary to ask the following questions:

1 Which account should *receive* this transaction (i.e. which account should be debited?
2 Which account has *given* this amount (i.e. which account should be credited?

Accounts have been designed to keep the debit entries separate from the credit entries. This helps to emphasize the opposite, albeit equal, effect that each transaction has within the recording system. The separation is achieved by recording the debit entries on the left-hand side of the page, and the credit entries on the right-hand side. In a handwritten system, each account is normally kept on a separate page (known as a folio) in a book of account (although if there are a lot of accounts, it may be necessary to keep several books of account). A book of account is also sometimes known as a ledger, and hence accounts are often referred to as *ledger accounts*. The format of a typical hand-written ledger account is illustrated in Exhibit 3.1.

There is no logical reason why debits should be entered on the left-hand side of an account, and credits on the right-hand side. It is purely a matter of custom, like driving on either the left-hand or the right-hand side of the road.

In the next section we will show you how particular transactions are recorded in appropriate ledger accounts.

Exhibit 3.1 Example of a ledger account

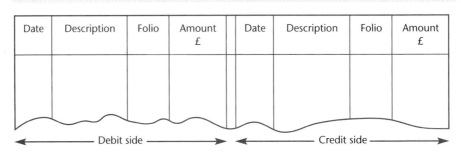

Tutorial notes

1 The columnar headings would normally be omitted.
2 The description of each entry is usually limited to the *title* of the corresponding account in which the equal entry and opposite entry may be found.
3 The folio column is used to refer to the folio (or page) number of the corresponding account.
4 This example of a ledger account may nowadays only be found in a fairly basic handwritten book-keeping system. Computerized systems of recording information usually necessitate an alternative format.

Working with accounts

It would not be helpful to the owners or the managers of a business if data were not recorded systematically. What has evolved, is a practical method of capturing the twofold nature of all transactions in separate accounts. The book-keeper has then to decide in which two accounts to enter a particular transaction. The following subsections illustrate the procedure that the book-keeper will adopt.

Choice of accounts

Most transactions can be easily assigned to an appropriate account. The total number and type will depend partly upon the amount of information that the owner wants (for example, salaries and wages might be kept in separate accounts), and partly upon the nature of the business (a manufacturing entity will probably need more accounts than a service entity). In practice, there are a number of accounts that are common to most entities, but if you do not know which account to use, you should adopt the following rule:

If in doubt, open another account.

If an account does eventually prove unnecessary, it can always be closed down. While some accounts are common to most entities, it will not always be clear what they should be used for. An idea of the overall system is shown in Figure 3.1, and we also list below a brief summary of the main types of accounts:

Capital   The **Capital Account** records what the owner has contributed (or given) to the entity out of his private resources in order to start the business and keep it going. In other words, it shows what the business owes him.

Cash at bank   The **Bank Account** records what money the entity keeps at the bank. It shows what has been put in (usually in the form of cash and cheques) and what has been taken out (usually by cheque payments).

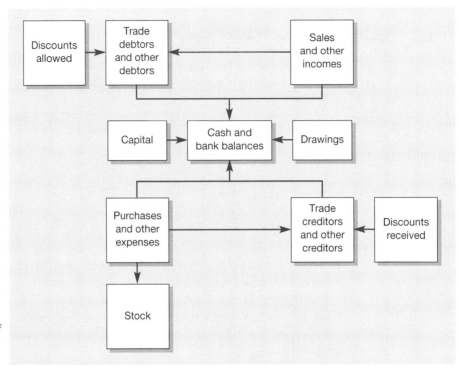

**Figure 3.1
The inter-linking of
different types
of accounts**

Cash in hand

The **Cash Account** works on similar lines to that of the Bank Account, except that it records the physical cash received (such as notes, coins and cheques) before they are paid into the bank. The cash received may be used to purchase goods and services, or it may be paid straight into the bank. From a control point of view, it is best not to pay for purchases directly out of cash receipts, but to draw an amount out of the bank specifically for sundry cash purchases. Any large amount should be paid by cheque.

Creditors

Creditor Accounts record what the entity owes its suppliers for goods or services purchased or supplied on credit (see also trade creditors).

Debtors

Debtor Accounts record what is owed to the entity by its customers for goods or services sold to them on credit (see also trade debtors).

**Discounts
allowed**

Discounts allowed are cash discounts granted to the entity's customers for the prompt settlement of any debts due to the entity. The amount of cash received from debtors who claim a cash discount will then be less than the total amount for which they have been involved.

**Discounts
received**

Discounts received relate to cash discounts given by the entity's suppliers for the prompt payment of any amounts due to them. Thus, the amount paid to the entity's creditors will be less than the invoiced amount.

Drawings

The term *drawings* has a special meaning in accounting. The **Drawings Account** is used to record what cash (or goods) the owner has withdrawn from the business for the owner's personal use.

Petty Cash

The **Petty Cash Account** is similar to both the Bank Account and the Cash Account. It is usually limited to the recording of minor cash transactions, such as bus fares, or tea and coffee for the office. The cash used to finance this account will normally be transferred from the Bank Account.

Purchases

The term *purchases* has a restricted meaning in accounting. It relates to those goods that are bought primarily with the intention of selling them (normally at a profit). The purchase of some motor cars, for example, would not usually be recorded in the **Purchases Account** unless they have been bought with the intention of selling them to customers. Goods not intended for resale are usually recorded in separate accounts. Some purchases may also require further work to be done on them before they are eventually sold.

Trade creditors

Trade Creditor Accounts are similar to Creditor Accounts except that they relate specifically to trading items, i.e. purchases.

Trade debtors

Trade Debtor Accounts are similar to Debtor Accounts except that they also relate specifically to trading items, i.e. sales.

Trade discounts

Trade discounts are a form of special discount. They may be given for placing a large order, for example, or for being a loyal customer. Trade discounts are deducted from the normal purchase or selling price. They are not recorded in the books of account and they will not appear on any invoice.

Sales

The **Sales Account** records the value of goods sold to customers during a particular accounting period. The account includes both cash and credit sales. It does not include receipts from (say) the sale of a motor car purchased for use within the business.

Stock

Stock includes the value of goods which have not been sold at the end of an accounting period. In accounting terminology, this would be referred to as *closing stock*. The closing stock at the end of one period becomes the *opening stock* at the beginning of the next period.

Once the book-keeper has chosen the accounts in which to record all the transactions for a particular accounting period, it is then necessary to decide which account should be debited and which account should be credited. We examine this problem in the next subsection.

Entering transactions in accounts

There is one simple rule that should be followed when entering a transaction in an account.

Debit the account which receives
and
Credit the account which gives.

This rule is illustrated in Exhibit 3.2, which contains some common ledger account entries.

Exhibit 3.2 Example of some common ledger account entries

Example 1

The proprietor contributes some cash to the business.

Debit: Cash Account   *Credit*: Capital Account

Reason: The Cash Account receives some cash given to the business by the owner. His Capital Account is the giving account and the Cash Account is the receiving account.

Example 2

Some cash in the till is paid into the business bank account.

Debit: Bank Account   *Credit*: Cash Account

Reason: The Cash Account is the giving account because it is releasing some cash to the Bank Account.

Example 3

A van is purchased for use in the business; it is paid for by cheque.

Debit: Van Account   *Credit*: Bank Account

Reason: The Bank Account is giving some money in order to pay for a van, so the Bank Account must be credited as it is the giving account.

Example 4

Some goods are purchased for cash.

Debit: Purchases Account   *Credit*: Cash Account

Reason: The Cash Account is giving up an amount of cash in order to pay for some purchases. The Cash Account is the giving account, and so it must be credited.

Example 5

Some goods are purchased on credit terms from Fred.

Debit: Purchases Account   *Credit*: Fred's Account.

Reason: Fred is supplying the goods on credit terms to the business. He is, therefore, the giver and his account must be credited.

Example 6

Some goods are sold for cash.

Debit: Cash Account   *Credit*: Sales Account

Reason: The Cash Account receives the cash from the sale of goods, the Sales Account being the giving account.

Example 7

Some goods are sold on credit terms to Sarah.

Debit: Sarah's Account   *Credit*: Sales Account

Reason: Sarah's Account is debited because she is receiving the goods, and the Sales Account is credited because it is supplying (or giving) them.

It is not easy for beginners to think of the receiving and of the giving effect of each transaction. You will find that it is very easy to get them mixed up and to then reverse the entries. If we look at Examples 6 and 7 in Exhibit 3.3, for example, it is difficult to understand why the Sales Account should be credited. Why is the Sales Account the giving account? Surely it is *receiving* an amount and not giving anything? In one sense, it is receiving something, but that applies to any entry in any account. So, in the case of the sales account, regard it as a *supplying* account, because it gives (or releases) something to another account.

If you find this concept difficult to understand, think of the effect on the opposite account. A cash sale, for example, results in cash being increased (not decreased). The cash account must, therefore, be the receiving account, and it must be debited. Somebody (say Jones) must have given the cash, but as it is a cash sale, we credit it straight to the sales account. If you find it easier, think of the Sales Department having supplied, given or sold the goods to Jones.

Most students find it easier, in fact, to work out the double-entry effect of respective transactions by relating them to the movement of cash. You might find it useful, therefore, to remember the following procedure:

> *Either*   DEBIT: the Cash (or Bank) Account and
> CREDIT: the corresponding account, if the
> entity *receives* some cash.
> *Or*   DEBIT: the corresponding account and
> CREDIT: the Cash (or Bank) Account, if
> the entity *gives* some cash.

If a movement of cash is not involved in a particular transaction, work out the effect on the corresponding account on the assumption that one account is affected by a cash transaction. In the case of a credit sale, for example, the account that benefits from the receipt of the goods must be that of an individual, so that individual's account must be debited (instead of the cash account, as it would be in the case of a cash sale). The corresponding entry must, therefore, be credited to some account. In this case it will be to the sales account.

You might also find it useful to remember another general rule used in double-entry book-keeping:

> **For every debit there must be a credit**
> and
> **For every credit there must be a debit.**

There are no exceptions to this rule – think back to the accounting equation covered earlier in this chapter. As this chapter develops, more practice will be obtained in deciding which account to debit and which account to credit. After some time, it becomes largely a routine exercise, and you will find yourself making the correct entries automatically.

It would now be helpful to illustrate the entry of a number of transactions in specific ledger accounts. We do so in the next section.

A ledger account example

This section illustrates the procedure adopted in entering various transactions in ledger accounts. The section brings together the basic material covered in the earlier part of this chapter. It demonstrates the use of various types, and the debiting and crediting effect of different types of transactions.

The example shown in Exhibit 3.3 relates to a sole trader commencing business on his own account. As we explained in earlier chapters, while most non-accountants will not be involved in sole-trader entities, this type of entity is useful in illustrating the basic principles of double-entry book-keeping. Indeed, a more complex form of entity would only obscure those principles.

The example is also confined to a business that purchases and sells goods on cash terms. Businesses that buy and sell goods on credit terms will be a feature of later examples.

It is unnecessary for you as a non-accountant to spend too much time on detailed ledger account work, but before moving on to the next section, you are recommended to work through Exhibit 3.3 without reference to the answer. This exercise will help you to familiarize yourself with the dual aspect concept, and therefore enable you to understand much more clearly the basis on which accounting information is recorded.

Exhibit 3.3 Joe Simple: a sole trader

The following information relates to Joe Simple, who started a new business on 1 January 2001:

1	1.1.01	Joe started the business with £5000 in cash.
2	3.1.01	He paid £3000 of the cash into a business bank account.
3	5.1.01	Joe bought a van for £2000 paying by cheque.
4	7.1.01	He bought some goods, paying £1000 in cash.
5	9.1.01	Joe sold some of the goods, receiving £1500 in cash.

Required:
Enter the above transactions in Joe's ledger accounts.

Answer to Exhibit 3.3

Joe Simple's books of account:

Cash Account

		£			£
1.1.01	Capital (1)	5 000	3.1.01	Bank (2)	3 000
9.1.01	Sales (5)	1 500	7.1.01	Purchases (4)	1 000

Capital Account

		£			£
			1.1.01	Cash (1)	5 000

Bank Account

		£			£
3.1.01	Cash (2)	3 000	5.1.01	Van (3)	2 000

Van Account

		£		£
5.1.01	Bank (3)	2 000		

Purchases Account

		£		£
7.1.01	Cash (4)	1 000		

Sales Account

	£			£
		9.1.01	Cash (5)	1 500

Tutorial notes

1 The numbers in brackets after each entry refer to the exhibit notes; they have been inserted for tutorial guidance only.
2 The narration relates to that account in which the equal and opposite entry may be found.

After entering all the transactions for a particular period in appropriate ledger accounts, the next stage in the exercise is to calculate the balance on each account as at the end of each accounting period.

Balancing the accounts

During a particular accounting period, some accounts (such as the bank and cash accounts) will contain a great many debit and credit entries. Some accounts may contain either mainly debit entries (e.g. the purchases account), or largely credit entries (e.g. the sales account). It would be somewhat inconvenient to allow the entries (whether mainly debits, credits, or a mixture of both) to build up without occasionally striking a balance. Indeed, the owner will almost certainly want to know not just what is in each account, but also what its overall or *net balance* is (i.e the total of all the debit entries less the total of all the credit entries). Thus, at frequent intervals, it will be necessary to calculate the balance on each account.

Balancing an account requires the book-keeper to add up all the respective debit and credit entries, take one total away from the other, and arrive at the net balance.

Accounts may be balanced fairly frequently, e.g. once a week or once a month, but some entities may only do so when they prepare their annual accounts. However, in order to keep a tight control on the management of the business, it is advisable to balance the accounts at reasonably short intervals. The frequency will depend upon the nature and the size of the entity, but once a month is probably sufficient for most entities.

The balancing of the accounts is part of the double-entry procedure, and the method is quite formal. In Exhibit 3.4 we show how to balance an account with a *debit* balance on it (i.e. when its total debit entries exceed its total credit entries).

Exhibit 3.4 Balancing an account with a debit balance

Cash Account

			£				£
1.1.01	Sales (1)		2 000	10.1.01	Jones (1)		3 000
15.1.01	Rent received (1)		1 000	25.1.01	Davies (1)		5 000
20.1.01	Smith (1)		4 000				
31.1.01	Sales (1)		8 000	31.1.01	Balance c/d (2)		7 000
		(3)	15 000			(3)	15 000
1.2.01	Balance b/d (4)		7 000				

Note: The number shown after each narration relates to the tutorial notes below.

Tutorial notes

1 The total debit entries equal £15 000 (2000 + 1000 + 4000 + 8000). The total credit entries equal £8000 (3000 + 5000). The net balance on this account, therefore, at 31 January 2001 is a *debit balance* of £7000 (15 000 – 8000). Until both the debit entries and the credit entries have been totalled, of course, it will not usually be apparent whether the balance is a debit one or a credit one. However, it should be noted that there can never be a credit balance in a cash account, because it is impossible to pay out more cash than has been received.

2 The debit balance of £7000 is inserted on the *credit* side of the account at the time that the account is balanced (in the case of Exhibit 3.4, at 31 January 2001). This then enables the total of the credit column to be balanced so that it agrees with the total of the debit column. The abbreviation 'c/d' means carried down. In this exhibit

the debit balance is carried down in the account in order to start the new period on 1 February 2001.

3 The £15 000 shown as a total in both the debit and the credit columns demonstrates that the columns balance (they do so, of course, because £7000 has been inserted in the credit column to make them balance). The totals are double-underlined in order to signify that they are a final total.

4 The balancing figure of £7000 is brought down ('b/d') in the account to start the new period on 1 February 2001. The double entry has been completed because £7000 has been debited *below* the line (i.e. below the £15 000 debit total), and the £7000 balancing figure credited *above* the line (i.e. above the £15 000 total).

Exhibit 3.4 demonstrates how an account with a debit entry is balanced. In Exhibit 3.5, we illustrate a similar procedure, but this time the account has a *credit* balance.

Exhibit 3.5 Balancing an account with a credit balance

Scott's Account

		£			£
31.1.01	Bank (1)	20 000	15.1.01	Purchases (1)	10 000
31.1.01	Balance c/d (2)	5 000	20.1.01	Purchases (1)	15 000
	(3)	25 000		(3)	25 000
			1.2.01	Balance b/d (4)	5 000

Note: The number shown after each narration relates to the tutorial notes below.

Tutorial notes

1 Apart from the balance, there is only one debit entry in Scott's account: the bank entry of £20 000. The total credit entries amount to £25 000 (10 000 + 15 000). Scott has a *credit balance*, therefore, in his account as at 31 January 2001 of £5000 (10 000 + 15 000 – 20 000). With many more entries in the account it would not always be possible to tell immediately whether the balance was a debit one or a credit one.

2 The credit balance of £5000 at 31 January 2001 is inserted on the *debit* side of the account in order to enable the account to be balanced. The balance is then carried down (c/d) to the next period.

3 The £25 000 shown as the total for both the debit and the credit columns identifies the balancing of the account. This has been made possible because of the insertion of the £5000 balancing figure on the debit side of the account.

4 The balancing figure of £5000 is brought down (b/d) in the account in order to start the account in the new period beginning on 1 February 2001. The double-entry has been completed because the debit entry of £5000 above the £25 000 line on the debit side equals the credit entry below the £25 000 line on the credit side.

Exhibits 3.4 and 3.5 demonstrate the importance of always obeying the cardinal rule of double-entry book-keeping:

For every debit there must be a credit
and
For every credit there must be a debit.

This rule must still be followed even if the two entries are made in the same account (as is the case when an account is balanced). If this rule is not obeyed, the accounts will not balance. This could mean that a lot of time is spent looking for an apparent error, or it could even mean that some incorrect information is given to the owner or managers of the business, since there is bound to be a mistake in at least one account.

The next stage after balancing each account is to check that the double entry has been completed throughout the entire system. This is done by compiling what is known as a *trial balance*.

The trial balance

A trial balance is a statement compiled at the end of a specific accounting period. It is a convenient method of checking that all the transactions and all the balances have been entered correctly in the ledger accounts. The trial balance is, however, a working paper, and it does not form part of the double-entry process.

A trial balance lists all of the debit balances and all of the credit balances extracted from each of the accounts throughout the ledger system. The total of all the debit balances is then compared with the total of all the credit balances. If the two totals agree, we can be reasonably confident that the book-keeping procedures have been carried out accurately.

We illustrate the preparation of a trial balance in Exhibit 3.6. We also take the opportunity of giving some more examples of how transactions are entered in ledger accounts. You are recommended to work through part (a) of Exhibit 3.6 before moving on to part (b). When you are confident that you understand the procedures involved, have a go at doing the question without looking at the solution.

Exhibit 3.6 Edward – compilation of a trial balance

Edward started a new business on 1 January 2001. The following transactions took place during his first month in business:

2001
1.1   Edward commenced business with £10 000 in cash.
3.1   He paid £8000 of the cash into a business bank account.

6.1 He bought a van on credit from Perkin's garage for £3000.

9.1 Edward rented shop premises for £1000 per quarter; he paid for the first quarter immediately by cheque.

12.1 He bought goods on credit from Roy Limited for £4000.

15.1 He paid shop expenses amounting to £1500 by cheque.

18.1 Edward sold goods on credit to Scott and Company for £3000.

21.1 He settled Perkin's account by cheque.

24.1 Edward received a cheque from Scott and Company for £2000; this cheque was paid immediately into the bank.

27.1 Edward sent a cheque to Roy Limited for £500.

31.1 Goods costing £3000 were purchased from Roy Limited on credit.

31.1 Cash sales for the month amounted to £2000.

Required:

(a) Enter the above transactions in appropriate ledger accounts, balance off each account as at 31 January 2001, and bring down the balances as at that date; and

(b) extract a trial balance as at 31 January 2001.

Cash Account

		£			£
1.1.01	Capital (1)	10 000	3.1.01	Bank (2)	8 000
31.1.01	Sales (12)	2 000	31.1.01	Balance c/d	4 000
		12 000			12 000
1.2.01	Balance b/d	4 000			

Capital Account

		£			£
			1.1.01	Cash (1)	10 000

Bank account

		£			£
3.1.01	Cash (2)	8 000	9.1.01	Rent payable (4)	1 000
24.1.01	Scott and		15.1.01	Shop expenses (6)	1 500
	Company (9)	2 000	21.1.01	Perkin's garage (8)	3 000
			27.1.01	Roy Limited (10)	500
			31.1.01	Balance c/d	4 000
		10 000			10 000
1.2.01	Balance b/d	4 000			

Van Account

		£			£
6.1.01	Perkin's Garage (3)	3 000			

Perkin's Garage Account

		£			£
21.1.01	Bank (8)	3 000	6.1.01	Van (3)	3 000

Rent Payable Account

		£			£
9.1.01	Bank (4)	1 000			

Purchases Account

		£			£
12.1.01	Roy Limited (5)	4 000			
31.1.01	Roy Limited (11)	3 000	31.1.01	Balance c/d	7 000
		7 000			7 000
1.2.01	Balance b/d	7 000			

Roy Limited Account

		£			£
27.1.01	Bank (10)	500	12.1.01	Purchases (5)	4 000
31.1.01	Balance c/d	6 500	31.1.01	Purchases (11)	3 000
		7 000			7 000
			1.2.01	Balance b/d	6 500

Shop Expenses Account

		£			£
15.1.01	Bank (6)	1 500			

Sales Account

		£			£
			18.1.01	Scott & Company (7)	3 000
31.1.01	Balance c/d	5 000	31.1.01	Cash (12)	2 000
		5 000			5 000
			1.2.01	Balance b/d	5 000

Scott and Company Account

		£			£
18.1.01	Sales (7)	3 000	24.1.01	Bank (9)	2 000
			31.1.01	Balance c/d	1 000
		3 000			3 000
1.2.01	Balance b/d	1 000			

Tutorial notes

1 The number shown after each narration has been inserted for tutorial guidance only in order to illustrate the insertion of each entry in the appropriate account.

2 There is no need to balance an account and carry down the balance when there is only a single entry in one account (for example, Edward's Capital Account).

3 Note that some accounts may have no balance in them at all as at 31 January 2001 (for example, Perkin's Garage Account).

Answer to Exhibit 3.6 (b)

Trial Balance at 31 January 2001

	Dr	Cr
	£	£
Cash	4 000	
Capital		10 000
Bank	4 000	
Van	3 000	
Rent payable	1 000	
Purchases	7 000	
Roy Limited		6 500
Shop expenses	1 500	
Sales		5 000
Scott and Company	1 000	
	21 500	21 500

Tutorial notes

1 The total debit balance agrees with the total credit balance, and therefore the trial balance balances. This confirms that the transactions appear to have been entered in the books of account correctly.
2 The total amount of £21 500 shown in both the debit and credit columns of the trial balance does not have any significance, except to prove that the trial balance balances.

Did you manage to get your trial balance to balance? If not, reread the earlier parts of this chapter and then have another attempt at Exhibit 3.6.

It should be noted that there are some errors that do not affect the balancing of the trial balance. These are as follows:

1 *Omission*: a transaction could have been completely omitted from the books of account.
2 *Complete reversal of entry*: a transaction could have been entered in (say) Account A as a debit and in Account B as a credit, when it should have been entered as a credit in Account A and as a debit in Account B.
3 *Principle*: a transaction may have been entered in the wrong *type* of account, e.g. the purchase of a new delivery van may have been debited to the purchases account, instead of the delivery vans account.
4 *Commission*: a transaction may have been entered in the correct type of account, but in the wrong *personal* account, e.g. in Bill's Account instead of in Ben's Account.
5 *Compensating*: an error may have been made in (say) adding the debit side of one account, and an identical error made in adding the credit side of another account; the two errors would then cancel each other out.
6 *Original entry*: a transaction may be entered incorrectly in both accounts, e.g. as £291 instead of as £921.

Even allowing for the types of errors listed above, the trial balance still serves three useful purposes. These are as follows:

1 it enables the accuracy of the transactions entered in the accounts to be checked;
2 a summary of the balance on each account can be obtained; and
3 it provides the information needed in preparing the annual accounts.

We shall be dealing with the third purpose in some detail in the next two chapters.

Conclusion

As a non-accountant, it is most unlikely that you will become involved in having to write up ledger accounts or enter transactions into a computerized accounting system. In this chapter, therefore, we have avoided going into too much detail about double-entry book-keeping that is irrelevant for your purposes. As part of your managerial role, you will almost certainly be supplied with information that has been extracted from a ledger system. In order to assess its real benefit to you, we believe that it is most important that you should know something about where it has come from, what it means, and what reliability can be placed on it.

We recommend that before leaving this chapter, you make absolutely sure that you are familiar with the following features of a double-entry book-keeping system:

- the accounting equation;
- the type of accounts generally used in practice;
- the meaning of the terms *debit* and *credit*;
- the definition of the terms *debtor* and *creditor*;
- the method of entering transactions in ledger accounts;
- the balancing of ledger accounts;
- the importance of the trial balance.

This chapter has provided you with the basic information necessary to become familiar with the seven features listed above. If you are reasonably confident that you now have a basic grasp of double-entry book-keeping, you can move on to an examination of how financial accounts are prepared. Before doing so, however, you are recommended to test your understanding of the contents of this chapter by attempting some of the questions at the end of the chapter.

Key points

1 The accounting equation is represented by the formula: Assets = Capital + Liabilities. The equation underpins the dual-aspect rule and it forms the basis of a conventional accounting recording system.

2 An account is an explaination, a record, or a history of a particular event.

3 A book of account is known as a ledger.

4 A page is referred to as a folio.

5 A transaction is the carrying out and the performance of any business.

6 All transactions have a twofold effect.

7 A double-entry system records that twofold effect.

8 A debit means a transaction is received into an account.

9 A credit means that a transaction is given by an account.

10 Debits are entered on the left-hand side of an account.

11 Credits are entered on the right-hand side of an account.

12 For every debit entry, there must be a credit entry.

13 Accounts are balanced periodically.

14 The accuracy of the book-keeping is tested by preparing a trial balance.

15 The trial balance does not reveal all possible book-keeping errors.

Check your learning

1 Fill in the missing blanks in the following statements:
   (a) The accounting equation is represented by _____ = _____ + _____ .
   (b) A debit entry goes on the ____ -hand side of a ledger account, and a ____ entry goes on the right-hand side.

2 Which two ledger accounts would you use in recording each of the following transactions?
   (a) cash sales
   (b) rent paid by cheque
   (c) wages paid in cash
   (d) a supplier of goods paid by cheque
   (e) goods sold on credit to Ford.

3 State which account would be debited and which account would be credited in respect of each of the following items:
   (a) cash paid to a supplier
   (b) office rent paid by cheque
   (c) cash sales
   (d) dividend received by cheque.

4 Is there anything wrong with the following abbreviated bank account?

Debit		£000	Credit		£000
10.3.06	Wages paid	1 000	6.6.06	Interest received	500

5 State whether each of the following errors would be discovered as a result of preparing a trial balance:
   (a) £342 has been entered in both ledger accounts instead of £432.   Yes/No
   (b) The debit column in Prim's account has been overstated by £50.   Yes/No
   (c) £910 has been put in Anne's account instead of in Agnes's.   Yes/No

[*The answers to these questions may be found at the back of the book.*]

Group discussion questions

3.1 Do you think that non-accounting managers need to know anything about double-entry book-keeping?

3.2 'My accountant has got it all wrong,' argued Freda. 'She's totally mixed up all her debits and credits.'
'But what makes you say that?' queried Dora.
'Oh! I've only to look at my bank statement to see that she's wrong,' responded Freda. 'I know I've got some money in the bank, and yet she tells me I'm in debit when she means I'm in credit.'
Is Freda right?

3.3 'Double-entry book-keeping is a waste of time and money because everything has to be recorded twice.' Discuss.

Practice questions

[*Note: The questions marked with an asterisk have answers at the back of the book.*]

3.4* Adam has just gone into business. The following is a list of his transactions for the month of January 2001:

   (a) Cash paid into the business by Adam.
   (b) Goods for resale purchased on cash terms.
   (c) Van bought for cash.
   (d) One quarter's rent for premises paid in cash.
   (e) Some goods sold on cash terms.
   (f) Adam buys some office machinery for cash.

Required:
State which account in Adam's books of account should be debited and which account should be credited for each transaction.

3.5* The following is a list of Brown's transactions for February 2002:

Transfer of cash to a bank account.
Cash received from sale of goods.
Purchase of goods paid for by cheque.
Office expenses paid in cash.
Cheques received from customers from sale of goods on cash terms.
A motor car for use in the business paid for by cheque.

Required:
State which account in Brown's books of account should be debited and which account should be credited for each transaction.

3.6 Corby is in business as a retail distributor. The following is a list of his transactions for March 2003:

Goods purchased from Smith on credit.
Corby introduces further capital in cash into the business.
Goods sold for cash.
Goods purchased for cash.
Cash transferred to the bank.
Machinery purchased, paid for in cash.

Required:
State which account in Corby's books of account should be debited and which account should be credited for each transaction.

3.7 Davies buys and sells goods on cash and credit terms. The following is a list of her transactions for April 2004:

1 Capital introduced by Davies paid into the bank.
2 Goods purchased on credit terms from Swallow.
3 Goods sold to Hill for cash.
4 Cash paid for purchase of goods.
5 Dale buys goods from Davies on credit.
6 Motoring expenses paid by cheque.

Required:
State which account in Davies's books of account should be debited and which account should be credited for each transaction.

3.8 The following transactions relate to Gordon's business for the month of July 2007:

1 Bought goods on credit from Watson.
2 Sold some goods for cash.
3 Sold some goods on credit to Moon.
4 Sent a cheque for half the amount owing to Watson.
5 Watson grants Gordon a cash discount.
6 Moon settles most of his account in cash.
7 Gordon allows Moon a cash discount that covers the small amount owed by Moon.
8 Gordon purchases some goods for cash.

Required:

State which accounts in Gordon's books of accounts should be debited and which account should be credited for each piece of information.

3.9 Harry started a new business on 1 January 2000. The following transactions cover his first three months in business:

1   Harry contributed an amount in cash to start the business.
2   He transferred some of the cash to a business bank account.
3   He paid an amount in advance by cheque for rental of business premises.
4   Bought goods on credit from Paul.
5   Purchased a van paying by cheque.
6   Sold some goods for cash to James.
7   Bought goods on credit from Nancy.
8   Paid motoring expenses in cash.
9   Returned some goods to Nancy.
10   Sold goods on credit to Mavis.
11   Harry withdrew some cash for personal use.
12   Bought goods from David paying in cash.
13   Mavis returns some goods.
14   Sent a cheque to Nancy.
15   Cash received from Mavis.
16   Harry receives a cash discount from Nancy.
17   Harry allows Mavis a cash discount.
18   Cheque withdrawn at the bank in order to open a petty cash account.

Required:

State which accounts in Harry's books of account should be debited and which account should be credited for each transaction.

3.10* The following is a list of transactions which relate to Ivan for the first month that he is in business:

1.9.00	Started the business with £10 000 in cash.
2.9.00	Paid £8000 into a business bank account.
3.9.00	Purchased £1000 of goods in cash.
10.9.00	Bought goods costing £6000 on credit from Roy.
12.9.00	Cash sales of £3000.
15.9.00	Goods sold on credit terms to Norman for £4000.
20.9.00	Ivan settles Roy's account by cheque.
30.9.00	Cheque for £2000 received from Norman.

Required:

Enter the above transactions in Ivan's ledger accounts.

3.11* Jones has been in business since 1 October 2001. The following is a list of her transactions for October 2001:

1.10.01	Capital of £20 000 paid into a business bank account.
2.10.01	Van purchased on credit from Lang for £5000.
6.10.01	Goods purchased on credit from Green for £15 000.

10.10.01   Cheque drawn on the bank for £1000 in order to open a petty cash account.

14.10.01   Goods sold on credit for £6000 to Haddock.

18.10.01   Cash sales of £5000.

20.10.01   Cash purchases of £3000.

22.10.01   Miscellaneous expenses of £500 paid out of petty cash.

25.10.01   Lang's account settled by cheque.

28.10.01   Green allows Jones a cash discount of £500.

29.10.01   Green is sent a cheque for £10 000.

30.10.01   Haddock is allowed a cash discount of £600.

31.10.01   Haddock settles his account in cash.

Required:

Enter the above transactions in Jones's ledger accounts.

3.12   The transactions listed below relate to Ken's business for the month of November 2002:

1.11.02   Started the business with £150 000 in cash.

2.11.02   Transferred £14 000 of the cash to a business bank account.

3.11.02   Paid rent of £1000 by cheque.

4.11.02   Bought goods on credit from the following suppliers:
    Ace   £5000
    Mace   £6000
    Pace   £7000

10.11.02   Sold goods on credit to the following customers:
    Main   £2000
    Pain   £3000
    Vain   £4000

15.11.02   Returned goods costing £1000 to Pace.

22.11.02   Pain returned goods sold to him for £2000.

25.11.02   Additional goods purchased from the following suppliers:
    Ace   £3000
    Mace   £4000
    Pace   £5000

26.11.02   Office expenses of £2000 paid by cheque.

27.11.02   Cash sales for the month amounted to £5000.

28.11.02   Purchases paid for in cash during the month amounted to £4000.

29.11.02   Cheques sent to the following suppliers:
    Ace   £4000
    Mace   £5000
    Pace   £6000

30.11.02   Cheques received from the following customers:
    Main   £1000
    Pain   £2000
    Vain   £3000

30.11.02   The following cash discounts were claimed by Ken:
    Ace   £200
    Mace   £250
    Pace   £300

      30.11.02   The following cash discounts were allowed by Ken:

                 Main   £100

                 Pain   £200

                 Vain   £400

      30.11.02   Cash transfer to the bank of £1000.

Required:

Enter the above transactions in Ken's ledger accounts.

3.13*   The following transactions relate to Pat's business for the month of December 2003:

      1.12.03   Started the business with £10 000 in cash.

      2.12.03   Bought goods on credit from the following suppliers:

                 Grass   £6000

                 Seed   £7000

      10.12.03   Sold goods on credit to the following customers:

                 Fog   £3000

                 Mist   £4000

      12.12.03   Returned goods to the following suppliers:

                 Grass   £1000

                 Seed   £2000

      15.12.03   Bought additional goods on credit from Grass for £3000 and from Seed for £4000.

      20.12.03   Sold more goods on credit to Fog for £2000 and to Mist for £3000.

      24.12.03   Paid office expenses of £5000 in cash.

      29.12.03   Received £4000 in cash from Fog and £6000 in cash from Mist.

      31.12.03   Pat paid Grass and Seed £6000 and £8000, respectively, in cash.

Required:

(a) Enter the above transactions in Pat's ledger accounts.

(b) Balance off the accounts as at 31 December 2003.

(c) Bring down the balances as at 1 January 2004.

(d) Compile a trial balance as at 31 December 2003.

3.14*   Vale has been in business for some years. The following balances were brought forward in his books of account as at 31 December 2002:

	£ Dr	£ Cr
Bank	5 000	
Capital		20 000
Cash	1 000	
Dodd		2 000
Fish	6 000	
Furniture	10 000	
	22 000	22 000

During the year to 31 December 2003 the following transactions took place:

1 Goods bought from Dodd on credit for £30 000.
2 Cash sales of £20 000.
3 Cash purchases of £15 000.
4 Goods sold to Fish on credit for £50 000.
5 Cheques sent to Dodd totalling £29 000.
6 Cheques received from Fish totalling £45 000.
7 Cash received from Fish amounting to £7000.
8 Office expenses paid in cash totalling £9000.
9 Purchase of delivery van costing £12 000 paid by cheque.
10 Cash transfers to bank totalling £3000.

Required:
(a) Compile Vale's ledger accounts for the year 31 December 2003, balance off the accounts and bring down the balances as at 1 January 2004.
(b) Extract a trial balance as at 31 December 2003.

3.15 Brian started in business on 1 January 2004. The following is a list of his transactions for his first month of trading:

1.1.04   Opened a business bank account with £25 000 obtained from private resources.
2.1.04   Paid one month's rent of £2000 by cheque.
3.1.04   Bought goods costing £5000 on credit from Linda.
4.1.04   Purchased motor car from Savoy Motors for £4000 on credit.
5.1.04   Purchased goods costing £3000 on credit from Sydney.
10.1.04   Cash sales of £6000.
15.1.04   More goods costing £10 000 purchased from Linda on credit.
20.1.04   Sold goods on credit to Ann for £8000.
22.1.04   Returned £2000 of goods to Linda.
23.1.04   Paid £6000 in cash into the bank.
24.1.04   Ann returned £1000 of goods.
25.1.04   Withdrew £500 in cash from the bank to open a petty cash account.
26.1.04   Cheque received from Ann for £5500; Ann also claimed a cash discount of £500.
28.1.04   Office expenses of £250 paid out of petty cash.
29.1.04   Sent a cheque to Savoy Motors for £4000.
30.1.04   Cheques sent to Linda and Sydney for £8000 and £2000, respectively. Cash discounts were also claimed from Linda and Sydney of £700 and £l00, respectively.
31.1.04   Paid by cheque another month's rent of £2000.
31.1.04   Brian introduced £5000 additional capital into the business by cheque.

Required:
(a) Enter the above transactions in Brian's ledger accounts for January 2004, balance off the accounts and bring down the balances as at 1 February 2004.
(b) Compile a trial balance as at 31 January 2004.

3.16   An accounts clerk has compiled Trent's trial balance as at 31 March 2006 as follows:

	Dr	Cr
	£	£
Bank (overdrawn)	2 000	
Capital	50 000	
Discounts allowed		5 000
Discounts received	3 000	
Dividends received	2 000	
Drawings		23 000
Investments		14 000
Land and buildings	60 000	
Office expenses	18 000	
Purchases	75 000	
Sales		250 000
Suspense (unexplained balance)		6 000
Rates		7 000
Vans	20 000	
Van expenses		5 000
Wages and salaries	80 000	
	310 000	310 000

Required:
Compile Trent's corrected trial balance as at 31 March 2006.

3.17   Donald's transactions for the month of March 2009 are as follows:

	£
Cash receipts	
Capital contributed	6 000
Sales to customers	3 000
Cash payments	
Goods for sale	4 000
Stationery	500
Postage	300
Travelling	600
Wages	2 900
Transfers to bank	500

	£
Bank receipts	
Receipts from trade debtors:	
Smelt	3 000
Tait	9 000
Ure	5 000

Bank payments	£
Payments to trade creditors:	
Craig	2 800
Dobie	5 000
Elgin	6 400
Rent and rates	3 200
Electricity	200
Telephone	100
Salaries	2 000
Miscellaneous expenses	600

Other transactions	
Goods purchased from:	
Craig	3 500
Dobie	7 500
Elgin	7 500

Goods returned to Dobie	400
Goods sold to:	
Smelt	4 000
Tait	10 000
Ure	8 000
Goods returned by Ure	900
Discounts allowed:	
Smelt	200
Tait	500
Ure	400
Discounts received:	
Craig	50
Dobie	100
Elgin	200

Required:

(a) Enter the above transactions in appropriate ledger accounts;

(b) balance each account as at 31 March 2009; and

(c) extract a trial balance as at that date.

4 Trading entity accounts

AOL to pay $3.5m for accounting claims

By Thomas Catán and agencies, New York

America Online, the world's largest internet company, yesterday agreed to pay regulators $3.5m (£2.3m) to settle civil charges that it improperly accounted for its advertising costs between 1995 and 1996.

In a case that highlighted the complexity of applying traditional accountancy standards to the rapidly evolving world of internet companies, analysts said the Securities and Exchange Commission was keen to show it was maintaining a tight grip on the sector.

According to the SEC, AOL wrongly capitalised the costs of acquiring new customers – including sending out thousands of free computer discs – and reported them as an asset rather than an expense. As a result, the SEC said, the company posted profits for six of eight quarters in the financial years 1995 and 1996, instead of the losses it would have reported had the costs been shown correctly.

The internet services provider, based in Dulles, Virginia, said it discontinued the controversial accounting practice of capitalising its advertising costs in October 1996 and took a $385m charge at the time. In settling the charges, AOL did not admit wrongdoing and stressed the agreement would have no impact on its results since 1997. However, it promised to restate its results from 1995 to 1997 to reflect the agreed changes to its accounts. AOL also agreed to an order preventing further violations of securities laws.

Financial Times, 16 May 2000. Reprinted with permission.

Capital versus revenue: an important distinction in accounting

We suggested in Chapter 1 that the owners of a business want to know the answers to three fundamental questions:

1 What profit has the business made?
2 How much does the business owe?
3 How much is owed to it?

The last chapter finished with an explanation of how to prepare a trial balance. A trial balance has two important functions:

1 it enables the accuracy of book-keeping to be checked; and
2 it provides the basic data for the preparation of the financial accounts.

The composition of the financial accounts will depend upon whether the entity is in the profit-making sector or the not-for-profit sector, and whether it is a manufacturing, trading or service entity. Most profit-making entities usually prepare a *profit and loss account* and a *balance sheet*. The profit and loss account enables the question to be answered: *'What profit has the business made?'* A balance sheet answers the questions: *'How much does the business owe?'* and *'How much is owed to it?'*

In this chapter we are going to concentrate on *trading entities* because their accounts enable us to demonstrate a comprehensive range of procedures involved in preparing a set of basic financial accounts. In addition to the profit and loss account, a trading entity also prepares a *trading account*. A trading account shows the difference between what the entity paid for goods purchased from outside suppliers and what they were sold for to its own customers. The elements of a set of financial accounts for a trading entity are shown in diagrammatic form in Figure 4.1.

Before we show you how to prepare a basic set of financial accounts for a trading entity, we need to examine in a little more detail what accountants mean by 'profit'. We do so in the next section.

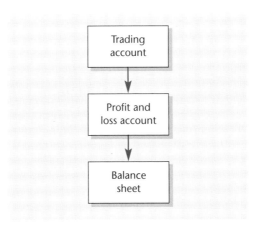

Figure 4.1
Basic accounts of a
trading entity

Learning
objectives

By the end of this chapter, you should be able to:

● **describe what accountants mean by profit;**

● **prepare a basic set of financial accounts for a trading entity.**

Cash versus profit

The owners of a business often try to measure the profit that it has made (i.e. how well it has done) by deducting the cash held at the end of a period from cash held at the beginning (after allowing for capital introduced or withdrawn during the period). It is then assumed that the difference represents profit (if the cash has increased) or loss (if the cash has decreased). This is *not* what accountants mean by profit.

As was outlined in Chapter 2, accounts are normally prepared by adopting a certain number of accounting rules. You will remember that the realization rule requires us to match the sales revenue for a particular period against the cost of selling those goods during the same period. The matching rule requires a similar procedure to be adopted for other types of incomes and expenses. It is unlikely that the difference between cash received and cash paid will be the same as the difference between income and expenditure. Cash transactions may relate to earlier or later periods, whereas incomes and expenditure (as defined in accounting) measure the *actual* economic activity that has taken place during a clearly defined period of time. By *income* we mean something that the entity has gained during a particular period, and by *expenditure* we mean something the entity has lost during the same period.

There are a great many problems, of course, in trying to measure income and expenditure in this way, rather than on a cash receipts and cash payments basis. In calculating profit, expenditure is especially difficult to determine. If the entity purchases a machine, for example, that has an estimated life of 20 years, how much of the cost should be charged against the income for (say) Year 1 compared with Year 20?

Accountants deal with this sort of problem by attempting to classify expenditure into *capital* and *revenue*. *Capital expenditure* is expenditure that is likely to provide a benefit to the entity for more than one accounting period, and *revenue expenditure* is expenditure that is likely to provide a benefit for only one period. As the basic financial accounts are normally prepared on an annual basis, we can regard revenue expenditure as being virtually the same as annual expenditure. If a similar benefit is required the next year, then the service will have to be reordered and another payment made.

Examples of revenue expenditure include goods purchased for resale, electricity charges, business rates paid to the local authority, and wages and salaries. Examples of capital expenditure include land and buildings, plant and machinery, motor vehicles, and furniture and fittings. Such items are described as *fixed assets*, because they are owned by the entity and they are intended for long-term use within it.

It is also possible to classify income into *capital* and *revenue*, although the terms capital income and capital revenue are not normally adopted. *Income of a revenue nature* would include the revenue from the sale of goods to customers, dividends and rents received. *Income of a capital nature* would include the resources invested by the owner in the business, and long-term loans made to it (such as bank loans).

Figure 4.2
Accounting profit

In practice, it is not always easy to distinguish between capital and revenue items, and the distinction is often an arbitrary one. Some items of expenditure are particularly difficult to determine, although most transactions fall into recognizable categories.

The distinction between capital and revenue items is very important because, essentially, accounting profit is the difference between revenue income and revenue expenditure (see Figure 4.2). If capital and revenue items are not classified accurately, the accounting profit will be incorrectly calculated. This could be extremely misleading, especially if the amount was overstated, because the owner might then draw too much out of the business, or have to pay more tax. Bearing in mind the prudence rule, it would be much less serious if the profit was understated, because it is likely that more cash would then have been retained within the business.

Preparation

We are now in a position to examine how a set of basic financial accounts for a trading entity are compiled, and hence how to calculate the amount of profit a business has made. We will assume that a trial balance has been prepared and that the books balance. There are then two main stages we have to go through in order to compile the accounts. We will deal with each stage separately.

The trading and profit and loss account stage

Once the trial balance has been compiled, the next step is to prepare a trading account and a profit and loss account. In order to do so, all the revenue income and expenditure items are extracted from the trial balance. These are then matched against each other in the form of a statement called (as you would expect) a *trading and profit and loss account*. By deducting the total of the revenue balances from the total of the revenue expenditure balances, we can determine the level of the profit (or loss) for the period. There are two important points to note. These are as follows:

1 The **trading account** comes before the profit and loss account. It matches the sales revenue for a certain period against the cost of goods sold (i.e. purchases) for the same period. The difference between the sales revenue and

the cost of goods sold is known as *gross profit*. The gross profit is then transferred to the profit and loss account, where it is added to the other revenue incomes of the business. That total is then matched against the other expenses of the business (such as heat and light, and wages and salaries). The difference between the gross profit plus other non-trading incomes, less the other expenses is known as *net profit* (or net loss). This all sounds very complicated, but we can express it in the form of two equations:

$$\text{Sales revenue} - \text{Cost of goods sold} = \text{Gross profit}$$

$$(\text{Gross profit} + \text{Revenue income}) - \text{Revenue expenditure} = \text{Net profit (or net loss)}$$

2 Both the trading account and the profit and loss account are accounts in their own right. This means that any transfer to or from them forms part of the double-entry procedure, and so a corresponding and equal entry has to be made in some other account.

The balance sheet stage

Once the trading account and profit and loss account balances have been extracted, all the balances left in the trial balance are summarized in the form of a statement called a *balance sheet*. A balance sheet is simply a listing of all the remaining balances left in the ledger account system following the preparation of the trading account and the profit and loss account. Unlike trading and profit and loss accounts, a balance sheet does not form part of the double-entry system: it is merely a listing of the remaining balances in the ledger system at the end of an accounting period. We could also describe it another way, and suggest that it is a listing of all the capital revenue and capital expenditure balances.

We are now in a position to show you how to prepare a set of basic trading entity accounts.

An illustrative example

In this section, we explain how to compile a trading account, a profit and loss account, and a balance sheet. The procedure is illustrated in Exhibit 4.1.

Exhibit 4.1 Preparation of basic financial accounts

The following trial balance has been extracted from Bush's books of account as at 30 June 2001:

Name of account		Dr £	Cr £
Bank (1)		5 000	
Capital (at 1 July 2000) (2)			11 000
Cash (3)		1 000	
Drawings (4)		8 000	
Motor vehicle at cost (5)		6 000	
Motor vehicle expenses (6)	(R)	2 000	
Office expenses (7)	(R)	3 000	
Purchases (8)	(R)	30 000	
Trade creditors (9)			4 000
Trade debtors (10)		10 000	
Sales (11)	(R)		50 000
		65 000	65 000

Notes: There were no opening or closing stocks.

R = revenue items.

Required:

(a) Prepare Bush's trading and profit and loss account for the year to 30 June 2001.

(b) Prepare a balance sheet as at that date.

Answer to Exhibit 4.1 (a)

Bush
Trading and profit and loss account for the year to 30 June 2001

	£		£
Purchases (8)	30 000	Sales (11)	50 000
Gross profit c/d	20 000		
	50 000		50 000
Motor vehicle expenses (6)	2 000	Gross profit b/d	20 000
Office expenses (7)	3 000		
Net profit c/d	15 000		
	20 000		20 000
		Net profit b/d	15 000

Tutorial notes

1 The number shown in brackets after each narration refers to the account number of each balance extracted from the trial balance.

2 Both the trading account and the profit and loss account cover a period of time. In this exhibit it is for the year to (or alternatively, *ending*) 30 June 2001.

3 It is not customary to keep the trading account totally separate from the profit and loss account. The usual format is the one shown above whereby the trading account balance (that is, the gross profit) is carried down straight into the profit and loss account.

4 Note that the proprietor's drawings (4), are not an expense of the business. They are treated as an *appropriation*, i.e. an amount withdrawn by the proprietor in advance of any profit that the business might have made.

The above trading and profit and loss account has been prepared in a ledger account format. This is known as the *horizontal format* because the debit entries (expenses) are shown on the left-hand side of the page, while the credit entries (incomes) are shown on the right-hand side. Trading and profit and loss accounts are ledger accounts in their own right, but they are also used to pass on information to parties who are not involved in the detailed recording procedures. Research evidence suggests that this format is not particularly helpful for those users who are not trained in double-entry book-keeping. A more acceptable presentation is when the information is presented on a line-by-line basis, starting from the top of the page and working downwards towards the bottom of the page. This is known as the *vertical format*. In accordance with modern practice, we will adopt this format throughout the rest of the book for the presentation of financial statements.

In the vertical account format, therefore, Bush's trading and profit and loss account would appear as set out in Exhibit 4.2.

Exhibit 4.2 Basic financial accounts in vertical format

Bush
Trading and profit and loss account for the year to 30 June 2001

	£	£
Sales		50 000
Less: cost of goods sold:		
Purchases		30 000
Gross profit		20 000
Less: expenses		
Motor vehicle expenses	2 000	
Office expenses	3 000	5 000
Net profit for the year		15 000

Answer to Exhibit 4.1 (b)

Bush's balance sheet, also prepared in the vertical format, would appear as follows.

Bush
Balance sheet at 30 June 2001

	£	£
Fixed assets		
Motor vehicles at cost (5)		6 000
Current assets		
Trade debtors (10)	10 000	
Bank (1)	5 000	
Cash (3)	1 000	
	16 000	
Current liabilities		
Trade creditors (9)	4 000	12 000
		18 000
Capital		
Balance at 1 July 2000 (2)		11 000
Add: Net profit for the year*	15 000	
Less: Drawings (4)	8 000	7 000
		18 000

* = obtained from the profit and loss account

Tutorial notes

1 The balance sheet is prepared at a particular moment in time. It depicts the balances as they were at a specific date. In this example, the balances are shown as at 30 June 2001.

2 The balance sheet is divided into two main sections. The first section shows the net assets that the entity owned at 30 June 2001. The net assets include the fixed assets plus the current assets less the current liabilities. The net assets total of £18 000 shows how much was invested in the business as at the balance sheet date. The second section shows how the net assets have been financed, i.e. by a combination of capital and retained profits. The total amount of £18 000 is, of course, the same amount as the total of the net assets. In other words, as the net assets section equals the capital section, the balance sheet balances!

3 This arrangement of the balance sheet is a little different from the way that we presented the accounting equation in Chapter 3, i.e. Assets = Capital + Liabilities. Here, the balance sheet is presented in the format: Assets – Liabilities = Capital. This format is quite common and we shall be adopting it for the presentation of most balance sheets throughout the rest of this book.

4 The fixed assets represent those assets that are intended for long-term use within the business. Fixed assets are usually shown at their original (i.e. their historic) cost, and this should be stated on the balance sheet

5 The current assets include those assets that are constantly being turned over, e.g. stock, debtors, and cash.

6 Both fixed assets and current assets should be listed in the order of the least liquid (or realizable) assets being placed first, e.g. property should come before machinery, and stock before trade debtors. The total of fixed assets and current assets is known as *total assets*.

7 The current liabilities section shows the amounts owed to various parties outside the entity due for payment within the next 12 months. They should be listed in the order of those that are going to be paid last being placed first, e.g. a short-term loan should come before trade creditors.

8 The capital section of the balance sheet shows the capital at the beginning of the year. This is then increased by the profit earned for the year (the balance is extracted from the profit and loss account). The profit and loss account balance has to be added to the capital balance (or deducted if there is a loss) because it is a summary balance, i.e. it is a net balance obtained after matching the revenue income and expenditure balances. However, the profit for the year is reduced by the total of the proprietor's 'drawings' for the year. It is then possible to see how much profit was left in the business out of the current year's profit. Proprietor's *drawings* represent the amounts of cash and the value of any goods withdrawn by the owner of the business during the year in anticipation of any profit that might be made (or was made in previous years).

You are now recommended to work through Exhibits 4.1 and 4.2 again, but this time without reference to the answers.

Conclusion

In this chapter we have examined the preparation and format of a basic set of financial accounts for a trading entity. In practice, once a trial balance has been agreed, a number of end-of-year adjustments would normally be made before the financial accounts are eventually finalized. These adjustments will be examined in the next chapter.

Key points

1 A trial balance provides the basic data for the preparation of the financial accounts.

2 The basic financial accounts for a trading entity normally consist of a trading account, a profit and loss account, and a balance sheet.

3 Revenue transactions are transferred to either the trading account or the profit and loss account, and capital items to the balance sheet.

4 The trading account and the profit and loss account form part of the double-entry system. The balance sheet is merely a listing of the balances that remain in the ledger system once the trading and profit and loss accounts have been prepared.

5 The basic financial accounts are nowadays normally prepared in a vertical format.

Check your learning

1 Are the following statements true or false?
   (a) Accounting profit is normally the difference between cash
       received and cash paid.   True/False
   (b) Capital expenditure only provides a short-term benefit.   True/False
   (c) Fixed assets are normally written off to the trading account. True/False

2 Name two stages in the preparation of a set of basic financial accounts.

3 What description is given to the balances on (a) the trading account; and (b) the profit and loss account?

4 What format is usually adopted for presenting financial accounts?

[*The answers to these questions may be found at the back of the book.*]

Group discussion questions

4.1 Explain why an increase in cash during a particular accounting period does not necessarily mean that an entity has made a profit.

4.2 'The differentiation between so-called capital and revenue expenditure is quite arbitrary and unnecessary.' Discuss.

4.3 How far does a balance sheet tell users how much an entity is worth?

Practice questions

[*Note: The questions marked with an asterisk have answers at the back of the book.*]

4.4* The following trial balance has been extracted from Ethel's books of accounts as at 31 January 2001:

	Dr £	Cr £
Capital		10 000
Cash	3 000	
Creditors		3 000
Debtors	6 000	
Office expenses	11 000	
Premises	8 000	
Purchases	20 000	
Sales		35 000
	48 000	48 000

Required:
Prepare Ethel's trading and profit and loss account for the year to 31 January 2001 and a balance sheet as at that date.

4.5* Marion has been in business for some years. The following trial balance has been extracted from her books of account as at 28 February 2002:

	Dr	Cr
	£000	£000
Bank	4	
Buildings	50	
Capital		50
Cash	2	
Creditors		24
Debtors	30	
Drawings	55	
Heat and light	10	
Miscellaneous expenses	25	
Purchases	200	
Sales		400
Wages and salaries	98	
	474	474

Required:
Prepare Marion's trading and profit and loss account for the year to 28 February 2002 and a balance sheet as at that date.

4.6 The following trial balance has been extracted from Jody's books of account as at 30 April 2004:

	Dr	Cr
	£000	£000
Capital (as at 1 May 2003)		30
Cash	1	
Electricity	2	
Maintenance	4	
Miscellaneous expenses	7	
Purchases	40	
Rent and rates	6	
Sales		85
Vehicle (at cost)	30	
Wages	25	
	115	115

Required:
Prepare Jody's trading and profit and loss account for the year to 30 April 2004 and a balance sheet as at that date.

4.7 The following trial balance has been extracted from the books of Garswood as at 31 March 2003:

	Dr	Cr
	£	£
Advertising	2 300	
Bank	300	
c/f	2 600	

		Dr	Cr
		£	£
	b/f	2600	
Capital			55700
Cash		100	
Discounts allowed		100	
Discounts received			600
Drawings		17000	
Electricity		1300	
Investments		4000	
Investment income received			400
Office equipment		10000	
Other creditors			800
Other debtors		1500	
Machinery		20000	
Purchases		21400	
Purchases returns			1400
Sales			63000
Sales returns		3000	
Stationery		900	
Trade creditors			5200
Trade debtors		6500	
Wages		38700	
		127100	127100

Required:

Prepare Garswood's trading and profit and loss account for the year to 31 March 2003 and a balance sheet as at that date.

4.8 Pete has extracted the following trial balance from his books of account as at 31 May 2005:

	debit Dr	*credit* Cr
	£000	£000
Bank		"15
Building society account	100	
Capital (as at 1 June 2004)		200
Cash	2	
Heat, light and fuel	18	
Insurances	10	
Interest received		1
Land and property (at cost)	200	
Long-term loan		50
Long-term loan interest paid	8	
Motor vehicles (at cost)	90	
Motor vehicle expenses	12	
Plant and equipment (at cost)	100	
	c/f 540	c/f 266

	Dr	Cr
	£000	£000
	b/f 540	b/f 266
Property maintenance	7	
Purchases	300	
Repairs to machinery	4	
Rent and rates	65	
Sales		900
Wages and salaries	250	
	1 166	1 166

Required:

Prepare Pete's trading and profit and loss account for the year to 31 May 2005 and a balance sheet as at that date.

5 Accounting for adjustments

Semple hit by contract row

Final offer for work on naval supply vessel forces firm to consider accounts provision

By Mark Williamson

SEMPLE Cochrane's ambitious expansion plans could be brought to a standstill as the company is forced to consider making a provision against contract income which would cut a swathe through first-half profits.

The Paisley-based services company may have to write off nearly £2m in respect of an ill-fated contract to refurbish a naval auxiliary vessel after negotiations with the contractor reached deadlock.

Industry sources say Babcock Rosyth Defence Limited has made a final offer in respect of the Sir Bedivere which would see Semple recover only about £1m out of a total of £3m which it is seeking.

BRDL refused to comment on the reports last night.

Semple, which announces interim results next week, could take the matter to arbitration. But such a move would entail heavy costs and could see the dispute drag on for years.

Either way, Semple may have to include a substantial provision in its accounts this year, which could see the company's £34m market value slashed.

Accounting rules require that companies do not take credit for income which they cannot be reasonably certain they will receive.

Industry sources say the dispute regarding the Sir Bedivere has dogged Semple since January 1998, when BRDL threw the company off the contract.

Although the agreed value of the contract was less than £5m, Semple is believed to have recorded turnover of nearly £9m for work on the ship's electrical systems.

But BRDL, which is said to have incurred costs completing the contract itself, has never agreed the amount accounted for by Semple.

It is thought that BRDL has now made a final offer of about £7m.

As a result Semple may have to make a hefty provision which would take a heavy toll on its results and cast into question the company's aggressive acquisition strategy. Last year it posted pre-tax profits of £2.7m.

Scotland on Sunday, 5 March 2000. Reprinted with permission.

Provisions can have a major impact on profits

In the last chapter, we explained how the trial balance provides the basis for the preparation of a trading account, a profit and loss account, and a balance sheet. At the end of an accounting period, however, a number of adjustments are usually required. These adjustments are not normally incorporated into the trial balance (although they can be). Instead, the financial accounts themselves will be amended, and it is only after they have been finalized that any post-trial adjustments will then be entered in the ledger accounts.

In this chapter, we shall be dealing with four main types of year-end adjustments. These are shown in Figure 5.1, and they may be summarized as follows:

1 closing stock adjustments;
2 depreciation adjustments;
3 accruals and prepayment adjustments;
4 adjustments for bad and doubtful debts.

Learning objectives

By the end of this chapter, you should be able to:

- **make post-trial balance adjustments for stock, depreciation, accruals and prepayments, and bad and doubtful debts;**

- **prepare a set of financial accounts incorporating such adjustments;**

- **list five main defects of conventional financial accounts.**

Stock

It is most unlikely that all of the purchases that have been made during a particular period will have been sold by the end of it. There almost certainly will still be some purchases in the stores at the period end. In accounting terminology, purchases still on hand at the period end are referred to as *stock*.

In calculating the gross profit for the period, therefore, it is necessary to make some allowance for closing stock, since we want to match the cost of

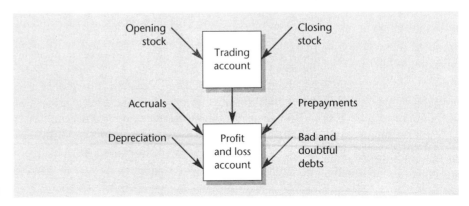

Figure 5.1
Main adjustments

goods sold (and not the cost of all of those goods actually purchased during the period) with the sales revenue earned for the period. Consequently, we have to check the quantity of stock we have on hand at the end of the accounting period, and then put some value on it. In practice, this is an extremely difficult exercise, and we shall be returning to it in a little more detail in Chapter 14. Most examples used in this part of the book assume that the value of the closing stock is readily available.

We also have another problem in dealing with stock. Closing stock at the end of one period becomes the opening stock at the beginning of the next period. In calculating the cost of goods sold, therefore, we have to allow for opening stock. The cost of goods sold can be quite easily calculated by adopting the following formula:

$$\text{Cost of goods sold} = (\text{Opening stock} + \text{Purchases}) - \text{Closing stock}$$

The book-keeping entries are not quite as easy to understand, but they may be summarized as follows:

1 Enter the opening stock in the trading account. To do so, make the following entries: DEBIT the trading account; CREDIT the stock account; with the value of the opening stock as estimated at the end of the previous period. This should have been brought down as a debit balance in the stock account at the beginning of the current period.
2 Estimate the value of the closing stock (using one of the methods described in Chapter 14).
3 Enter the closing stock in the trading account. To do so, make the following entries: DEBIT the stock account; CREDIT the trading account; with the value of the closing stock as estimated in stage 2 above.

By making these adjustments the trading account should now appear as in Exhibit 5.1

Exhibit 5.1 Example of a trading account with stock adjustments

	£		£
Opening stock	1 000	Sales	4 000
Purchases	2 000	Closing stock	1 500
Gross profit c/d	2 500		
	5 500		5 500
		Gross profit b/d	2 500

This format does not show clearly the cost of goods sold, and so it is customary to *deduct the closing stock* from the total of opening stock and purchases. The information will then be presented as follows:

	£	£
Sales		4 000
Less: Cost of goods sold		
Opening stock	1 000	
Purchases	2 000	
	3 000	
Less: Closing stock	1 500	1 500
Gross profit		2 500

Study this format very carefully; it will be encountered frequently in subsequent examples.

Depreciation

As we have already explained, expenditure that covers more than one account-ing period is known as *capital expenditure*. Capital expenditure is not normally included in either the trading account or the profit and loss account, but it would be misleading to exclude it altogether from the calculation of profit.

Expenditure on fixed assets (such as plant and machinery, motor vehicles, and furniture) is necessary in order to help provide a general service to the busi-ness. The benefit received from the purchase of fixed assets must (by definition) extend beyond at least one accounting period. The cost of the benefit provided by fixed assets ought, therefore, to be charged to those accounting periods that benefit from such expenditure. The problem is in determining what charge to make. In accounting terminology, such a charge is known as *depreciation*.

There is also another reason why fixed assets should be depreciated. By *not* charging each accounting period with some of the cost of fixed assets, the level of profit will be correspondingly higher. Thus, the owner will be able to with-draw a higher level of profit from the business. If this is the case, insufficient cash may be left in the business, and the owner may then find it difficult to buy new fixed assets.

In practice, it is not easy to measure the benefit provided to each accounting period by some groups of fixed assets. Most depreciation methods tend to be somewhat simplistic. The one method most commonly adopted is known as *straight-line depreciation*. This method charges an equal amount of depreci-ation to each accounting period that benefits from the purchase of a fixed asset. The annual depreciation charge is calculated as follows:

Annual depreciation charge =

$$\frac{\text{Original cost of the asset} - \text{Estimated residual value}}{\text{Estimated life of the asset}}$$

You can see that in order to calculate the annual depreciation charge it is nec-essary to work out (a) how long the asset is likely to last, and (b) what it can be sold for when its useful life is ended.

Although it is customary to include fixed assets at their historic (i.e. original) cost in the balance sheet, some fixed assets (such as property) may be revalued at regular intervals. If this is the case, the depreciation charge will be based on the revalued amount, and not on the historic cost. It should also be noted that even if the asset is depreciated on the basis of its revalued amount, there is still no guarantee that it can be replaced at that amount. A combination of inflation and obsolescence may mean that the eventual replacement cost is far in excess of either the historic cost or the revalued amount. It follows that when the fixed asset eventually comes to be replaced, the entity may still not have sufficient cash available to replace it.

Besides straight-line depreciation, there are other methods that may be adopted. One other method that is sometimes used (although it is far less common than the straight-line method) is known as the *reducing balance method*. This method is similar to the straight-line system in that it is based on the historic cost of the asset. It also requires an estimate to be made of the life of the asset and of its estimated residual value. The depreciation rate is usually expressed as a percentage, and the rate is then applied to the reducing balance of the asset, i.e. after the depreciation charge in previous years has been deducted. The procedure is illustrated in Exhibit 5.2.

Exhibit 5.2 Illustration of the reducing balance method of depreciating fixed assets

Assume that an asset costs £1000, and that the depreciation rate is 50 per cent of the reduced balance. The depreciation charge per year would then be as follows:

Year		£
1. 1. 01	Historic cost	1 000
31.12.01	Depreciation charge for the year (50%)	500
	Reduced balance	500
31.12.02	Depreciation charge for the year (50%)	250
	Reduced balance	250
31.12.03	Depreciation charge for the year (50%)	125
	Reduced balance	125

. . . and so on, until the asset has been written down to its estimated residual value.

The reducing balance depreciation rate can be calculated by using the following formula:

$$r = 1 - \sqrt[n]{\frac{R}{C}}$$

where: r = the depreciation rate to be applied;
n = the estimated life of the asset;
R = its estimated (residual or scrap) value; and
C = its historic cost.

The reducing balance method results in a much higher level of depreciation in the first few years of the life of an asset, and a much lower charge in later years. It is a suitable method to adopt when calculating the depreciation rate for such fixed assets as vehicles, because vehicles tend to have a high depreciation rate in their early years, and a low rate towards the end of their life. In addition, maintenance costs tend to be low initially, and become greater as the vehicles become older. Consequently, the combined depreciation charge plus maintenance costs produce a more even pattern of total vehicle costs than does the straight-line method.

There are other methods of depreciating fixed assets, but since these are rarely used, we do not think that it is necessary for us to go into them in this book.

The ledger account entries for depreciation are quite straightforward. The annual charge for depreciation will be entered into the books of account as follows:

DEBIT   Profit and loss account.
CREDIT   Accumulated depreciation account with the depreciation charge for the year.
(*Note*: Each group of fixed assets will normally have its own accumulated depreciation account.)

As far as the balance sheet is concerned, it is customary to disclose the following details for each group of fixed assets:

1 historic cost (or revalued amount), i.e. the gross book value (GBV);
2 accumulated depreciation;
3 net book value (NBV).

(In other words, line 1 minus line 2 = line 3.)

We illustrate how this is normally shown in a balance sheet in Exhibit 5.3. The exhibit shows how the accumulated depreciation is deducted from the original cost for each group of assets, thereby arriving at the respective net book value for each group. The total net book value (£80 000 in Exhibit 5.3) forms part of the balancing of the balance sheet. The total cost of the fixed assets and the total accumulated depreciation are shown purely for information. Such totals do not form part of the balancing process.

Exhibit 5.3 Balance sheet disclosure of fixed assets

Fixed assets	Historic cost	Accumulated depreciation	Net book value
	£	£	£
Buildings	100 000	30 000	70 000
Equipment	40 000	25 000	15 000
Furniture	10 000	7 000	3 000
	150 000	62 000	88 000

	Historic cost £	Accumulated depreciation £	Net book value £
Current assets			
Stocks		10 000	
Debtors		8 000	
Cash		2 000	
			20 000
			108 000

Accruals and prepayments

We explained in Chapter 2 why it is sometimes necessary at the end of an accounting period to make an adjustment for accruals and prepayments. We will now examine this procedure in a little more detail.

Accruals

An accrual is an amount outstanding for a service provided during a particular accounting period that is still to be paid for at the end of it. It is expected that the amount due will normally be settled in cash in a subsequent accounting period. The entity may, for example, have paid the last quarter's electricity bill one week before the year end. In its accounts for that year, therefore, it needs to allow for (or *accrue*) the amount that it will owe for the electricity consumed during the last week of the year.

The accrual will be based on an estimate of the likely cost of one week's supply of electricity, or, as a proportion of the amount payable (if it has already received the invoice).

The ledger account entries are reasonably straightforward. It is not normal practice to open a separate account for accruals, the double-entry being completed within the account that relates to that particular service. Exhibit 5.4 illustrates the procedure.

Exhibit 5.4 Accounting for accruals

Electricity account

		£			£
1.4.01	Bank	400	1.4.01	Balance b/d*	400
1.7.01	Bank	300			
1.9.01	Bank	100			
1.1.02	Bank	500			
31.3.02	Balance c/d**	600	31.3.02	Profit and loss account	1 500
		1 900			1 900
			1.4.02	Balance b/d	600

* This balance is assumed to be an accrual made in the year to 31 March 2001.
** This amount is an accrual for the year to 31 March 2002.

You will note from Exhibit 5.4 that the balance on the electricity account at 31 March 2002 is transferred to the profit and loss account. The ledger account entries are as follows:

DEBIT   Profit and loss account.
CREDIT Electricity account with the electricity charge for the year.

The double entry has been completed for the accrual by debiting it in the accounts for the year to 31 March 2002 (i.e. above the line), and crediting it in the following year's account (i.e. below the line). The accrual of £600 will be shown on the balance sheet at 31 March 2002 in the current liabilities section under the subheading 'accruals'.

Prepayments

A prepayment is an amount paid in cash during an accounting period for a service that has not yet been provided. For example, if a company's year end is 31 December and it buys a van halfway through (say) 2001 and licences it for 12 months, half of the fee paid will relate to 2001 and half to 2002. It is necessary, therefore, to adjust 2001's accounts so that only half of the fee is charged in that year. The other half will eventually be charged to 2002's accounts. The book-keeping procedure is illustrated in Exhibit 5.5.

Exhibit 5.5 Accounting for prepayments

Van tax account

		£			£
1.1.01	Balance b/d*	40	31.12.01	Profit and	
1.7.01	Bank	100		loss account	90
			31.12.01	Balance c/d**	50
		140			140
1.1.02	Balance b/d	50			

*   This balance is assumed to be a prepayment arising in the previous year.
** This amount is assumed to be a prepayment as at 31 December 2001.

You will note from Exhibit 5.5 that the balance on the van tax account is transferred to the profit and loss account. The double-entry procedure is as follows:

DEBIT   Profit and loss account.
CREDIT Van tax account with the annual cost of the tax on the van.

The double entry has been completed by debiting the prepayment in next year's accounts (i.e. below the line) and crediting it to this year's accounts (i.e. above the line).

The prepayment of £50 made at 31 December 2001 will be shown in the balance sheet at that date in the current assets section under the subheading 'prepayments'.

Bad and doubtful debts

The fourth main adjustment made in finalizing the annual accounts relates to bad debts and provisions for bad and doubtful debts.

It was explained in Chapter 2 that the realization rule allows us to claim profit for any goods that have been sold, even if the cash for them is not received until a later accounting period. This means that we are taking a risk in claiming the profit on those goods in the earlier period, even if the legal title has been passed to the customer. If the goods are not eventually paid for, we will have overestimated the profit for that period. The owner might already have taken the profit out of the business (e.g. by increasing his cash drawings), and it then might be too late to do anything about it.

Fortunately, there is a technique whereby we can build in an allowance for any possible *bad debts* (as they are called). This is quite a tricky operation, and so we will need to explain it in two stages: (a) how to account for bad debts; and (b) how to allow for the possibility that some debts may be *doubtful*.

Bad debts

Once it is clear that a debt is bad (in other words, that it is highly unlikely it will ever be paid), then it must be written off immediately. This means that we have to charge it to the current year's profit and loss account, even though it may relate to an earlier period. It is usually impractical to change accounts once they have been finalized because the owner may have already drawn a share of the profits out of the business.

The double-entry procedure for writing off bad debts is quite straightforward. The entries are as follows:

DEBIT   Profit and loss account.
CREDIT Trade debtor's account with the amount of the bad debt to
             be written off.

Trade debtors will be shown in the balance sheet *after* deducting any bad debts that have been written off to the profit and loss account.

Provisions for bad and doubtful debts

The profit in future accounting periods would be severely distorted if the entity suffered a whole series of bad debts. It seems prudent, therefore, to allow for the possibility that some debts may become bad. We can do this by seting up a provision for bad and doubtful debts (a *provision* is simply an amount set aside for something that is highly likely to happen), and opening a special account for that purpose.

In order to do so, it is necessary to estimate the likely level of bad debts. The estimate will normally be based on the experience that the entity has had in dealing with specific bad debts. In simple book-keeping exercises, the provision is usually expressed as a percentage of the outstanding trade debtors. The double-entry procedure is as follows:

> DEBIT   Profit and loss account.
> CREDIT Provision for bad and doubtful debts account with the amount of the provision needed to meet the expected level of bad and doubtful debts.

The procedure is illustrated in Exhibit 5.6.

Exhibit 5.6 Accounting for bad and doubtful debts

You are presented with the following information for the year to 31 March 2003:

	£
Trade debtors at 1 April 2002	20 000
Trade debtors at 31 March 2003 (including £3000 of specific bad debts)	33 000
Provision for bad and doubtful debts at 1 April 2002	1 000

Note: A provision for bad and doubtful debts is maintained equivalent to 5 per cent of the trade debtors as at the end of the year.

Required:
(a) Calculate the increase required in the bad and doubtful debts provision account for the year to 31 March 2003; and
(b) show how both the trade debtors and the provision for bad and doubtful debts account would be featured in the balance sheet at 31 March 2003.

Answer to Exhibit 5.6

	£
(a) Trade debtors as at 31 March 2003	33 000
Less: Specific bad debts to be written off to the profit and loss account for the year to 31 March 2003	3 000
	30 000

Provision required: 5% thereof	1 500
Less: Provision at 1 April 2002	1 000
Increase in the bad and doubtful debts provision account to be charged to the profit and loss account for the year to 31 March 2003	500

Tutorial note

The balance on the provision for bad and doubtful debts account will be higher at 31 March 2003 than it was at 1 April 2002. This arises because the level of trade debtors is higher at the end of 2003 than it was at the end of 2002. The required increase in the provision of £500 will be *debited* to the profit and loss account. If it had been possible to reduce the provision (because of a lower level of trade debtors at the end of 2003 compared with 2002), the decrease would have been *credited* to the profit and loss account.

(b) Balance sheet extract at 31 March 2003

	£	£
Current assets		
Trade debtors	30 000	
Less: Provision for bad and doubtful debts	1 500	
		28 500

The treatment of bad debts and doubtful debts in ledger accounts is a fairly complicated and technical exercise. However, as a non-accountant it is important for you to grasp just two essential points:

1 A debt should never be written off until it is absolutely certain that it is bad because, once written off, no further attempt will probably ever be made to recover it.

2 It is prudent to allow for the possibility of some doubtful debts although, as sometimes happens, it is rather a questionable decision to reduce profit by an arbitrary amount, e.g. by guessing whether it should be 3 per cent or 5 per cent of outstanding debtors. Obviously, the level that you choose can make a big difference to profit!

We have covered a great deal of technical matter in this chapter, and so it would now be helpful to bring all the material together in the form of a comprehensive example.

A comprehensive example

In this section, we use a comprehensive example to cover all the basic procedures that we have outlined in both this chapter and the preceding one. The example used in Exhibit 5.7 is a fairly detailed one, so take your time in working through it.

Exhibit 5.7 Example of basic accounting procedures

Wayne has been in business for many years. His accountant has extracted the following trial balance from his books of account as at 31 March 2005:

	£	£
Bank	1 200	
Capital		33 000
Cash	300	
Drawings	6 000	
Insurance	2 000	
Office expenses	15 000	
Office furniture at cost	5 000	
Office furniture: accumulated depreciation at 1 April 2004		2 000
Provision for bad and doubtful debts at 1 April 2004		500
Purchases	55 000	
Salaries	25 000	
Sales		100 000
Stock at 1 April 2004	10 000	
Trade creditors		4 000
Trade debtors	20 000	
	139 500	139 500

Notes: The following additional information is to be taken into account:

1 Stock at 31 March 2005 was valued at £15 000.
2 The insurance included £500 worth of cover which related to the year to 31 March 2006.
3 Depreciation is charged on office furniture at 10 per cent per annum of its original cost (it is assumed not to have any residual value).
4 A bad debt of £1000 included in the trade debtors balance of £20 000 is to be written off.
5 The provision for bad and doubtful debts is to be maintained at a level of 5 per cent of outstanding trade debtors as at 31 March 2005, i.e. after excluding the bad debt referred to in note 4 above.
6 At 31 March 2005, there was an amount owing for salaries of £1000.

Required:
(a) Prepare Wayne's trading and profit and loss account for the year to 31 March 2005; and
(b) prepare a balance sheet as at that date.

Answer to Exhibit 5.7

(a)

Wayne
Trading and profit and loss account for the year to 31 March 2005

	£	£	(Source of entry)
Sales		100 000	(TB)
Less: Cost of goods sold:			
Opening stock	10 000		(TB)
Purchases	55 000		(TB)
	65 000		
Less: Closing stock	15 000		(QN 1)
		50 000	
Gross profit		50 000	
Less: Expenses:			
Insurance (2000 − 500)	1 500		(Wkg 1)
Office expenses	15 000		(TB)
Depreciation: office furniture (10% × 5000)	500		(Wkg 2)
Bad debt	1 000		(QN 4)
Increase in provision for bad and doubtful debts	450		(Wkg 3)
Salaries (25 000 + 1000)	26 000		(Wkg 4)
		44 450	
Net profit for the year		5 550	

(b)

Wayne
Balance sheet at 31 March 2005

	£	£	£	(Source of entry)
Fixed assets	Cost	Accumulated depreciation	Net book value	
Office furniture	5 000	2 500	2 500	(TB and Wkg 5)
Current assets				
Stock		15 000		(QN 1)
Trade debtors				
(20 000 − 1000)	19 000			(Wkg3)
Less: Provision for bad and				
doubtful debts	950	18 050		(Wkg 3)
Prepayment		500		(QN2)
Cash at bank		1 200		(TB)
Cash in hand		300		(TB)
	c/f	35 050	2 500	

	£	£	£	(Source of entry)
		b/f 35 050	2 500	
Less: Current liabilities				
Trade creditors	4 000			(TB)
Accrual	1 000			(QN 6)
		5 000	30 050	
			32 550	
Financed by:				
Capital				
Balance at 31 March 2004			33 000	(TB)
Add: Net profit for the year		5 550		(P&L A/c)
Less: Drawings		6 000	(450)	
			32 550	

Key:
TB = from trial balance;
QN = extracted straight from the question and related notes;
Wkg = workings (see below);
P&L A/c = balance obtained from the profit and loss account.

Workings

		£
1	Insurance:	
	As per the trial balance	2 000
	Less: Prepayment (QN 2)	500
	Charge to the profit and loss account	1 500
2	Depreciation:	
	Office furniture at cost	5 000
	Depreciation: 10% of the original cost	500
3	Increase in provision for bad and doubtful debts:	
	Trade debtors at 31 March 2005	20 000
	Less: Bad debt (QN 4)	1 000
		19 000
	Provision required: 5% thereof	950
	Less: Provision at 1 April 2004	500
	Increase in provision: charge to profit and loss	450
4	Salaries:	
	As per the question	25 000
	Add: Accrual (QN 6)	1 000
		26 000
5	Accumulated depreciation:	
	Balance at 1 April 2004 (as per TB)	2 000
	Add: Depreciation for the year (Wkg 2)	500
	Accumulated depreciation at 31 March 2005	2 500

After you have worked your way through Exhibit 5.7 as carefully as you can, try to do the question without referring to the answer.

We are nearly at the end of a difficult chapter, but before we move on to other matters, we ought to examine somewhat critically what we have done in both this chapter and the preceding one.

Estimating accounting profit

In previous sections of the book, we have emphasized that the calculation of accounting profit calls for a great deal of subjective judgement. Accounting involves much more than merely being very good at mastering some complicated arithmetical exercises, and so we think that it will be helpful (indeed essential) for us to summarize the major defects inherent in the traditional method of calculating accounting profit.

As a non-accountant, it is most important that you appreciate one vital fact: the method that we have outlined results in an *estimate* of what the accountant thinks the profit should be. You must not place too much reliance on the *absolute* level of accounting profit. It can only be as accurate and as reliable as the assumptions upon which it is based. If you accept the assumptions, then you can be fairly confident that the profit figure is reliable. You will then not go too far wrong in using the information for decision-making purposes. But you must know what the assumptions are, and you must support them. The message can, therefore, be put as follows:

Always question accounting information before accepting it.

A summary of the main reasons why you should not place too much reliance on the actual level of accounting profit (especially if you are unsure about the assumptions upon which it is based) is outlined below:

1 Goods are treated as being sold when the legal title to them changes hands, and not when the customer has paid for them. In some cases, the cash for some sales may never be received.
2 Goods are regarded as having been purchased when the legal title to them is transferred to the purchaser, although there are occasions when they may not be received or paid for (e.g. if a supplier goes into receivership).
3 Goods that have not been sold at the period end have to be quantified and valued. This procedure involves a considerable amount of subjective judgement.
4 There is no clear distinction between so-called capital and revenue items.
5 Estimates have to be made to allow for accruals and prepayments.
6 The cost of fixed assets is apportioned between different accounting periods using methods that are fairly simplistic and highly questionable.
7 Arbitrary reductions in profit are made to allow for bad and doubtful debts.

8 Historic cost accounting makes no allowance for inflation. In a period of inflation, for example, the value of £100 at 1 January 2001 is not the same as £100 at 31 December 2001. Hence, profit tends to be overstated, partly because of low closing stock values and partly because depreciation charges will be based on the historic cost.

The above disadvantages of historic cost accounting are fairly severe, but accountants have not yet been able to suggest anything better. If at this stage you are feeling somewhat disillusioned, therefore, then take comfort in the old adage that 'it is better to be vaguely right than precisely wrong'!

Conclusion

In this chapter, we have examined in some detail the main adjustments made to financial accounts at the end of an accounting period. You should now be in a far better position to assess the relevance and reliability of any accounting information that is presented to you.

The material that we have covered has provided a broad foundation for all the remaining chapters. It is essential that before moving on to them you satisfy yourself that you really do understand the mechanics behind the preparation of a set of basic financial accounts. To test your understanding of this subject, you are recommended to work through all of the Exhibits contained in this chapter and the preceding one once again, and then to attempt some of the exercises that end this chapter.

Key points

1 Following the completion of the trial balance, some last-minute adjustments have usually to be made to the financial accounts. The main adjustments are: closing stock, depreciation, accruals and prepayments, and bad and doubtful debts.

2 Accounting profit is merely an estimate. The method used to calculate it is highly questionable, and it is subject to very many criticisms. Undue reliance should not be placed on the actual level of profit shown in the accounts. The assumptions upon which profit is based should be carefully examined, and it should be viewed merely as a guide to decision making.

Check your learning

1 Are the following statements true or false?
   (a) A provision for bad and doubtful debts results in cash leaving the business.   True/False
   (b) An amount owing for rent at the year end is an accrual.   True/False
   (c) There is no such thing as the correct level of accounting profit.   True/False

2 Fill in the missing word(s) in each of the following statements:
   (a) opening stock + _____ – closing stock = gross profit.
   (b) gross profit + other incomes – total expenditure = _____ _____.
   (c) _____ – liabilities = capital.

3 A company buys a machine for £12 000 expecting it to have a life of ten years and an estimated residual value of £2000. If the company uses the straight-line method of depreciation, what is the annual charge to the profit and loss account?
   (a) £12 000
   (b) £1000
   (c) £2000
   (d) none of these.

4 List five basic defects of conventional accounting statements.

[*The answers to these questions may be found at the back of the book.*]

Group discussion questions

5.1 'Depreciation methods and rates should be prescribed by law.' Discuss.

5.2 Explain why it is quite easy to manipulate the level of gross profit when preparing a trading account.

5.3 How far is it possible for an entity to build up hidden amounts of profit (known as *secret reserves*) by making some adjustments in the profit and loss account for bad and doubtful debts?

Practice questions

[*Note: The questions marked with an asterisk have answers at the back of the book.*]

5.4* The following information has been extracted from Lathom's books of account for the year to 30 April 2004:

	£
Purchases	45 000
Sales	60 000
Stock (at 1 May 2003)	3 000
Stock (at 30 April 2004)	4 000

Required:
(a) Prepare Lathom's trading account for the year to 30 April 2004; and
(b) state where the stock at 30 April 2004 would be shown on the balance sheet as at that date.

5.5 Rufford presents you with the following information for the year to 31 March 2005:

	£
Purchases	48 000
Purchases returns	3 000
Sales	82 000
Sales returns	4 000
Stock at 1 April 2004	4 000

He is not sure how to value the stock as at 31 March 2005. Three methods have been suggested. They all result in different closing stock values, namely:

	£
Method 1	8 000
Method 2	16 000
Method 3	4 000

Required:
(a) Calculate the effect on gross profit for the year to 31 March 2005 by using each of the three methods of stock valuation; and
(b) state the effect on gross profit for the year to 31 March 2006 if method 1 is used instead of method 2.

5.6* Standish has been trading for some years. The following trial balance has been extracted from his books of account as at 31 May 2006:

	Dr £	Cr £
Capital		22 400
Cash	1 200	
Creditors		4 300
Debtors	6 000	
Drawings	5 500	
Furniture and fittings	8 000	
Heating and lighting	1 500	
Miscellaneous expenses	6 700	
Purchases	52 000	
Sales		79 000
Stock (at 1 June 2005)	7 000	
Wages and salaries	17 800	
	105 700	105 700

Note: Stock at 31 May 2006: £12 000.

Required:
Prepare Standish's trading and profit and loss account for the year to 31 May 2006 and a balance sheet as at that date.

5.7 Witton commenced business on 1 July 2006. The following trial balance was extracted from his books of account as at 30 June 2007:

	Dr	Cr
	£	£
Capital		3 000
Cash	500	
Drawings	4 000	
Creditors		1 500
Debtors	3 000	
Motor car at cost	5 000	
Office expenses	8 000	
Purchases	14 000	
Sales		30 000
	34 500	34 500

Additional information:
1 Stock at 30 June 2007: £2000.
2 The motor car is to be depreciated at a rate of 20 per cent per annum on cost; it was purchased on 1 July 2006.

Required:
Prepare Witton's trading and profit and loss account for the year to 30 June 2007 and a balance sheet as at that date.

5.8 The following is an extract from Barrow's balance sheet at 31 August 2008:

Fixed assets	Cost	Accumulated depreciation	Net book value
	£	£	£
Land	200 000	–	200 000
Buildings	150 000	60 000	90 000
Plant	55 000	37 500	17 500
Vehicles	45 000	28 800	16 200
Furniture	20 000	12 600	7 400
	470 000	138 900	331 100

Barrow's depreciation policy is as follows:

1 a full year's depreciation is charged in the year of acquisition, but none in the year of disposal;
2 no depreciation is charged on land;
3 buildings are depreciated at an annual rate of 2 per cent on cost;
4 plant is depreciated at an annual rate of 5 per cent on cost after allowing for an estimated residual value of £5000;
5 vehicles are depreciated on a reduced balance basis at an annual rate of 40 per cent on the reduced balance;
6 furniture is depreciated on a straight-line basis at an annual rate of 10 per cent on cost after allowing for an estimated residual value of £2000.

Additional information:

1 During the year to 31 August 2009, new furniture was purchased for the office. It cost £3000 and it is to be depreciated on the same basis as the old furniture. Its estimated residual value is £300.

2 There were no additions to, or disposals of, any other fixed assets during the year to 31 August 2009.

Required:

(a) Calculate the depreciation charge for each of the fixed asset groupings for the year to 31 August 2009; and

(b) show how the fixed assets would appear in Barrow's balance sheet as at 31 August 2009.

5.9* Pine started business on 1 October 2001. The following is his trial balance at 30 September 2002:

	£	£
Capital		6 000
Cash	400	
Creditors		5 900
Debtors	5 000	
Furniture at cost	8 000	
General expenses	14 000	
Insurance	2 000	
Purchases	21 000	
Sales		40 000
Telephone	1 500	
	51 900	51 900

The following information was obtained after the trial balance had been prepared:

1 Stock at 30 September 2002: £3000.

2 Furniture is to be depreciated at a rate of 15 per cent on cost.

3 At 30 September 2002, Pine owed £500 for telephone expenses and insurance had been prepaid by £200.

Required:

Prepare Pine's trading and profit and loss account for the year to 30 September 2002 and a balance sheet as at that date.

5.10 Dale has been in business for some years. The following is his trial balance at 31 October 2003:

	Dr	Cr
	£	£
Bank	700	
Capital		85 000
Depreciation (at 1 November 2002):		
Office equipment		14 000
Vehicles		4 000
c/f	700	103 000

		Dr	Cr
		£	£
	b/f	700	103 000
Drawings		12 300	
Heating and lighting		3 000	
Office expenses		27 000	
Office equipment, at cost		35 000	
Rates		12 000	
Purchases		240 000	
Sales			350 000
Stock (at 1 November 2002)		20 000	
Trade creditors			21 000
Trade debtors		61 000	
Vehicles at cost		16 000	
Wages and salaries		47 000	
		474 000	474 000

Additional information (not taken into account when compiling the above trial balance):
1 Stock at 31 October 2003: £26 000.
2 Amount owing for electricity at 31 October 2003: £1500.
3 At 31 October 2003, £2000 had been paid in advance for rates.
4 Depreciation is to be charged on the office equipment for the year to 31 October 2003 at a rate of 20 per cent on cost and on the vehicles at a rate of 25 per cent on cost.

Required:
Prepare Dale's trading and profit and loss account for the year to 31 October 2003 and a balance sheet as at that date.

5.11 The following information relates to Astley for the year to 30 November 2004:

Item	Cash paid during the year to 30 November 2004	As at 1 December 2003 Accruals/ Prepayments		As at 30 November 2004 Accruals/ Prepayments	
	£	£	£	£	£
Electricity	26 400	5 200	–	8 300	–
Gas	40 100	–	–	–	4 900
Insurance	25 000	–	12 000	–	14 000
Rates	16 000	–	4 000	6 000	–
Telephone	3 000	1 500	–	–	200
Wages	66 800	1 800	–	–	–

Required:
(a) Calculate the charge to the profit and loss account for the year to 30 November 2004 for each of the above items.
(b) Demonstrate what amounts for accruals and prepayments would be shown in the balance sheet as at 30 November 2004.

5.12 Duxbury started in business on 1 January 2003. The following is his trial balance as at 31 December 2003:

	Dr	Cr
	£	£
Capital		40 000
Cash	300	
Delivery van, at cost	20 000	
Drawings	10 600	
Office expenses	12 100	
Purchases	65 000	
Sales		95 000
Trade creditors		5 000
Trade debtors	32 000	
	140 000	140 000

Additional information:
1 Stock at 31 December 2003 was valued at £10 000.
2 At 31 December 2003 an amount of £400 was outstanding for telephone expenses, and the business rates had been prepaid by £500.
3 The delivery van is to be depreciated at a rate of 20 per cent per annum on cost.
4 Duxbury decides to set aside a provision for bad and doubtful debts equal to 5 per cent of trade debtors as at the end of the year.

Required:
Prepare Duxbury's trading and profit and loss account for the year to 31 December 2003 and a balance sheet as at that date.

5.13 Beech is a retailer. Most of his sales are made on credit terms. The following information relates to the first four years that he has been in business:

	2004	2005	2006	2007
Trade debtors as at 31 January:	£60 000	£55 000	£65 000	£70 000

The trade is one that experiences a high level of bad debts. Accordingly, Beech decides to set aside a provision for bad and doubtful debts equivalent to 10 per cent of trade debtors as at the end of the year.

Required:
(a) Show how the provision for bad and doubtful debts would be disclosed in the respective balance sheets as at 31 January 2004, 2005, 2006 and 2007; and
(b) calculate the increase/decrease in provision for bad and doubtful debts transferred to the respective profit and loss accounts for each of the four years.

5.14   The following is Ash's trial balance as at 31 March 2005:

	Dr £	Cr £
Bank		4 000
Capital		20 500
Depreciation (at 1 April 2004): furniture		3 600
Drawings	10 000	
Electricity	2 000	
Furniture, at cost	9 000	
Insurance	1 500	
Miscellaneous expenses	65 800	
Provision for bad and doubtful debts (at 1 April 2004)		1 200
Purchases	80 000	
Sales		150 000
Stock (at 1 April 2004)	10 000	
Trade creditors		20 000
Trade debtors	21 000	
	199 300	199 300

Additional information:
1   Stock at 31 March 2005: £15 000.
2   At 31 March 2005 there was a specific bad debt of £6000. This was to be written off.
3   Furniture is to be depreciated at a rate of 10 per cent per annum on cost.
4   At 31 March 2005 Ash owes the electricity board £600, and £100 had been paid in advance for insurance.
5   The provision for bad and doubtful debts is to be set at 10 per cent of trade debtors as at the end of the year.

Required:
Prepare Ash's trading and profit and loss account for the year to 31 March 2005 and a balance sheet as at that date.

5.15   Lime's business has had liquidity problems for some months. The following trial balance was extracted from his books of account as at 30 September 2007:

	Dr £	Cr £
Bank		15 200
Capital		19 300
Cash from sale of office equipment		500
Depreciation (at 1 October 2006): office equipment		22 000
Drawings	16 000	
Insurance	1 800	
Loan (long-term from Cedar)		50 000
Loan interest	7 500	
Miscellaneous expenses	57 700	
c/f	83 000	107 000

		Dr £	Cr £
	b/f	83 000	107 000
Office equipment, at cost		44 000	
Provision for bad and doubtful debts (at 1 October 2006)			2 000
Purchases		320 000	
Rates		10 000	
Sales			372 000
Stock (at 1 October 2006)		36 000	
Trade creditors			105 000
Trade debtors		93 000	
		586 000	586 000

Additional information:

1 Stock at 30 September 2007: £68 000.

2 At 30 September 2007, accrual for rates of £2000 and insurance prepaid of £200.

3 Depreciation on office equipment is charged at a rate of 25 per cent on cost. During the year, office equipment costing £4000 had been sold for £500. Accumulated depreciation on this equipment amounted to £3000. Lime's depreciation policy is to charge a full year's depreciation in the year of acquisition and none in the year of disposal.

4 Specific bad debts of £13 000 are to be written off.

5 The provision for bad and doubtful debts is to be made equal to 10 per cent of outstanding trade debtors as at 30 September 2007.

Required:

Prepare Lime's trading, and profit and loss account for the year to 30 September 2007, and a balance sheet as at that date.

6 Company accounts

The presentation of accounts is an important matter

The last three chapters, have dealt mainly with the sole-trader type of entity. However, as was argued in Chapter 1, this term is not to be taken too literally. The term *sole trader* means that the entity is *owned* by one individual, although hundreds of employees may work for it. The owner can also be engaged in any kind of business, and not just one that relates to trading. Sole-trader entities are quite common, especially among very small businesses (e.g. those employing less than 20 people), but partnerships and limited liability companies are almost as common.

You will recall that a partnership entity is very similar to that of a sole trader, except that the business is owned and managed by more than one individual, and the profits and losses are shared among the partners in agreed proportions. As the basic financial procedures are also similar to those of a sole trader, it is not necessary to go into any further detail about partnerships in this book. Instead, we will concentrate on limited liability companies which, as a non-accountant, you are far more likely to come across in your day-to-day work.

Learning objectives

By the end of this chapter, you should be able to:

- **describe the nature of limited liability;**
- **distinguish between private and public limited companies;**
- **prepare a basic set of company accounts.**

Limited liability

There is a great personal risk in operating a business as a sole trader or as a partnership. If the business runs short of funds, the owners may be called upon to settle the business's debts out of their own private resources. This type of risk can have an inhibiting effect on the development of new businesses. Hence the need for a different type of entity that will neither make the owners bankrupt nor inhibit new developments. This need became apparent in the 19th century as a result of the Industrial Revolution, when, in order to finance new and rapidly expanding industries (such as the railways, and iron and steel), enormous amounts of capital were required.

These sorts of ventures were undertaken at great personal risk. By agreeing to become involved in them, investors often faced bankruptcy if the ventures were unsuccessful (as they often were). It became apparent that the development of industry would be severely restricted unless some means could be devised of restricting the personal liability of prospective investors.

Hence the need for a form of *limited liability*. In fact, the concept of limited liability was not entirely an innovation of the 19th century but it did not receive legal recognition until the Limited Liability Act was passed in 1855. The Act only remained in force for a few months before it was repealed and incorporated into the Joint Stock Companies Act 1856.

By accepting the principle of limited liability, the 1855 Act also recognized the *entity* concept. By distinguishing between the private and public affairs of business proprietors, it effectively created a new form of entity. Since the 1850s, Parliament has passed a number of other Companies Acts, all of which have continued to give legal recognition to the concept of limited liability.

The important point about a limited liability company is that no matter what financial difficulties a company may get into, its members cannot be required to contribute more than an agreed amount of capital. Thus, there is no risk of members being forced into bankruptcy.

The concept of limited liability is often very difficult for business owners to understand, especially if they have formed a limited liability company out of what was originally a sole trader or a partnership entity. Unlike such entities, companies are bound by some fairly severe legal restrictions that affect their operations.

The legal restrictions can be somewhat burdensome, but they are necessary for the protection of all those parties who might have dealings with the company (such as creditors and employees), since if a limited liability company runs short of funds the creditors and employees might not get paid. It is only fair, therefore, to warn all those people who might have dealings with the company that they run a risk in dealing with it. Consequently, companies have to be more open about their affairs than do sole traders and partnerships.

Structure and operation

In this section, the structure and operation of limited liability companies is briefly examined. In order to make it easier to follow, we have broken down our examination into a number of subsections.

Share capital

Although the law recognizes that limited liability companies are separate beings with a life of their own (i.e. separate from those individuals who collectively own and manage them), it also accepts that someone has to take responsibility for promoting the company, i.e. bringing it into being. Only one person is now required to form a private company (two for a public company), and that person (or persons, if there is more than one), agrees to make a capital contribution by buying a number of shares. The capital of a company is known as its *share capital*. The share capital will be made up of a number of shares of a certain denomination, such as 10p, 50p, and £1. A member may hold only one share, or many hundreds or thousands, depending upon the total share capital of the company, the denomination of the shares, and the amount that he wishes to contribute.

The maximum amount of capital that the company envisages ever raising has to be stated. This is known as its *authorized share capital*, although this does not necessarily mean that it will issue shares up to that amount. In practice, it will probably only issue sufficient capital to meet its immediate and foreseeable requirements. The amount of share capital that it has actually issued is known as the *issued share capital*. Sometimes when shares are issued, prospective shareholders are only required to contribute to them in instalments. Once all of the issued share capital has been received in cash, it is described as being *fully paid*.

There are two main types of shares: *ordinary shares* and *preference shares*. Ordinary shares do not usually entitle the shareholder to any specific level of dividend (see definition below), and the rights of other types of shareholders always take precedence over the rights of the ordinary shareholders, e.g. if the company goes into liquidation. Preference shareholders are normally entitled to a fixed level of dividend, and they usually have priority over the ordinary shareholders if the company is liquidated. Sometimes the preference shares are classed as *cumulative*; this means that if the company cannot pay its preference dividend in one year, the amount due accrues until such time as the company has the profits to pay all of the accumulated dividends.

There are many other different types of shares, but in this book we need only concern ourselves with ordinary shares and preference shares.

Types of companies

A prospective shareholder may invest in either a public company or a private company. A *public company* must have an authorized share capital of at least £50 000, and it becomes a public company merely by stating that it is a public company. In fact, most public limited companies in the United Kingdom have their shares listed on the London Stock Exchange, and hence they are often referred to as *listed* companies.

As a warning to those parties who might have dealings with them, public companies have to include the term 'public limited liability company' after their name (or its abbreviation 'plc').

Any company that does not make its shares available to the public is regarded as being a *private company*. Like public companies, private companies must also have an authorized share capital, although no minimum amount is prescribed. Otherwise, they are very similar to public companies in respect of their share capital requirements.

Private companies also have to warn the public that their liability is limited. They must do so by describing themselves as 'limited liability companies', and attaching the term 'limited' after their name (or the abbreviation 'Ltd').

Loans

Besides obtaining the necessary capital from their shareholders, companies often borrow money in the form of *debentures*. A company may invite the public to loan it some money for a certain period of time (although the period can be unspecified) at a certain rate of interest. A debenture loan may be secured on specific assets of the company, on its assets generally, or it might not be secured at all. If it is secured and the company cannot repay it on its due repayment date, the debenture holders may sell the secured assets and use the amount to settle the amount owing to them.

Debentures, like shares, may be bought and sold freely on the Stock Exchange. The nearer the redemption date for the repayment for the debentures, the closer the market price will be to their nominal (i.e. their face, or stated paper) value, but sometimes if they are to be redeemed at a premium (i.e. in excess of their nominal value), the market price may exceed the nominal value.

Debenture holders are not shareholders of the company, and they do not have voting rights. From the company's point of view, one further advantage of raising capital in the form of debenture loans is that for taxation purposes the interest can be charged as a business expense against the profit for the year (unlike dividends paid to shareholders).

Disclosure of information

It is necessary for both public and private companies to supply a minimum amount of information to their members. The detailed requirements will be examined in later chapters. You might find it surprising to learn that shareholders have neither a right of access to the company's premises, nor a right to receive any information that they demand. This might not seem fair, but it would clearly be difficult for a company's managers to cope with thousands of shareholders, all of whom suddenly all turned up one day demanding to be let into the buildings in order to inspect the company's books of account!

Instead, shareholders in both private and public companies have to be supplied with an annual report containing at least the minimum amount of information required by the Companies Act 1985. The company also has to file (as it is called) a copy of the report with the Registrar of Companies. This means that, on payment of a small fee, the report is open for inspection by any member of the public who wants to consult it. Some companies (defined as small or medium-sized) are permitted to file an abbreviated version of their annual report with the Registrar, although the full report must still be sent to their shareholders.

Company accounts

Company accounts are very similar to those of sole traders. They do, however, tend to be more detailed, and some modifications have to be made in order to comply with various legal requirements. We shall be looking at company accounts in more detail a little later on in the chapter.

Directors

It must be clearly understood that any limited liability company is regarded as being a separate entity, i.e. separate from those shareholders who own it collectively, and separate from anyone who works for it. This means that all those who are employed by it (no matter how senior) are its employees. None the less, someone has to take responsibility for the management of the company, of course, and so the shareholders usually delegate that responsibility to *directors*.

Directors are the most senior level of management. They are responsible for the day-to-day running of the company, and they answer to the shareholders. Directors are officers of the company, and any remuneration paid to them as directors is charged as an expense of the business. Directors may also be shareholders, but any payment that they receive as such is regarded as being a private matter, and it must not be confused with any income that they receive as directors.

The distinction between employees and shareholder-employees is an important one, although it is one that is not always understood. This is especially the case in very small companies where both employees and shareholders may be one and the same. As we have tried to emphasize, in law the company is regarded as being a separate entity. Even if there are just two shareholders, for example, who both work full-time for the company, the company is still treated as distinct from that of the two individuals who happen to own it. They may take decisions that appear to affect no one else except themselves, but because they operate the company under the protection of limited liability, they have certain obligations as well as rights. Consequently, they are not as free to operate the company as they might be if they ran it as a partnership.

Dividends

Profits are usually distributed to shareholders in the form of a dividend. A dividend is calculated on the basis of so many pence per share. The actual dividend will be recommended by the directors to the shareholders. It will depend upon the amount of net profit earned during the year, and how much profit the directors want to retain in the business.

A dividend may have been paid during the year as an *interim dividend*, i.e. a payment on account. In preparing the annual accounts, the directors recommend a proposed dividend (sometimes referred to as the *final dividend*). The proposed dividend has to be approved by the shareholders at a general meeting.

Taxation

Taxation is another feature which clearly distinguishes a limited liability company from that of a sole-trader entity.

Sole-trader entities do not have tax levied on them as entities. Instead, tax is levied on the amount of profit the owner has made during the year. The tax payable is a private matter and, in accordance with the entity rule, it lies outside the boundary of the entity. Any tax that appears to have been paid by the entity on the owner's behalf is treated as part of the owner's drawings (i.e. an amount paid as part of the share of the profits).

Companies are treated quite differently. Companies are taxed in their own right, like individuals. They have their own form of taxation, known as *corporation tax*. Corporation tax was introduced in 1965 and all companies are eligible to pay it. It is based on the company's accounting profits for a particular financial year. The accounting profit has to be adjusted, however, because some items are treated differently for tax purposes, for example the depreciation of fixed assets. The corporation tax due at the year end is treated as a current liability.

Now that the basic structure and operation of limited liability companies have been outlined, we can begin to examine company accounts in some detail. We start with the profit and loss account.

The profit and loss account

As was suggested earlier, the preparation of a company's, trading and profit and loss account is basically no different from that of sole-trader entities. Almost an identical format may be adopted, and it is only after the net profit stage that some differences become apparent. Company accounts usually include, for example, a profit and loss appropriation account. The profit and loss appropriation account follows on after the profit and loss account, although no clear dividing line is usually drawn between where the profit and loss account ends and the appropriation account begins. An example of a company's profit and loss appropriation account is shown in Exhibit 6.1.

Exhibit 6.1 Example of a company's profit and loss appropriation account

	£000
Net profit for the year before taxation	1 000
Taxation	(300)
Net profit for the year after taxation	700
Dividends	(500)
Retained profit for the year	200

As can be seen from Exhibit 6.1, the company's net profit for the year is used (or appropriated) in three ways:

1 to pay tax;
2 to pay dividends;
3 for retention within the business.

The balance sheet

The structure of a limited liability company's balance sheet is also very similar to that of a sole trader. The main differences arise because of the company's share capital structure. There are, however, some other features that are not usually found in non-company balance sheets.

We illustrate the main features of a company's balance sheet in Exhibit 6.2. Study this exhibit carefully but please note that the information has been kept to a minimum; we have not given the full details where there are insignificant differences between a company's balance sheet and those of other entities.

Exhibit 6.2 Example of a company's balance sheet

Exhibitor Ltd
Balance sheet at 31 March 2001

	£000	£000	£000
Fixed assets			600
Investments (1)			100
Current assets		6 000	
Less: Current liabilities			
Trade creditors	2 950		
Accruals	50		
Corporation tax (2)	300		
Proposed dividend (3)	500	3 800	2 200
			2 900

Financed by:

Capital and reserves (4):	Authorized	Issued and fully paid
	£000	£000
Ordinary shares of £1 each (5)	2 000	1 500
Preference shares of £0.50 each (5)	500	500
	2 500	2 000
Capital reserves (6)		200
Revenue reserves (7)		600
Shareholders' funds (8)		2 800
Loans (9)		100
		2 900

Note: The number shown after each narration refers to the tutorial notes below.

Tutorial notes

1 *Investments*. This item usually represents long-term investments in the shares of other companies. Short-term investments (such as money invested in bank deposit accounts) would be included in current assets. The shares may be either in public limited liability companies or in private limited companies. It is obviously more difficult to buy shares in private companies and to obtain current market prices for them. The market price of the investments should be stated or, where this is not available, a directors' valuation should be obtained.

2 *Corporation tax*. Corporation tax represents the tax due on the company's profits for the year. It will be due for payment after the company's year end.

3 *Proposed dividend*. A proposed dividend will probably be due for payment very shortly after the year end, and so it will usually be shown as a current liability.

4 *Capital and reserves*. Details of the authorized, issued and fully paid-up share capital should be shown.

5 *Ordinary shares and preference shares*. Details about the different types of shares that the company has issued should be disclosed.

6 *Capital reserves*. This section may include several different reserve accounts of a capital nature, that is, amounts that are not available for distribution to the shareholders as dividend. It might include, for example, a share premium account, i.e. the extra amount paid by shareholders in excess of the nominal value of the shares. This extra amount does not rank for dividend, but shareholders are sometimes willing to pay a premium if they think that the shares are particularly attractive. Another asset may have been revalued, and the difference between the original cost and the revalued amount will be credited to this account.

7 *Revenue reserves*. Revenue reserve accounts are amounts that are available for distribution to the shareholders. At one time profits that could be distributed to shareholders were put into a general reserve account, although no real purpose was served in classifying them in this way.

8 *Shareholders' funds*. The total amount available to shareholders at the balance sheet date is equal to the share capital originally subscribed, plus all the capital, reserve and revenue reserve account balances.

9 *Loans*. The loans section of the balance sheet will include all the long-term loans obtained by the company, i.e. those loans that do not have to be repaid for at least twelve months, such as debentures and long-term bank loans.

A comprehensive example

In this section, the structure of a company's accounts is examined in a little more detail. Exhibit 6.3 is used as an example. The example assumes that the accounts are being prepared for internal management purposes (accounts for external purposes are dealt with later in the book). Work through the answer to Exhibit 6.3 making sure that you understand each step in its construction.

Exhibit 6.3 Preparation of a company's accounts

The following information has been extracted from the books of Handy Ltd as at 31 March 2005:

	Dr	Cr
	£	£
Bank	2 000	
Capital: 100 000 issued and fully paid ordinary shares of £1 each		100 000
50 000 issued and fully paid 8% preference shares of £1 each		50 000
Debenture loan stock (10%: repayable 2020)		30 000
Debenture loan stock interest	3 000	
Dividends received		700
Dividends paid: Ordinary interim	5 000	
Preference	4 000	
Freehold land at cost	200 000	
Investments (listed: market value at 31 March 2005 was £11 000)	10 000	
Office expenses	47 000	
Motor van at cost	15 000	
Motor van: accumulated depreciation at 1 April 2004		6 000
Motor van expenses	2 700	
Purchases	220 000	
Retained profits at 1 April 2004		9 000
Sales		300 000
Share premium account		10 000
Stocks at cost (at 1 April 2004)	20 000	
Trade creditors		50 000
Trade debtors	27 000	
	555 700	555 700

Additional information:

1 The stocks at 31 March 2005 were valued at cost at £40 000.
2 Depreciation is to be charged on the motor van at a rate of 20 per cent per annum on cost. No depreciation is to be charged on the freehold land.
3 The corporation tax for the year has been estimated to be £10 000.
4 The directors propose a final ordinary dividend of 10p per share.
5 The authorized share capital of the company is as follows:
    (a) 150 000 ordinary shares of £1 each; and
    (b) 75 000 preference shares of £1 each.

Required:

Prepare (a) Handy Ltd's trading and profit and loss account for the year to 31 March 2005; and
         (b) a balance sheet as at that date.

Answer to Exhibit 6.3

(a)

Handy Ltd
Trading and profit and loss account for the year to 31 March 2005

	£	£	£
Sales			300 000
Less: Cost of goods sold:			
Opening stocks		20 000	
Purchases		220 000	
		240 000	
Less: Closing stocks		40 000	200 000
Gross profit			100 000
Add: Incomes:			
Dividends received			700
			100 700
Less: Expenditure:			
Debenture loan stock interest		3 000	
Motor van depreciation (1)	3 000		
Motor van expenses	2 700	5 700	
Office expenses		47 000	
			55 700
Net profit for the year future taxation			45 000
Less: Corporation tax (2)			10 000
Net profit future year after taxation			35 000
Less: Dividends (3):			
Preference dividend paid (8%)		4 000	
Interim ordinary paid (5p per share)		5 000	
Proposed final ordinary dividend			
(10p per share)		10 000	19 000
Retained profit for the year			16 000
Retained profits brought forward			9 000
Retained profits carried forward (4)			25 000

(b)

Handy Ltd
Balance sheet at 31 March 2005

	Cost	Accumulated depreciation	Net book value
Fixed assets	£	£	£
Freehold land (5)	200 000	–	200 000
Motor van (6)	15 000	9 000	6 000
	215 000	9 000	206 000
Investments			
At cost (market value at 31 March 2005: £11 000) (7)			10 000
Current assets			
Stocks at cost		40 000	
Trade debtors		27 000	
Bank		2 000	
		69 000	
Less: Current liabilities			
Trade creditors	50 000		
Corporation tax (8)	10 000		
Proposed ordinary dividend (9)	10 000	70 000	
Net current assets			(1 000)
			215 000

	Authorized	Issued and fully paid
Financed by:		
Capital and reserves		
Ordinary shares of £1 each (10)	150 000	100 000
Preference shares of £1 each (10)	75 000	50 000
	225 000	150 000
Share premium account (11)		10 000
Retained profits (12)		25 000
Shareholders' funds (13)		185 000
Loans (14)		
10% debenture stock (repayable 2009)		30 000
		215 000

Note: The number shown after each narration refers to the following tutorial notes.

Tutorial notes

1 Depreciation has been charged on the motor van at a rate of 20 per cent per annum on cost (as instructed in question note 2).
2 Question note 3 requires £10 000 to be charged as corporation tax. Remember that the corporation tax rate is applied to the *taxable* profit and not to the *accounting* profit. The taxable profit has not been given in the question.
3 A proposed ordinary dividend of 10p has been included as instructed in question note 4.

4   The total retained profit of £25 000 is carried forward to the balance sheet (see tutorial note 12 below).

5   Question note 2 states that no depreciation is to be charged on the freehold land.

6   The accumulated depreciation for the motor van of £9000 is the total of the accumulated depreciation brought forward at 1 April 2004 of £6000, plus the £3000 written off to the profit and loss account for the current year (see tutorial note 1 above).

7   Note that the market value of the investments has been disclosed on the face of the balance sheet.

8   The corporation tax charged against profit (question note 3) will be due for payment in 2006. It is treated as a current liability.

9   The proposed ordinary dividend will be due for payment shortly after the year end, and so it is also a current liability. The interim dividend and the preference dividend have already been paid, and so they are not current liabilities.

10 Details of the authorized, issued and fully paid share capital should be disclosed.

11 The share premium is a capital account: it cannot be used for the payment of dividends. This account will tend to remain unchanged in successive balance sheets, although there are a few highly restricted purposes for which it may be used.

12 The retained profits become part of a revenue account balance that the company could use for the payment of dividends. The total retained profits of £25 000 is the amount brought in to the balance sheet from the profit and loss account.

13 The total amount of shareholders' funds should always be shown.

14 The loans are long-term loans. Loans are not part of shareholders' funds, and they should be shown in the balance sheet as a separate item.

You are now recommended to work through Exhibit 6.3 again without reference to the answer.

Conclusion

This chapter has briefly examined the background to the legislation affecting limited liability companies. This was followed by some examples of how company accounts are prepared for *internal* purposes.

Although a great deal of information can be obtained from studying the annual accounts of a company, it is difficult to extract the most relevant and significant features. Some further guidance is needed, therefore, in how to make the best use of the financial accounting information presented to you. That guidance will be provided in Chapters 8 and 9, but in the meantime we need to examine some other types of account. We do so in the next chapter.

Key points

1 Company accounts have to be adapted in order to meet certain legal requirements. Basically, the structure of the annual accounts is similar to those of sole traders.

2 The profits of a company are taxed separately (like an individual). The tax is based on the accounting profit for the year. Any tax due at the year end will be shown in the balance sheet as a current liability.

3 The net profit after tax may be paid to shareholders in the form of a dividend (although some profit may still be retained within the business). Any proposed dividend (i.e. one recommended but not yet paid) should be shown in the balance sheet as a creditor.

Check your learning

1 Fill in the blank spaces in each of the following statements:
  (a) Limited liability is a ____ concept.
  (b) The shares in a ____ company can be bought and sold on a Stock Exchange.
  (c) There are two main types of shares, ____ and ____.
  (d) Debentures are a form of ____ .

2 Complete the following equations:
  (a) Sales – cost of goods sold = ____
  (b) Profit for the year after taxation – ____ retained profit for the year
  (c) ____ – current liabilities = net current assets
  (d) Ordinary shares + share premium account + retained profits = ____
  (e) Retained profits brought forward + _____ = retained profits carried forward

3 State in which section of the balance sheet you are likely to find the following items:
  (a) amount owing for corporation tax
  (b) debenture stock
  (c) plant and machinery
  (d) preference shares
  (e) trade debtors.

[*The answers to these questions may be found at the back of the book.*]

Group discussion questions

6.1 'The concept of limited liability is an out-of-date nineteenth-century concept.' Discuss.

6.2 Appleton used to operate her business as a sole-trader entity. She has recently converted it into a limited liability company. Appleton owns 80 per cent of the ordinary (voting) shares, the remaining 20 per cent being held by various relatives and friends. Explain to Appleton why it is now inaccurate for her to describe the company as 'her' business.

6.3 How far do you think that the information presented in a limited liability company's profit and loss account and balance sheet is useful to the owners of a small business?

Practice questions

[*Note: The questions marked with an asterisk have answers at the back of the book.*]

6.4* The following balances have been extracted from the books of Margo Ltd for the year to 31 January 2001:

	Dr £000	Cr £000
Cash at bank and in hand	5	
Plant and equipment:		
At cost	70	
Accumulated depreciation (at 31.1.01)		25
Profit and loss account (at 1.2.00)		15
Profit for the financial year (to 31.1.01)		10
Share capital (issued and fully paid)		50
Stocks (at 31.1.01)	17	
Trade creditors		12
Trade debtors	20	
	112	112

Additional information:
1 Corporation tax owing at 31 January 2001 is estimated to be £3000.
2 Margo Ltd's authorized share capital is £75 000 of £1 ordinary shares.
3 A dividend of 10p per share is proposed.

Required:
Prepare Margo Ltd's profit and loss account for the year to 31 January 2001 and a balance sheet as at that date.

6.5* Harry Ltd was formed in 2000. The following balances as at 28 February 2002 have been extracted from the books of account after the trading account has been compiled:

	Dr £000	Cr £000
Administration expenses	65	
Cash at bank and in hand	10	
Distribution costs	15	
Dividend paid (on preference shares)	6	
Furniture and equipment:		
At cost	60	
Accumulated depreciation at 1.3.01		36
c/f	156	36

		Dr	Cr
		£000	£000
	b/f	156	36
Gross profit for the year			150
Ordinary share capital (shares of £1 each)			100
Preference shares (cumulative 15% of £1 shares)			40
Profit and loss account (at 1.3.01)			50
Share premium account			20
Stocks (at 28.2.02)		130	
Trade creditors			25
Trade debtors		135	
		421	421

Additional information:
1 Corporation tax owing at 28 February 2002 is estimated to be £24 000.
2 Furniture and equipment is depreciated at an annual rate of 10 per cent of cost and it is all charged against administrative expenses.
3 A dividend of 20p per ordinary share is proposed.
4 All of the authorized share capital has been issued and is fully paid.

Required:
Prepare Harry Ltd's profit and loss account for the year to 28 February 2002 and a balance sheet as at that date.

6.6* The following balances have been extracted from the books of Jim Ltd as at 31 March 2003:

	Dr	Cr
	£000	£000
Advertising	3	
Bank	11	
Creditors		12
Debtors	118	
Furniture and fittings:		
At cost	20	
Accumulated depreciation (at 1.4.02)		9
Directors' fees	6	
Profit and loss account (at 1.4.02)		8
Purchases	124	
Rent and rates	10	
Sales		270
Share capital (issued and fully paid)		70
Stock (at 1.4.02)	16	
Telephone and stationery	5	
Travelling expenses	2	
Vehicles:		
At cost	40	
Accumulated depreciation (at 1.4.02)		10
Wages and salaries	24	
	379	379

Additional information:

1 Stock at 31 March 2002 was valued at £14 000.

2 Furniture and fittings and the vehicles are depreciated at a rate of 15 per cent and 25 per cent, respectively on cost.

3 Corporation tax owing at 31 May 2005 is estimated to be £25 000.

4 A dividend of 40p per share is proposed.

5 The company's authorized share capital is £100 000 of £1 ordinary shares.

Required:

Prepare Jim Ltd's trading and profit and loss account for the year to 31 March 2003 and a balance sheet as at that date.

6.7 The following trial balance has been extracted from Carol Ltd as at 30 April 2004:

	Dr	Cr
	£000	£000
Advertising	2	
Bank overdraft		20
Bank interest paid	4	
Creditors		80
Debtors	143	
Directors' remuneration	30	
Freehold land and buildings:		
At cost	800	
Accumulated depreciation at 1.5.03		102
General expenses	15	
Investments at cost	30	
Investment income		5
Motor vehicles:		
At cost	36	
Accumulated depreciation (at 1.5.03)		18
Preference dividend paid	15	
Preference shares (cumulative 10% shares		
of £1 each)		150
Profit and loss account (at 1.5.03)		100
Purchases	480	
Repairs and renewals	4	
Sales		900
Share capital (authorized, issued and fully paid		
ordinary shares of £1 each)		500
Share premium account		25
Stock (at 1.5.03)	120	
Wages and salaries	221	
	1 900	1 900

Additional information:

1 Stock at 30 April 2004 was valued at £140 000.

2 Depreciation for the year of £28 000 is to be provided on buildings and £9000 for motor vehicles.

3 A provision of £6000 is required for the auditors' remuneration.

4 £2000 had been paid in advance for renewals.
5 Corporation tax owing at 30 April 2004 is estimated to be £60 000
6 The directors propose an ordinary dividend of 10p per share.
7 The market value of the investments at 30 April 2004 was £35 000.

Required:
Prepare Carol Ltd's trading and profit and loss account for the year to 30 April 2004 and a balance sheet as at that date.

6.8 Nelson Ltd was incorporated in 2000 with an authorized share capital of 500 000 £1 ordinary shares, and 200 000 5% cumulative preference shares of £1 each. The following trial balance was extracted as at 31 May 2005:

	Dr £000	Cr £000
Administrative expenses	257	
Auditor's fees	10	
Cash at bank and in hand	5	
Creditors		85
Debentures (12%)		100
Debenture interest paid	6	
Debtors	225	
Directors' remuneration	60	
Dividends paid:		
Ordinary interim	20	
Preference	5	
Furniture, fittings and equipment:		
At cost	200	
Accumulated depreciation at 1.6.04		48
Investments at cost (market value at 31.5.05:		
£340 000)	335	
Investment income		22
Ordinary share capital (issued and fully paid)		400
Preference share capital		200
Profit and loss account (at 1.6.04)		17
Purchases	400	
Sales		800
Share premium account		50
Stock at 1.6.04	155	
Wages and salaries	44	
	1 722	1 722

Additional information:
1 Stock at 31 May 2005 was valued at £195 000.
2 Administrative expenses owing at 31 May 2005 amounted to £13 000.
3 Depreciation is to be charged on the furniture and fittings at a rate of 12½% on cost.
4 Salaries paid in advance amounted to £4000.
5 Corporation tax owing at 1.6.05 is estimated to be £8000.
6 Provision is to be made for a final ordinary dividend of 1.25p per share.

125

Required:
Prepare Nelson Ltd's trading and profit and loss account for the year to 31 May 2005 and a balance sheet as at that date.

6.9 The following trial balance has been extracted from the books of Keith Ltd as at 30 June 2006:

	Dr £000	Cr £000
Advertising	30	
Bank	7	
Creditors		69
Debentures (10%)		70
Debtors (all trade)	300	
Directors' remuneration	55	
Electricity	28	
Insurance	17	
Investments (quoted)	28	
Investment income		4
Machinery:		
At cost	420	
Accumulated depreciation at 1.7.05		152
Office expenses	49	
Ordinary share capital (issued and fully paid)		200
Preference shares		50
Preference share dividend	4	
Profit and loss account (at 1.7.05)		132
Provision for bad and doubtful debts		8
Purchases	1 240	
Rent and rates	75	
Sales		2 100
Stock (at 1.7.05)	134	
Vehicles:		
At cost	80	
Accumulated depreciation (at 1.7.05)		40
Wages and salaries	358	
	2 825	2 825

Additional information:
1 Stock at 30 June 2006 valued at cost amounted to £155 000.
2 Depreciation is to be provided on machinery and vehicles at a rate of 20 per cent and 25 per cent respectively on cost.
3 Provision is to be made for auditors' remuneration of £12 000.
4 Insurance paid in advance at 30 June 2006 amounted to £3000.
5 The provision for bad and doubtful debts is to be made equal to 5 per cent of outstanding trade debtors as at 30 June 2006.
6 Corporation tax owing at 30 June 2006 is estimated to be £60 000.
7 An ordinary dividend of 10p per share is proposed.

8   The investments had a market value of £30 000 at 30 June 2006.

9   The company has an authorized share capital of 600 000 ordinary shares of £0.50 each and of 50 000 8% cumulative preference shares of £1 each.

Required:

Prepare Keith Ltd's trading and profit and loss account for the year to 30 June 2006 and a balance sheet as at that date.

7 Other accounts

Resource accounting is 'too little, too late'

The Public Accounts Select Committee has condemned the government's plan to introduce resource accounting – which will see government departments produce commercial-style balance sheets for the first time – as 'a missed opportunity'.

The Government Resources and Accounts Bill was published to great fanfare at the beginning of January, when it was described by Andrew Smith, chief secretary to the Treasury, as 'the biggest reform and modernisation programme in the management of the country's public finances since the Gladstone era'. The Bill introduces resource accounting and budgeting into government accounts and allows for the preparation and audit of consolidated accounts for the whole public sector.

All government departments conducted a dry run of the new procedures during 1999 and, as a result, a decision was made to introduce resource accounting in two stages. Large non-cash elements will be included as part of annually managed expenditure until 2002, when they will be moved into departmental expenditure limits. This will allow departments to develop a track record in forecasting items such as depreciation and provisions.

Accountancy, February 2000. Reprinted with permission.

Governmental accounts are being brought up to date

In Chapter 3 we demonstrated how to record financial data in books of accounts. Chapter 4 showed how to prepare a basic trading and profit and loss account and balance sheet. Chapter 5 then illustrated the impact of various year-end adjustments. In the last chapter, Chapter 6, we were involved in the preparation of the financial accounts for a limited liability company. Thus, so far, we have been primarily concerned with financial accounts relating to trading entities in the profit-making sector.

In this chapter, we want to show you how the basic financial accounts may be adapted to suit the requirements of different types of entities in both the profit-making and the not-for-profit sectors. We are going to concentrate on three main types of entities but we will also refer briefly to governmental accounting.

By the end of this chapter, you should be able to:

- outline the contents of a manufacturing account;
- prepare a simple manufacturing account;
- describe the type of accounts required by service-sector entities;
- compare and contrast accounts in the profit-making sector with those in the not-for-profit sector;
- itemize the distinctive nature of governmental accounting.

Manufacturing accounts

A manufacturing entity is an entity that purchases or obtains raw materials and converts them to a finished goods state. The finished goods are then sold to customers. Manufacturing entities are normally to be found in the private sector and they may be organized as sole traders, partnerships or companies.

Unlike the examples we have used in the previous chapters, manufacturing entities are not likely to use a *purchases account*. This is because they normally buy raw materials and then process them before they are sold in a *finished goods state*. Hence before the trading account can be compiled it is necessary to calculate the cost of converting the raw materials into a finished goods state. The conversion cost is called the *manufacturing cost* and it is the equivalent of a trading entity's purchases.

In order to calculate an entity's manufacturing cost, we need to open (not surprisingly) a *manufacturing account*. A manufacturing account forms part of the double-entry system and it is included in the periodic financial accounts. It normally only contains manufacturing *costs* since it is rare to have any manufacturing *incomes*.

Manufacturing costs are debited to the manufacturing account. They are usually classified into *direct* and *indirect* costs. Direct costs are those costs that can be easily and economically identified with a particular segment. A segment may be a department, a section, a product or a unit. Indirect costs are those costs that cannot be easily and economically identified with a particular segment. Indirect costs are sometimes referred to as 'overhead' or 'overheads'.

The format of the manufacturing account is straightforward. Normally, it contains two main sections comprising the direct and the indirect costs. Each section is then analyzed into what are called the *elements of cost*. The elements of cost include materials, labour, and other expenses.

Exhibit 7.1 illustrates the format of a typical manufacturing account. A detailed explanation of its contents then follows the exhibit.

Exhibit 7.1 Format of a basic manufacturing account

	£000	£000
Direct costs (1)		
Direct materials (2)	20	
Direct labour (3)	70	
Other direct expenses (4)	5	
Prime cost (5)		95
Manufacturing overhead (6)		
Indirect material cost (7)	3	
Indirect labour cost (7)	7	
Other indirect expenses (7)	10	
Total manufacturing overhead incurred (8)		20
Total manufacturing costs incurred (9)		115
Work-in-progress (10)		
Opening work-in-progress	10	
Closing work-in-progress	(15)	(5)
Manufacturing cost of goods produced (11)		110
Manufacturing profit (12)		11
Market value of goods produced transferred to the trading account (13)		121

Notes:
(a) The number shown after each item refers to the tutorial notes immediately below. The amounts have been inserted purely for illustrative purposes.
(b) The term 'factory' or 'work' is sometimes substituted for the term *manufacturing*.

Tutorial notes

1 *Direct costs.* The exhibit relates to a *company's* manufacturing account. It is assumed that the direct costs listed for materials, labour and other expenses relate to those expenses that have been easy to identify with the specific products that the company manufactures.

2 *Direct materials.* The charge for direct materials will be calculated as follows:

Direct material cost = (Opening stock of raw materials + purchases of raw materials)
– Closing stock of raw materials

The total of direct material cost is sometimes referred to as *materials consumed*. Direct materials will include all the raw material costs and component parts that have been easy to identify with particular products.

3 *Direct labour.* Direct labour will include all those employment costs that have been easy to identify with particular products.

4 *Other direct expenses.* Besides direct materials and direct labour costs, there are sometimes other direct expenses that are easy to identify with particular products – for example, the cost of hiring a specific machine. Such expenses are relatively rare.

5 *Prime cost.* The total of direct material costs, direct labour costs and other direct expenses is known as prime cost.

6 *Manufacturing overhead.* Overhead is the collective term given to represent the total of all indirect costs, and so any manufacturing costs that are not easy to identify with specific products will be classified separately under this heading.

7 *Indirect material cost, indirect labour cost* and *other indirect expenses.* Manufacturing overhead will probably be shown separately under these three headings.

8 *Total manufacturing overhead incurred.* This item represents the total of indirect material cost, indirect labour cost and other indirect expenses.

9 *Total manufacturing costs incurred.* The total of prime cost and total manufacturing overhead incurred equals the total manufacturing costs incurred.

10 *Work-in-progress.* Work-in-progress represents the estimated cost of incomplete work that is not yet ready to be transferred to finished stock. There will usually be some opening and closing work-in-progress.

11 *Manufacturing cost of goods produced.* The manufacturing cost of goods produced equals the total manufacturing costs incurred plus (or minus) the difference between the opening and closing work-in-progress.

12 *Manufacturing profit.* The manufacturing cost of goods produced is sometimes transferred to the finished goods stock account without any addition for manufacturing profit. If this is the case, the double-entry effect is as follows:

> DEBIT   Finished goods stock account.
> CREDIT   Manufacturing account
>   with the manufacturing cost of goods produced.

The finished goods stock account is the equivalent of the purchases account in a trading organization.

Sometimes, however, a manufacturing profit is added to the manufacturing cost of goods produced before it is transferred to the trading account. The main purpose of this adjustment is to enable management to compare more fairly the company's total manufacturing cost – inclusive of profit – with outside prices (since such prices will also be normally inclusive of profit). The profit added to the manufacturing cost of goods produced may simply be an appropriate percentage, or it may represent the level of profit that the industry generally expects to earn. Any profit element added to the manufacturing cost (irrespective of how it is calculated) is an internal book-keeping arrangement, because the profit has not been earned or *realized* outside the business. The double-entry is affected as follows:

> DEBIT   Manufacturing account.
> CREDIT   Profit and loss account
>   with the manufacturing profit.

13 *Market value of goods produced.* As explained in note 12 above, the market value of goods produced is the amount that will be transferred (that is, debited) to the trading account.

You are now recommended to study Exhibit 7.1 most carefully. If you are not sure about a particular item, then refer to the accompanying tutorial notes. Once you are clear about the basic structure of a manufacturing account, you can move on to the next section.

Construction of the account

In this section, we are going to explain how to construct a manufacturing account. This can best be understood by reference to an example. We use one in Exhibit 7.2.

Exhibit 7.2 Constructing a manufacturing account

The following balances, *inter alia*, have been extracted from the Wren Manufacturing Company as at 31 March 2005:

	Dr £
Carriage inwards (on raw materials)	6 000
Direct expenses	3 000
Direct wages	25 000
Factory administration	6 000
Factory heat and light	500
Factory power	1 500
Factory rent and rates	2 000
Factory supervisory costs	5 000
Purchase of raw materials	56 000
Raw materials stock (at 1 April 2004)	4 000
Work-in-progress (at 1 April 2004)	5 000

Additional information:
1 The stock of raw materials at 31 March 2005 was valued at £6000.
2 The work-in-progress at 31 March 2005 was valued at £8000.
3 A profit loading of 50 per cent is added to the total cost of manufacture.

Required:
Prepare Wren's manufacturing account for the year to 31 March 2005.

Answer to Exhibit 7.2

Wren Manufacturing Company
Manufacturing account for the year to 31 March 2005

	£	£	£
Direct materials			
Raw material stock at 1 April 2004		4 000	
Purchases	56 000		
Carriage inwards (1)	6 000	62 000	
		66 000	
Less: Raw material stock at 31 March 2005		6 000	
Cost of materials consumed			60 000
Direct wages			25 000
Direct expenses			3 000
Prime cost			c/f 88 000

	£	£	£
			b/f 88 000
Other manufacturing costs (2)			
Administration		6 000	
Heat and light		500	
Power		1 500	
Rent and rates		2 000	
Supervisory		5 000	
Total manufacturing overhead expenses			15 000
Total manufacturing costs incurred			103 000
Work-in-progress			
Add: Work-in-progress at 1 April 2004		5 000	
Less: Work-in-progress at 31 March 2005		(8 000)	(3 000)
Manufacturing cost of goods produced			100 000
Manufacturing profit (50%) (3)			50 000
Market value of goods produced (4)			150 000

Tutorial notes

1 Carriage inwards (i.e. the cost of transporting goods to the factory) is normally regarded as being part of the cost of purchases.
2 Other manufacturing costs include production overhead expenses. In practice, there would be a considerable number of other manufacturing costs.
3 A profit loading of 50 per cent has been added to the manufacturing cost (see note 3 of the question). The manufacturing profit is a debit entry in the manufacturing account. The corresponding credit entry will eventually be made in the profit and loss account.
4 The market value of goods produced will be transferred to the finished goods stock account.

You are now recommended to work through Exhibit 7.2 again, but this time without reference to the answer.

Links with the other accounts

Exhibit 7.2 deals with the manufacturing account in isolation. However, once the manufacturing account has been prepared, it will then be linked with the trading account and the profit and loss account by transferring either the manufacturing cost of the goods produced or the market value of the goods produced to the trading account. Thus the manufacturing cost or the market value of the goods produced is the equivalent of the entry for 'purchases' which may be found in the trading account of a non-manufacturing entity. Apart from this slight amendment, the preparation of a trading account for a manufacturing entity is exactly the same as it is for a trading entity.

The relationship between a manufacturing account and the other main financial statements is shown in Figure 7.1.

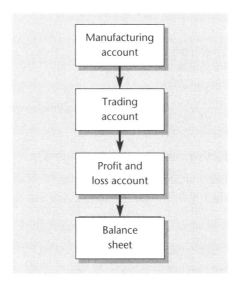

**Figure 7.1
The relationship
between the main
accounts**

Service entity accounts

The profit-making sector is made up of a great many other types of entities beside those that may be classified as manufacturing or trading. For convenience, we will describe them as *service entities*. Service entities do not normally deal in physical or tangible goods, unlike manufacturing or trading entities; instead, they offer advice and provide assistance to their customers, clients, patients or passengers. In recent years, the manufacturing sector in the United Kingdom has declined and the service sector has become much more important.

The service sector is extremely diverse, but there are a number of recognizable categories. These are as follows:

1 *Hotels and catering*. Such entities are generally regarded as being part of the service sector although the service they offer includes a physical or tangible element, e.g. the supply of food and drink.

2 *Leisure and recreational activities*. Services included in this category include cinema, concerts and theatre productions, leisure and sports centres, and travel agencies.

3 *Personal*. Examples of personal services include beauticians, hairdressing, and manicuring.

4 *Professional*. The more common professional services include accounting, legal, and medical (including chiropody and optical).

5 *Transportation*. Transportation services include the movement of goods and passengers by air, land, and sea.

It will be apparent from the above list that there is an extremely wide variety of different types of service entities. This means that the accounts of different entities will also be somewhat different, e.g. the accounts of a beautician will not be identical to those of a railway company. None the less, there are some basic features that are common to all service sector entities and that distinguish them from manufacturing and trading entities. These may be summarized as follows:

1 *Manufacturing and trading accounts are irrelevant.* Such accounts are irrelevant in service entities because such entities do not normally manufacture products or trade in tangible goods.
2 *Gross profit not calculated.* As service entities do not prepare trading accounts, the calculation of gross profit is irrelevant.
3 *Primacy of the profit and loss account.* Details of the income and expenditure for a particular accounting period are shown in the profit and loss account.
4 *Format.* The format of a service-sector profit and loss account is very similar to that of trading entities. However, specific expenditure is sometimes deducted from specific income, the net amount then being highlighted in the profit and loss account. For example, suppose an entity sells some food for £1000 and the cost of providing it was £600. The £1000 income could be shown in the income section of the profit and loss account, with the £600 being shown separately as an expenditure item. However, as there is a close relationship between the income and the expenditure, it is helpful to users if the net amount earned on selling the food is disclosed. It would then be presented as shown in Exhibit 7.3.
5 *Segmentation.* Similar categories of income or expenditure are usually grouped together in the same part of the profit and loss account with the subtotal of each category being shown separately.

Exhibit 7.3 Extract from the profit and loss account

	£	£
Income from sale of food	1 000	
Less: cost of provision	600	400

We illustrate the presentation of a set of financial statements for a service entity in Exhibit 7.4. As you will see, the presentation of the profit and loss account and the balance sheet is very similar to the examples used in previous chapters.

Exhibit 7.4 Example of a service entity account

Mei Loon: Educational training consultant
Profit and loss account for the year to 31 March 2002

	£	£
INCOME (1)		
Article fees	5 000	
Author's licensing and collecting payments	2 000	
Consultation fees	90 000	
Lecture fees	30 000	
Public lending right payment	1 000	
Royalties	20 000	148 000
EXPENDITURE (2)		
Computing	5 000	
Depreciation : equipment (3)	2 000	
: furniture (3)	500	
Heat and light	1 000	
Insurances	600	
Photocopying	200	
Postage	100	
Rates	1 500	
Secretarial	30 000	
Stationery (4)	700	
Subscriptions	400	
Travelling	6 000	48 000
Net profit for the year (5)		100 000

Balance sheet at 31 March 2002

	£	£
FIXED ASSETS (6)		
Office equipment	10 000	
Less: accumulated depreciation	4 000	6 000
Office furniture	5 000	
Less: accumulated depreciation	1 500	3 500
		9 500
CURRENT ASSETS		
Stock of stationery (7)	200	
Debtors (8)	15 000	
Prepayments (9)	3 000	
Cash at bank and in hand	52 300	
	70 500	
CURRENT LIABILITIES		
Creditors (10)	2 000	
Accruals (11)	1 000	
	3 000	67 500
		77 000

	£	£
CAPITAL		
At 1 April 2001 (12)		17 000
Net profit for the year (13)	100 000	
Less: drawings (14)	40 000	60 000
		77 000

Balance at 31 March 2002

Tutorial notes

1   All six of the listed income items will have been compiled on an accruals and prepayments basis, i.e. the cash received during the period will have been adjusted for any opening and closing debtors.

2   Apart from depreciation, the expenditure items will have been adjusted for any opening or closing accruals and prepayments.

3   Mei Loon appears to be depreciating her office furniture by 10 per cent per annum on cost [(£500 ÷ £5000) × 100%], and her office equipment by 20 per cent per annum on cost [(£2000 ÷ £10 000) × 100%].

4   The stationery costs for the year have been reduced by the stock at 31 March 2002 (see note 7).

5   The net profit for the year has been added to Mei Loon's capital at 1 April 2001 (see note 12).

6   The fixed assets are shown at their gross book value less the accumulated depreciation. Sometimes additional information would be provided by inserting separate columns for (a) the gross book value; (b) the accumulated depreciation; and (c) the net book value.

7   Mei Loon appears to have valued the stock of stationery that she held at 31 March 2002 at £200.

8   The debtors entry probably represents what is owed to Mei Loon for various fees as at 31 March 2001.

9   The prepayments represent what she has paid in advance at the end of the year for various services, such as insurances or heat and light, from which she would expect to benefit in the year to 31 March 2003.

10   The creditors represent what she owes at the end of the year for various goods and services supplied during the year.

11   The accruals are similar to the creditors, but they probably relate to services such as insurances or heat and light (see note 9).

12   Mei Loon's opening capital balance is shown as £17 000. This would be composed of her original capital contribution plus previous years' profits that she had not drawn out of the business.

13   The net profit for the year is the balance on the profit and loss account.

14   Mei Loon has drawn £40 000 out of the business during the year for her own private use. Some of the £40 000 probably relates to previous years' profits that she has drawn out during the current year, along with various amounts drawn out in advance of this year's profits.

Not-for-profit entity accounts

As the term suggests, not-for-profit entities are those whose primary objective is non-profit-making, for example various voluntary associations, charities, clubs, pressure groups and societies. The main objective of such entities may be to provide leisure, social or welfare facilities for their members. It is possible that they may be involved in some trading (or even manufacturing) activities, but the profit motive would not be their main consideration.

If not-for-profit entities have some manufacturing or trading activities, they will prepare manufacturing and trading accounts. The balance on the manufacturing account would be transferred to the trading account, and the balance on the trading account (i.e. the gross profit) would be transferred to an *income and expenditure account*. An income and expenditure account is almost identical to a profit and loss account, the main difference being in the title. The change of terminology also means that the balance on the account is described as the *excess of income over expenditure* (or expenditure over income) instead of *profit* (or loss).

An example of an income and expenditure account and a balance sheet for a social club is shown in Exhibit 7.5. The preparation of such accounts is very similar to that used in compiling accounts for trading entities.

Exhibit 7.5 Example of a social club's accounts

Balli social club
Income and expenditure account for the year to 31 March 2003

	£	£
INCOME (1)		
Bar sales (2)	60 000	
Less: purchases	40 000	20 000
Building society interest		200
Dances (2)	1 600	
Less expenses	900	700
Food sales (2)	8 000	
Less: purchases	4 500	3 500
Members' subscriptions		36 200
		60 600
EXPENDITURE (3)		
Accountants' fees	250	
Depreciation: furniture and fittings	3 900	
Insurances	600	
Electricity	1 400	
Office expenses	22 000	
Rates	2 000	
Salaries and wages	14 000	
Telephone	3 100	
Travelling expenses	13 000	60 250
Excess of income over		
expenditure for the year (4)		350

Balance sheet at 31 March 2003

	Cost	Accumulated depreciation	Net book value
FIXED ASSETS (5)	£	£	£
Club premises	18 000	–	18 000
Furniture and equipment	39 000	17 900	21 100
	57 000	17 900	39 100
CURRENT ASSETS (5)			
Stocks	1 500		
Prepayments	200		
Members' subscriptions (in arrears)	7 000		
Building society account	2 700		
Cash	5 500	16 900	
CURRENT LIABILITIES (5)			
Trade creditors	2 000		
Members' subscriptions (paid in advance)	800		
Accruals	1 250	4 050	12 850
			51 950
ACCUMULATED FUND (6)			
Balance at 1 April 2002 (7)			51 600
Excess of income over expenditure for the year (8)			350
Balance at 31 March 2003 (9)			51 950

Tutorial notes

1 The income items will have been calculated on an accruals and prepayments basis.
2 Details relating to the bar, dances, and food sales (and other similar activities) may require separate disclosure. If so, individual accounts would be prepared for these activities, the balance on such accounts then being transferred to the income and expenditure account.
3 Expenditure items would be calculated on an accruals and prepayments basis.
4 The balance on the account (the excess of income over expenditure for the year) is transferred to the Accumulated Fund account (see note 6).
5 Fixed assets, current assets, and current liabilities are calculated and presented in exactly the same way that they are for profit-making entities.
6 The Accumulated Fund is the equivalent of the Capital element in the accounting equation. The total amount of £51 950 represents what the members have invested in the club as at the 31 March 2003 and what could have been paid back to them (in theory) if the club had been closed down at that date. In practice, of course, the various items on the balance sheet would not necessarily have been sold at their balance sheet values.
7 This was the balance in the Accumulated Fund at the beginning of the club's financial year.
8 This balance has been transferred from the income and expenditure account.
9 This is the balance in the Accumulated Fund as at the end of the club's financial year.

Governmental accounts

Another important set of entity accounts is that relating to the governmental sector of the economy. Such accounts may generally be regarded as part of the not-for-profit service sector. There are three broad categories: (1) central government accounts; (2) local government accounts; and (3) quasi-governmental accounts.

Central government accounts incorporate the results of major departments such as defence, the environment, social security, and trade and industry. Until fairly recently, they were prepared on a cash flow basis, i.e. cash received for the year less cash paid during that year. The government has now adopted what they call *resource accounting*. This is just another term for accounts prepared on an accruals and prepayments basis.

Local government accounts include income and expenditure details relating to major services such as education, housing, police and social services. The annual budget (running from 1 April to 31 March) determines the amount of cash that the local authority needs to raise from its council tax payers in order to finance its projected expenditure for the forthcoming year. This is a highly political consideration and councillors are usually more concerned about the impact that a forthcoming budget may have on the electorate than about expenditure that has already been incurred.

Quasi-government entities include those bodies that are owned by the government but operated at arm's length (i.e. indirectly) through specially appointed authorities and councils. Examples, include the British Broadcasting Corporation (the BBC), secondary or tertiary education colleges, the Post Office, and universities. Such bodies are often heavily dependent on the government for providing them with a great deal of their operational income.

Government accounting generally is a highly specialist activity, although the basics are similar to the procedures used in the private sector. As it is so specialized, we will not consider it any further in this book.

Conclusion

In describing and illustrating the nature and purpose of accounting, there is a danger that too much emphasis is placed on manufacturing industry in the profit-making sector of the economy. There are three main reasons for this tendency: (1) modern accounting practice grew out of the requirements of 19th-century manufacturing industry; (2) twenty or so years ago manufacturing formed a major part of the economy; and (3) a complete range of accounting techniques may be applied in manufacturing industries.

The position has changed rapidly in recent years. Manufacturing industries have declined in importance and service sector industries have taken their place. Government activities have become much more important and greater attention has been given to them. Such activities are largely financed by taxpayers in one form or another. Taxpayers appear increasingly reluctant to contribute more and more of their income in taxes, and the government has had to search for economies and efficiencies in the way that it operates.

The profession of accountancy has not been immune from the changes taking place in the economic and political sectors, and it has had to adapt in recent years to a rapidly changing environment. This has meant moving away from traditional accounting practices that relate largely to profit-making manufacturing industries and adapting them to a service economy monitored very closely by an anxious government.

We began the chapter by describing the nature and purpose of manufacturing accounts and demonstrating how they may be compiled. We then moved the focus away from manufacturing and trading accounts toward other types of accounts used in the service sector, the non-for-profit sector, and in government.

You will have noticed that there is a great deal of similarity between manufacturing and trading accounts and the accounts of service sector entities. Manufacturing, trading and service-sector entities all usually adopt an accruals and prepayments basis for preparing their financial statements, and they are presented in the form of a profit and loss account (or equivalent) and a balance sheet.

The main differences are in the detail. Non-manufacturing and trading entities have few (if any) raw material stocks, work-in-progress or finished goods, and product costing is largely irrelevant. There are also a few differences in the way that information is presented in the profit and loss account (alternatively the income and expenditure account) and the balance sheet. Thus if you can work your way through a manufacturing entity's accounts, you should not have too much difficulty with non-manufacturing, non-trading and service-sector accounts.

In the next chapter we move on to examine another type of financial statement called a *cash flow statement*. Cash flow statements are now used widely in all sectors of the economy and in all types of entities, and they are regarded as one of the main financial statements.

Key points

1 Entities that convert raw materials and component parts into finished goods may need to prepare a manufacturing account.

2 A manufacturing account is part of the double-entry system. Normally, it will be prepared annually along with the other main financial accounts. It usually comes before the trading account.

3 The main elements of a manufacturing account include: direct materials, direct labour, direct expenses, and various indirect manufacturing costs.

4 A direct cost is a cost that can be easily and economically identified with a particular department, section, product, process or unit. An indirect cost is a cost that cannot be so easily and economically identified.

5 The type of manufacturing account described in this chapter would not be necessary if an entity operated a management accounting system. Management accounting is covered in Part 3 of this book.

6 Service-sector entities do not normally deal in physical or tangible goods or services. Hence they do not need to prepare a manufacturing or a trading account, their basic accounts consisting of a profit and loss account and a balance sheet. The preparation of such financial statements is similar to that required for compiling manufacturing and trading entity accounts.

7 The accounts of not-for-profit entities are very similar to those of service entities, except that the profit and loss account is referred to as an income and expenditure account.

8 Governmental accounts are highly specialized although, in essence, their basic structure is similar to that adopted in the private sector.

Check your learning

1 State whether each of the following assertions is true or false:
   (a) A manufacturing account will normally be required if an entity make a product.   True/False
   (b) An indirect cost is a cost that can be easily and economically identified with a specific department.   True/False
   (c) Opening work-in-progress has to be added to the total of manufacturing costs incurred.   True/False
   (d) Service sector accounts will not normally prepare a trading account.   True/False
   (e) The accounts of not-for-profit entities will normally be similar to those of profit-making entities.   True/False

2 Put the following items in the order that you would expect to find them in a manufacturing account:
   (a) Closing work-in-progress
   (b) Direct labour
   (c) Direct materials
   (d) Indirect labour
   (e) Indirect materials
   (f) Opening work-in-progress

3 To which element of cost does the following definition refer?

'Goods purchased for incorporation into products for sale.'

4 Fill in the blanks in each of the following statements:
   (a) The basic accounts of a not-for-profit entity will consist of an _____ and _____ account and a _____ sheet.
   (b) The total amount of capital contributed by members of a voluntary organization is usually to be found in the _____ Fund.
   (c) The balance on the profit and loss account of a private-sector service entity is described as the _____ /(_____) for the _____ _____ .
   (d) _____ government, _____ government, and _____ governmental accounts form the three main categories of governmental accounting.

[*The answers to these questions may be found at the back of the book.*]

Group discussion questions

7.1 A direct cost has been defined as 'a cost that that can be easily and economically identified with a particular department, section, product or unit'. Critically examine this definition from a non-accounting manager's perspective.

7.2 Although a manufacturing account may contain a great deal of information, how far do you think that it helps managers who are in charge of production cost-centres?

7.3 It has been asserted that the main objective of a profit-making entity is to make a profit while that of not-for-profit entity is to provide a service. Discuss this assertion in the context of the accounting requirements of different types of entities.

Practice questions

[*Note: The questions marked with an asterisk have answers at the back of the book.*]

7.4* The following information relates to Megg for the year to 31 January 2001:

	£000
Stocks at 1 February 2000:	
Raw material	10
Work-in-progress	17
Direct wages	65
Factory: Administration	27
Heat and light	9
Indirect wages	13
Purchases of raw materials	34
Stocks at 31 January 2001:	
Raw material	12
Work-in-progress	14

Required:
Prepare Megg's manufacturing account for the year to 31 January 2001.

7.5* The following balances have been extracted from the books of account of Moor for the year to 28 February 2002:

	£
Direct wages	50 000
Factory indirect wages	27 700
Purchases of raw materials	127 500
Stocks at 1 March 2001:	
Raw material	13 000
Work-in-progress	8 400
Stocks at 28 February 2002:	
Raw material	15 500
Work-in-progress	6 300

Required:
Prepare Moor's manufacturing account for the year to 28 February 2002.

7.6 The following balances have been extracted from the books of Stuart for the year to 31 March 2003:

	£000
Administration: Factory	230
Direct wages	330
Purchases of raw materials	1 123
Stocks at 1 April 2002:	
Raw material	38
Work-in-progress	29

Additional information:

Stocks at 31 March 2003:	
Raw material	44
Work-in-progress	42

Required:
Prepare Stuart's manufacturing account for the year to 31 March 2003.

7.7 The following balances have been extracted from the books of the David and Peter Manufacturing Company as at 30 April 2004:

	£000
Direct wages	70
Factory equipment: at cost	360
General factory expenses	13
Heat and light (factory $\frac{3}{4}$; general $\frac{1}{4}$)	52
Purchases of raw materials	100
Stocks at 1 May 2003:	
Raw material	12
Work-in-progress	18
Rent and rates (factory $\frac{2}{3}$; general $\frac{1}{3}$)	42

Additional information:

	£000
1 Stocks at 30 April 2004:	
Raw material	14
Work-in-progress	16

2 The factory equipment is to be depreciated at a rate of 15 per cent per annum on cost.

Required:

Prepare the David and Peter Manufacturing Company's manufacturing account for the year to 30 April 2004.

8 Cash flow statements

Calluna appoints Arthur Andersen

Three firms interested in saving disk drive maker

By Christopher Hope

CALLUNA, the struggling Scottish computer disk drive manufacturer, last night appointed the accountants, Arthur Andersen, as administrators one day after it suspended trading in its shares because of a cash flow crisis.

Iain Watters and Gordon Christie, both partners at Andersens, were appointed as interim managers following a request by Calluna's directors to the Court of Session.

The administrators, whose appointment was revealed in *The Scotsman* yesterday, must now find a buyer or joint venture for the Glenrothes-based business.

Under the order, Calluna's directors will be able to run the business and look for a cash injection or a buyer while being protected from any proceedings from the company's creditors.

One business from the Far East and two from the US are understood to have expressed an interest in either buying the business or injecting cash in a joint venture agreement.

Calluna is understood to have enough cash to survive until April but the move will cast a question-mark over the job prospects of its 100 staff.

The Scotsman, 20 January 2000. Reprinted with permission.

Monitoring cash flow is vital for survival

In the previous three chapters we have been concerned with the preparation of financial accounts for various types of entity. Such accounts are normally prepared on the basis of the accounting rules outlined in Chapter 2. A profit and loss account tells us how well a business has done during the accounting period reported on, and a balance sheet shows how much the business owes and is owed to it at the end of the period.

Profit and loss accounts do not provide much information about the movements of cash during the period they represent. The frequent monitoring of cash is a vital management function because entities cannot continue in business for very long if they do not have sufficient cash to meet their day-to-day requirements. Thus while in the long run an entity needs to make an adequate profit, it must have the cash resources to keep it going in the short term.

We may use the analogy of football to make the point. The main long-term objective of a football match is to make sure that your team scores more goals than the opposition, but you will not do so if you keep taking your eye of the ball. Similarly with a profit-making entity: the main long-term objective is to make a profit, but this is unlikely to happen unless you keep a constant eye on the day-to-day cash position. Thus it is vital for managers and owners to be supplied regularly with details of the entity's cash position. This can be done by preparing what is known as a *cash flow statement* (CFS). CFSs form the subject of this chapter.

The chapter is divided into three main sections. In the first section we examine the nature of accounting profit and its relationship to cash. In the second section we explain how to construct a simple cash flow statement. The third section shows how to convert that cash flow statement into a format required by FRS 1 – *Cash Flow Statements*. Although much of the chapter is concerned with the mechanics of preparing a cash flow statement, we have tried to emphasize its relevance and usefulness for non-accountants.

Learning objectives	**By the end of this chapter, you should be able to:**
	● **distinguish between profitability and liquidity;**
	● **outline the importance of cash in ensuring the long-term viability of an entity;**
	● **prepare a basic cash flow statement;**
	● **specify the main requirements of FRS 1 –** *Cash Flow Statements*;
	● **assess the relevance of cash flow statements for non-accounting managers.**

Accounting profit and cash

In Chapter 3 we demonstrated how financial accounting data were recorded in a system of double-entry book-keeping. Chapters 4, 5, 6, and 7 then explained how to use that data in preparing a set of basic financial statements. The format and content of such statements varies, depending upon whether an entity is in the profit-making sector or the not-for-profit sector, or whether it is a manufacturing, service or trading entity. In general, however, most entities will normally prepare a profit and loss account (or an income and expenditure account) and a balance sheet based on the accounting rules outlined in Chapter 2.

The information included in a typical set of financial statements is useful for medium to long-term planning and control purposes but it is inadequate for control of the cash position in the short term. This is because the basic accounts do not contain much specific information about the entity's cash position. The profit and loss account discloses the profit for the period, while the balance sheet lists the entity's assets, liabilities and capital balances. Such balances will include cash in hand, cash at the bank and bank overdrafts (for convenience, we will class all such balances as 'cash') but no information is given about the movement of cash during the period. At this stage you may be asking *'Why is this necessary? Surely the calculation of profit gives us that information?'* Unfortunately, this is not the case.

Monitoring the cash position

A profit-making entity needs to make a profit if it is to have a long-term future. It can often survive some periods when it is making a loss provided that they are balanced by some profit-making periods. By contrast, it cannot survive for very long if it runs short of cash. There are some short-term measures that it could adopt, for example, it could delay paying its creditors for a few months – but eventually they will either refuse to supply any more goods or they will take legal action. Indeed, it is unlawful for companies to continue operating if they knowingly cannot settle their debts when they fall due. The entity may perhaps borrow some money on a short-term or a long-term basis, although such measures could take some time to organize.

It follows that in order to ensure that an entity does not run short of cash, it is most important that it monitors regularly (possibly weekly, or even daily) the cash coming in and the cash going out. This means that managers should be presented with frequent reports disclosing the entity's cash position. It is also helpful to present an annual statement containing similar information

You may now be asking a further question, *'OK. But why can't the information be obtained from the profit and loss account?'* The reason is that the profit and loss account does not provide us with the information needed. Why is this the case?

Accounting profit The adoption of the accounting rules outlined in Chapter 2 means that accounting profit for a particular period is *not* necessarily the same as a movement in cash for the same period. There are three main reasons why this is the case and these are explained below.

1 *Adoption of the realization and matching rules.* You will recall that two of the measurement rules that we examined in Chapter 2 were the realization rule and the matching rule. The realization rule requires transactions to be accounted for when the legal title has been transferred from one party to another, regardless of when a cash settlement takes place. Similarly, the matching rule involves adjusting the cash received and the cash paid during a particular period to reflect the actual economic activity, i.e. opening and closing accruals and prepayments are added to or deducted from the cash transactions.

These rules mean that there is usually delay between the time when the economic activity is measured and when a cash settlement takes place. As a result, the profit or loss for a particular period (which measures economic activity) will not normally be the same as the increase or decrease in cash for that same period.

2 *Inclusion of non-cash items.* The profit and loss account usually contains some items that have not affected the cash position for that period. Such items include depreciation, bad debts written off, provisions for bad and doubtful debts, and profits or losses on the sale of fixed assets. The inclusion of such items are known as 'book entries' because they do not go through the cash book. If we take depreciation as an example, the entry in the books of account would be as follows:

> DEBIT   Profit and loss account.
> CREDIT Accumulated Depreciation account
> with the depreciation for the year.

As you can see, the entry of this transaction in the books of account has no impact on the cash position, although the profit for the year will be less.

3 *Exclusion of capital items.* Movements that take place in capital items, e.g. the issue of more shares or debentures, do not affect the profit because they are not credited to the profit and loss account. Similarly, some fixed assets may have been purchased and the cost will not have been debited to the profit and loss account.

It follows that it is impossible to assume that the profit (or loss) for a particular period will have seen a consequent increase (or decrease) in the cash position at the end of the period compared with the beginning. In other words:

The profit (or loss) for a period does not necessarily result in a cash increase (or decrease) during the same period.

Many proprietors of small businesses do not always understand this point. They often assume that because they have made a profit, the business is prospering. Thus they are puzzled when they suddenly go bankrupt. The reason is, of course, that they have not paid sufficient attention to the *cash* position – they have taken their eye off the ball.

Before you move on to the next section, make sure that you understand why profit is not necessarily the same as an increase in cash. The importance of monitoring the cash position cannot be sufficiently emphasized if a business is to survive on a long-term basis.

Construction

A cash flow statement is simply a summary of cash received for the period and cash paid. Such information could be obtained from the cash book but it is much more helpful to a general understanding of the financial accounts if it is integrated with the profit and loss account and the balance sheet. This means that we have to take the information in the financial accounts and convert it into cash terms. We do this by examining each item in the accounts and then adjusting each one for any opening and closing creditors and debtors, accruals and prepayments, and for any non-cash and capital items. Of course, not all items will require to be adjusted and so the procedure is not quite as complicated as it might appear! The relationship between the profit and loss account, the balance sheet and the cash flow statement is clearly very close and it is shown in diagrammatic format in Figure 8.1.

In order to demonstrate how to construct a cash flow statement, we will use a simple example. The details are contained in Exhibit 8.1.

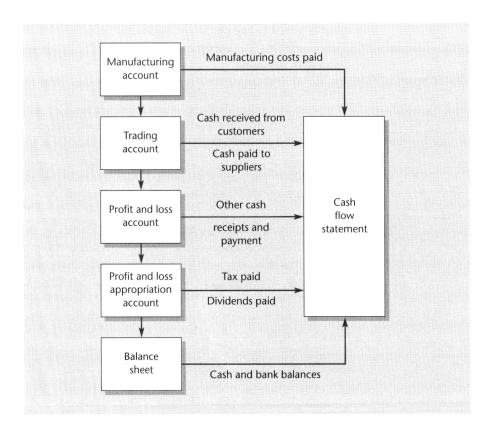

**Figure 8.1
The inter-
relationship
between the
main financial
statements**

Exhibit 8.1 Preparation of a cash flow statement

You are presented with the following information:

Durton Ltd
Trading and profit and loss account for the year to 31 December 2002

	£000	£000
Sales (1)		1 000
Less: Cost of goods sold:		
Opening stock (NA)	200	
Purchases (3)	700	
	900	
Less: Closing stock	300	600
Gross profit		400
Operating expenses (4)		(240)
Operating profit		160
Debenture interest (5)		(10)
Net profit before taxation		150
Taxation (6)		(50)
Net profit after taxation		100
Dividends (7)		(60)
Retained profit for the year		40

Durton Ltd
Balance sheet at 31 December 2002

	2001		2002	
	£000	£000	£000	£000
Fixed assets at cost (8)	900		1 050	
Less: Accumulated depreciation (4)	150	750	255	795
Current assets				
Stocks (NA)	200		300	
Trade debtors (1)	120		150	
Cash (NA)	20		45	
	340		495	
Less: Current liabilities				
Trade creditors (3)	70		90	
Taxation (4)	40		50	
Proposed dividend (7)	30		60	
	140	200	200	295
		950		1 090

	2001		2002	
	£000	£000	£000	£000
Capital and reserves				
Ordinary shares of £1 each (NA)		750		750
Profit and loss account (NA)		200		240
		950		990
Loans				
Debenture stock (10%: issued 1 January 2002 (2)		–		100
		950		1 090

Required:

Prepare a cash flow statement for the year to 31 December 2002.

Answer to Exhibit 8.1

Durton Ltd

Cash flow statement for the year to 31 December 2002

	£000
Cash receipts	
Sale of goods (£1000 + £120 – £150) (1)	970
Issue of debenture stock (£100 – £0) (2)	100
	1 070
Cash payments	
Purchases of goods (£700 + £70 – £90) (3)	(680)
Operating expenses (£240 – (£255 – £150)) (4)	(135)
Debenture interest paid (5)	(10)
Taxation (6)	(40)
Dividends (7)	(30)
Purchases of fixed assets (£1050 – £900) (8)	(150)
	(1 045)
Increase in cash during the year (9)	25
Cash at 1 January 2002 (9)	20
Cash at 31 December 2002 (9)	45

Notes: The number shown after each narration refers to the tutorial notes below. NA = no adjustment necessary.

Tutorial notes

1. The cash received from the sale of goods has been calculated by taking the sales figure of £1 000 000, adding the opening trade debtors of £120 000, and then deducting the closing trade debtors of £150 000.
2. The issue of debenture stock equals the closing balance of £100 000 as at 31 December 2002. As there was no opening balance, all of the debenture stock must have been issued during the year.
3. The cash payments to suppliers has been calculated as follows:
   Purchases + Opening trade creditors – Closing trade creditors, i.e £700 000 + £70 000 – £90 000.

4 The other cash payments relate to the operating expenses of £240 000 less the depreciation on the fixed assets of £105 000 (i.e. the closing accumulated balance of £255 000 less the opening accumulated depreciation balance of £150 000). As there were no opening or closing debtors or creditors for operating expenses, the whole of the £135 000 must have been paid during the year.

5 This is the total amount of debenture interest paid during the year.

6 The tax paid of £40 000 represents the taxation due for payment at 1 January 2002, since the amount outstanding at 31 December 2002 of £50 000 is the same as the figure for tax shown in the profit and loss account.

7 The dividend paid is the same as the proposed dividend at 1 January 2002, because the dividends shown in the profit and loss account as £60 000 had not been paid at 31 December 2002.

8 Purchase of fixed assets equals the closing balance of £1 050 000 less the opening balance of £900 000.

9 The increase in cash during the year of £25 000 plus the opening balance of £20 000 equals the closing balance of £45 000.

You are now recommended to work through Exhibit 8.1 again, but this time without reference to the answer.

Referring to Durton Limited's balance sheet in Exhibit 8.1, we can see that at 31 December 2001 it had a cash balance of £20 000. By 31 December 2002, the cash balance was £45 000, an increase of £25 000. Note that the retained profit for the year of £40 000 does not reflect the £25 000 increase in cash during the year. We do not, of course need to prepare a CFS to elicit such information but we do need some help in determining why the retained profit for the year was £40 000 while the cash only increased by £25 000. A CFS provides us with that guidance. As can be seen from the answer to Exhibit 8.1, most of the cash received for the year came from sales and much of it was spent on buying goods.

If you look at the CFS a little more closely, you will also see that £100 000 was raised by issuing some debenture stock and that £150 000 was incurred on purchasing some fixed assets. These items do not appear in the profit and loss account. There is probably a connection between them, i.e. the debentures might have been issued to finance the purchase of the fixed assets. Certainly, without them the cash position at the end of the year would have been very different, e.g. an overdrawn amount of £55 000 (45 000 – 100 000) instead of a favourable balance of £45 000. Similarly, if the taxation balance of £50 000 and the dividend balance of £60 000 as at 31 December 2002 had had to be paid early in 2003, the cash position would have been extremely vulnerable. Durton Ltd would then have to depend on its trade debtors (£150 000 at 31 December 2002) settling their debts before it needed to pay its trade creditors of £90 000.

Durton's CFS is a simplified example of a company's cash flow statement. None the less, it does enable the major cash items to be highlighted and to bring them to the attention of the managers and the owners of the entity. Although it is to be hoped that the cash position of Durton was being closely monitored during the year (a CFS would probably be prepared on a frequent basis), an annual CFS enables the year's results to be measured in cash terms and put into perspective. A CFS is nowadays considered as a very important financial statement. Indeed, you may regard it as being just as important as the profit and loss account and the balance sheet.

The format that we have adopted in preparing the solution to Exhibit 8.1 demonstrates the close relationship between the profit and loss account, the balance sheet and the CFS. The various changes that have been made are, however, somewhat difficult to trace. It would be useful, therefore, to present the CFS in such a way that its close relationship with the profit and loss account and the balance sheet is clearly apparent. The ASB has devised such a format and we can now examine it.

FRS 1 format

The very first financial reporting standard that the ASB issued dealt with cash flow statements. This was FRS 1 – *Cash Flow Statement* issued in 1991 and revised in 1996.

In this chapter we are only going to be concerned with cash flow statements that relate to a single entity. In Chapter 11 we will deal with CFSs for groups, i.e. companies that own a substantial number of shares in other companies.

FRS 1 requires the CFS to be set out under eight main headings. These headings are summarized in Table 8.1. The exhibit also contains some examples of what may be included under each heading.

FRS 1 requires the cash flow statement to be accompanied by a number of notes. These are as follows:

- a reconciliation between the operating profit and the net cash flow arising from operating activities;
- a reconciliation of net cash flow to movements in net debt;
- an analysis of the changes in net debt.

We deal with each of these notes below.

Reconciliation of operating profit to operating cash flows

This note to the CFS shows how the operating profit for the period has been converted into the respective cash flows, so that we measure the operating profit for the period in cash terms. There are two ways that this can be done. One way is to use what is called the *direct* method. If we adopt this method, all that we have to do is list for the period in question the cash received from customers and any other operating cash receipts, and the cash paid to suppliers together with any other operating cash payments. The information may be obtained from the cash book.

Table 8.1 Structure of a cash flow statement according to FRS 1

Heading[a]	Contents[b]
1 Net cash inflow from operating activities	Operating or trading activities.[c]
2 Returns on investments and servicing of finance	Investment income. Interest payments on loans. Dividends paid to preference shareholders.
3 Taxation	Tax paid on profits.
4 Capital expenditure and financial investment[d]	Purchases and sales of fixed assets. Loans to other entities received and paid.
5 Acquisitions and disposals	Sales and purchases of other entities or of investments in them.
6 Equity dividends paid	Dividents paid to ordinary shareholders.
7 Management of liquid resources[e]	Purchases and sales of current asset investments.
8 Financing[e]	Receipts and payments relating to share issues and redemptions, debentures, loans, and other long-term borrowings.

Notes:

(a) Headings may be omitted if no cash transaction has taken place either in the current period or the previous period. They must be in the order listed. A subtotal should be included for each heading.

(b) The contents only reflect the *cash* flow for each transaction. Cash includes cash in hand, deposits repayable on demand, and overdrafts. *Cash flow* is an increase or decrease in cash during the period.

(c) FRS 1 requires a reconciliation to be made between the operating profit and the net cash flows from operating activities. We deal with this requirement in the main text relating to this example.

(d) The heading 'capital expenditure' may be used if there are no cash flows relating to financial investment (such as loans).

(e) Headings 7 and 8 may be combined under one heading provided that each of their respective cash flows are shown separately and that separate subtotals are given for each heading.

FRS 1 prefers entities to use this method. However, even if this method is adopted, the standard still requires a reconciliation to be made between the operating profit shown in the profit and loss account and the operating cash flow for the period. In order to make this reconciliation, it is necessary to follow the procedures involved in adopting the other method, the *indirect* method. Most entities appear to have adopted the indirect method. There are two main reasons why this might be so. First, a clear link needs to be made between the CFS, the profit and loss account, and the balance sheet. Second, FRS 1 requires a reconciliation to be made between the operating profit and the operating cash for the period. Unlike the direct method, the indirect method automatically provides this reconciliation. We will follow common practice, therefore, and adopt the indirect method throughout the rest of the chapter.

In order to convert the operating activities for a period into the operating cash flows for the same period, we work from the current and previous period's profit and loss accounts and balance sheets. The following steps need to be taken in order to do so:

1 Extract the operating (or trading) profit from the profit and loss account for the current year.

2 Referring to the two balance sheets periods, calculate the movement between the following *operating* working capital balances:
   (a) stocks;
   (b) trade debtors;
   (c) other debtors;
   (d) prepayments;
   (e) trade creditors;
   (f) other creditors;
   (g) accruals.

3 Now comes the tricky bit. Determine whether in respect of each movement there has been either an increase or a decrease in cash during the period. In order to make it a little easier for you, we have summarized the various possibilities in Table 8.2.

4 If the cash movement has had the effect of *increasing* the cash for the period, add the difference to the operating profit for the year. If it has had the effect of *decreasing* the cash, then deduct it from the operating profit (deductions are usually shown in brackets).

5 Inspect the profit and loss account for any non-cash items. These should then either be added to, or deducted from, the operating profit. Additions will include losses on disposals of fixed assets, depreciation, increases in provisions for bad and doubtful debts, and bad debts written off. Deductions (shown in brackets) will include profits on sales of fixed assets and reductions in provisions for bad and doubtful debts.

6 Total the items included in the reconciliation. The balance should now represent the net cash inflow (or outflow) from operating activities. The balance is then inserted as the first item in the CFS.

The above steps may appear somewhat confusing, but do not worry at this stage. We will put them into context in a illustrative exhibit later in the chapter. We will now move on to the second note required by FRS1.

Reconciliation of net cash flow to movement in net debt

In order to help users assess the solvency and liquidity position of a company, FRS1 requires two notes to accompany the CFS. One note should show a reconciliation between the net debt at the beginning of the period and the net debt at the end of it. Basically, net debt is the difference between any long-term loans and cash and bank balances. If the cash and bank balances exceed the long-term funds, the balance would be referred to as *net funds*. Exhibit 8.2 illustrates the compilation of this particular note.

Table 8.2 The effect of working capital movements on cash flow

Item	Movement (Closing balance less opening balance)	Effect on cash
Stocks	Increase	Down (more cash has been spent on stocks). Insert the movement in brackets.
	Decrease	Up (less cash has been spent on stocks).
Trade debtors, other debtors, and prepayments	Increase	Down (less cash has been received). Insert the movement in brackets.
	Decrease	Up (more cash has been received).
Trade creditors, other creditors, and accruals (excluding taxation payable and proposed dividends	Increase	Up (less cash has been spent).
	Decrease	Down (more cash has been paid). Insert the movement in brackets.

An analysis of changes in net debt

The other additional note requires a detailed analysis of the changes that have taken place in the net debt position during the year. We will show you how to compile this note in Exhibit 8.2.

We can now illustrate how to prepare a cash flow statement as required by FRS 1.

An illustrative example

In order to demonstrate how a CFS is compiled in accordance with FRS 1 and how it should be presented, we are going to use the data contained in Exhibit 8.2. As explained earlier, FRS 1 gives a choice between the direct and indirect methods. We will be adopting the indirect method.

Exhibit 8.2 Preparation of a cash flow statement in accordance with FRS 1

Durton Ltd
Cash flow statement for the year to 31 December 2002

	£000
Net cash inflow from operating activities (1)	155
Returns on investments and servicing of finance	
Interest paid (7)	(10)
Taxation (8)	(40)
Capital expenditure	
Payments to acquire tangible fixed assets (9)	(150)
c/f	(45)

Durton Ltd
Cash flow statement for the year to 31 December 2002

		£000
	b/f	(45)
Equity dividends paid (10)		(30)
		(75)
Management of liquid resources and financing		
Issue of debenture stock (11)		100
Increase in cash (12)		25

Note 1 Reconciliation of operating profit to net cash inflow from operating activities

	£000
Operating profit (2)	160
Depreciation (3)	105
(Increase) in stocks (4)	(100)
(Increase) in trade debtors (5)	(30)
Increase in trade creditors (6)	20
Net cash inflow from operating activities (1)	155

Note 2 Reconciliation of net cash flow to movement in debt

	£000
Increase in cash during the period (12)	25
Cash from issuing debentures (13)	(100)
Change in net debt (14)	(75)
Net funds at 1 January 2002 (15)	20
Net debt at 31 December 2002 (16)	55

Note 3 Analysis of change in net debt

	At 1.1.02	Cash flows	At 31.12.02
	£000	£000	£000
Cash	20 (15)	25 (12)	45 (17)
Debt due after			
one year	– (15)	(100) (13)	(100) (13)
Total	20 (15)	(75) (14)	(55) (16)

[Note: the number in brackets after each amount refers to the tutorial notes.]

Tutorial notes

1 The calculation of the net cash inflow from operating activities totalling £155 000 is shown in Note 1 to the CFS (as required by FRS 1).
2 The operating profit of £160 000 has been obtained from the profit and loss account.
3 The depreciation charge has been obtained from the balance sheet. It is the difference between the accumulated depreciation of £255 000 as at 31 December 2002 and £150 000 as at 31 December 2001. Note that, in more advanced examples, the depreciation charge may require some detailed calculations.

4   The increase in stocks has been obtained from the two balance sheets. It is the movement between the two balances of £300 000 and £200 000. Note that an *increase* in stocks is the equivalent of a *reduction* in cash because more cash will have been paid out.

5   The increase in trade debtors of £30 000 represents the movement between the opening and closing trade debtors as obtained from the two balance sheets. An *increase* in trade debtors represents a *reduction* in cash because less cash has been received by the entity.

6   The increase in trade creditors of £20 000 is again obtained from the balance sheets. The £20 000 represents an *increase* in cash because less cash has been paid out of the business.

7   The interest paid of £10 000 has been obtained from the profit and loss account.

8   The taxation amount of £40 000 is the balance shown on the previous year's balance sheet. As £50 000 was charged to this year's profit and loss account for taxation and this amount features on this year's balance sheet, only £40 000 must have been paid during the year. In more advanced questions, more detailed adjustments would probably be required.

9   The capital expenditure amount of £150 000 is the difference between the two balance sheet amounts for fixed assets, of £1 050 000 and £900 000 respectively. No further details are given. In practice, the calculation of this amount would normally be more complex.

10 The equity dividends of £30 000 represent the dividends paid out to ordinary shareholders during the year (there are no other groups of shareholders in this example). The amount has been obtained from the 2001 balance sheet. The 2002 balance sheet shows an amount of £60 000, which is the same amount as disclosed in the profit and loss account. This means that only last year's dividend has been paid during the current year. Normally, there would also be other payments during the year.

11 The debenture stock balance has been obtained from the 2002 balance sheet. There was no such balance at the end of 2001, and so all the debenture must have (as stated) been issued during 2002.

12 After making all the above adjustments to the financial accounts, the net increase in cash during 2002 is found to be £25 000.

13 See Tutorial note (11) above.

14 Without the issue of the debentures, there would have been a £75 000 net *outflow* of cash during the year.

15 The company only had cash at 1 January 2002; it did not have any debt.

16 The entity's net debt at 31 December 2002 was £55 000, i.e. the debenture stock of £100 000 less the cash in hand of £45 000.

17 This was the cash balance at 31 December 2002, as shown in the balance sheet at that date.

Note that FRS 1 permits the detailed items included under each of the main headings on the cash flow statement to be shown in notes.

Although we have tried to simplify Exhibit 8.2 as much as possible, it is still fairly complicated, so it might be as well if you worked through it again. It might then be advisable to have another go at it but this time without looking at the solution.

As a non-accountant, what are your views about what the CFS shown in Exhibit 8.2 tells you? The format adopted is now well established, and so it should make comparisons between different entities reasonably straightforward. There are, however, two major difficulties as we see them: (1) the terminology is not easy to understand; and (2) the reconciliation notes relating to net debt are extremely difficult to sort out. Normally, of course, you will not have to prepare your own CFS. None the less, we feel that, by your knowing something about its construction, it will be easier for you to understand what a CFS is telling you. Remember that because cash flow is so important, your accountant will probably supply you (as a senior manager) with a CFS on a regular basis, perhaps as frequently as once a month.

Conclusion

A cash flow statement using the indirect method links directly with the profit and loss account and the balance sheet. Unlike the traditional financial statements, it contains some extremely useful information because it gives a lot more detail about the movement in the cash position. This is vital as it is possible for an entity to be profitable without necessarily having the cash resources to keep it going. Strict control over cash resources is absolutely essential, and a cash flow statement can help in this respect.

This chapter is closely linked with the next one, which deals with the interpretation of accounts. Before moving on, however, you are recommended to test your understanding of cash flow statements by attempting some of the chapter questions below.

Key points

1 Entities may have a long-term profitable future, but in the short term they may be short of cash. This may curb their activities, and in extreme cases they may be forced out of business.

2 To avoid this happening, owners and managers should be supplied with information about the cash movement and resources of the entity, i.e. about its liquidity. This can be done by preparing a cash flow statement.

3 A cash flow statement can be presented in any format, but most companies are required to adopt the recommendations contained in FRS 1.

4 FRS 1 permits the cash flow statement to be presented in either: (a) a direct method format, or (b) an indirect method format. The indirect method is preferred, because it can be more obviously linked to the profit and loss account and the balance sheet.

Check your learning

1 State whether each of the following assertions is true or false:

(a) Operating activities reflect total cash inflows.		True/False
(b) Depreciation reduces the cash position.		True/False
(c) Tax paid decreases the cash position.		True/False
(d) A proposed dividend increases the cash position.		True/False
(e) A decrease in debtors increases the cash position.		True/False
(f) An increase in creditors decreases the cash position.		True/False

2 Fill in the missing blanks in each of the following statements:

(a) There are _____ main sections in a cash flow statement as prepared under FRS 1.

(b) If stocks go up, cash goes _____.

(c) If accruals go up, cash goes _____.

(d) If the opening cash was £15 000, and the closing cash was £20 000, there was a _____ _____ _____ of £5000.

[*The answers to these questions may be found at the back of the book.*]

Group discussion questions

8.1 'Proprietors are more interested in cash than profit.' Discuss.

8.2 Unlike traditional financial accounting, cash flow accounting does not require the accountant to make a series of arbitrary assumptions, apportionments and estimates. How far, therefore, do you think that there is a case for abandoning traditional financial accounting?

8.3 Does a cash flow statement serve any useful purpose?

Practice questions

[*Note: The questions marked with an asterisk have answers at the back of the book.*]

8.4* You are presented with the following information:

DENNIS LIMITED
Balance sheet at 31 January 2002

		31 January 2001		31 January 2002	
		£000	£000	£000	£000
Fixed assets					
Land at cost			600		700
Current assets					
Stock		100		120	
Debtors		200		250	
Cash		6		10	
	c/f	306		380	

DENNIS LIMITED
Balance sheet at 31 January 2002

		31 January 2001		31 January 2002	
		£000	£000	£000	£000
	b/f	306		380	
Less: Current liabilities					
Creditors		180	126	220	160
			726		860
Capital and reserves					
Ordinary share capital			700		800
Profit and loss account			26		60
			726		860

Required:

Prepare Dennis Limited's cash flow statement for the year ended 31 January 2002.

8.5* The following balance sheets have been prepared for Frank Limited:

Balance sheets at:		28.2.01		28.2.02	
	£000	£000	£000	£000	
Fixed assets					
Plant and machinery at cost		300		300	
Less: Depreciation		80		100	
		220		200	
Investments at cost		–		100	
Current assets					
Stocks	160		190		
Debtors	220		110		
Bank	–		10		
	380		310		
Less: Current liabilities					
Creditors	200		160		
Bank overdraft	20		–		
	220	160	160	150	
		380		450	
Capital and reserves					
Ordinary share capital		300		300	
Share premium account		50		50	
Profit and loss account		30		40	
		380		390	
Shareholders' funds					
Loans					
Debentures		–		60	
		380		450	

Additional information:
There were no purchases or sales of plant and machinery during the year.

Required:
Prepare Frank Limited's cash flow statement for the year ended 28 February 2002.

8.6 You are presented with the following information:

STARTER
Profit and loss account for the year to 31 March 2003

	£	£
Sales		10 000
Purchases	5 000	
Less: Closing stock	1 000	4 000
Gross profit		6 000
Less: Depreciation		2 000
Net profit for the year		4 000

Balance sheet at 31 March 2003

	£	£
Van		10 000
Less: Depreciation		2 000
		8 000
Stock	1 000	
Trade debtors	5 000	
Bank	12 500	
	18 500	
Less: Trade creditors	2 500	16 000
		24 000
Capital		20 000
Add: Net profit for the year		4 000
		24 000

Note: Starter commenced business on 1 April 2002.

Required:
Compile Starter's cash flow statement for the year ended 31 March 2003.

8.7 The following is a summary of Gregory Limited's accounts for the year ended 30 April 2004.

Profit and loss account for the year ended 30 April 2004

	£000
Net profit before tax	75
Taxation	25
	50
Dividend (proposed)	40
Retained profit for the year	10

163

Balance sheet at 30 April 2004

	30.4.03		30.4.04	
	£000	£000	£000	£000
Fixed assets				
Plant at cost		400		550
Less: Depreciation		100		180
		300		370
Current assets				
Stocks	50		90	
Debtors	70		50	
Bank	10		2	
	130		142	
Less: Current liabilities				
Creditors	45		55	
Taxation	18		25	
Proposed dividend	35		40	
	98	32	120	22
		332		392
Capital and reserves				
Ordinary share capital		200		200
Profit and loss account		132		142
		332		342
Loans		–		50
		332		392

Additional information:
There were no sales of fixed assets during the year ended 30 April 2004.

Required:
Prepare Gregory Limited's cash flow statement for the year ended 30 April 2004.

8.8 The following summarized accounts have been prepared for Pill Limited:

Profit and loss account for the year ended 31 May 2005

	2004	2005
	£000	£000
Sales	2 400	3 000
Less: Cost of goods sold	1 600	2 000
Gross profit	800	1 000
Less: Expenses:		
Administrative expenses	310	320
Depreciation: vehicles	55	60
furniture	35	40
	400	420
Net profit	400	580
Taxation	120	150
	280	430
Dividends	200	250
Retained profits for the year	80	180

Balance sheet at 31 May 2005

	31.5.04		31.5.05	
	£000	£000	£000	£000
Fixed assets				
Vehicles at cost	600		800	
Less: Depreciation	200	400	260	540
Furniture	200		250	
Less: Depreciation	100	100	140	110
Current assets	——		——	
Stocks	400		540	
Debtors	180		200	
Cash	320		120	
	900		860	
Less: Current liabilities				
Creditors	270		300	
Corporation tax	170		220	
Proposed dividends	150		100	
	590	310	620	240
		810		890
Capital and reserves				
Ordinary share capital		500		550
Profit and loss account		120		300
Shareholders' funds		620		850
Loans				
Debentures (10%)		190		40
		810		890

Additional information:
There were no sales of fixed assets during the year ended 31 May 2005.

Required:
Compile Pill Limited's cash flow statement for the year ended 31 May 2005.

8.9 The following information relates to Brian Limited for the year ended 30 June 2006:

Profit and loss account for the year to 30 June 2006

	£000	£000
Gross profit		230
Administrative expenses	76	
Loss on sale of vehicle	3	
Increase in provision for doubtful debts	1	
Depreciation on vehicles	35	115
Net profit		115
Taxation		65
		50
Dividends		25
Retained profit for the year		25

Balance sheet at 30 June 2006

	2005 £000	2005 £000	2006 £000	2006 £000
Fixed assets				
Vehicle at cost		150		200
Less: Depreciation		75		100
		75		100
Current assets				
Stocks		60		50
Trade debtors	80		100	
Less: Provision for bad and doubtful debts	4	76	5	95
Cash		6		8
		142		153
Less: Current liabilities				
Trade creditors	60		53	
Taxation	52		65	
Proposed dividend	20	132	25	143
		85		110
Capital and reserves				
Ordinary share capital		75		75
Profit and loss account		10		35
		85		110

Additional information:

1 The company purchased some new vehicles during the year for £75 000.
2 During the year the company sold a vehicle for £12 000 in cash. The vehicle had originally cost £25 000, and £10 000 had been set aside for depreciation.

Required:

Prepare a cash flow statement for Brian Limited for the year ended 30 June 2006.

9 Interpretation of accounts

Selfridges sales rise by 12%

By Lucy Killgren

Selfridges, the upmarket department store chain, has maintained its position as one of the strongest UK retail performers, announcing sales growth yesterday of 12 per cent for the first 15 weeks of the new financial year.

Analysts had been concerned that a difficult April might have affected sales. But Selfridges said a re-stocking programme at its 18-month old Manchester store, where Selfridges had tweaked its offering, helped boost sales there by 23 per cent over the period.

The refurbishment of its flagship store in Oxford Street helped push sales there up by 10 per cent.

However, analysts cautioned that comparative growth could slow as the year progresses.

One said: "This is a strong performance, but I think things will get increasingly difficult for them and there will be tougher comparisons as the year goes on."

Peter Williams, finance director said: "I think that's fair comment. However, while the sales line is likely to be affected in the second half, we are in a much better stock position than last year."

Financial Times, 19 May 2000. Reprinted with permission.

But what about its profits?

In previous chapters, we have shown that a set of basic financial accounts can tell you a great deal about an entity's performance. In this chapter, we are going to explain how you can use those accounts to an even greater effect, i.e. how to squeeze out the maximum possible amount of information. Accountants call this process 'interpretation', and it forms the subject of this chapter.

In order to understand the importance of this topic, we need to review some of the material covered in the earlier part of the book. We do so in the next section.

By the end of this chapter, you should be able to:

- explain the usefulness and importance of ratio analysis;
- calculate at least nine basic accounting ratios;
- apply those ratios in interpreting a set of accounts.

Background

You will recall that, in Chapter 1, we suggested that owners of entities want to know the answers to three basic questions. As these questions are so important, we will remind you of them again. They are as follows:

1 How much profit has the business made?
2 How much does the business owe?
3 How much is owed to the business?

In Chapters 3 to 7 we described how an accountant would go about trying to answer these questions, but as we have seen, the method is far from satisfactory. The profit and loss account provides only an *estimate* of an entity's profitability, while the balance sheet is a mixture of different costs and values.

If such results are used in isolation, the owner could be misled by the apparent long-term trend of his profits, and by his current liquidity (i.e. cash) position. For example, his debtor and creditor balances do not tell him very much: are they too high or too low? A debtor's balance of £200 000 would appear be a very large amount for a small business, but it would be insignificant for a large international company. The results, therefore, need to be put into context and we need to go into them in much greater detail.

It might also be necessary to do this in order to satisfy the demand for information from other groups of interested parties, e.g. analysts, creditors, employees, the general public, the government, investors, journalists, management, shareholders, and trade unions. All of these groups will have some interest in how an entity performs (especially if it is a public company), and the information contained within the basic statements may not tell them what they want to know.

If you are asked to interpret a set of accounts, therefore, the amount of work you will have to undertake will depend upon the reasons for your investigation. For example, if you are asked to examine a company's accounts because your own company is considering making a take-over bid, you will probably need all the information that you can get. However, if you are a creditor, your main interest will be in finding out whether the company is in a position to pay what it owes you.

It might be helpful if we give you some general guidance that you can follow in carrying out your investigation, but obviously you will need to adapt it to suit the circumstances.

Obtaining information

You are recommended to look at the economic environment in which the company operates. In which countries is it based? What is the state of their economies? What are the prospects for the economic sector in which the company is placed? How does it compare with other companies in the same sector?

Then try to obtain as much information about the company as you can. It is not usually difficult to do so if you search for it. You can start with the company's annual report and accounts. The company's own public relations department may also be willing to supply you with additional information about the company. There are also a number of commercial agencies that specialize in obtaining company information, and you may be able to find some information in newspaper and journal articles.

You will find that by assimilating information about the company from such a wide range of sources, you will already have got some idea of its performance.

Calculating trends and ratios

It is desirable to look at the company's progress over a number of years. As a general rule, it is recommended that you think in terms of a three- to a five-year period. Anything less than three years does not enable you to plot a reasonable trend, and beyond five years the data can become somewhat out of date.

Once you have collected some data, you can use them to establish some trends and to calculate some statistics. The exact number and type will depend upon the purpose of your investigation, and some of them may need to be fairly specialized. For example, if you were dealing with a hotel's accounts, you might want to calculate the rooms occupied as a proportion of the total number of rooms in the hotel or, in the case of a retailing organization, the staff salaries of the sales personnel as a proportion of sales revenue.

You can begin to assess the trends and calculate the ratios by using a number of different techniques, but they all have one overriding purpose: *they attempt to put the accounting information into context*. The four main techniques are shown in Figure 9.1, and they may be summarized as follows:

1 *Horizontal analysis*. This technique involves making a line-by-line comparison of the company's accounts for each accounting period chosen for investigating. You might observe, for example, that the sales were £100m in 2000, £110m in 2001, and £137.5m in 2002. Thus, they have increased by 10 per cent in 2001, and by 25 per cent in 2002. This type of comparison is

something that we tend to do naturally when we look at a set of accounts, although if you are going to calculate the percentage changes, you will probably need a calculator.

2 *Trend analysis.* Trend analysis is similar to horizontal analysis, except that the first set of accounts in the series is given a weighting of 100. Subsequent accounts are then related to the base of 100. In the example used above, the 2000 sales would be expressed as 100, the 2001 sales as 110, and the 2002 sales as 137.5. This method enables us to see what changes have taken place much more easily than by inspecting the absolute amounts. For example, it is much easier to grasp the significance of, say, 159 than it is £323 739 392.

3 *Vertical analysis.* This technique requires all of the profit and loss account, and all of the balance sheet items to be expressed as a percentage of their respective totals. For example, if trade debtors in 2002 were £20m and the balance sheet total was £50m, trade debtors would be expressed as 40 per cent, compared with (say) 35 per cent in 2001, and 30 per cent in 2000. Again, the reason for adopting this method is that it is much easier to grasp the significance of the figures.

4 *Ratio analysis.* We are shortly going to deal with ratio analysis in some detail, but for the moment, all you need note is that a ratio attempts to relate one item to another item, e.g. 20 to 40. This relationship is then perhaps expressed as a percentage, i.e. 50% ($\frac{20}{40} \times 100\%$).

If you had adopted all of the above techniques in your analysis, you would already have a great deal of information about the company, and so you would be in a position to begin a detailed assessment of it. It is likely, however, that you would be selective in adopting the above four techniques. For example, in trend analysis you probably would not need to calculate a trend for literally every line in the accounts: you would be much more likely to choose only the most significant items.

There is one further point that we need to make before moving on to the next section. It is probable that the annual accounts have not been adjusted for inflation, and so to make a fairer comparison between different accounting periods, you should make some allowance for inflation. We return to this subject in Chapter 12, but we suggest that for the moment, you could use the Retail Price Index (RPI) as a rough guide.

In the next section, we take a closer look at ratio analysis.

Ratio analysis

In this section we are going to deal with ratio analysis in some detail. We need to do so, for otherwise it is unlikely that you will understand it! But don't be put off! You will find that the time spent studying this topic will be well worth while. Indeed, you will find it useful in both your business and your private life, e.g. if you ever want to buy some shares.

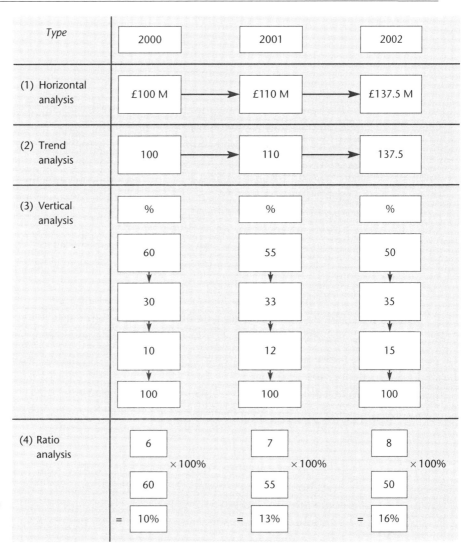

Figure 9.1
Main analytical techniques used in interpreting accounts

We will start our study by examining what is meant by a *ratio*. Data may be extracted from accounting statements and converted into statistics. These statistics can then be used to examine an entity's performance over a given period of time. They may also be used to compare the current year's performance with that for previous years, or with similar entities. Such comparisons may be done on a percentage basis or by using simple factors. For example, we might report that the net profit is 7 per cent of annual sales, or that the dividend for the year represents three times the profit for that year. In order to make such statistics easier to understand, we will refer to them all as *ratios*.

In order to establish clearly the concept underpinning a ratio, we will assume that you have put £1000 in a building society account on 1 January 2000. During the year to 31 December 2000, you leave the £1000 in your account. You do not withdraw any of it, and you do not add to it. At the end of the year, the building society credits you with £100 of interest. If we express the interest received as a *ratio*, the calculation will be as follows:

$$\frac{£100}{£1000} \times 100\% = 10\%$$

This might all seem quite obvious, but it is worth labouring the point. The £100 received represents 10 per cent of the £1000 invested. In other words, there is a clear relationship between the interest earned and what it took to earn it.

You will find that as we go through this chapter we are going to express many other accounting relationships in the form of percentages. Make sure, therefore, that you always establish a clear, meaningful relationship between the numerator (the £100 in the above example), and the denominator (the £1000 in the example). This is not always easy, so be careful, and make sure that you do not try to link some quite spurious relationships, such as dividends received to the cost of goods sold.

It would be possible to produce hundreds of recognized accounting ratios, but for the purposes of this book, we will limit ourselves to just a small number of key ones. We do so for three main reasons:

1 we do not need to use very many ratios in demonstrating the *principles* of ratio analysis;
2 a select number of ratios will give sufficient information;
3 experience suggests that, in analyzing the ratios, it is difficult to deal with more than just a select few.

For convenience, we will examine the main ratios under four main headings: (a) profitability ratios; (b) liquidity ratios; (c) efficiency ratios; and (d) investment ratios. This classification is, however, somewhat arbitrary, and some ratios could be included in another grouping. A diagrammatic version of the classification adopted is shown in Figure 9.2. Some of these ratios will not be appropriate for non-manufacturing, non-trading, or not-for-profit entities, while others may need to be adapted to suit the particular circumstances of specialized types of entities. We are, however, going to concentrate on *basic* ratio analysis and the procedures that we cover will be helpful for you irrespective of the type of entity in which you are employed.

Profitability ratios

Users of accounts will want to know how much profit a business has made, and then to compare it with previous periods or with other entities. The absolute level of accounting profit will not be of much help, because it needs to be related to the size of the entity and how much capital it has got invested in it. There are four main profitability ratios, and they are examined in the following sections.

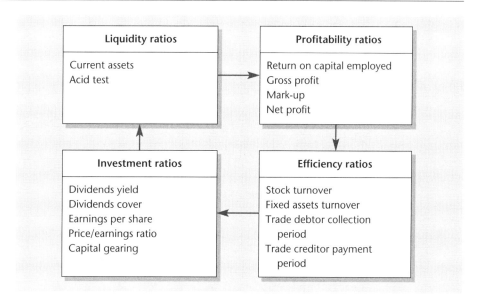

Figure 9.2
Classification of
accounting ratios

Return on capital employed ratio

The best way of assessing profitability is to calculate a ratio known as the
return on capital employed (ROCE) ratio. It can be expressed quite simply as:

$$\frac{\text{Profit}}{\text{Capital}} \times 100\% = X\%$$

This ratio (like most other ratios) is usually expressed as a percentage, and it is
one of the most important. Even so, there is no common agreement about how
it should be calculated. The problem is that both 'profit' and 'capital' can be
defined in several different ways. As a result, a variety of ROCE ratios can be
produced merely by changing the definitions of either profit or capital. The
main definitions are listed in Table 9.1.

Table 9.1 Possible elements in ROCE ratios

Profit	Capital
1 Operating profit	1 Total assets
2 Net profit before interest and taxation	2 Total assets less intangible assets
3 Net profit before taxation	3 Total assets less current liabilities
4 Net profit after taxation	4 Shareholders' funds
5 Net profit after taxation and preference dividend	5 Shareholders' funds less preference shares
	6 Shareholders' funds plus long-term loans
	7 Shareholders' funds plus total liabilities (this might be the same as total assets)

Which definitions should you adopt? Provided that the numerator and denominator are compatible, that really depends upon your purpose. If you are looking at profit from the point of view of the entity as a whole, we would suggest that you should select the *net profit before interest and taxation*. This should then be related to the total amount of capital needed to generate it, i.e. *shareholders' funds plus long-term loans* (long-term loans are included because we have taken the profit *before* interest). However, if we were looking at profit from only an ordinary shareholder's point of view, we might define profit as being the *net profit after taxation and preference dividends* (i.e. the amount available for distribution to ordinary shareholders), and capital as *shareholders' funds less preference shares* (i.e. the total amount of capital that the ordinary shareholders have invested in the business). Does this latter relationship make sense to you? Net profit after taxation and preference dividends reflect what *could* be distributed to ordinary shareholders. Shareholders' funds less preference shares gives the total amount of capital contributed (or financed) by the ordinary shareholders (ordinary shares + capital reserves + revenue reserves + other reserves + retained profits).

Irrespective of the definitions, ROCE is often calculated using the capital as at the year end. However, as profit builds up during the year, we really ought to take the *average* capital invested in the entity during the year. If so, it is customary to take a simple average, i.e. $\frac{1}{2}$ (opening capital + closing capital).

You may need to calculate ROCE for different purposes, and so it would be useful if we were to summarize the main methods used in calculating this most important ratio. Here they are:

1 $$\frac{\text{Net profit before taxation}}{\text{Average shareholders' funds}} \times 100\% = X\%$$

2 $$\frac{\text{Net profit after taxation}}{\text{Average shareholders' funds}} \times 100\% = X\%$$

3 $$\frac{\text{Net profit after taxation and preference dividends}}{\text{Average shareholders' funds less preference shares}} \times 100\% = X\%$$

4 $$\frac{\text{Profit before taxation and interest}}{\text{Average shareholders' funds plus long-term loans}} \times 100\% = X\%$$

By calculating the return on capital employed, we can get a far better idea of the entity's profitability than we can by merely looking at the absolute level of profit. ROCE means that we can avoid making sweeping assertions about (say) a profit of £500 million being high (for it might be thought rather poor if the capital employed was £10 billion), or a profit of £500 being low (it might be acceptable if the capital invested was only £2000). 'High' and 'low' in this context can only be viewed in a relative sense.

Gross profit ratio

The *gross profit ratio* enables us to judge how successful the entity has been at trading. It is calculated as follows:

$$\frac{\text{Gross profit}}{\text{Total sales revenue}} \times 100\% = X\%$$

The gross profit ratio measures how much profit the entity has earned in relation to the amount of sales that it has made. The definition of gross profit does not usually cause any problems. Most entities adopt the definition which we have used in this book, namely sales less the cost of goods sold, and so meaningful comparisons can usually be made between different entities.

Mark-up ratio

The gross profit ratio complements another main trading ratio: for convenience, we will refer to it as the *mark-up ratio*. The mark-up ratio is calculated as follows:

$$\frac{\text{Gross profit}}{\text{Cost of goods sold}} \times 100\% = X\%$$

Mark-up ratios measure the amount of profit added to the cost of goods sold. The cost of goods sold is defined as opening stock + purchases – closing stock, and the cost of goods sold plus profit equals the sales revenue. The mark-up may be reduced to stimulate extra sales activity, but this will have the effect of reducing the gross profit. However, if extra goods are sold, there may be a greater volume of sales and this will help to compensate for the reduction in the mark up on each unit.

Net profit ratio

Owners sometimes like to compare their net profit with the sales revenue. This can be expressed in the form of the *net profit ratio*, which is calculated as follows:

$$\frac{\text{Net profit before taxation}}{\text{Total sales revenue}} \times 100\% = X\%$$

It is difficult to compare fairly the net profit ratio for different entities. Individual operating and financing arrangements vary so much that entities are bound to have different levels of expenditure, no matter how efficient one entity is compared with another. Thus it may only be realistic to use the net profit ratio in making *internal* comparisons. Over a period of time, a pattern may emerge, and it might then be possible to establish a trend. If you use the net profit ratio to make inter-company comparisons, make sure you allow for different circumstances.

We can now turn to our second main category of accounting ratios: liquidity ratios.

Liquidity ratios

Liquidity ratios measure the extent to which assets can be quickly turned into cash. In other words, they try to assess how much cash the entity has available in the short term (this usually means within the next twelve months). For example, it is easy to extract the total amount of trade debtors and trade creditors from the balance sheet, but are they perhaps too high? We cannot really tell until we put them into context. We can do this by calculating two liquidity ratios known as the *current assets ratio* and the *acid test ratio*.

Current assets ratio

The *current assets ratio* is calculated as follows:

$$\frac{\text{Current assets}}{\text{Current liabilities}}$$

It is usually expressed as a factor, e.g. 3 to 1, or 3 : 1, although you will sometimes see it expressed as a percentage (300% in our example).

In most circumstances we can expect that current assets will be in excess of current liabilities. The current assets ratio will then be at least 1 : 1. If this is not the case, the entity may not have sufficient liquid resources (i.e. current assets that can be quickly turned into cash) available to meet its immediate financial commitments. Some textbooks argue that the current assets ratio must be at least 2 : 1, but there is no evidence to support this assertion. You are not, therefore, advised to accept that a 2 : 1 relationship is required.

The term 'current' means receivable or payable within the next twelve months, and so the entity may not always have to settle all of its current debts within the next week or even the next month. Be careful, then, before you assume that a factor of (say) 1 : 2 suggests that the company will be going into immediate liquidation! For example, tax and dividends may not have to be paid for some months after the year end. In the meantime, the company may receive regular receipts of cash from its debtors and it may be able to balance these against what it has to pay to its creditors. In other instances, some entities (such as supermarkets), do not do much trade on credit terms, and so it is not uncommon for them to have a current assets ratio of less than 2 : 1. This is not likely to be a problem for them, because they are probably collecting sufficient amounts of cash daily through the checkouts. In some cases, however, a current assets ratio of less than 2 : 1 may signify a serious financial position, especially if the current assets consist of a very high proportion of stocks. This leads us on to the second liquidity ratio: the acid test ratio.

Acid test ratio

It may not be easy to dispose of stocks in the short term as they cannot always be quickly turned into cash. In any case, the entity would then be depriving itself of those very assets that enable it to make a trading profit. It seems sensible, therefore, to see what would happen to the current ratio if stocks were not included in the definition of current assets. This ratio is called the acid test (or quick) ratio. It is calculated as follows:

$$\frac{\text{Current assets} - \text{Stocks}}{\text{Current liabilities}}$$

Like the current ratio, the acid test ratio is usually expressed as a factor (or occasionally as a percentage). It is probably a better measure of the entity's immediate liquidity position than the current assets ratio because it may be difficult to dispose of the stocks in the short term. Do not assume, however, that if current assets less stocks are less than current liabilities, the entity's cash position is vulnerable. As we explained above, some of the current liabilities may not be due for payment for some months. Some textbooks suggest that the acid test ratio must be at least 1 : 1, but there is no evidence to support this idea, so you are advised not to accept it.

Efficiency ratios

Traditional accounting statements do not tell us how *efficiently* an entity has been managed, that is, how well its resources have been looked after. Profit may, to some extent, be used as a measure of efficiency, but as we have explained in earlier chapters, accounting profit is subject to too many arbitrary adjustments to be entirely reliable. What we need to do, therefore, is to put whatever evidence we have into context, and then to compare it with earlier accounting periods and with other similar entities.

There are very many different types of ratios that we can use to measure the efficiency of an entity, but in this book we will cover only the more common ones.

Stock turnover ratio

The stock turnover ratio may be calculated as follows:

$$\frac{\text{Cost of goods sold}}{\text{Average stock}} = \text{X times}$$

The average stock is usually calculated as follows:

$$\frac{\text{Opening stock} + \text{Closing stock}}{2}$$

The stock turnover ratio is normally expressed as a number (e.g. 5 or 10 times) and not as a percentage. Note that there are also various other ways in which this ratio can be calculated.

Sometimes the sales revenue is substituted for the cost of goods sold, but it should not be used if it can be avoided because the sales contain a profit loading that can cause the ratio to become distorted. Many accountants also prefer to substitute a more accurate average stock level than the simple average shown above (particularly if goods are purchased at irregular intervals). It is also quite common to compare the *closing* stock with the cost of sales in order to gain a clearer idea of the stock position at the end of the year. This may be misleading, however, if the company's trade is seasonal, and the year end falls during a quiet period.

The greater the turnover of stock, the more efficient the entity would appear to be in purchasing and selling goods. A stock turnover of 2 times, for example, would suggest that the entity has about six months of sales in stock. In most circumstances, this would appear to be a high relative volume, whereas a stock turnover of (say) 12 would mean that the entity had only a month's normal sales in stock.

Fixed assets turnover ratio

Another important area to examine, from the point of view of efficiency, relates to fixed assets. Fixed assets (such as plant and machinery) enable the business to function more efficiently, and so a high level of fixed assets ought to generate more sales. We can check this by calculating a ratio known as the *fixed assets turnover ratio*. This may be done as follows:

$$\frac{\text{Total sales revenue}}{\text{Fixed assets at net book value}} = X$$

The fixed assets turnover ratio may also be expressed as a percentage. The more times that the fixed assets are covered by the sales revenue, the greater the recovery of the investment in fixed assets.

This ratio is really only useful if it is compared with previous periods or with other entities. In isolation, it does not mean very much. For example, is a turnover of 5 good and 4 poor? All we can suggest is that if the trend is upwards, then the investment in fixed assets is beginning to pay off, at least in terms of increased sales. Note also that the ratio can be strongly affected by the entity's depreciation policies. There is an argument, therefore, for taking the gross book value of the fixed assets, and not the net book value.

Trade debtor collection period ratio

Investing in fixed assets is all very well, but there is not much point in generating extra sales if the customers do not pay for them. Customers might be encouraged to buy more by a combination of lower selling prices and generous credit terms. If the debtors are slow at paying, the entity might find that it has run into cash flow problems. It is important, therefore, for it to watch its trade debtor position very carefully. We can check how successful it has been by calculating the average *trade debtor collection period*. The ratio is calculated as follows:

$$\frac{\text{Average trade debtors}}{\text{Total credit sales}} \times 365 \text{ days} = \text{X days}$$

The average trade debtors are usually calculated by using a simple average [i.e. $\frac{1}{2}$ (opening trade debtors + closing trade debtors)]. The closing trade debtors figure is sometimes substituted for average trade debtors. This is acceptable, provided that the figure is representative of the overall period.

It is important to relate trade debtors to credit sales if possible, and so cash sales should be excluded from the calculation. The method shown above for calculating the ratio would relate the average trade debtors to X days' sales, but it would be possible to substitute weeks or months for days. It is not customary to express the ratio as a percentage.

An acceptable debtor collection period cannot be suggested, as much depends upon the type of trade in which the entity is engaged. Some entities expect settlement within 28 days of delivery of the goods, or on immediate receipt of the invoice. Other entities might expect settlement within 28 days following the end of the month in which the goods were delivered. On average, this adds another 14 days (half a month) to the overall period of 28 days. If this is the case, a company would appear to be highly efficient in collecting its debts if the average debtor collection period was about 42 days (the United Kingdom experience is that the *median* debtor collection period is 50 days).

Like most of the other ratios, however, it is important to establish a trend, and if the trend is upwards, then it might suggest that the company's credit control has begun to weaken.

Trade creditor payment period

A similar ratio can be calculated for the average trade creditor payment period. The formula is as follows:

$$\frac{\text{Average trade creditors}}{\text{Total credit purchases}} \times 365 \text{ days} = \text{X days}$$

The average trade creditors amount would again be a simple average of the opening and closing balances, although it is quite common to use the closing trade creditors. The trade creditors must be related to credit purchases, and weeks or months may be substituted for the number of days. Like the trade debtor collection period, it is not usual to express it as a percentage.

An upward trend in the average level of trade creditors would suggest that the entity is having some difficulty in finding the cash to pay its creditors. Indeed, it might be a sign that it is running into financial difficulties.

Investment ratios

The various ratios examined in the previous sections are probably of interest to all users of accounts, such as creditors, employees and managers, as well as to shareholders. There are, however, some other ratios that are primarily (although not exclusively) of interest to prospective investors. These ratios are known as *investment ratios*.

Dividend yield

The first investment ratio that you might find useful is the *dividend yield*. It usually applies to ordinary shareholders, and it may be calculated as follows:

$$\frac{\text{Dividend per share}}{\text{Market price per share}} \times 100\% = X\%$$

The dividend yield measures the rate of return than an investor gets by comparing the cost of his shares with the dividend receivable (or paid). For example, if an investor buys 100 £1 ordinary shares at a market rate of 200p per share, and the dividend was 10p, his yield would be 5 per cent (10/200 × 100%). As far as the company is concerned, while he may have invested £200 (100 × £2 per share), he will be registered as holding 100 shares at a nominal value of £1 each (100 shares × £1). He would be entitled, therefore, to a dividend of £10 (10p × 100 shares), but from the shareholder's individual point of view, he will only be getting a return of 5 per cent, i.e. £10 for his £200 invested.

Dividend cover

Another useful investment ratio is called *dividend cover*. It is calculated as follows:

$$\text{Divided cover} = \frac{\text{Net profit after taxation and preference dividend}}{\text{Paid and proposed ordinary dividends}} = X \text{ times}$$

This ratio shows the number of times that the ordinary dividend could be paid out of current earnings. The dividend is usually described as being X times covered by the earnings. Thus, if the dividend is covered twice, the company would be paying out half of its earnings as an ordinary dividend.

Earnings per share

Another important investment ratio is that known as *earnings per share* (EPS). This ratio enables us to put the profit into context, and to avoid looking at it in simple absolute terms. It is usually looked at from the ordinary shareholder's point of view, and it may be calculated as follows:

$$\frac{\text{Net profit after taxation and preference dividend}}{\text{Number of ordinary shares in issue during the year}} = X\text{p}$$

It is customary to calculate this ratio by taking the net profit after taxation, although there is no reason why it could not be taken before taxation. Preference dividends are deducted because they are usually paid before ordinary shareholders receive a dividend.

EPS enables a fair comparison to be made between one year's earnings and another by relating the earnings to something tangible, i.e. the number of shares in issue.

Price/earnings ratio

Another common investment ratio is the *price/earnings ratio* (or P/E ratio). It is calculated as follows:

$$\frac{\text{Market price per share}}{\text{Earnings per share}} = X$$

The P/E ratio enables a comparison to be made between the earnings per share (as defined above) and the market price. It tells us that the market price is X times the earnings. It means that it would take X years before we recovered the market price paid for the shares out of the earnings (assuming that they remained at that level, and that they were all distributed). Thus the P/E ratio is a multiple of earnings, and a high or low ratio can only be judged in relation to other companies in the same sector of the market.

Capital gearing ratio

We come finally to our last investment ratio: the *capital gearing ratio*. This is usually a most difficult one for students to understand, possibly because (like ROCE) there are so many ways of calculating it.

As we outlined in Chapter 6, companies are financed out of a mixture of share capital, retained profits and loans. Loans may be long-term (such as debentures), or short-term (such as credit given by trade creditors). In addition, the company may have set aside all sorts of provisions (e.g. for taxation) which it expects to meet sometime in the future. These may also be regarded as a type of loan. From an ordinary shareholder's point of view, even preference share capital can be classed as a loan, because the preference shareholders may have priority over ordinary shareholders, both in respect of dividends and upon liquidation.

If a company, therefore, finances itself from a high level of loans, there is obviously a higher risk in investing in it. This arises for two main reasons:

1 the higher the loans, the more interest that the company will have to pay, and that may affect the company's ability to pay an ordinary dividend;
2 if the company cannot find the cash to repay its loans, the ordinary shareholders may not get any money back if the company goes into liquidation.

As far as item 1 is concerned, there will be no particular problem arising if profits are increasing, because the interest on its loans will become a smaller and smaller proportion of the total profit. But it could become a problem if profits are falling and the interest is having to be paid out of a continuing decline in profit. It might then be difficult to pay out any ordinary dividend.

There are many different ways of calculating capital gearing. As we indicated above, the entity will have been financed by a combination of shareholders' funds and loans. The relationship between them can be expressed in many ways. The two most common methods are as follows:

1
$$\frac{\text{Loans}}{\text{Shareholders' funds} + \text{Loans}}$$

2
$$\frac{\text{Loans}}{\text{Shareholders' funds}}$$

We prefer the first method, since if we express it as a percentage, it appears clearer, i.e. 'X% of the company has been financed by loans'. The second method tells us that the loans represent a certain proportion of the shareholders' funds (including preference shares). You might not agree with our reasoning, and if you prefer the second method there is no reason why you should not use it.

Irrespective of which method we adopt, we now have to decide what we mean by 'shareholders' funds' and loans. It is not too difficult to define shareholders' funds. They include the following items:

- Ordinary share capital
- Preference share capital (see the Note 1 below)
- Share premium account
- Capital reserves
- Revenue reserves
- Other reserves
- Profit and loss account.

Loans may (but will not necessarily) include the following items:

- Preference share capital (see the Note 1 below)
- Debentures
- Loans
- Overdrafts
- Provisions
- Accruals
- Current liabilities
- Other amounts due for payment.

Notes: (1) Some accountants exclude preference share capital from shareholders' funds because they regard it as a type of loan.

(2) In a complex group structure, you might also come across other items that could be classed as loans.

As we do not want to complicate the calculation of the ratio by getting involved in too much technical detail, we recommend that you go for a fairly straightforward approach and adopt the following definition of capital gearing:

$$\frac{\text{Preference shares} + \text{Long-term loans}}{\text{Shareholders' funds} + \text{Long-term loans}} \times 100\% = X\%$$

A company that has financed itself out of a high proportion of loans (e.g. in the form of a combination of preference shares and long-term loans) is known as a highly geared company. Conversely, a company with a low level of loans is regarded as being low-geared. Note that high and low in this context are relative terms. As we indicated above, a highly-geared company is potentially a higher risk investment, as it has to earn sufficient profit to cover the interest payments and the preference dividend before it can pay out any ordinary dividend. This should not be a problem when profits are rising, but if they are falling, then they may not be sufficient to cover even the preference dividend.

We have now defined 18 common accounting ratios, and there are many others that could also have been included! However, the 18 selected are enough for you to be able to interpret a set of accounts. If the ratios are used in isolation, many of them are not particularly helpful, but you will find that as part of a detailed analysis they are invaluable.

An illustrative example

In this section, we use the ratios outlined above to interpret a set of accounts. In order to establish a reasonable trend, we really need to adopt something like a three- to five-year period. It would also be useful to compare our results with the ratios obtained from similar entities (there are some commercial organizations that provide such comparative data). However, for our purposes, such a long period would be impractical, and it would also obscure the basic procedures that we want to illustrate. Consequently, we shall limit our data to a single company for a two-year period. We do so in Exhibit 9.1.

Exhibit 9.1 Interpreting company accounts

You are provided with the following summarized information relating to Gill Limited for the year to 31 March 2003:

Gill Ltd
Trading and profit and loss account for the year to 31 March 2003

		2002		2003	
		£000	£000	£000	£000
Sales			160		180
Less: Cost of goods sold:					
Opening stock		10		14	
Purchases		100		130	
	c/f	110	160	144	180

		2002		2003	
		£000	£000	£000	£000
	b/f	110	160	144	180
Less: Closing stock		14	96	24	120
Gross profit			64		60
Less: Expenses:					
Administration		18		24	
Loan interest		1		1	
Selling and distribution		12	31	16	41
Net profit before taxation			33		19
Taxation			15		6
Net profit after taxation			18		13
Dividends: preference (paid)		2		2	
ordinary (proposed)		8	10	5	7
Retained profit for the year			8		6
Retained profit brought forward			4		12
Retained profit for the year			12		18

Gill Ltd
Balance sheet at 31 March 2003

	2002			2003		
	Cost	Depreci-ation	Net book value	Cost	Depreci-ation	Net book value
	£000	£000	£000	£000	£000	£000
Fixed assets						
Freehold property	60	–	60	60	–	60
Vehicles	42	14	28	48	22	26
	102	14	88	108	22	86
Current assets						
Stocks		14			24	
Trade debtors		20			60	
Bank		3			1	
		37			85	
Less: Current liabilities						
Trade creditors	10			62		
Taxation	15			6		
Proposed dividend	8	33	4	5	73	12
			92			98
Capital and reserves						
Authorized, issued and fully paid ordinary shares of £1 each			40			40
Preference shares (10%)			20			20
Profit and loss account			12			18
Shareholders' funds		c/f	72			78

	£000	£000	£000	£000	£000
Shareholders' funds	b/f	72			78
Loans					
Debenture stock (5%)		20			20
		92			98

Additional information:

1 Purchases and sales are made evenly throughout the year.
2 All purchases and all sales are made on credit terms.
3 You may assume that price levels are stable.
4 The company only sells one product: in 2002 it sold 40 000 units and in 2003 60 000 units.
5 There were no sales of fixed assets during the year.
6 The market value of the ordinary shares was estimated to be worth £2.30 per share at 31 March 2002 and £1.80 per share at 31 March 2003.

Required:

(a) Compute significant ratios for the two years to 31 March 2002 and 2003 respectively; and
(b) using the ratios that you have calculated in part (a) of the question, comment upon the results for the year to 31 March 2003.

Answer to Exhibit 9.1

(a) Significant ratios

Gill Ltd

	2002	*2003*

Profitability ratios:

● Return on capital employed (ROCE):

$$\frac{\text{Net profit before taxation}}{\text{Shareholders' funds*}} \times 100\% = \frac{33\,000}{72\,000} \times 100\% = \frac{19\,000}{78\,000} \times 100\%$$

$$= \underline{45.83\%} \qquad = \underline{24.36\%}$$

* The opening balance for shareholders' funds for 2002 has not been given, and so the closing balance has been used.

● Gross profit:

$$\frac{\text{Gross profit}}{\text{Total sales revenue}} \times 100\% \qquad = \frac{64\,000}{160\,000} \times 100\% = \frac{60\,000}{180\,000} \times 100\%$$

$$= \underline{40.00\%} \qquad = \underline{33.33\%}$$

● Mark up:

$$\frac{\text{Gross profit}}{\text{Cost of goods sold}} \times 100\% \qquad = \frac{64\,000}{96\,000} \times 100\% = \frac{60\,000}{120\,000} \times 100\%$$

$$= \underline{66.67\%} \qquad = \underline{50.00\%}$$

	2002	*2003*

- Net profit:

$$\frac{\text{Net profit before taxation}}{\text{Total sales revenue}} \times 100\% = \frac{33\,000}{160\,000} \times 100\% = \frac{19\,000}{180\,000} \times 100\%$$

$$= 20.63\% \qquad = 10.56\%$$

Liquidity ratios:

- Current assets:

$$\frac{\text{Current assets}}{\text{Current liabilities}} = \frac{37\,000}{33\,000} \qquad = \frac{85\,000}{73\,000}$$

$$= 1.12 \text{ to } 1 \qquad = 1.16 \text{ to } 1$$

- Acid test:

$$\frac{\text{Current assets} - \text{stocks}}{\text{Current liabilities}} = \frac{37\,000 - 14\,000}{33\,000} = \frac{85\,000 - 24\,000}{73\,000}$$

$$= 0.70 \text{ to } 1 \qquad = 0.84 \text{ to } 1$$

Efficiency ratios:

- Stock turnover:

$$\frac{\text{Cost of goods sold}}{\text{Average stock*}} = \frac{96\,000}{\frac{1}{2}(10\,000 + 14\,000)} = \frac{120\,000}{\frac{1}{2}(14\,000 + 24\,000)}$$

$$= 8.0 \text{ times} \qquad = 6.3 \text{ times}$$

* $\frac{1}{2}$ (Opening stocks + closing stocks)

- Fixed assets turnover:

$$\frac{\text{Total sales revenue}}{\text{Fixed assets at net book value}} = \frac{160\,000}{88\,000} \qquad = \frac{180\,000}{86\,000}$$

$$= 1.82 \text{ times} \qquad = 2.09 \text{ times}$$

- Trade debtor collection period:

$$\frac{\text{Closing trade debtors*}}{\text{Total credit sales}} \times 365 \text{ days} = \frac{20\,000}{160\,000} \times 365 \text{ days} = \frac{60\,000}{180\,000} \times 365 \text{ days}$$

$$= 46 \text{ days} \qquad = 122 \text{ days}$$

* Opening trade debtors have not been given for 2002, and so closing trade debtors have been used.

- Trade creditor payment period:

$$\frac{\text{Closing trade creditors*}}{\text{Total credit purchases}} \times 365 \text{ days} = \frac{10\,000}{100\,000} \times 365 \text{ days} = \frac{62\,000}{130\,000} \times 365 \text{ days}$$

$$= 37 \text{ days} \qquad = 175 \text{ days}$$

* Opening trade creditors have not been given for 2002, so closing trade creditors have been used.

Investment ratios:	*2002*	*2003*

- Dividend per share:

$$\frac{\text{Dividend}}{\text{Ordinary share capital}} \times 100p \quad = \frac{8000}{40\,000} \times 100p \quad = \frac{5000}{40\,000} \times 100p$$

$$= \underline{\underline{20p}} \qquad = \underline{\underline{12.5p}}$$

- Dividend yield:

$$\frac{\text{Dividend per share}}{\text{Market price per share}} \times 100\% \quad = \frac{20}{230} \times 100\% \quad = \frac{12.5}{180} \times 100\%$$

$$= \underline{\underline{8.70\%}} \qquad = \underline{\underline{6.94\%}}$$

- Dividend cover:

$$\frac{\substack{\text{Net profit after taxation and}\\ \text{preference dividend}}}{\substack{\text{Paid and proposed}\\ \text{ordinary dividends}}} \quad = \frac{18\,000 - 2000}{8000} \quad = \frac{13\,000 - 2000}{5000}$$

$$= \underline{\underline{2.00 \text{ times}}} \qquad = \underline{\underline{2.20 \text{ times}}}$$

- Earnings per share (EPS):

$$\frac{\substack{\text{Net profit after taxation and}\\ \text{preference dividend}}}{\substack{\text{Number of ordinary shares}\\ \text{in issue during the year}}} \quad = \frac{18\,000 - 2000}{40\,000} \quad = \frac{13\,000 - 2000}{40\,000}$$

$$= \underline{\underline{40.00p}} \qquad = \underline{\underline{27.50p}}$$

- Price/earnings (P/E) ratio:

$$\frac{\text{Market price per share}}{\text{Earnings per share}} \quad = \frac{2.30}{0.40} \quad = \frac{1.80}{0.275}$$

$$= \underline{\underline{5.75}} \qquad = \underline{\underline{6.55}}$$

- Capital gearing:

$$\frac{\substack{\text{Preference shares +}\\ \text{long-term loans}}}{\substack{\text{Shareholders' funds +}\\ \text{Long-term loans}}} \times 100\% = \frac{20\,000 + 20\,000}{72\,000 + 20\,000} \times 100\% = \frac{20\,000 + 20\,000}{78\,000 + 20\,000} \times 100\%$$

$$= \underline{\underline{43.48\%}} \qquad \qquad = \underline{\underline{40.82\%}}$$

(b) Comments on the ratios

Profitability

1 The selling price of the product in 2002 must have been £4.00 per unit since the company sold 40 000 units and its total sales revenue was £160 000 (£160 000 ÷ 40 000). In 2003 the company sold 60 000 units and its total sales revenue was £180 000. The selling price per unit must, therefore, have been £3.00. It would appear that Gill Limited deliberately reduced its selling price per unit by 25 per cent (1 × 100%/4 = 25 per cent). There was thus a 50 per cent increase in sales volume (from 40 000 units to 60 000), but its total sales revenue only increased by £20 000 (or 12.5%).

2 The relatively modest increase in sales revenue did not help to increase the gross profit (down from £64 000 to £60 000), largely because the reduction in mark-up (down from 66.67% to 50%) did not generate sufficient extra sales.

3 The large increase in sales volume also affected overall profitability. The net profit on sales was reduced from 20.63% to 10.56%, partly because of the reduction in gross profit and partly because other expenses increased by £10 000. Consequently, the return on capital employed was much reduced, from 45.83% to 24.36%. This is still a favourable rate of return when compared with alternative forms of investment, but the company's management must view the downward trend with some concern.

Liquidity

1 Gill's current assets position does not appear to have been greatly affected by the overall decline in profitability. In fact the current assets ratio has improved slightly, from 1.12 to 1 to 1.16 to 1. The current assets are in excess of current liabilities in both years, and so provided that receipts from trade debtors can be kept in step with payments to trade creditors, the company would appear not to have an immediate liquidity problem.

2 If stocks are excluded from current assets, however, the position is a little more worrying. The acid test ratio was 0.71 to 1 in 2002, and 0.84 to 1 in 2003, so there has been an improvement in Gill's immediate liquidity position. Even so, by the end of 2003 the company did not have sufficient cash to pay its proposed dividend, and so it was dependent on either being able to obtain overdraft facilities from the bank or cash receipts from its trade debtors. (Note that there was a similar situation in 2002.) Fortunately, the tax would probably not have to be paid until well into 2004.

Efficiency

1 Gill was not as efficient at trading in 2003 as it had been in 2002. Its stock turnover was down from 8.0 to 6.3, which means that it was not turning over its stocks as quickly in 2003 as it did in 2002.

2 The company's investment in fixed assets (as measured by its sales activity) has improved from 1.82 times in 2002 to 2.09 times in 2003. This arose largely because the purchase of new assets only increased the gross book value of its fixed assets by £6000, whereas the depreciation charge for the year reduced the total net book value by £8000, a net difference of £2000.

3 The extra sales generated during 2003 were made at some cost to its potential liquidity position. At the end of 2003 its outstanding trade debtors represented 46 days' sales, but at the end of 2003, they represented 122 days' sales. This suggests that Gill encouraged a greater sales volume by reducing both its selling prices and by offering more generous credit terms. It is also possible that the company was so busy coping with the increased operational activity that it did not have time to control its debtor position.

4 Gill appears to have been fortunate in 2003 in not having to pay its trade creditors as promptly as it did in 2002. At the end of 2002, its trade creditors represented about 37 days' purchases. If Gill had had to pay its creditors as quickly in 2003 as it had done in 2002, its total trade creditors at the end of 2003 would have amounted to about £13 000 (130 000 × 37/365), instead of the £62 000 actually owing at that date. By paying its trade creditors more quickly, Gill would probably have had a bank overdraft of some £48 000 [(62 000 − 13 000) = 49 000 − 1000], instead of the favourable balance of £1000.

Investment

1 Gill Limited is a private company, and so its shares would not be freely available on a recognized stock exchange. The market price of the shares given in the question is bound to be rather a questionable one, and it probably does not reflect the earnings potential of the company.

2 The dividend yield has fallen from 8.7% in 2002 to 6.94% in 2003. Compared with the yield currently available from other investments, these yields are about average, although the reduction in the dividend for 2003 could be the start of a downward trend.

3 Whilst the reduction in the dividend from 20p per share in 2002 to 12.5p per share in 2003 is worrying, the dividend is well covered by the earnings. Indeed, the company could have paid the same dividend in 2003 as it did in 2002, and the dividend would still have been covered 1.38 times (13 000 – 2000/8000). It would appear that the company's policy is to pay less than half of its earnings as dividend, even if it means reducing the dividend. This would not matter as much to a private company as it would to a public one. In a public company a reduction in dividend can result in a fall in the market value of its shares, thus reflecting the reduction in confidence that the market has in the company.

4 No new shares were issued during the year. Thus, as a result of the reduction in profits, the earnings per share declined from 40.00p to 27.50p.

5 The increase in the price/earnings ratio (up from 5.75 to 6.55) is surprising. It was probably caused by the market's view (albeit a rather restricted one) that the company's future is a reasonably good one, notwithstanding the reduction in the company's profit. However, this company is a private one, and so we cannot be certain how the market price of its shares has been determined.

6 Gill Limited is a fairly highly-geared company. In 2002, nearly 44 per cent of its financing had been raised in the form of fixed interest stock, but in 2003 this was reduced to just under 41 per cent. By financing itself in this way, the company is committed to making annual payments of £3000 (£2000 of preference dividend + £1000 of debenture interest). In absolute terms, this amount is not large, and so although it is a relatively high-geared company, its earnings should be sufficient to cover its interest commitments.

Summary

1 In 2003 Gill Limited achieved its presumed objective of increasing its sales. It did this partly by reducing its unit selling price, and partly by offering extended credit terms to its customers. The effect of this policy has been to reduce gross profit by £4000 and its net profit by £14 000.

2 The new policy did not affect its liquidity position, largely because the extended credit terms (leading to delays in the settlement of its trade debts) were offset by similar delays in paying its trade creditors.

3 As a result of the reduction in its profits for 2003, the company reduced its dividend, although its earnings would still have enabled it to maintain the same dividend as in 2002.

4 The market (such as it is) does not seem to agree that the reduction in the profit or of the dividend is serious. Indeed, it can be argued the company's future is healthy provided that it can persuade its trade debtors to pay their debts more promptly.

You are now advised to go through Exhibit 9.1 again most carefully. Make sure that you know how to calculate the ratios, and that you know what they mean. Then try to list your own views on Gill Limited's progress during 2003. The comments listed above are only brief ones, and much more could have been written about the company. However, we hope that we have been able to demonstrate that ratio analysis enables us to extract a great deal more information about the company than could be obtained merely by attempting to 'read' the profit and loss account and the balance sheet.

Although ratios help us to put the information into context, they must then be used as part of a detailed overall analysis. Think of ratios as signposts. They point us in the right direction, but they are not a substitute for the journey itself. We now need to undertake that journey. In other words, we must look a little closer at what we mean by 'interpretation'.

Interpretation

Once you have collected all the data that you need about a company, and you have established a considerable number of trends and calculated innumerable ratios, you have to write a story. This means that you have to use the data to interpret what *has* happened and possibly predict what *will* happen. It is important that you appreciate that ratios themselves are not particularly useful unless they are incorporated into an overall analysis. What can you do to make some sense out of all the information that you have got? Much depends, of course, upon the reason for your investigation, but the following questions might help you to come to some provisional conclusions:

1 *The market for the company's products.* Has this expanded or contracted in recent years? How has the company coped with the changes in market conditions? What is the market likely to be like over (say) the next five years? How will it be affected by general demographic, economic, political, and social factors? Does the company seem attuned to these possible changes?
2 *Sales and profits.* Have these increased or decreased over the period? If there has been any growth, has it been because of internal expansion or because of acquisition? Does the management seem keen enough to pursue growth, or is the company stagnating?
3 *Capital investment.* What capital investment has there been and what is planned? How would future investments be financed? What retained reserves has the company built up?
4 *Management.* What is the record of the management? Are the senior managers near retirement? Are they young enough to want change? Are they ambitious? How well do they seem to have managed the company's resources? Is its liquidity position secure? How good are they at portraying a favourable public image for the company?

5 *Employees and industrial relations.* Does the company appear to have a stable workforce? Has it had any industrial disputes? What is its attitude and relationship as far as the trade unions are concerned? How does the output and profit record per employee compare with other companies?

6 *The 'feel good' factor.* Having found out a great deal about the company, does it inspire you with some confidence about its future? Is it likely to expand in the short term and survive in the long term ? Overall, do you feel 'good' about the company?

The above questions are not exhaustive, but they should be a help to you in your analysis. There is no doubt that having extensively researched a company's history and examined its future, you will already have formed a provisional view before you come to make your recommendations. All that remains for you to do is to commit your thoughts to paper. You might have to produce only a *brief* report, and so you then will have the difficult task of summarizing all that you have learned about the company in just a few pages. You may well find that this is almost as difficult as carrying out the original investigation!

Conclusion

This chapter has explained how you can go about interpreting a set of accounts by using a variety of techniques, namely horizontal analysis, trend analysis, vertical analysis, and ratio analysis. The use of these techniques can help to put all the data that you have obtained about a particular company into perspective, but remember that the ratios that you produce are based on accounting information that is somewhat questionable. Furthermore, remember to use the ratios as signposts: they are not a substitute for an analytical assessment of the company's performance.

Note that we have concentrated almost exclusively on ratios that relate to the profit-making manufacturing and trading sectors. In the service sector or the not-for-profit sector, not all of the ratios that we have covered will be relevant, and you may either have to adapt them or substitute ratios that are specific to the sector in question.

Summary of the main ratios

Profitability ratios

$$\text{ROCE} = \frac{\text{Net profit before taxation}}{\text{Average shareholders' funds}} \times 100\%$$

$$\text{ROCE} = \frac{\text{Net profit after taxation}}{\text{Average shareholders' funds}} \times 100\%$$

$$\text{ROCE} = \frac{\text{Net profit after taxation and preference dividends}}{\text{Average shareholders' funds less preference shares}} \times 100\%$$

$$\text{ROCE} = \frac{\text{Profit before taxation and interest}}{\text{Average shareholders' funds} + \text{Long-term loans}} \times 100\%$$

$$\text{Gross profit ratio} = \frac{\text{Gross profit}}{\text{Total sales revenue}} \times 100\%$$

$$\text{Mark-up ratio} = \frac{\text{Gross profit}}{\text{Cost of goods sold}} \times 100\%$$

$$\text{Net profit ratio} = \frac{\text{Net profit before taxation}}{\text{Total sales revenue}} \times 100\%$$

Liquidity ratios

$$\text{Current assets ratio} = \frac{\text{Current assets}}{\text{Current liabilities}}$$

$$\text{Acid test ratio} = \frac{\text{Current assets} - \text{Stocks}}{\text{Current liabilities}}$$

Efficiency ratios

$$\text{Stock turnover} = \frac{\text{Cost of goods sold}}{\text{Average stock}}$$

$$\text{Fixed assets turnover} = \frac{\text{Total sales revenue}}{\text{Fixed assets at net book value}}$$

$$\text{Trade debtor collection period} = \frac{\text{Average trade debtors}}{\text{Total credit sales}} \times 365 \text{ days}$$

$$\text{Trade creditor payment period} = \frac{\text{Average trade creditors}}{\text{Total credit purchases}} \times 365 \text{ days}$$

Investment ratios

$$\text{Dividend yield} = \frac{\text{Dividend per share}}{\text{Market price per share}} \times 100\%$$

$$\text{Dividend cover} = \frac{\text{Net profit after taxation and preference dividend}}{\text{Paid and proposed ordinary dividends}}$$

$$\text{Earnings per share} = \frac{\text{Net profit after taxation and preference dividend}}{\text{Number of ordinary shares in issue during the year}}$$

$$\text{Price/earnings ratio} = \frac{\text{Market price per share}}{\text{Earnings per share}}$$

$$\text{Capital gearing} = \frac{\text{Preference shares} + \text{Long-term loans}}{\text{Shareholders' funds} + \text{Long-term loans}} \times 100\%$$

Key points

1 The interpretation of accounts involves examining accounts in some detail so as to be able to explain what has happened and to predict what is likely to happen.

2 The examination can be undertaken by using a number of techniques, such as horizontal analysis, trend analysis, vertical analysis, and ratio analysis.

3 Ratio analysis, in particular, is a popular method of interpreting accounts. It involves comparing one item in the accounts with another closely related item. Ratios are normally expressed in the form of a percentage or a factor. There are literally hundreds of recognized accounting ratios (the main ones being summarized at the very end of the chapter), as well as those that relate only to specific industries.

4 Not all of the ratios covered in this chapter will be relevant for non-manufacturing, non-trading or not-for-profit entities. You will therefore need to be selective in your choice of ratios.

5 When relating one item to another item, and then expressing it in the form of a ratio, be careful to make sure that there is a close and logical correlation between the two items.

6 Remember that, in the case of some ratios, different definitions can be adopted. This applies particularly to ROCE and capital gearing. In other cases, remember that sometimes only year-end balances are used, and not an annual average. This applies especially to ratios relating to stocks, debtors, and creditors.

Check your learning

1 State whether the following assertions are true or false:
  (a) Ratio analysis aims to put the financial results of an entity into perspective.　　　　　　　　　　　　　　　　　　　True／False
  (b) Ratio analysis is only one form of analysis that can be used in interpreting accounts.　　　　　　　　　　　　　　　　True／False
  (c) Ratio analysis helps establish whether or not an entity is a going concern.　　　　　　　　　　　　　　　　　　　　True／False

2 Fill in the missing blanks in the following equations:

  (a) $\dfrac{\text{Gross profit (50)}}{\text{Sales (200)}} \times \underline{\hspace{2cm}} \% = 25\%$.

  (b) $\dfrac{\text{Profit}}{\text{Capital}} \times 100\% = \underline{\hspace{1cm}}\ \underline{\hspace{1cm}}\ \underline{\hspace{1cm}}\ \underline{\hspace{1cm}} \%$.

  (c) $\dfrac{\text{Trade debtors}}{\underline{\hspace{2cm}}} \times 365 \text{ days} = \text{Trade debtor collection period}$.

  (d) $\dfrac{\underline{\hspace{1cm}}\ \underline{\hspace{1cm}}\ \underline{\hspace{1cm}}\ \underline{\hspace{1cm}}}{\text{Average stock}} = \text{Stock turnover ratio}$.

193

(e) $\dfrac{\text{Net profit after taxation and preference dividend}}{\underline{\hspace{2cm}}\quad\underline{\hspace{2cm}}} = $ Dividend cover.

(f) $\dfrac{\text{Preference shares} + \underline{\hspace{2cm}}}{\text{Shareholders' funds} + \text{Long-term loans}} \times 100\% = $ Capital gearing.

3 State how each of the following ratios would normally be classed:
   (a) Gross profit ratio: 70%   High/Low/Neither
   (b) Net profit ratio: 3%   High/Low/Neither
   (c) Return on capital employed: 30%   High/Low/Neither
   (d) Trade debtors collection period: 125 days   High/Low/Neither
   (e) Capital gearing: 40%   High/Low/Neither

[*The answers to these questions may be found at the back of the book.*]

Group discussion questions

9.1 Accounting ratios are only as good as the data on which they are based.' Discuss.

9.2 How far do you accept the argument that the return on capital employed ratio can give a misleading impression of an entity's profitability?

9.3 Is ratio analysis useful in understanding how an entity has performed?

Practice questions

[*Note: The questions marked with an asterisk have answers at the back of the book.*]

9.4* The following information has been extracted from the books of account of Betty for the year to 31 January 2001:

Trading and profit and loss account for the year to 31 January 2001

	£000	£000
Sales (all credit)		100
Less: Cost of goods sold:		
Opening stock	15	
Purchases	65	
	80	
Less: Closing stock	10	70
Gross profit		30
Administrative expenses		16
Net profit		14

Balance sheet at 31 January 2001

		£000	£000
Fixed assets (net book value)			29
Current assets			
Stock		10	
Trade debtors		12	
Cash		3	
	c/f	25	29

		£000	£000
	b/f	25	29
Less: Current liabilities			
Trade creditors		6	19
			48

Financed by:		
Capital at 1 February 2000		40
Add: Net profit	14	
Less: Drawings	6	8
		48

Required:

Calculate the following accounting ratios:

1 gross profit;
2 net profit;
3 return on capital employed;
4 current ratio;
5 acid test;
6 stock turnover; and
7 debtor collection period.

9.5* You are presented with the following summarized accounts:

James Ltd
Profit and loss account for the year to 28 February 2002

	£000
Sales (all credit)	1 200
Cost of sales	600
Gross profit	600
Administrative expenses	(500)
Debenture interest payable	(10)
Profit on ordinary activities	90
Taxation	(30)
	60
Dividends	(40)
Retained profit for the year	20

James Ltd
Balance sheet at 28 February 2002

	£000	£000	£000
Fixed assets (net book value)			685
Current assets			
Stock		75	
Trade debtors		200	
	c/f	275	685

	£000		£000		£000
		b/f	275		685
Less: Current liabilities					
Trade creditors	160				
Bank overdraft	10				
Taxation	30				
Proposed dividend	40		240		35
					720
Capital and reserves					
Ordinary share capital					600
Profit and loss account					20
Shareholders' funds					620
Loans:					
10% debentures					100
					720

Required:

Calculate the following accounting ratios:

1 return on capital employed;
2 gross profit;
3 mark up;
4 net profit;
5 acid test;
6 fixed assets turnover;
7 debtor collection period; and
8 capital gearing.

9.6 You are presented with the following information relating to three companies:

Profit and loss accounts for the year to 31 March 2003

	Mark Limited £000	Luke Limited £000	John Limited £000
Profit before tax	64	22	55

Balance sheet (extracts) at 31 March 2003

	Mark Limited £000	Luke Limited £000	John Limited £000
Capital and reserves			
Ordinary share capital of £1 each	100	177	60
Cumulative 15% preference shares of £1 each	–	20	10
Share premium account	–	70	20
Profit and loss account	150	60	200
Shareholders' funds	250	327	290
Loans			
10% debentures	–	–	100
	250	327	390

Required:
Calculate the following accounting ratios:
1 return on capital employed; and
2 capital gearing.

9.7 The following information relates to Helena Limited:

Trading account year to 30 April

	2001 £000	2002 £000	2003 £000	2004 £000	2005 £000	2006 £000
Sales (all credit)	–	130	150	190	210	320
Less: Cost of goods sold:						
Opening stock	–	20	30	30	35	40
Purchases (all in credit terms)	–	110	110	135	145	305
	–	130	140	165	180	345
Less: Closing stock	–	30	30	35	40	100
	–	100	110	130	140	245
Gross profit	–	30	40	60	70	75
Trade debtors at 30 April	40	45	40	70	100	150
Trade creditors at 30 April	20	20	25	25	30	60

Required:
Calculate the following accounting ratios for each of the five years from 30 April 2002 to 2006 inclusive:
1 gross profit;
2 mark-up;
3 stock turnover;
4 trade debtor collection period; and
5 trade creditor payment period.

9.8 You are presented with the following information relating to Hedge public limited company for the year to 31 May 2005:
(a) The company has an issued and fully paid share capital of £500 000 ordinary shares of £1 each. There are no preference shares.
(b) The market price of the shares at 31 May 2005 was £3.50.
(c) The net profit after taxation for the year to 31 May 2005 was £70 000.
(d) The directors are proposing a dividend of 7p per share for the year to 31 May 2005.

Required:
Calculate the following accounting ratios:
1 dividend yield;
2 dividend cover;
3 earnings per share; and
4 price/earnings ratio.

9.9 The following information relates to Style Limited for the two years to 30 June 2005 and 2006, respectively:

Trading and profit and loss accounts for the years

	2005		2006	
	£000	£000	£000	£000
Sales (all credit)		1 500		1 900
Less: Cost of goods sold:				
Opening stock	80		100	
Purchases (all on credit terms)	995		1 400	
	1 075		1 500	
	100	975	200	1 300
Gross profit		525		600
Less: Expenses		250		350
Net profit		275		250

Balance sheet at 30 June

	2005		2006	
	£000	£000	£000	£000
Fixed assets (net book value)		580		460
Current assets				
Stock	100		200	
Trade debtors	375		800	
Bank	25		–	
	500		1 000	
Less: Current liabilities				
Bank overdraft	–		10	
Trade creditors	80		200	
	80	420	210	790
		1 000		1 250
Capital and reserves				
Ordinary share capital		900		900
Profit and loss account		100		350
Shareholders' funds		1 000		1 250

Required:
(a) Calculate the following accounting ratios for the two years 2005 and 2006 respectively:
   1 gross profit;
   2 mark-up;
   3 net profit;
   4 return on capital employed;
   5 stock turnover;
   6 current ratio;
   7 acid test;
   8 trade debtor collection period; and
   9 trade creditor payment period.
(b) Comment upon the company's performance for the year to 30 June 2006.

Not so secure

Learning objectives	**By the end of this case study, you should be able to:** ● analyse financial statements; ● extract additional information from a set of financial statements; ● summarize information contained within them; ● prepare a report based on your observations.

Background	**Location**	Security Systems Limited: Head Office
	Personnel	Alan Pymn: Joint Managing Director Frank Lynch: Joint Managing Director

Synopsis

Some years ago, Alan Pymn and Frank Lynch went into partnership marketing and installing security alarm systems. Both Alan and Frank had previously worked at the local brewery, Alan in plant maintenance and Frank in the sales office.

They lived in Stutfield, a quiet north-country town of about 80 000 inhabitants. Stutfield was within easy travelling distance of several major cities. At that time, the town was suffering from an increasing amount of crime and vandalism and house owners were extremely worried by the number of houses being burgled.

The two partners were neighbours. They were also both keen members of the local squash club. Talking at the bar one night about the latest burglary, they had the idea of forming their own security system business. The idea appealed to them, especially as neither of them wanted to work for someone else for the rest of their lives.

They thought about the idea for a little while. In the meantime, by working for a friend at the weekend, Alan was able to gain some experience of installing security systems and Frank learned something about the administrative and marketing side of the security business. Financial backing was promised from various friends and   relatives, and within just a few months they were able to set up their business.

The business was an instant success as everyone in the town seemed to want some form of protection. After a few years of rapid growth they decided to convert the partnership into a limited liability company called 'Security Systems Limited'.

The charge for installing a security system was based partly on the size of the property and partly on the complexity of the installation. The policy of the company was to invoice customers 30 days after a job had been satisfactorily completed.

After the first year, a fixed annual maintenance charge became payable. This charge covered all further inspections and repairs. Customers were contracted to pay this charge for five years, but after that time only a nominal annual charge was made. All contracts had a maximum life of ten years.

Following the formation of the company, the business continued to grow, although at a slower rate than had previously been experienced. By the time that Security Systems Ltd was formed, most householders in Stutfield had obtained a burglar alarm, and so the company began to conduct more of its business in the nearby cities.

It proved to be much more difficult to operate outside Stutfield. Although there was quite a demand for such services, the competition was extremely tough. Furthermore, city customers always argued about the effectiveness of the system, and both operative and office staff spent a great deal of time persuading customers to settle their accounts.

An additional worrying feature first became apparent as the business developed. Contrary to expectations, those security systems installed in the earlier years of the business proved increasingly expensive to maintain, and the operative staff spent more and more of their time repairing old systems instead of installing new ones. Under the terms of the contract, it was not possible to increase the annual maintenance charge.

The company's accounting policy had always been to claim any profit made on the installation of a system in the year of installation and to credit maintenance fees receivable to each year's profit and loss account. Separate records were not kept of installation expenses and maintenance costs, and no provision had been made for maintenance and repairs.

Required:

1 Inspect the summarized financial statements for Security Systems Limited for the five-year period 1 April 2003 to 31 March 2008 (Appendix A). Make a note of any obvious changes or features that become apparent as you read through the accounts.

2 For the five-year period 1 April 2003 to 31 March 2008, prepare the following analyses:
   (a) Horizontal analysis: installation fees, maintenance fees and direct labour.
   (b) Trend analysis: installation fees, maintenance fees and direct labour.
   (c) Vertical analysis: direct labour as a proportion of total income.
   (d) Ratio analysis: calculate the following ratios:
      (i)   current assets ratio.
      (ii) trade debter collection period (in days).
      (iii) operating profit as a percentage of total income.
      (iv) net profit ratio.
      (v)   return in capital employed.

3 Using the information obtained in completing 1 and 2 above, prepare a report for the Board of Directors of Security Systems Limited examining the company's efficiency, liquidity and profitability during the five-year period 1 April 2003 to 31 March 2008 inclusive. Be careful to state what recommendations you would make to the Board of Directors in order to enable the company to continue in business.

Appendix A

Profit and loss accounts (extracts) for the year to 31 March

	2004 £000	2005 £000	2006 £000	2007 £000	2008 £000
INCOME:					
Installation fees	1 250	1 500	2 100	2 400	2 500
Maintenance fees	1 000	1 500	1 920	2 340	2 600
	2 250	3 000	4 020	4 740	5 100
EXPENDITURE:					
Direct materials	250	306	437	528	575
Direct labour	795	1 254	1 753	2 182	3 060
Direct expenditure	40	40	70	90	120
Operational overheads	140	200	280	370	470
	1 225	1 800	2 540	3 170	4 225
OPERATING PROFIT	1 025	1 200	1 480	1 570	875
Directors' emoluments	80	100	130	150	150
Loan interest	–	–	–	75	75
Office expenses	675	780	995	1 040	1 085
Office salaries	120	140	155	180	210
	875	1 020	1 280	1 445	1 520
NET PROFIT (LOSS)	150	180	200	125	(645)
Taxation	45	60	65	70	–
	105	120	135	55	(645)
Dividends	100	115	115	120	–
RETAINED PROFIT/(LOSS)	5	5	20	(65)	(645)

Balance sheet (extracts) at 31 March

	2004 £000	2005 £000	2006 £000	2007 £000	2008 £000
FIXED ASSETS:					
At cost	1 400	1 450	1 500	1 550	1 900
Less: Accumulated depreciation	275	355	440	530	695
	1 125	1 095	1 060	1 020	1 205
CURRENT ASSETS:					
Stocks at cost (2003 £15 000)	20	25	40	50	80
Trade debtors	200	240	363	434	806
Other debtors	25	25	30	40	50
Cash and bank	–	–	–	278	–
	245	290	433	802	936
	1 370	1 385	1 493	1 822	2 141

Balance sheet (extracts) at 31 March

	2004 £000	2005 £000	2006 £000	2007 £000	2008 £000
CAPITAL AND RESERVES:					
Ordinary shares of					
£1 each	1 000	1 000	1 000	1 000	1 000
Retained profits/(losses)	55	60	80	15	(630)
	1 055	1 060	1 080	1 015	370
DEBENTURE LOANS (15%)	–	–	–	500	500
CURRENT LIABILITIES:					
Trade creditors	26	31	43	52	66
Other creditors	40	50	60	65	80
Bank overdraft	104	69	130	–	1 125
Taxation	45	60	65	70	–
Proposed dividend	100	115	115	120	–
	315	325	413	307	1 271
	1 370	1 385	1 493	1 822	2 141

Note:
There were no sales of fixed assets during the period 1 April 2003 to 31 March 2008 inclusive.

Cash flow statements for the year to 31 March

	2005 £000	2006 £000	2007 £000	2008 £000
Net cash inflow/(outflow) from				
operating activities	230	164	213	(788)
Returns on investments and servicing				
of finance				
Interest paid	–	–	(75)	(75)
Taxation				
Corporation tax paid	(45)	(60)	(65)	(70)
Capital expenditure				
Payments to acquire tangible fixed assets	(50)	(50)	(50)	(350)
	135	54	23	(1 283)
Equity dividends paid	(100)	(115)	(115)	(120)
	35	(61)	(92)	(1 403)
Management of liquid				
resources and financing	–	–	500	–
Increase/(decrease) in cash	35	(61)	408	(1 403)

	2005	2006	2007	2008
	£000	£000	£000	£000
Reconciliation of operating profit to net cash inflow/outflow from operating activities				
Operating profit/(loss)	180	200	200	(570)
Depreciation charges	80	85	90	165
Increase in stocks	(5)	(15)	(10)	(30)
Increase in debtors	(40)	(128)	(81)	(382)
Increase in creditors	15	22	14	29
Net cash inflow/(outflow) from operating activities	230	164	213	(788)

10 Disclosure of information

E-mail results for private investors?   FT

Your e-mail inbox could soon be filling up with company results reports.

A government accounting committee has reinforced proposals by the Accounting Standards Board (ASB) calling for electronic delivery of company accounts to private investors.

The idea is part of a government drive to give them a fairer chance to compete with institutional investors.

The committee says companies should have to post their results on the internet and send e-mails to private shareholders at the same time as they release them to the stock exchange.

Although few would criticise the idea of speedy electronic delivery of results in addition to being sent the full annual report by normal mail, there could be concern among private investors that abbreviated electronic information could replace a full report service and deprive them of the full picture.

Financial Times, 11/12 March 2000. Reprinted with permission.

Disclosing
information
electronically

In previous chapters, we have been mainly concerned with collecting and summarizing information for *internal* management purposes. In order to illustrate some of the basic principles of accounting, we have concentrated on problems dealing with sole traders and companies. However, it would be as well to remind you again that the accounting principles with which we have been dealing can similarly be applied to non-profit-making entities (such as a local authority or a hospital) or to service industries (such as an electrical contractor or a chain of garages).

Nevertheless, *any* entity constituted as a limited liability company also has a statutory duty to disclose some information about its financial affairs to parties external to the company (mainly to its shareholders). The main aim of this chapter is to explore that requirement.

By the end of this chapter, you should be able to:
- **list seven user groups of financial information;**
- **state the main sources of authority for company disclosure of information.**

User groups

In Chapter 1, we indicated that there were seven main user groups of accounting information. These groups were identified in a report published in 1999 by the ASB called *Statement of Principles for Financial Reporting*. The report listed seven user groups. The groupings are summarized below and they are also shown in Figure 10.1.

1 *Investors*. The investors group includes both present and potential investors. Investors provide the risk capital and as shareholders they are, of course, also the owners of the company. None the less, the law has always regarded it as being impractical for every shareholder (in some large companies, there could be hundreds of thousands of individual shareholders) to have an automatic right of access to the company's premises to inspect the books of account, and to demand an unrestricted amount of information. Thus, since shareholders' rights are legally defined, they may be regarded as one of the main *external* user groups.

2 *Lenders*. Lenders are groups of people who have loaned funds to the business under some formal agreement, e.g. by buying debentures in the company. It is considered that they need to be supplied with some information about the company's affairs in order to be reassured that the company will be able to continue paying interest on their debt, and that their loans will eventually be repaid.

3 *Suppliers and other trade creditors*. This group is similar to the lenders group. Suppliers and trade creditors need some information about the company in order to decide whether to sell to it. Thereafter, they need some reassurance that they will be paid what is owed to them.

4 *Employees*. Without an appropriate amount of *financial* capital, a company could not be formed, but it would soon go out of business without the input of some *human* capital, i.e. someone to manage and operate it. It follows that employees must be an important user group of financial information, because they need some assurance about the stability and profitability of the company. It could be argued, of course, that employees are hardly an *external* group since they work within the company. However, this does not necessarily mean that they have ready access to the type of information

about the company that is of interest to them; e.g. the stability and profitability of the company.

5 *Customers*. Customers often have a long-term involvement with a company, and like many of the other groupings they too need some reassurance about its long-term future. They may, for example, have long-term warranties and might require parts of machinery to be replaced.

6 *Governments and their agencies*. Governments and their agencies (as the ASB puts it) is another important user group interested in a company's progress, whether this is in respect of employment prospects, the collection of taxes (such as value added tax or corporation tax), or the compilation of statistics.

7 *The public*. A company does not work in isolation, and its success or otherwise does have an indirect impact on many other people with whom it comes into contact. A company that happens to be a major employer in a small town, for example, helps to generate employment outside the company itself, since other entities provide services to the company's employees and their families. Hence the public, in the form of the local community, has an interest in a company's performance and future prospects.

It should be noted that not all observers accept the above groupings. It could be argued, for example, that the public's interest is too remote for a company to be required to inform the local community about its affairs (although it may be good public relations to do so). Similarly, the government can obtain all the information it wants about a company by other means, without necessarily having to establish a separate reporting system. The *Statement* is also primarily concerned with what it calls 'profit-oriented reporting entities' (whereas we have referred largely to 'companies'), although it also states that it is broadly relevant for not-for-profit entities.

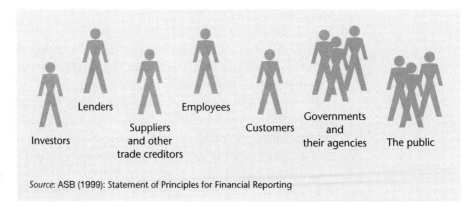

**Figure 10.1
The main users of
financial reports**

Source: ASB (1999): Statement of Principles for Financial Reporting

Sources of authority

In the United Kingdom, the reporting of information to parties external to a limited liability company is governed by three main sources of authority:

1 *Statutory*: those requirements covered by Acts of Parliament.
2 *Professional*: those requirements determined by the business community acting in conjunction with the accountancy profession.
3 *Stock exchange*: those requirements laid down by the capital markets.

Statutory requirements

For well over 150 years the United Kingdom has adopted what might be called a *permissive* system of financial reporting. This means that Parliament lays down a body of general accounting law but the detailed implementation of it is left mainly to those parties who have a direct interest in the legislation. Until recently, this meant mainly the accountancy profession, but nowadays the wider business and professional community has also become involved. The permissive system is in marked contrast to the *prescriptive* system of financial reporting, which is found in most Continental European countries (such as France and Germany). In a prescriptive system, some very detailed accounting rules and regulations are laid down in law. Hence there is not the same opportunity for individual interpretation of the law as there is in a permissive system.

The present British statutory requirements are contained in an Act of Parliament known as the Companies Act 1985. This Act is a consolidating measure. It includes the earlier Companies Acts of 1948, 1967, 1976, 1980, and 1981, respectively, although some provisions have been amended by the Companies Act 1989.

Companies Act legislation since 1981 has been brought about mainly by the UK's membership of the European Union. Strictly speaking, therefore, it is no longer UK law but European law that sets the pace and direction for change.

The Companies Act 1985 (as amended by the Companies Act 1989) lays down the *minimum* disclosure requirements that companies must disclose to their investors. It should be noted that, apart from some brief references to creditors and employees, the other user groups discussed earlier in this chapter are barely mentioned. Although the Act lays down the minimum requirements, the inclusion of additional professional and stock exchange requirements means that shareholders are now supplied with a considerable amount of detailed information about a company's affairs.

In effect, the statutory disclosure of information to external parties takes two forms:

1 *The Annual Report.* Shareholders are automatically supplied with a copy of the company's annual report, of which they can elect to receive a summary version (see Chapter 12 for more detail).

2 *Filing*. The annual report has also to be 'filed' with the Registrar of Companies. The reports are left in Companies House (there is one in Edinburgh and one in Cardiff) and anyone can go along to have a look at them. 'Large' companies must file the full annual report, but 'medium' and 'small' companies may file a modified version. The terms 'large', 'medium', and 'small' are defined in the Act, but they can be amended from time-to-time by means of a 'statutory instrument'. The definitions are based on a combination of size criteria, namely turnover, gross assets, and number of employees.

Professional requirements

As mentioned in Chapter 2, the professional requirements that govern the disclosure of information by limited liability companies are issued by a body called the Accounting Standards Board (ASB). The ASB was set up in 1990. It succeeded an earlier body known as the Accounting Standards Committee (ASC), which was created in 1970 (originally as the Accounting Standards Steering Committee, or ASSC).

The main aim of the ASC was to narrow the areas of difference in accounting practice. It has been traditional in the United Kingdom for only broad principles of company law to be laid down by Parliament. Thus accountants and other interested parties have been relatively free to interpret the law quite broadly (leading to a practice known as 'creative accounting'). Not surprisingly, this eventually led to a number of accounting 'scandals' that were well publicized. The profession was forced into taking some action. It did so by setting up the ASSC, although it was not until 1976 that all the six main professional accountancy bodies had become members of it.

The ASC issued what were known as 'Statements of Standard Accounting Practice' (SSAPs). SSAPs laid down some fairly general guidelines which professionally qualified accountants were expected to follow when preparing financial accounts and it was possible for transgressors to be disciplined by their respective professional body. Accountants were also expected to encourage their clients and their employers to adopt and abide by the spirit of the standards programme.

By the time of its demise in 1990, the ASC had issued 25 SSAPs (although three had been withdrawn). The ASC fell into disrepute, partly because many of the standards enabled a great deal of interpretation (hence defeating their objective) and partly because the ASC was perceived to be very slow in reacting to events, as all the six bodies had to approve a draft standard before it could be issued.

The ASB's position is somewhat different. It is one of the main committees of the *Financial Reporting Council* (FRC). The FRC comprises members from industry, commerce, and the public sector, and unlike the ASC its membership is not dominated by the accountancy profession. The ASB issues what are called 'Financial Reporting Standards' (FRSs). At its inception in 1990 it also adopted the 22 SSAPs that were still outstanding. It is the intention of the ASB in due course to replace all the SSAPs with FRSs. By December 1999, 14 SSAPs were still in existence and 16 FRSs had been issued. Unlike SSAPs, FRSs do not need to be approved by all six professional bodies before they are issued. Hence, in theory, the ASB can react to events much more quickly than did the ASC, although in practice a great deal of discussion and argument is still required.

Like SSAPs, FRSs are meant to give guidance on how certain matters should be dealt with in preparing financial reports. Some FRSs permit various options, whereas others prescribe a specific method. They normally also include a great deal of information to be disclosed. Most of the FRSs that have been issued so far deal with some extremely complex issues and are very difficult to understand.

The ASB's job is also supported by an *Urgent Issues Task Force* (UITF). No doubt at this stage you are finding all of these initials somewhat confusing, but since you are likely to come across them it is necessary to refer to them. In order to help you sort them out, the standard-setting process in the United Kingdom (through the FRC) is shown in diagrammatic format in Figure 10.2.

The UITF's role is to react quickly to any new or emerging financial reporting issue that requires some immediate response to be given. In other words, it acts as a 'fire-fighting' body.

As can be seen from Figure 10.2, besides the ASB the FRS has another main arm attached to it. This is known as the Financial Reporting Review Panel (FRRP). The FRRP's job is to examine apparent defects in published accounts and to decide what it should do about them. It is usually successful in persuading companies to accept its recommendations. If, however, its

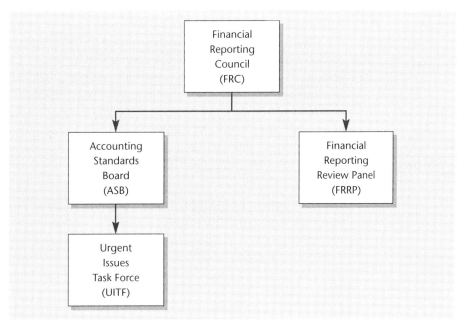

Figure 10.2
The structure of standard setting in the United Kingdom

intervention is unsuccessful, it has the power to ask for the accounts to be re-issued. Thereafter, court proceedings may be instituted.

This possibility arises because the Companies Act 1985 (as amended by the Companies Act 1989) requires companies (other than small and medium-sized ones) to state whether their accounts have been prepared in accordance with applicable accounting standards. Otherwise, details have to be given of all material departures from such standards. If a company has not abided by a particular standard, it is possible for the court to ask the directors of the company for an explanation; they might then be ordered to comply with that standard. This was the first time in British law that accounting standards were given some legal recognition. It is possible to argue, therefore, that accounting standards now have a semi-statutory status.

The Companies Act 1985 also has an overriding clause that requires accounts to give 'a *true and fair view* of the state of affairs of the company'. As no one is quite sure what is meant by the phrase 'true and fair', directors can always argue that they have not followed a particular standard because to do so would not present a 'true and fair view'. Although this phrase has been enshrined in company law for over 50 years, its meaning has never been tested in a court of law and no company has ever been challenged if it has adopted it as an overriding rule. It is also interesting to note that the phrase has been incorporated into European law and the other member states have tended to translate it literally. Hence it is open to quite different interpretations throughout the European Union.

Stock exchange requirements

The stock exchange regulations covering disclosure of information no longer carry the same significance that they once did. This is because most of what used to be required is now contained within either statutory or professional requirements. However, for certain categories of companies (such as those that are listed), there are a few additional disclosure requirements, e.g. some extra information has to be provided about creditors and an interim report has to be issued.

Conclusion

In this chapter, we have provided you with some background information about the external disclosure requirements relating to limited liability companies. Although it is possible to recognize at least seven user groups of published financial information, the Companies Act 1985 (which contains the main statutory disclosure requirements) almost exclusively concentrates on the investor group. Indeed, it is only in the event of liquidation of the company that two other groups (suppliers and other trade creditors, and employees) are given some recognition.

In addition to statutory requirements, SSAPs and FRSs add to the amount of information to be disclosed. Listed companies are also bound by a few extra stock exchange requirements. As will be seen in the next chapter, all these requirements mean that the amount of information supplied to shareholders in the form of an annual report results in a document of daunting proportions.

Key points

1 The Companies Act 1985 lays down the minimum amount of information that must be supplied to company shareholders.

2 This is supplemented by professional requirements issued by the ASB in the form of SSAPs and FRSs.

3 Such accounting and financial reporting standards have semi-statutory status.

4 Listed companies are also bound by a number of additional stock exchange requirements.

5 Accounts should be prepared in such a way that they represent a 'true and fair view' of the company's affairs. This is an overriding rule of the Companies Act 1985. It takes precedence over other legislative, professional and stock exchange requirements.

Check your learning

1 What are the three main sources of authority for the disclosure of information to shareholders?

2 What is the main source of company legislation in the United Kingdom?

3 What do the following initials mean:
   (a) ASC
   (b) SSAP
   (c) FRC
   (d) ASB
   (e) FRS?

4 What statutory rule overrides all other disclosure requirements?

[*The answers to these questions may be found at the back of the book.*]

Group discussion questions

10.1 What type of information do you think a company should disclose to its shareholders?

10.2 Should Parliament lay down rigid accounting procedures for supplying information to company shareholders?

10.3 'Accounting standards should become enshrined in company law.' Discuss.

10.4 Do you think that the 'true and fair view' rule should be abandoned?

11 The annual report

Published accounts: a mystery to shareholders

The annual accounts of a company must be supplied to shareholders at least 21 days before the accounts are due to be considered at a general meeting of the company. The accounts comprise the company's balance sheet, a profit and loss account, the directors' report, the auditors' report and, if required, *group* accounts. However, 'the accounts' are often accompanied by other types of reports and reviews. In this chapter, we are going to examine the contents of what, for convenience, we will call 'the annual report'.

By the end of this chapter, you should be able to:

- identify the main sections of an annual report;
- list the main contents of a chairman's statement, an auditor's financial report, and a directors' report;
- locate the major items contained in a group profit and loss account, a statement of total recognized gains and losses, a group balance sheet, a group cash flow statement, and notes to the accounts;
- trace the notes to the accounts back to the main financial statements.

Background

An annual report received from a large multinational company can be somewhat off-putting, especially to those shareholders who have had no training in basic accounting. It will usually arrive in a large brown or white envelope, and it will feel very heavy. Assuming that the envelope is opened and the pages flicked through, the average shareholder is likely to be totally bewildered by what is inside the report. Some reports may be well over 100 pages long. They will usually be printed in a wide variety of print sizes and colours, and they will contain a great many narrative reports, as well as many pages of statistical data. Fortunately, the sheer off-putting nature of such information is often relieved by a series of eye-catching glossy diagrams and photographs.

None the less, it is difficult for even experienced and trained users of annual reports to make much sense of them. It is probably almost impossible, therefore, for the average shareholder to do so unless he or she has had some training in accounting. In this chapter we aim to offer you some clear guidance about the contents of annual reports so that you will be able to find your way round them relatively easily. However, you will appreciate that since not all annual reports necessarily follow the same format and structure, we can only offer you some *general* guidance. Nevertheless, by the end of the chapter you should have sufficient confidence to be able to adapt the knowledge that you have gained so as to be able to cope with different types of annual reports.

For convenience, our study of annual reports will be divided into four main sections. In practice, no such clear differentiation will normally be apparent. These sections will be referred to as *introductory material, operational reports and reviews, the accounts,* and *shareholder information.* They are shown in diagrammatic format in Figure 11.1 and described further below.

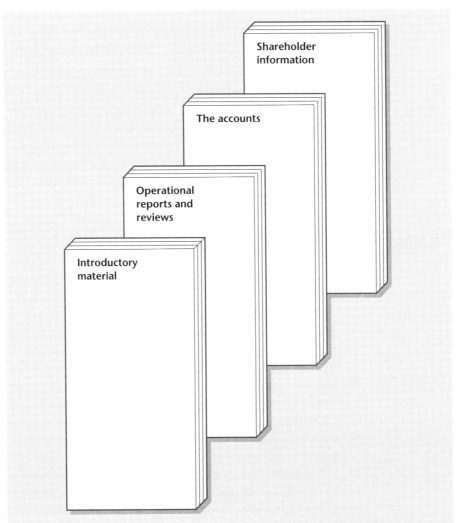

Figure 11.1
The main sections
of an annual report

Introductory material

Many annual reports begin with a brief summary of the history of the company and its objectives. These may then be followed by a review of the year's financial and operating results which may be supported by a series of charts, graphs, photographs, and statistical tables comparing the year's achievements with previous years.

None of this information is statutory or professionally required and sometimes it is presented in a somewhat misleading fashion. A carefully constructed graph, for example, can often disguise the fact that an apparent rise in sales has not been particularly spectacular.

Operational reports and reviews

This section will nearly always contain a report from the chairman and it may also contain a report from the chief executive, as well as individual reports from other senior officers of the company. These various reports often include many pages detailing the company's operational activities, especially those relating to production and marketing. They are also frequently accompanied by a series of vivid photographs proclaiming the virtues of the company's products.

This section of an annual report might, therefore, be regarded as more in the nature of a public relations exercise than an attempt to communicate financial information. Indeed, such material is normally a fairly blatant form of advertising. It is especially prominent in consumer-orientated companies, since it is to the company's advantage to encourage the shareholders to buy the company's own products.

The above comments might now, however, be a little unfair, because in 1993, the ASB issued a statement of good practice that supported the idea of companies including an *Operating and Financial Review* (OFR) in their annual report. The suggestion had come from the *Cadbury Report*, which was published in 1992 by the 'Committee on the Financial Aspects of Corporate Governance'. This Committee was set up in 1991 by the FRC, the London Stock Exchange and the accountancy profession to examine the ways in which companies were governed. An OFR is supposed to cover, *inter alia*, the business as a whole, discuss individual aspects of the business, give an insight into matters that underpin the financial results and consider factors that might affect the company's future performance.

It follows that the operational report and review section of an annual report may contain some interesting information, e.g. about the development of a new product. However, because such promotional material can take up many pages, the financial reports may have less impact. This is unfortunate because, after all, the main reason for publishing an annual report is to report to shareholders on the financial performance of the company.

In this context, probably the most interesting report contained in this section is the chairman's report. Indeed, from the research undertaken into the usefulness of annual reports, it would appear that the chairman's report is the one that is most likely to be read. As there are no statutory, professional, or stock exchange requirements for a chairman to prepare a report, there is no specified format and the contents will vary from company to company. Some chairman's reports are very long (although most chairmen manage to limit their comments to one or two pages) and a chairman is quite free to include almost anything that he or she likes. The chairman should, however, be mindful of the effect that the remarks in the report may have on the company's share price. Indeed, a great deal of trouble can be stored up for the company if the chairman is too optimistic about its future prospects.

A typical chairman's report will, among other things, review the results for the year, give some details about the dividend, highlight the major changes in the company's activities for the year, and comment on the achievements of the directors and other employees. It may also give an indication of how the chairman views the company's future.

The report will normally be found within the first few pages of most annual reports, but in order to find its exact position you may need to consult the contents page of the annual report (assuming that there is one).

One other narrative report that may be included in this section is a brief biography of each of the company's directors. Such a report will not tell you very much. Each biography will probably give you no more than the director's age, profession, specific company responsibilities and the directorships held in other companies.

Two interesting points to note at this stage are (a) whether the Chairman is also the Chief Executive (the Cadbury Committee recommended that the roles should be separate); and (b) whether the company has a number of 'non-executive directors' (i.e. those without specific operational managerial duties within the company). The Cadbury Committee considered that a strong group of non-executive directors was essential if companies were to set and maintain high standards of corporate governance. This kind of information will, therefore, give you a strong indication of the type of company with which you are dealing. For example, is it one that has a strong sense of responsibility to all those groups that have an interest in the company besides its investors?

The accounts

This is the main section of the actual report. It contains the statutory and professionally required information – the reason for issuing the report in the first place. Such information is both detailed and complex, and so we will break it down into a number of subsections to make it easier for you to follow. This breakdown is also shown in diagrammatic format in Figure 11.2.

As the exact position of the various subsections within an overall annual report will vary from company to company, each of them will be dealt with below in alphabetical order.

Accounting policies

This is a statement required by SSAP 2. It is important to digest it thoroughly in order to gain a fundamental understanding of the financial result for the year. As the term suggests, it lays down the accounting policies that the company has adopted in compiling the financial accounts. It should state, for example, which accounting model has been used in preparing the accounts (normally historic or original cost, but it could be at replacement cost), as well as such matters as consolidation policies, foreign currency translations, the

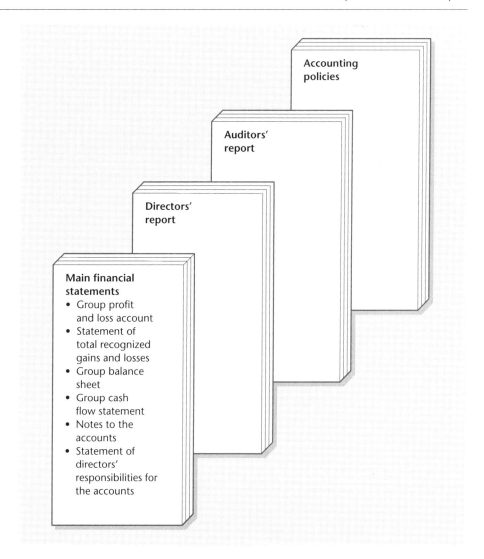

Accounting
policies

Auditors'
report

Directors'
report

**Main financial
statements**
- Group profit
  and loss account
- Statement of
  total recognized
  gains and losses
- Group balance
  sheet
- Group cash
  flow statement
- Notes to the
  accounts
- Statement of
  directors'
  responsibilities for
  the accounts

**Figure 11.2
The accounts
section of an
annual report**

definition of turnover, research and development expenditure, depreciation, the stock valuation method, and taxation and pension contributions.

In some annual reports, the accounting policies' statement is not prepared as a separate statement and it may be incorporated in 'Notes to the accounts' (see below).

Auditors' report

The auditors' report will be fairly short, and most auditors' reports that you are likely to come across will be very similar. A typical example is shown in Figure 11.3.

AUDITORS' REPORT TO THE SHAREHOLDERS OF ENERGY PLC

We have audited the financial statements on pages XX to XX which have been prepared under the historical cost convention as modified by the revaluation of certain fixed assets and the accounting policies set out on pages XX to XX.

Respective responsibilities of directors and auditors
As described on page XX, the company's directors are responsible for the preparation of financial statements. It is our responsibility to form an independent opinion, based on our audit, on those statements, and to report our opinion to you.

Basis of opinion
We conducted our audit in accordance with Auditing Standards issued by the Auditing Practices Board. An audit includes examination, on a test basis, of evidence relevant to the amounts and disclosures in the financial statements. It also includes an assessment of the significant estimates and judgements made by the directors in the preparation of the financial statements, and of whether the accounting policies are appropriate to the company's circumstances, consistantly applied and adequately disclosed.

We planned and performed our audit so as to obtain all the information and explanations which we considered necessary in order to provide us with sufficient evidence to give reasonable assurance that the financial statements are free from material mis-statement, whether caused by fraud or other irregularity or error. In forming our opinion we also evaluated the overall adequacy of the presentation of information in the financial statements.

Opinion
In our opinion the financial statements give a true and fair view of the state of the company's and the group's affairs as at 31 March 2001 and of its profit for the year then ended and have been properly prepared in accordance with the Companies Act 1985.

Cope & Co.,	Cope Court
Registered Auditors	London
31 May 2001	EC9 9CC

Figure 11.3 Example of a typical auditors' financial report

Directors' report

The directors' report is a statutory requirement, and a copy must be attached to the accounts sent to shareholders. It contains a great deal of information, such as details of the company's activities, its auditors, some information about the directors, charitable and political donations paid, the proposed dividend, the company's employment policy, a note about any major changes or values affecting its fixed assets, and a reference to any changes in its share capital. The London Stock Exchange also requires a section to be included in 'corporate governance', i.e. on how the company is managed. This section will include details about the directors and its board, its committees, accountability and audit procedures, and considerable material on how the directors are remunerated.

Main financial statements

You will find at least six main financial statements contained within a listed company's annual report. These are a profit and loss account, a statement of total recognized gains and losses, a balance sheet, a cash flow statement, some notes to the accounts, and a statement of directors' responsibilities. Most of these statements are extremely complex and quite hard to understand. However, based on the knowledge gained in the earlier part of this book and by working carefully through this chapter, you should not have much difficulty in locating the information you need.

The main parts of the financial statements will be dealt with in each of the following subsections. However, there are three points that we need to cover before we do so. They are as follows.

1 *Format.* Companies have slightly different ways of presenting the required information, and so you must not expect to find accounts that are necessarily identical to the ones that are used as examples in this chapter.

2 *Structure.* The published accounts of most large listed companies will relate to a *group* of companies. A group of companies is like a family. One company (say Company A) may buy shares in another company (say Company B). When Company A owns more than 50 per cent of the voting shares in Company B, B becomes a *subsidiary* of A. If A were to own more than 20 per cent but less than 50 per cent of the voting shares in B, B would be known as an *associated company* of A. In effect, B is considered to be the offspring of A. Of course B might have children of its own), say Company C and Company D, and thus C and D become part of the family, i.e. part of the A group of companies. It is also the case that sometimes one company is in a position to *control* the affairs of another company, even if it does not necessarily own a substantial number of shares in the other company. If this is the case, then companies that are controlled by other companies will be included as part of the group. An example of this type of group structure is shown in Figure 11.4.

    The Companies Act 1985 actually uses the term *group undertaking* to describe a subsidiary company. Associate companies are defined as *undertakings in which the company has participating interest.* This is because the Companies Act 1989 brought in a requirement to include other types of entities (and not just companies) in the group accounts.

    The main significance of these relationships is that the Companies Act 1985 then requires the accounts to be published for the *group,* i.e. in effect, as though it was one entire entity, thereby ignoring any inter-group activities (such as sales made or transfers of funds between group companies). It follows that, when inspecting a set of published accounts for a listed company, you can normally expect to see a *group* profit and loss account, a *group* balance sheet and a *group* cash flow statement.

    The Companies Act 1985 permits group accounts to be presented in several ways. The most common method of satisfying the statutory requirements is to prepare a group profit and loss account and a group balance

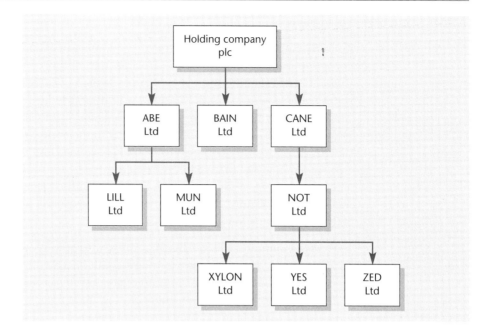

**Figure 11.4
A group of
companies**

sheet, accompanied by a balance sheet for the *holding* company. Cash flow statements are not required by law. They are a professional requirement (at least for large companies) covered by FRS1 (Cash Flow Statements).

In order to prepare group accounts, it is necessary to add together, i.e. *consolidate*, all of the company accounts within the group. As a result, the subsidiary company results are absorbed into the holding company's accounts (the treatment being slightly different for associated companies). This may sound a fairly routine arithmetical task, but in practice it is extremely complicated. Hence it has become somewhat of a specialism even among accountants.

3 *Comparative figures.* The Companies Act 1985 requires the previous year's accounts to be included alongside the current year's results. This adds to the amount of information given in the accounts, although there is some advantage in being able to make comparisons between the two years. However, it does appear to make the accounts even more complicated!

**Group profit
and loss account**

In presenting the profit and loss account, the Companies Act 1985 allows a choice to be made between two formats:

1 *Horizontal.* In this format, expenditures are listed on the left-hand side of the page and incomes on the right-hand side.
2 *Vertical.* This format presents the income and expenditure on a line-by-line basis.

The vertical format should be familiar to you. It has been used exclusively throughout this book and most UK companies have adopted it. Consequently, it is the format that you are most likely to meet.

The Companies Act 1985 also permits expenditure to be disclosed using either an 'operational' format or a 'type of expenditure' format. These formats are shown in Exhibit 11.1.

Exhibit 11.1 Examples of the vertical profit and loss account expenditure formats

(a) 'Operational' format		(b) 'Type of expenditure' format		
	£000		£000	£000
Turnover	9 000	Turnover		9 000
Cost of sales	(5 500)	Change in stocks of finished goods and work-in-progress		200
Gross profit	3 500	Own work capitalized		50
		Other operating income		100
				9 350
Distribution costs	(1 000)	Raw materials and consumables	(4 000)	
Administrative expenses	(1 600)	Other external charges	(400)	
Operating profit	900	Staff costs	(3 000)	
		Depreciation and other amounts written off tangible and intangible fixed assets	(900)	
Other operating income	100	Other operating charges	(50)	(8 350)
Operating profit	1 000	Operating profit		1 000

Notes:
1 The exhibit contains dummy information.
2 After the operating profit stage the two formats are identical.

As can be seen from Exhibit 11.1, the type of expenditure format is very much more detailed than the operational format. Both types are used in the UK. The operational format is more common, probably because it is a little easier to follow. It is basically the same format that we have used throughout the book. It is also easier to adapt it to suit the requirements of FRS 3 (Reporting Financial Performance) which deals with the presentation of financial statements.

Following this introduction, we can now examine a published profit and loss account in some detail. We do this in Exhibit 11.2.

Exhibit 11.2 Example of a published profit and loss account

Energy plc
Group profit and loss account for the year to 31 March 2002

	£000	£000
Turnover (1)		
Continuing operations	44 000	
Acquisitions	2 000	
	46 000	
Discontinued operations	3 000	49 000
Cost of sales (2)		(40 000)
Gross profit (3)		9 000
Distribution costs (4)		(4 000)
Administrative expenses (5)		(2 000)
Other operating income (6)		20
Operating profit (7)		
Continuing operations	2 740	
Acquisitions	250	
	2 990	
Discontinued operations	30	
Profit on ordinary activities before interest		3 020
Other interest receivable and other income (8)		295
Interest payable and similar charges (9)		(260)
Profit on ordinary activities before taxation (10)		3 055
Tax on profit on ordinary activities (11)		(145)
Profit on ordinary activities after taxation (12)		2 910
Minority interests (13)		(110)
Profit for the financial year (14)		2 800
Dividends paid and proposed (15)		(2 400)
Retained profit for the year (16)		400
Earnings per ordinary share (17)		2.85p

Notes:
(a) The numbers in brackets after each item refer to the tutorial notes below.
(b) References to the formal notes and the notes themselves are not included.
(c) Comparative figures have been ignored.
(d) The Exhibit contains dummy information.

Tutorial notes

1 Turnover is usually defined as being sales to customers outside the group, less returns by customers, exclusive of trade discounts and value added tax. You will notice that turnover has been analyzed between continuing operations, acquisitions and discontinued operations. In other words, sales from entities taken over

during the year, and sales arising from activities prior to their disposal during the year. FRS 3 (Reporting Financial Performance) requires this breakdown of turnover.

2   The detailed calculation for the cost of sales does not have to be disclosed. The term is not defined in the Companies Act 1985.

3   The gross profit may not be identical to that shown in the internal accounts because of the definition used for the cost of sales.

4   The Companies Act 1985 does not define what is meant by distribution costs.

5   Similarly, administrative expenses are not defined in the 1985 Act.

6   Other operating income includes income from rentals and royalties.

7   Operating profit. This is the point at which the operational and type of expenditure formats become identical. Note that FRS 3 requires the operating profit to be broken down into operating profit from continuing operations, acquisitions, and discontinued operations.

8   Other interest receivable and similar income includes interest received on loans.

9   Interest payable and similar charges includes interest payable on bank and other short-term borrowings.

10   The profit on ordinary activities before taxation will require a detailed formal note to the accounts. It will include such information as the auditors' remuneration, wages and salaries, depreciation charges, and social security and pension costs.

11   The tax on the profit on ordinary activities will consist largely of the company's corporation tax, but it may also include a number of technical accounting adjustments affecting taxation.

12   The amount shown for profit on ordinary activities after taxation is simply a subtotal.

13   A proportion of the after-tax profits may be due to non-group shareholders if the holding company has not purchased all of the shares in a subsidiary company.

14   The profit for the financial year is the total amount of net profit for the year that could be distributed to group members.

15   Dividends paid and proposed will include dividends paid or payable on all types of shares.

16   The retained profit for the year will be transferred to the revenue reserves (the balance of which will be shown in the balance sheet). The retained profit will be used to help finance the future expansion of the company.

17   The formal definition of earnings per ordinary share is quite complex. In simple terms, the earnings per share may be defined as the profit after tax less the preference dividends, divided by the number of issued ordinary shares. In practice, you may find that companies disclose a number of calculations for their earnings per ordinary share.

Statement of total recognized gains and losses

FRS 3 requires companies to prepare a statement called a *statement of total recognized gains and losses*. This statement will normally be presented immediately after the profit and loss account. It should include *all* the gains and losses that the company has made during the year, and not just those that are debited or credited to the profit and loss account. It is possible for some gains or losses (such as deficits or surpluses arising from the revaluation of fixed assets, and foreign currency exchange gains or losses) to be taken straight to a balance sheet reserve account. Hence they may never appear in the profit and loss account. An example of a statement of total recognized gains and losses as shown in Exhibit 11.3.

Exhibit 11.3 Example of a statement of total recognized gains and losses

	£000
Profit for the financial year (1)	2 800
Unrealized surplus on revaluation of properties (2)	100
Unrealized loss/gain on trade investments (3)	(30)
Currency translation difference on foreign currency net investments (4)	(10)
Total recognized gains relating to the year (5)	2 860

Tutorial notes

1　These figures are extracted from the profit and loss account.
2　Revaluation surpluses on properties will be added to the revaluation reserve account shown on the balance sheet.
3　Trade investment losses and gains will be dealt with similarly.
4　Currency translation differences will be adjusted against the profit and loss account balance shown on the balance sheet.
5　These figures show the total gain (or loss) from all sources that the company has made during the year.
6　Comparative figures are not shown.

Group balance sheet

As with the profit and loss account, the Companies Act 1985 allows a choice to be made between adopting a horizontal or a vertical format for the balance sheet. The horizontal format requires the assets to be laid out on the left-hand side of the page and the capital on the right-hand side. The vertical format lists the assets then the liabilities on a line-by-line basis. The vertical format will be most familiar to you as it has been adopted almost exclusively throughout this book. It is also common among many UK companies, although some companies do use the horizontal type.

Published balance sheets do not look very different from those prepared for internal purposes. The main differences are that: (1) they will normally be prepared for a group of companies; (2) they will be far more detailed than a sole trader's balance sheets; (3) they will include comparative figures; and (4) a great many pages of formal notes will be attached to them.

An example of a group balance sheet is shown in Exhibit 11.4 (comparative figures are not disclosed).

Exhibit 11.4 Example of a published balance sheet

Energy plc
Group balance sheet at 31 March 2002

	Group	Company
	£000	£000
Fixed assets (1)		
Intangible assets (2)	90	–
Tangible assets (3)	1 400	1 300
Investments (4)	70	1 300
(5)	1 560	2 600
Current assets (6)		
Stocks (7)	6 500	3 300
Debtors (8)	7 500	4 800
Investments (9)	60	–
Cash in bank and in hand (10)	700	20
(11)	14 760	8 120
Creditors: Amounts falling due within one year (12)	(8 500)	(7 000)
Net current assets (13)	6 260	1 120
Total assets less current liabilities (14)	7 820	3 720
Creditors: Amounts falling due after more than one year (15)	(3 000)	–
Provisions for liabilities and charges (16)	(1 200)	–
(17)	3 620	3 720
Capital and reserves (18)		
Called up share capital (19)	1 000	1 000
Share premium account (20)	500	500
Revaluation reserve (21)	600	900
Other reserves (22)	360	300
Profit and loss account (23)	1 040	1 020
(24)	3 500	3 720
Minority interests (25)	120	–
(26)	3 620	3 720

Approved by the board on XX June 2002

_____Director (27)

Notes:

(a) The numbers in brackets after each item refer to the tutorial notes below.

(b) Reference to the formal notes, and the notes themselves, are not included.

(c) Comparative figures have been ignored.

(d) The Exhibit contains dummy information.

Tutorial notes

1 The net book value of the fixed assets must be shown under three headings: (a) intangible assets; (b) tangible assets; and (c) investments.

2 Intangible assets are those assets that are not of a physical nature, such as goodwill, patents and development costs.

3 Tangible assets include land and buildings, plant and machinery, fixtures, fittings, tools and equipment.

4 Fixed assets investments are those that are intended to be held for the long term, i.e. in excess of 12 months.

5 This line is the total of all the fixed assets.

6 Current assets have to be analyzed into a number of categories (see notes 7 to 10 below).

7 Stocks must be disclosed into, e.g. raw materials and consumables, work-in-progress, finished goods and payments on account. The detail will be shown in a formal note.

8 Debtors have to be analyzed under trade debtors, other debtors, prepayments and accrued income. These will be included in a formal note.

9 Current assets investments are those investments held for the short term, i.e. normally for less than 12 months.

10 Cash at bank and in hand. This will be the same amount that will be included in the balance sheet prepared for internal purposes.

11 This line represents the total of current assets.

12 Creditors have to be analyzed between short-term creditors (i.e. those payable within the next 12 months), and long-term creditors (i.e. those that do not have to be paid for at least 12 months). Both short- and long-term creditors are analyzed into categories such as trade creditors, other creditors, and accruals and deferred income. The details will be found in a formal note.

13 The net current assets line is a subtotal of current assets (11) less creditors: amounts falling due within one year (12).

14 This is another subtotal: fixed assets (1) plus net current assets (13).

15 See 12 above.

16 Provisions for liabilities and charges include provisions for pensions and similar obligations, taxation and other provisions that are not specified in the Companies Act 1985.

17 This line represents the balance sheet totals.

18 The capital and reserves section is the other main part of the balance sheet. It explains how the net assets (17) have been financed.

19 The called up share capital represents all of the shares that have been issued, details of which will be shown in a formal balance sheet note.

20 The share premium account records the extra amount on top of the nominal value of their shares which shareholders were willing to pay when they bought their shares. It does not attract a dividend and the Companies Act permits only a few highly selected uses.

21 Some fixed assets, such as land and buildings, may be revalued. The difference between the revalued amount and the net book value will be credited to a revaluation reserve account. The balance cannot be distributed to shareholders.

22 Other reserves. This balance may include a number of other reserve accounts both of a capital nature (i.e. reserves that cannot be distributed to shareholders) and of a revenue nature (i.e. amounts that may be distributed to shareholders).

23 This is the total of all the profits that have not been distributed to shareholders, less those that have been put into special reserve accounts.

24 This is the total of the capital and reserves' section of the balance sheet. It represents shareholders' funds.

25 The minority interests represent that proportion of the net assets of subsidiary companies owned by shareholders outside the group.

26 This line should balance with line 17.

27 The balance sheet should be signed by at least one director.

Group cash flow statement

The construction of a cash flow statement (CFS) has already been examined in some detail in Chapter 8. Apart from reflecting the activities of a group of companies and the inclusion of comparative figures, published CFSs differ little from the format that was adopted in that chapter.

Unlike the profit and loss account and the balance sheet, CFSs do not have any statutory backing. They are, however, now considered so important that they are usually regarded as being one of the main financial statements. Indeed, FRS 1 requires most companies (small companies are the notable exception) to prepare a CFS. It is highly unlikely that you will come across a set of published accounts that does not include one.

An example of a group CFS is shown in Exhibit 11.5.

Exhibit 11.5 Example of a group cash flow statement

Energy plc
Group cash flow statement for the year ended 31 March 2002

	£000	£000
Cash flow from operating activities		2 820
Returns on investments and servicing of finance		(680)
Taxation		(660)
Capital expenditure and financial investment		(410)
Acquisitions and disposals		(180)
Equity dividends paid		(1 000)
Cash outflow before use of liquid resources and financing		(110)
Management of liquid resources		100
Financing – Issue of shares	100	
Increase in debt	490	590
Increase in cash in the period		580

Tutorial notes

1 The exhibit contains dummy information.
2 The formal notes that would normally be attached to the statement have not been included. Such notes (along with various reconciliations) give details about the make-up of each heading.
3 The above format is only a guide: it is not mandatory.
4 Apart from some items that relate only to a group, e.g. dividend received from associated undertakings, and purchase of subsidiary undertakings, the statement is very similar to the one used in Chapter 8.
5 Comparative figures have not been included.

Exhibit 11.5 is based upon the example given in FRS 1 but it is likely that you will come across other slightly amended formats. Some can be a little confusing, especially when some figures are shown in brackets. It might help to remember that the basic idea of a CFS is to show where the cash has come from and where it has gone to. A non-group CFS should contain seven main sections and a group CFS eight, namely:

1 operating activities;
2 returns on investments and servicing of finance;
3 taxation;
4 capital expenditure and financial investment;
5 acquisitions and disposals (group CFS only);
6 equity dividends paid;
7 management of liquid resources;
8 financing.

Heading 7 (management of liquid resources) and heading 8 (financing) may be combined provided that the cash flows relating to each heading are shown separately.

Most of the above sections will contain both cash received and cash paid. Items representing cash paid are normally inserted in brackets.

Notes to the accounts

The profit and loss account, the balance sheets and the cash flow statement are usually supported by a great deal of additional information in as 'Notes to the accounts'. Such notes serve two main purposes:
(1) they avoid too much detail being shown on the face of the accounts; and
(2) they make it easier to provide supplementary information.

One important point to remember is that the notes form an integral part of the accounts and that they are an essential element in the total amount of information that has to be disclosed. However, it is only fair to warn you that it is sometimes difficult to understand how some of the information fits into the overall accounts (such as the movement of the various reserve accounts). By contrast, some information is straightforward. For example, a note giving details about the company's profit before taxation will include such items as the depreciation charged to the profit and loss account for the year, the auditors' remuneration, and the amount of research and development expenditure.

Statement of directors' responsibilities for the accounts

In accordance with corporate governance principles, directors are required to state the nature of their responsibility for preparing the accounts. You should therefore find a statement to that effect somewhere within the accounts. Normally, it will appear immediately before the auditors' report. It should include information relating to the directors' legal requirements to prepare financial statements, their responsibility to maintain adequate accounting records, the adoption of suitable accounting policies, and the applicable accounting standards adopted in preparing the accounts.

Shareholder information

Towards the end of an annual report you might find some additional data. For convenience, we will refer to this as 'shareholder information'. Shareholder information may include some details about the financial results of the company over a five- or ten-year period, an analysis of the different types of shareholders, the company's financial calendar, notice of the annual general meeting, various names and addresses, and some information about the company's share price.

Conclusion

You are now recommended to study the contents of a published annual report with great care. (Most companies will supply you with a copy if you write to the Company Secretary.) Work through the report and see if it breaks down broadly into the various sections that we have used in this chapter, namely:

1 introductory material;
2 operational reports and reviews;
3 the accounts; and
4 shareholder information.

As far as the accounts are concerned, first read through the various reports, e.g. the statement of directors' responsibilities and the auditors' report. Then work your way through the statement of accounting policies. Next, tackle the main financial statements (the profit and loss account, the balance sheet and the cash flow statement) along with the accompanying notes to the accounts.

The amount of time that you will need to spend on perusing the various accounts, statements and reports will depend partly upon the size of the company and partly upon your own objectives. If you are thinking of investing in the company, for example, it may be necessary for you to take some of the data contained in the accounts and convert them into the types of accounting ratios covered in Chapter 9. However, if you are only interested in an overview of the company's results, you may need to check only the earnings per ordinary share, the liquidity position and the gearing.

Irrespective of your purpose, do not be put off by the sheer volume of information contained in an annual report. Cadbury Schweppes' Annual Report for 1999, for example, contained 148 pages. However, only 48 pages related directly to the financial statements. None the less, those 48 pages included a great deal of complex technical information that would take even an expert some time to sort out. Fortunately, as a non-accountant, you have now reached the stage in your studies where you should have sufficient knowledge about financial accounting and reporting to be able to extract all the information that you need.

Key points

1 An annual report contains a great many statements and reports. Some of these are not statutory or professional requirements.

2 A typical annual report may be divided into four main sections: introductory material, operational reports and reviews, the main accounts, and shareholder information.

3 The accounts of a group company will include a group profit and loss account, a statement of total recognized gains and losses, a group balance sheet (including the holding company's balance sheet), and a group cash flow statement. These statements will be supported by many pages of notes.

4 The accounts section will include a statement of accounting policies, an auditors' report and a statement outlining the directors' responsibilities for the preparation of the accounts.

5 An annual report will also include a directors' report. This report will contain a great deal of information about the company's management, operations and financial results.

Check your learning

1 What is the main section of an annual report?

2 Name four financial statements contained in the main section of an annual report.

3 Name five other statements or reports that you might find in an annual report.

4 What report/statement is regarded as being the one that is most likely to be consulted?

[*The answers to these questions may be found at the back of the book.*]

Group discussion questions

11.1 'A limited liability company's annual report should be made comprehensible to the average shareholder.' Discuss.

11.2 Examine the argument that annual reports are a costly irrelevance because hardly anyone refers to them.

11.3 Should companies be banned from including non-financial data in their annual report?

Assignment

11.4 Carry out the assignment as set out below.

Objectives:
1 to enable you to familiarize yourself with what is contained in a company's annual report; and
2 to know where to look for information within it.

Required:
(a) Obtain a copy of the annual report of a public limited liability company. You are encouraged to choose a manufacturing company or a retail company. Avoid banks, insurance companies and investment trusts as their reports are somewhat specialized.
(b) Using the report that you have obtained, complete the following schedule:

NAME OF COMPANY

YEAR END

MAIN OPERATING ACTIVITIES

CHAIRMAN'S NAME

CHIEF EXECUTIVE'S NAME

CHAIRMAN'S STATEMENT
  Tone of the Chairman's statement in respect of the company's future:
    highly optimistic ☐ optimistic ☐ neutral ☐ pessimistic ☐ highly pessimistic ☐

DIRECTORS' REPORT
  Amount of the recommended final dividend
  Charitable donations
  Political donations
  Job title of officer signing the report

ACCOUNTING POLICIES
  Accounting convention
  Depreciation rates for each major class of fixed assets

CONSOLIDATED PROFIT AND LOSS ACCOUNT
Turnover
Gross profit
Net profit before taxation
Net profit after taxation
Dividends paid and proposed
Retained profits
Earnings per ordinary share

CONSOLIDATED BALANCE SHEET
Fixed assets (total)
Cash at bank and in hand
Current assets (total)
Creditors: Amounts falling due within one year (total)
Net current assets/(liabilities) (total)
Creditors: Amounts falling due after more than one year (total)
Provisions for liabilities (total)
Shareholders' funds (total)

CONSOLIDATED CASH FLOW STATEMENT
Opening balance of cash in hand and at bank
Increase/(decrease) in cash in the period
Closing balance of cash in hand and at bank

NOTES TO THE ACCOUNTS
Geographical analysis of turnover:

Total operating profit
Geographical analysis of operating profit:

Total of tangible fixed assets' depreciation
Auditors' remuneration
Total of directors' emoluments
Average number of employees during the year

Debtors receivable after more than one year
Bank loans and overdrafts:
  in one year or less
  between one and two years
  between two and five years
  after five years
Issued share capital (total)
Profit and loss account balance

AUDITORS' REPORT
List any qualifications:

OTHER REPORTS AND STATEMENTS
List:

ACCOUNTING RATIOS

Calculate the following accounting ratios for the current year and (if possible) the previous year:

Current ratio

Acid test ratio

Gearing

Gross profit ratio

Net profit before tax

Net profit after tax

Return on capital employed

Stock turnover

Trade debtor collection period

Trade creditor payment period

Fixed assets ratio

OVERALL ASSESSMENT

Liquidity

very strong ☐ strong ☐ neutral ☐ weak ☐ very weak ☐

Profitability

very healthy ☐ healthy ☐ neutral ☐ sick ☐ very sick ☐

Efficiency

very efficient ☐ efficient ☐ neutral ☐ inefficient ☐ highly inefficient ☐

CONCLUSION

Insert below your conclusions on the overall financial strength of the company:

Elizabeth Lo and friends

Learning objectives

After preparing this case study, you should be able to:
- state the desirable characteristics of financial reports;
- design a questionnaire;
- interview the users of accounts;
- write up the results of your survey.

Background

Location   The University of East Cheshire: The Main Lecture Theatre

Personnel   Dale Galloway: Accounting Lecturer
Heather Watt: Student
Elizabeth Lo: Student

Synopsis

Elizabeth Lo was a first-year student in Business Studies at the University of East Cheshire. She had been born and brought up in Lighton, a small market town in the Midlands. Elizabeth was a bright and popular young woman, and she had many sports and activities in which she was involved. She had been hoping to go to one of the ancient universities to read Philosophy, but her 'A' level results had been somewhat disappointing. In desperation, and rather at the last minute, her father had managed to get her a place at East Cheshire.

Elizabeth soon settled down at East Cheshire, but initially she had no more interest in Business Studies than she had in going to the moon. The course was reasonably varied and she got on well with her fellow students. Although there were one or two subjects that some of the class hated, everyone found accounting quite boring.

Dale Galloway, their accounting lecturer, did his best but it was hard going for all of them. During the first term, they ploughed through the mechanics of double-entry book-keeping and it took a long time before it began to make sense. The one golden rule in accounting seemed to be that the answer to any question was the opposite of whatever you first thought.

In the spring term, the class began to study the format and structure of published financial statements. There were lots of rules to learn that were based partly on the Companies Act 1985 and partly on 'financial reporting standards' and 'accounting standards'.

As it was a degree class, Dale was very keen that the students should be highly critical of such procedures. Elizabeth was not alone in finding it very difficult to understand what he was talking about. It was not easy to remember all that they were supposed to learn and it was almost impossible to criticize something that was not very clear to you in the first place.

As the term went by, Elizabeth began to realize that accounting was not like simple arithmetic. She came to appreciate that, although you were supposed to follow a lot of accounting rules, it was possible to interpret them in any way you wished. It was quite a shock to find out that accountants were just as fallible as anybody else. You could *fix* accounting statements so that they showed what you wanted and yet you could still be following the rules! It was all very confusing.

Dale was even more scathing about the contents of an annual report. 'Just get hold of an annual report,' he invited the class. 'You have now done some accounting. Tell me honestly: does it mean anything to you?' Heather Watt, one of Elizabeth's friends, *did* get hold of an annual report. They both had a good look at it and agreed with Dale: it did appear to be meaningless.

By this time the class was thoroughly disillusioned. Although the students found the subject boring, they had understood that accountancy was a highly regarded profession. Now it appeared to be nothing more than a sophisticated confidence trick.

Fortunately, Dale was a very experienced lecturer. He realized that some of the class did not understand him, while the remainder had perhaps been put off accounting for life. He tried to argue that while the current method of reporting financial results was open to question, neither the accountancy profession nor anyone else had anything better to put in its place. In other words, he stated, 'It's better to be vaguely right, than precisely wrong.'

'Well, why doesn't your profession try to do something about making it precisely *right*?', asked Heather (who was one of the bolder elements in the class). 'Why, for example, don't you ask people, such as shareholders, what they want, instead of supplying all this information that you say is rubbish?'

'Now that's a very good question,' replied Dale without a trace of sarcasm in his voice. 'Perhaps we *should* be able to design financial reports that will be useful to those who want to use them.' A thought struck him. 'I tell you what. We'll make this the subject of a tutorial exercise. I think it would be a lot more interesting for you and it might either prove or disprove my point. How about it?' The class agreed, and Dale began preparing a suitable assignment.

By the next week he had come up with a few ideas. 'I want you to work in your respective tutorial groups,' he said. Elizabeth was pleased, because she was in a good tutorial group of only eight students (they were lucky at East Cheshire). 'As part of a group exercise I want you to do two things: first, find out from looking at books in the library what are the desirable characteristics of financial reports. Now, I think you will find that, while it is relatively easy to put them down on paper, it is less easy to apply them in practice.'

'And that takes me on to the second part of the exercise. I want you to do a survey of what use shareholders make of their annual reports. I want each group to prepare a report on its findings, and then to present it to the rest of the class. There are one or two suggestions on how you should go about doing this exercise in the hand-out I circulated at the beginning of the lecture. I think that four weeks should be long enough for the project, particularly as we shall not be holding any accounting lectures or tutorials during that time.'

The class cheered and Elizabeth became quite excited. This seemed a lot more interesting than sitting in an uncomfortable lecture theatre taking notes from dozens of overhead slides.

Required:

1 Desirable characteristics of financial reports:

    (a) Consult a number of articles, books and reports on financial reporting in your library or through the Internet. List the desirable characteristics of financial reports as outlined in such sources.

    (b) Obtain three sets of limited liability companies' annual reports. (Most companies will let you have a copy of their latest report if you write to the Company Secretary). Examine such reports. Assess them to see how far in your view they appear to contain the desirable characteristics of financial reports as outlined in the sources you have consulted in answering part (a).

2 Shareholders' information needs and requirements:

It would be interesting to find out what use shareholders make of a company's annual report, and what improvements they would like to see in its presentation.

    (a) Prepare a questionnaire suitable for surveying a number of shareholders in limited liability companies. You may need to consult a book on questionnaire design, but some idea of the type of questions that you might ask are listed in the Appendix at the end of this Case Study. Be careful that you do not ask questions that suggest a particular answer.

    (b) The next stage of the exercise is even more difficult. It perhaps would not be wise to stop people in the street and ask them if they would be prepared to answer some questions about their shareholdings! You could, however, ask a few members of your family or friends who are shareholders in public limited liability companies whether they would be prepared to answer your questions. You will not have the time to survey a totally representative group of shareholders but try and survey about ten people.

    (c) Prepare a written report on your findings, and present it to your tutorial group. In your conclusions, answer the following questions:

       – To what extent do shareholders use their annual reports?

       – What particular items are they interested in?

       – Can they follow the structure of them?

       – Do they understand the terminology used in the report?

       – Would they like a different type of annual report? If so, what?

Appendix   **Shareholders' Questionnaire**

The type of questions to ask:

1 Would you mind answering a few questions?

2 Do you have any shares in a company?

3 Did you buy the shares on the Stock Exchange?

4 Have you received an annual report from the company?

5 Can you tell from the envelope that it is an annual report?

6 Do you take it out of the envelope?

7 Do you look at the report at all?

8 Do you flick through it?

9 Do you look at the pictures?

10 Do you look at the advertising material?

11 Do you look at the other pages?

12 Do you read through the Chairman's report?

13 Do you read through the directors' report?
14 Do you have a look at the profit and loss account?
15 Do you go through the profit and loss account notes?
16 Do you have a look at the balance sheet?
17 Do you go through the balance sheet notes?
18 Do you go through the cash flow statement?
19 Do you look at any other part of the report?
20 Is there anything else you would like to see given in the report?
21 Have you any knowledge of book-keeping or accounting?

12 Contemporary issues in financial reporting

US rules 'too costly'

80% of European businesses say they would resist adoption of US standards

By Gavin Hinks

European businesses would resist adoption of US GAAP because international accounting standards are far cheaper to implement, according to a new survey.

In the midst of growing tension between competing sets of accounting standards, chief financial officers at four out of five European businesses say unequivocally that IASs offer similar quality to US GAAP but at a much lower implementation cost.

The International Federation of Accountants hope to push ahead with the drive to global standards at its meeting in Edinburgh next month.

Mark Vaessen, IAS advisory services partner with KPMG, who carried out the survey, said; 'Choosing a new financial reporting language is a strategic decision. In making a choice between different sets of GAAP, various factors need to be considered, including regulatory developments and the preferences of investors and analysts, as well as more pragmatic issues such as implementation costs and internal reporting impact.'

Accountancy bodies across the world give the appearance of converging on a common set of standards, but many in the profession believe the US is holding out against using IASs because it believes its own are far more rigorous.

Adopting US standards may open the door to new markets for European businesses but they appear set on holding out for IASs despite those opportunities. Many national regulators already allow foreign companies to file financial statements in accordance with IASs or GAAP. Some countries even allow domestic companies to pick and choose their accounting standards.

With this diverse environment governments and regulators across Europe are in the process of deciding to implement just one of the standards whether it be domestic GAAP, IASs or US. Vaessen said: 'A majority of respondents contemplating a change are considering adopting IASs, while another 29% are considering US GAAP. The result underlines the urgent need for globally accepted financial reporting standards.'

Accountancy Age, 20 April 2000. Reprinted with permission.

Accounting practices are becoming increasingly internationalized

In this chapter we are going to examine some of the problems that have arisen in financial reporting during the last few years. The ASB has tackled some of the issues and it may be that they have been satisfactorily resolved. It is likely, however, that more work needs to be done on some of them, while in other cases little attention has yet been given to them.

Our main aim in this chapter is to demonstrate to non-accountants that there is a lively debate taking place in accountancy circles about the need for improving financial reporting practices. The topics selected for study are necessarily selective and it is not possible to go into too much depth. If you go on to take a more advanced course in accounting, you will probably deal with them (and others) in a great deal of detail.

For convenience, we have divided the chapter into four main sections. The first section deals with *measurement issues*, the second section considers *understandability (i.e. comprehension) issues*, the third section covers *international issues*, and the fourth section discusses some *liberalization issues*.

By the end of this chapter, you should be able to:

- **list nine topics relating to current financial reporting issues;**
- **outline the main deficiencies of the historic cost accounting model;**
- **summarize the problems that non-accountants may have when consulting published financial statements;**
- **recognize the increasing internationalization of financial accounting and reporting practices;**
- **advance a case for preparing other types of reports for use by shareholders and other interested parties.**

Measurement issues

By *measurement issues* we mean those problems that have arisen because of the adoption of the historic cost accounting rule. You will recall that conventional financial accounting practice is to record transactions at their original or historic cost. There are a number of optional models but the preferred option is to record transactions at their *replacement cost*, i.e. to record them at what would be paid today instead of what might have been paid in some previous period.

The main advantage of the historic cost approach is that it is factual. In other words, there is usually no doubt about what was paid (or received), whereas with replacement cost accounting it is usually necessary to estimate what *might* have been paid. Reporting events based on their historic cost, however, may be misleading. Current sales revenue will be matched against historic costs. Thus if prices are rising, profits tend to be overstated and yet the goods sold will need to be replaced at their *current* cost. The same point applies to fixed assets, such as plant and machinery and furniture: depreciation will be based on their historic cost but the amount eventually set aside may not be sufficient to meet the *current* cost of their replacement.

Note that this problem arises irrespective of whether there is a general rise in prices or whether price rises are specific to individual assets and costs. The opposite problem may occur if prices fall. This is much less common and less sustained than increases in prices but it sometimes occurs when new products gradually become subject to competitive pressures, such as has happened in the last decade with computers and mobile telephones.

This inherent weakness of historic cost accounting has caused enormous difficulties for the accountancy profession. What has been done to tackle it? We start with the phenomenon of changing prices.

Inflation

For convenience, we will now refer to the problem of changing prices as 'inflation'. Inflation is not a new phenomenon; it has been present in most societies for at least 1000 years but it has only become a major problem in recent times. Britain, like many other advanced industrialized countries, experienced high bouts of inflation during the late 1970s and the early 1980s. On at least two occasions, inflation rose above 20 per cent per annum. Although this was historically high for Britain, inflation at this level was minor compared with some South American countries; it was not unusual at that time for some of those to experience inflation rates of several thousand per cent per annum.

In more recent times, inflation rates in Britain and in many other countries have been very low, i.e. well below 5 per cent per annum. None the less, while an annual inflation rate of (say) 3 per cent may appear to be low, it should be put into context. An annual rate of inflation of 5 per cent means that prices double over a period of about 15 years. This may seem to be a very long time but it should be remembered that some financial statements are intended to cover periods of 10 years. This means that costs and revenues recorded in (say) 2001 price terms are substantially different from those recorded in 2011 price terms. The same point applies to a comparison between 2001 and 2002 price terms (i.e. a one-year span), although with a low inflation rate the contrast is far less obvious.

Even so, it is somewhat misleading to compare the financial results of an entity for one year with those of another year when prices are rising even at a modest rate. It is sometimes difficult to understand that prices in 2002 are *not* the same as prices as in 2001; effectively, they are two different currencies (although they *look* the same). Thus it is almost as nonsensical to compare 2002 prices with those of 2001 as it is to compare financial reports prepared in current-year dollars with those prepared in current-year francs.

This problem of reporting in what is, in effect, different currencies appeared to be a growing and major problem when inflation in Britain (and elsewhere) was at a very high level. In 1980, after long and protracted discussion and after several unsuccessful attempts, the accountancy profession put forward an accounting standard (SSAP 16) to deal with the problem. The details need not concern us now but its requirements were based mainly on a replacement cost accounting system. The standard was very unpopular and it was withdrawn in 1985. It has never been replaced.

Since 1985, little attention has been given to the problem of accounting for inflation, partly because the accountancy profession was exhausted after a long-running debate, partly because no one knows what to do for the best, and partly because inflation has become less of a problem since that time.

In our view, however, the problem is still there. Consequently, when comparing data that relate to different years, you should allow for them not being strictly comparable because of changes in the purchasing power of the currency. You can do this by using the retail prices index as a guide. For example, assume that a company's sales revenue was £100 in 2001 and £108 in 2002 and that the inflation rate over that period was 5 per cent per annum. Multiply the 2001 sales revenue of £100 by 105% (100% + 5%), i.e. £105 (£100 × 105/100). Then compare the adjusted sales revenue of £105 for 2001 with the sales revenue of £108 in 2002. This gives a much fairer comparison: while sales have still risen (from £105 in 2001 to £108 in 2002 at constant prices) the rise is much less significant when inflation is taken into account.

Fixed asset valuations

We indicated above that during periods of rising prices the value of fixed assets is understated if they are included at their historic cost. Some entities adopt a *modified form* of historic cost accounting. Fixed assets are valued at their replacement cost and depreciation is then calculated on that basis. This approach goes some way towards recognizing the problem of changing prices, but it is not a substitute for it because it only deals with fixed assets.

Note that if the fixed assets are revalued, the amounts shown in the balance sheet are likely to be more realistic. However, by revaluing them and basing depreciation on a value in excess of the historic cost, the depreciation charge in the profit and loss account will be greater. Hence, all other things being equal, the profit for the period will be lower. None the less, this policy is often adopted to avoid the apparent undervaluation of assets on the company's balance sheet. Companies that have undervalued assets on their balance sheets are prone to unwelcome takeover bids!

Tangible (i.e. physical) fixed assets have been subject of a recent financial reporting standard (*FRS 15 – Tangible Fixed Assets*), issued in February 1999. The standard aims to codify existing accounting practice. It breaks no new ground and it has merely regularized much of what has anyway been fairly common policy.

Goodwill and intangible assets

Goodwill and other intangible assets (e.g. copyrights, patents and trademarks) are the subject of another FRS (*FRS 10 – Goodwill and Intangible Assets*). It was issued in December 1997.

The treatment of goodwill in company balance sheets has been a contentious issue for many years. A company may generate goodwill simply by being in business for a long time and having a favourable relationship with its customers, employees, and suppliers. This is known as *internally generated goodwill* and the standard does not permit it to be capitalized, i.e. to be shown on the balance sheet. Internally generated goodwill is very difficult to quantify and it may only be possible to do so when the entity or part of the entity is sold.

The type of goodwill with which the standard is mainly concerned is known as *purchased goodwill*. It arises when a company purchases another entity at a price that is in excess of what is regarded as being a fair value for its assets and liabilities. Purchased goodwill may be capitalized but it may then remain on the balance sheet until the company ceases to exist. Retaining goodwill on the balance sheet may appear to inflate the company's value because, over a period of time, purchased goodwill will normally be replaced by internally generated goodwill.

How, does FRS 10 require goodwill (including similar intangible assets) to be treated in financial reports? The ASB's requirement is to amortize (or depreciate) purchased goodwill. Normally, this should be done over a period of 20 years or less but a longer period may be chosen. Amortizing purchased goodwill means that, other things being equal, the value of the company as depicted in its balance sheet would appear to decline; similarly, the profit for the periods in which the goodwill is written off will be reduced.

Thus you will now see why the required treatment of goodwill, as as set out by FRS 10, is such a contentious issue. A requirement to reduce balance-sheet asset values and cut profits is not a matter that any company would normally wish to recommend to its shareholders!

Understandability issues

The term 'understandability' is the one used by the ASB in its *Statement of Principles for Financial Reporting*, which we discussed in Chapter 10. It is a clumsy term but it is useful for our purposes. The statement argues that 'Information provided by financial statements needs to be understandable – in other words, users need to be able to perceive its significance.' (para. 3.26)

This is a laudable aim but, as the Statement goes on to explain, understandability (i.e. comprehension) depends on how that information is dealt with, the way that it is presented and the capabilities of the users. The Statement argues that preparers of financial statements are entitled to assume that users have 'a reasonable knowledge of business and economic activities and accounting and a willingness to study with reasonable diligence the information provided' (para. 3.27). This is a highly arguable point.

As you will have gathered from the material covered in the previous two chapters, the format of financial statements is not easy to follow and the technical content is highly complex. We have also not introduced you to *detailed* group statements (the most common set of published accounts that you are likely to meet) or the pages of detailed notes attached to them. Indeed, it is our contention that the Statement's authors are being quite unrealistic when they argue that it is reasonable to assume that users have a reasonable knowledge of accounting, and especially that they have a willingness to study the information with reasonable diligence!

In our view, the dozens of pages of information now provided in financial statements and its growing complexity means that only those users who are prepared to devote a considerable amount of time to studying them in some depth can ever hope to have a grasp of them. The training given in this book has provided you with the basic requirements but we do not pretend that it is anything other than a beginning!

So what has been done to help those users who do not have 'a reasonable knowledge of accounting'? We discuss below two approaches that have been introduced in recent years, even though they do not meet with universal approval.

Summary financial statements

Instead of allowing companies to supply their shareholders with a complete set of annual accounts, the Companies Act 1989 permits companies to substitute what is supposed to be a simplified version. This substitute is known as a *summary financial statement* (SFS). The 1989 Act lays down certain requirements that should be included in a SFS, e.g. the inclusion of a summarized directors' report, a summarized profit and loss account, a summarized balance sheet and an auditors' report.

The move towards introducing SFSs came about mainly as a result of a number of privatizations in the late 1980s (such as British Telecom and the Trustee Savings Bank). The privatization programme was very popular but it meant that some of the newly privatized companies had to supply millions of shareholders with a copy of their annual accounts. Rightly or wrongly, it was believed that most of their shareholders would not be interested in, or capable of understanding, the accounts. Companies were also concerned about the cost of supplying so many copies to so many shareholders. Consequently, Parliament decided to give the opportunity for shareholders to opt (if they so wished) for a slimmer version of a company's annual financial statements.

In order to comply with this requirement of the Companies Act 1989, most companies inform each shareholder that unless they hear to the contrary, it will be assumed that the shareholder does *not* wish to receive the full set of accounts.

Bearing in mind this rather negative approach, it is not surprising that some 95 per cent of shareholders 'opt' (passively) for the summarized version!

SFSs are usually much shorter than the full version. The information required by the 1989 Act (as updated in 1995) can be contained in two pages, although some companies produce SFSs that are 50 pages in length and such SFSs are nearly as long as the full version! However, the format, the language and the technical aspects still remain formidable and SFSs not particularly understandable even for those users who have some accounting knowledge. Although the 1995 regulations permit companies to replace the statutory headings with their own descriptions (provided that the statutory order of the headings is still followed), there is little evidence to indicate that companies have taken advantage of this opportunity to *simplify* their SFSs.

The issue of what, where and how to supply information to users who have little accounting knowledge remains an ongoing problem and one that still needs more attention to be given to it.

Smaller entities

External financial reporting requirements tend to be geared towards large listed companies. The Companies Act 1985 allows small and medium-sized companies to file abbreviated versions of their annual accounts with the Registrar of Companies, although the full version has still to be supplied to their shareholders. As far as FRSs are concerned, however, they are generally supposed to be of relevance for those accounts that are intended to give a ' true and fair view' (which presumably means *all* accounts).

Many of the requirements are considered unnecessarily burdensome for smaller companies, especially those where the shares are owned by family members who are also employed in the business. The ASB has given recognition to this problem, and in March 2000 it issued a *Financial Reporting Standard For Smaller Entities* (FRSSE). The FRSSE basically applies to small companies. Those companies that adopt it are exempt from having to comply with other accounting standards and similar pronouncements.

The FRSSE is a recognition, therefore, that the complexity and volume of information that has to be disclosed publicly is not of universal application and that it is not necessarily relevant to every type of company. Nonetheless, the technical requirement underpinning the FRSSE are still considerable and much still needs to be done to make financial statements understandable to non-accountants.

International issues

Financial reporting requirements in Britain do not operate in a vacuum. Indeed, as we have seen, UK company law is now effectively European Union (EU) company law. None the less, the European law still only provides a framework, and the accountancy profession and the business community have to provide the detail through the semi-statutory accounting standards programme. This programme is heavily influenced by two external sources: international accounting standards and American financial reporting requirements.

International accounting standards

An International Accounting Standards Committee (IASC) was formed in 1973, one of its founder members being the United Kingdom. The IASC is a private body, financed largely by its members. Its aim is to make financial statements more comparable on a worldwide basis.

The IASC's method of working is similar to that of the ASB. By Spring 2000 it had issued 40 international accounting standards, most of them dealing with issues covered by British standards. As economic, financial, legal and political considerations differ so markedly in member countries, IASC requirements tend to be much more general than specific British standards. As far as Britain is concerned, this means that where the ASB's requirements cover similar topics to those of the international accounting standards, observance of the British ones usually means automatic compliance with those set internationally.

Many countries are too poor or too small to have their own accounting standards programme, so they tend to opt for the international standards and adapt them to suit their own particular requirements. The IASC has struggled to ensure that its programme has become more widespread, partly because it is an enormously difficult task to encourage up to 200 nations to work together, partly because of language problems (the working language is English), and partly because the United States has not been a willing partner in the enterprise.

American considerations

As far as company financial reporting is concerned, the United States is somewhat of a paradox. Few US states have detailed company-law provisions, whereas at the federal level, a relatively small number of listed companies are bound by some very severe restrictions. The federal system reflects the Securities Act 1933 and the 1934 Securities Exchange Act which established a Securities and Exchange Commission (SEC) to administer the securities regulations. The SEC operates a standards-setting process through a private-sector board called the *Financial Accounting Standards Board* (FASB) The FASB issues accounting standards similar to those of the ASB, although there are many more of them and they are usually in considerably more detail.

The stringent financial regulations for companies that have a stock exchange listing in the United States have important repercussions for overseas companies. If they wish to list on the New York Stock Exchange, for example, they must comply with US Generally Accepted Accounting Principles (GAAP) *regardless of the requirements of their own country.* As New

York listing is a necessity for many international companies, there has been a tendency for US GAAP requirements to become the norm.

The European Union has attempted to ensure that US GAAP has not become the *de facto* requirement for European companies, and the IASC has also attempted to fight a similar battle on a worldwide basis. The objective of both these bodies is to gain acceptance of the IASC requirements (the European Union having abandoned any idea of formulating its own accounting standards) by the SEC, thus enabling non-US companies to gain a listing in the United States provided that they comply with IASC standards.

What are the lessons of these international developments for non-accountants in Britain? Basically, two very broad ones: first, UK companies that trade abroad cannot ignore accounting and financial reporting requirements overseas; and, second, such requirements are likely to add to the amount and complexity of information that needs to be disclosed publicly.

Liberalization issues

In this section we are going to examine what we have termed 'liberalization' issues, that is, the idea of extending reporting requirements beyond their traditional financial boundaries.

The last few chapters have concentrated almost exclusively on the financial accounting and reporting requirement in so far as they affect shareholders. This mirrors the Companies Act 1985 which hardly refers to any other user group. However, as we have outlined in Chapters 2 and 10, the *Statement of Principles for Financial Reporting* identifies *seven* user groups. Just to remind you, besides shareholders (the Statement referring to them as investors) there are lenders, suppliers and other trade creditors, employees, customers, governments and their agencies, and the public. Furthermore, the information required to be disclosed by the Companies Act 1985 is almost entirely of a financial nature.

Two questions arise from this scenario.

1 Should current financial accounting and reporting requirements be extended to include other groups besides shareholders?
2 Should the requirements include non-financial information? We will discuss two of the ideas that have been put forward in recent years in response to these two questions: *corporate governance* and *social reporting*.

Corporate governance

The term 'corporate governance' has increasingly been adopted in the accounting and business world over the last 10 years to describe the methods by which companies are controlled and directed. Increasingly, the way in which directors operate companies has been subject to much public criticism. This has arisen because there have been some well publicised cases where shareholders appear powerless to control their own directors. Shareholders' annoyance has been further inflamed as a result of the apparent high salaries, bonuses and share options that directors appeared to have awarded themselves, sometimes irrespective of how the company has performed.

Although, legally, directors report to their shareholders, shareholders have very little practical power. In large public companies the vast majority of shares are owned by institutional holders, such as investment trusts and pension funds. At general meetings the combined votes of all the small shareholders usually make very little difference to the eventual outcome of any proposal. It is rare for the institutional shareholders to disagree publicly with the board of a public company; indeed, there is sometimes a complex interlocking of directorships between various institutions, so there is little incentive for directors to oppose each other. Effectively, therefore, a small group of individuals controls the operation of most of Britain's large commercial, financial and industrial institutions.

In a free enterprise system this might be acceptable if there were some way of enabling directors to account for their actions. However, the public perception is that a director of a poorly performing company may be dismissed with a handsome 'golden handshake' and then be rewarded almost immediately with a directorship in another (or possibly several) other companies.

Whether this portrayal of corporate life is generally accurate or true is somewhat debatable, but public perceptions matter because they often trigger a political response. At best, company directors may then fail to gain prestigious public appointments, awards, decorations and honours; at worst, the government may introduce some highly unwelcome company legislation before Parliament. Consequently, in view of growing public concern nowadays about the way that directors operate, companies have been encouraged to introduce a number of suggested improvements.

An attempt was made at self-regulation following the report of the Cadbury Committee in 1992. This committee was set up by the Financial Reporting Council, the London Stock Exchange and the accountancy profession collectively to make recommendations for the improvement of corporate governance. The committee put forward an extremely detailed Code of Practice. The Code is voluntary but it has resulted in more companies disclosing more details about their directors' responsibilities, the control they exercise over the company's operations, and the ways by which their remuneration is determined.

Since that time three other committees have also put forward further recommendations on various aspects of corporate governance: the Greenbury Report in 1995, which dealt specifically with directors' remuneration; the Hampel Report in 1998, which refined Cadbury and Greenbury's recommendations; and the Turnbull Working Party in 1999, which dealt more specifically with the internal control mechanisms of companies.

The details of these various committees need not concern us here. From our point of view, we merely need to know that their recommendations are adding to the amount of information disclosed in a company's annual report and that it includes information that goes well beyond the conventional financial statements.

Social reporting

We have indicated on a number of occasions throughout this book that the Companies Act 1985 is almost exclusively concerned with shareholders and that it contains few provisions that deal with other user groups. The traditional belief has been that, as shareholders provide the necessary finance and take the ultimate risk, their rights should be paramount.

The modern view is that, while the shareholders' *financial stake* in a company is of vital importance, there are other groups whose contribution is just as vital, e.g. lenders, employees, suppliers, the government and society generally. Thus it can be argued that such groups have a *non-financial investment* in the company that is just as relevant as a financial one. Employees, for example, invest their time and energy in the company, while local traders may base their business around it. It follows that the lives of everyone connected with the company is partly dependent on it. For example, who has the biggest stake in a company: an investor who owns a small number of shares, or a trader 20 per cent of whose goods are purchased by the company?

There is an argument, therefore, that other user groups have just as much a need for information about the company as have shareholders. Hence the need for supplying them with their own special reports. Such reports are usually referred to as 'social reports'.

As there are no statutory or professional requirements covering social reports, we can only speculate about their format and contents. A comprehensive social report that has been prepared for use by all the stakeholder groups would probably be impracticable since it would be too unwieldy and contain a great deal of information that was of no interest to some users. Separate social reports prepared for different groups would perhaps be more appropriate. The information presented is likely to be more narrative than quantitative because research shows that most users find narrative statements easier to understand. They would also tend to concentrate on non-financial data (both current and projected) that closely matches the interest of the particular user group being addressed. The employees group, for example, will be particularly interested in details about company wages, salaries, pensions and working conditions, while suppliers and other trade creditors will be more concerned about the company's liquidity and prospects for the future.

A few companies are now producing social reports – or at least including some material in their annual report and accounts that may be classed as 'social'. Environmental matters, for example, are causing great concern to the public at the moment, and some companies are either addressing such concerns in their annual reports or producing a separate *environmental report*. An environmental report is likely to contain information about the company's success in dealing with pollution, its use of scarce resources, and the methods used to dispose of waste and scrap.

Social reports in general and environmental reports in particular are extremely wide-ranging. It is envisaged, therefore, that non-accountants are more likely to play a significant role in their compilation than has been the case with financial reports. There is thus an opportunity for you to become directly involved in a new form of reporting that is not constrained by legal or professional considerations.

Conclusion

In this chapter we have examined a number of contemporary issues in financial reporting.

First, there are a number of measurement issues that have arisen because of the adoption of the historic cost accounting model. While the ASB has tackled many of the problems that this model causes (such as the treatment of tangible fixed assets, and goodwill and other intangible assets), the problem of inflation accounting is still unresolved.

Second, current financial accounting practice raise considerable 'understandability' problems. In corporate reporting, for example, the annual report supplied to shareholders tends to be highly technical, written in an unfriendly language and takes a long time to absorb. Shareholders may opt to receive a Summary Financial Statement but this does not mean that it is a simplified version of the annual report. The technical and volume problems, however, have been recognized by the ASB and small companies now have their own financial reporting standard (FRSSE).

Third, British corporate reporting is becoming more internationalized. Company law is already effectively European law and the ASB's pronouncements are increasingly been affected by the work of the International Accounting Standards Committee and the Financial Accounting Standards Board in the United States.

Finally, there is a move to expand corporate reporting beyond the traditional boundaries. Indeed, there is ongoing pressure on the authorities to include both non-quantifiable and non-financial information in corporate reports, so that company directors can become much more accountable for their actions. At the same time, there is a move to prepare 'social reports' (including details of environmental considerations, for example) for supply to other user groups.

Key points

1 The traditional accounting model is known as the *historic cost convention*. In an advanced manufacturing and information technology era, this model is subject to a number of measurement problems, e.g. the valuation of fixed tangible and intangible assets and the instability of prices (especially when prices are rising).

2 The ASB is gradually issuing Financial Reporting Standards to deal with these measurement problems but it has not yet dealt with the problem of inflation.

3 Annual accounts at present supplied to shareholders are long and complex, although shareholders can opt for a summarized version. Other user groups have no legal right to receive either the annual accounts or the summarized version. The ASB has now issued a financial reporting standard specifically tailored for the needs of small companies (FRSSE).

4 British corporate reporting is based on European law and increasingly on international practice through the work of the International Accounting Standards Committee. It is also strongly influenced by US financial reporting requirements.

5 Attempts are being made to push back the traditional boundaries of corporate reporting so that reports are regularly prepared for users groups other than shareholders. Such reports are known as social reports. A social report may include matters relating to environment considerations or a separate environmental report may be prepared. Social reports are not covered by any legal, professional or other mandatory requirements and they are at an early stage of development.

Check your learning

1 State whether each of the following statements is true or false:
   (a) Non-purchased goodwill should be retained on the
       balance sheet.   True/False
   (b) Purchased goodwill should be written off the profit and loss
       account immediately it is acquired.   True/False
   (c) Fixed assets may be included on the balance sheet at their
       replacement cost.   True/False
   (d) By using the historic cost accounting model during a period of
       inflation, profits are normally reduced.   True/False

2 What do the following initials stand for?
   (a) HCA;   (b) SFS;   (c) FRSSE;   (d) IAS;   (e) FASB.

3 With what particular issue do you associate the Cadbury Committee?

4 Which accounting standard or financial reporting standard covers the preparation and presentation of a social report?

[The answers to these questions may be found at the end of the book.]

Group discussion questions

12.1 Discuss the proposition that, because inflation in Britain is now at a low level, there is no need for the accountancy profession to worry about inflation accounting.

12.2 How far do you think that it is possible to produce a simplified financial statement for shareholders that would be both relevant and reliable?

12.3 Should accounting practices be harmonized (i.e. brought closer together) or standardized (i.e. made the same)?

12.4 What should be included in an environmental report prepared by a company for issue to the local community?

PART 3

Management accounting

13 The framework of management accounting

XS finance chief quits after accounting errors

By David Blackwell

Philip Bunt resigned yesterday as finance director at XS Leisure, after the bowling alley and pool bar group announced that accounting errors would leave it nursing loses for the year to March 31.

The group said the monthly management accounts "appear to have overstated the company's profitability by a considerable margin."

The shares – 65p when the company moved from Ofex to Aim last summer – fell 14.5p to close at 54.5p.

The group said the losses for last year would be "exacerbated by abortive acquisition costs incurred in connection with a proposed acquisition that had to be abandoned in March as a result of the inaccuracies in the company's management accounts."

The directors are understood to have been unaware until late last week that its 10-pin bowling alley in Worsley, Manchester, was making a loss.

Financial Times, 28 March 2000. Reprinted with permission.

In previous chapters we have been almost exclusively concerned with *financial* accounting and reporting, In this part of the book we are going to deal with *management* accounting The part contains eight chapters, each dealing with various aspects of management accounting.

In this the first chapter, we provide a framework for the remaining seven chapters. The chapter falls into four main sections: the first section describes the nature and purpose of management accounting; the second provides a brief historical review of the development of the discipline; the third section outlines the main functions of management accounting; and the fourth section assesses the behavioural implications of management accounting.

Learning objectives

By the end of this chapter, you should be able to:

- describe the nature and purpose of management accounting;
- outline its historical development;
- summarize the six main functions of management accounting;
- assess the impact of management accounting on human behaviour.

Nature and purpose

Management accounting is one of the five main branches of accounting. Accounting, you will recall, is a specialized service function involving the collection, recording, storage and summary of data (primarily of a financial nature), and the communication of information to interested parties. *Financial accounting* deals mainly with information normally required by parties that are *external* to an entity, e.g. shareholders or government departments. *Management accounting* has a similar role, except that the information supplied is normally for parties *within* an entity, e.g. management. In summary, therefore, we put forward the following definition of management accounting:

> **Management accounting** is a functional activity involving the collection, recording, storage, and summary of both financial and non-financial data and the communication of information to interested parties working mainly within an entity.

It should be noted that financial accounting is not necessarily concerned exclusively with financial information, and it will also be of interest to various internal managerial parties such as the board of directors and divisional directors. Similarly, management accounting is not restricted solely to the supply of management information, and it may be of relevance to some external parties (e.g. the government). The essential points that make management accounting different from financial accounting, can be summarized as follows:

1 *Non-mandatory.* There are no statutory or compulsory professional requirements covering management accounting.

2 *Data volume.* More data are normally incorporated into a management accounting system.

3 *Qualitative data.* Management accounting information increasingly includes both quantitative and qualitative data.

4 *Non-monetary data.* Management accounting data that cannot be translated into monetary terms may still be used in reporting to interested parties.

5 *Forecasted and planned data.* Data of both a historic and a forecasted or planned nature is of considerable importance and relevance in management accounting.

6 *Users*. Management accounting is primarily concerned with providing information for use *within* an entity.

It is clear, therefore, that, unlike financial accountants, management accountants have considerably more freedom in providing information that meets the specific requirements of interested parties. The main parties interested will normally be the entity's junior and senior managers.

Historical review

Until the 18th century, Britain was primarily an agrarian society and there were comparatively few recognizable industrial entities (as we now call them). Furthermore, most entities (of whatever type) were relatively small, and they were largely financed and managed by individuals or their families. Consequently, it was largely unnecessary to have formal documentary systems for planning, control and reporting purposes because the entities were small enough for the owners to assess these considerations for themselves on a day-to-day basis.

During the 18th century, Britain became the first country in the world to undergo an Industrial Revolution. In just a short period of time she changed from a predominantly agricultural society to an industrial one, and by the 19th century she had become a major industrial power in the world. There were two specific consequences of this development that we should note. First, the new industrial enterprises needed large amounts of capital; individuals and their families could not provide the necessary funds. Capital had to be sought from 'investors' whose interest in the enterprise was largely financial. Such investments were extremely risky and there was the strong possibility of personal bankruptcy. Hence Parliament intervened and introduced the concept of *limited liability* into company law. Second, the new enterprises needed specialist staff to operate and manage them. Such staff had often to be recruited from outside the immediate family circle.

The above two factors resulted in the ownership of the enterprise being divorced from its management. In a number of Company Acts passed in the 19th and 20th centuries, Parliament decided that shareholders in limited liability companies should have a right to receive a minimum amount of information annually and that auditors should be appointed to report to shareholders on the information presented to them by the company's management.

The complexity, scale and size of the new industrial enterprises meant that it was difficult for professional managers to control them on the basis of personal knowledge and observation. Hence some form of documentary reporting system was required. At first this revolved round the statutory annual accounts, but it soon became clear that such accounts were produced too late, too infrequently, and in too little detail for effective day-to-day managerial control. As a consequence, during the period 1850 to about 1900, a more detailed recording and reporting system was devised. We now refer to this as a *cost accounting system*. Its main purposes were to provide sufficient information for the valuation of closing work-in-progress and finished goods, and for calculating the costs of individual products. In the early days, it was common for financial accounting systems and cost accounting systems to run side by side. As they incorporated much common data, they gradually became merged into just one system.

The main developments in management accounting occurred in the United States at the beginning of the 20th century and by 1925 most of the practices and techniques used today were established. Indeed, between 1925 and 1980 few new developments in management accounting took place. The position has changed somewhat during the last 20 years or so, and many new ideas have been put forward. Some of them have been incorporated into practice, albeit mainly by large companies.

While management accounting techniques were rapidly developed and practised fairly widely in the United States from the beginning of the 20th century, progress was much slower in Britain. Apart from the largest industrial companies, the application of management accounting did not become common until about 1970; even now, there is evidence that many smaller entities still depend on what is called 'back of the envelope' exercises for managerial planning and control purposes. It should also be noted that, over the same period, manufacturing industry in many industrial nations has given way to service industries. This means that many of the traditional management accounting issues, such as stock control and pricing, standard costing and product costing are of much less significance than they once were. None the less, they are still of some considerable relevance and we will be covering them in subsequent chapters.

Main functions

The overall role of a management accountant within an entity is to collect data and to provide information to management. Six specific functions can be readily identified, which we describe in further detail in the rest of this section. They are:

1 Planning;
2 Control;
3 Cost accounting;
4 Decision making;
5 Financial management;
6 Auditing.

Planning

Planning can be classified into two broad groupings: long-term planning and short-term planning.

Long-term planning

Long-term planning is commonly called *strategic planning* or *corporate planning*. We will refer to it as 'strategic planning' because this appears to be the most widely used term. *Strategy* is a military term meaning the ability to plan and organize manoeuvres in such a way that the enemy is put at a disadvantage. Over the last 20 years, strategic planning has become an important managerial function in both profit-making and not-for-profit entities. In essence, it involves working out what the entity wants to achieve in the long term, i.e. beyond a calendar year, and how it intends to achieve it.

Six basic steps are involved in preparing a strategic plan:

- *Step 1*: Establish the entity's objectives, for instance to earn a minimum of 20 per cent on capital employed. ('*Where do we want to be in x years' time?*')
- *Step 2*: Assess the entity's current position. ('*Where are we now?*')
- *Step 3*: Estimate the external (e.g. economic, financial and political) factors that will apply during the period of the plan. ('*What is the outside world likely to be like?*')
- *Step 4*: Specify the differences that there are between the current and the required future position. ('*What gaps are there between where we are now and where we want to be?*')
- *Step 5*: Conduct a SWOT analysis. ('*What are our strengths, weaknesses, opportunities and threats?*')
- *Step 6*: Prepare a strategic plan. ('*What do we have to do to get towards where we want to go?*')

Strategic planning is not specifically a management accounting function. The senior management of the entity will probably set up a multidisciplined strategic planning team that may include a management accountant. The management accountant's major role will be to collect data and provide information required by the strategic planning team. In particular, the strategic plan itself will normally include various financial statements, such as profit and loss accounts (or similar income statements), balance sheets, and cash flow statements.

Short-term planning

Accountants normally refer to short term planning as *budgeting*, the short-term being regarded as being a period of up to a calendar year. Budgeting is covered in Chapter 15.

Control

A clear plan of what an entity wants to do and how it intends to get there is clearly preferable to having no plan at all; otherwise the entity will just drift. However, an additional benefit of planning is that it can also form part of the control mechanism of the entity. What management accountants do is to measure what has actually happened over a certain period of time and then compare it with what was planned to happen. Any apparent significant differences, or *variances* as they are called, are investigated and, if they are not acceptable, action is taken to ensure that future actual events will better meet the agreed plan. It may be found, for example, that the actual price paid for some raw materials was £5 per kilo when the plan allowed for a payment of only £4.50 per kilo. Why was there a variance? Was it poor planning? Was it impossible to estimate the actual price more accurately? Was it inefficient purchasing? Were higher-quality materials purchased and, if so, was there less wastage?

Not all variances are unwelcome. For instance, 1000 units might have been sold when the plan only allowed for sales of 950 units. The reasons for this variance should still be investigated, and if this favourable trend were deemed likely to continue, it would be necessary to ensure that additional resources (e.g. production, administration, distribution, and finance) were made available to meet higher expected levels of sales.

Note that it would be the responsibility of the management accounting to co-ordinate the investigation of any variances and report back to the senior management of the entity. *It would not be the responsibility of the management accountant to take any disciplinary action if a variance had been caused by inefficient management.* This is a point that is not always understood by those employees who come into contact with management accountants!

Further aspects of control are covered in Chapters 15 and 16.

Cost accounting

Historically, cost accounting has been the main function of management accounting. It is now much less significant and other functions, such as the provision of information for decision making, have become much more important. The cost accounting function involves the collection of the entity's ongoing costs and revenues, the recording of them in a double-entry book-keeping system (a task that these days is normally done by computer), the balancing of the 'books', and the extraction of information as and when required by management. Cost accounting also involves the calculation of *actual costs* of products and services for stock valuation, control and decision-making purposes.

We return to the subject of cost accounting in Chapter 14.

Decision making

The provision of information for decision making is now one of the major functions of management accountants. Although actual costs collected in the cost accounting records may provide some guidance, decision-making information usually requires dealing with anticipated or expected future costs and revenues and it may include data that would not normally be incorporated in a traditional ledger system.

Most decisions are of a special or 'one-off' nature, and they may involve much ingenuity in obtaining information that is of assistance to managers in determining a particular decision. Note that it is the managers themselves who will (and should) take the decision, not the management accountants.

Various aspects of decision making are covered in Chapters 17, 18 and 19.

Financial management

The financial management function associated with management accounting generally is again one that has become much more significant in recent years. Indeed, financial management has almost become a discipline in its own right. Its main purpose is to seek out the funds necessary to meet the planning requirements of the entity, to make sure that they are available when required, and to that they are used efficiently and effectively.

Financial management is not covered in any depth in this book, although we do return briefly to it in Chapter 19.

Auditing

Auditing involves the checking and verification of accounting information and accounting reports. There are two main types of audit: external and internal.

External auditing may be regarded as part of the financial accounting function, while internal auditing is more of management accounting responsibility. External auditors are not employees of the entity that they happen to be auditing, whereas internal auditors are employed by, and answer to, the entity's management. Thus there is an essential difference between the two types. In practice they may work closely together. Furthermore, internal auditors may be involved in assessing the effectiveness and efficiency of management systems generally, rather than concentrating on the cost and financial records.

Auditing is not considered any further in this book.

Behavioural considerations

The collection of data and the supply of information are not neutral activities; that is, they have an impact on those who are involved in supplying and receiving such material. The impact can be strongly negative and it can adversely affect the quality of the data or information. In turn, this may cause management to take some erroneous decisions because of unreliable data and biased information. This is a feature of the job that accountants are now trained to recognize, so that they are aware of the *behavioural impact* that they have on other employees. What relevance is this for non-accountants?

A great deal of the data required for financial accounting and external auditing purposes is supported by legislation. Thus the requirements cannot be ignored, irrespective of whether the entity as a whole or individuals within it regard them as being irrelevant. Data will be required to meet any statutory requirements and, if necessary, the financial accountants and auditors can *demand* whatever information they need.

Management accountants do not have statutory backing, but their position is still an extremely powerful one because they usually receive strong support from the entity's senior management. This can cause a great deal of hostility because management accountants can make demands knowing that they will be backed by the senior managers. Furthermore, they often earn salaries and enjoy working conditions that are the envy of other employees. It is not surprising, therefore, that, as the following quotation indicates, there is often an assumption that the accountant 'runs things':

> *I'm sad that a way of life is disappearing – unfortunately it's accountants who run our lives today rather than the demands of mariners.*
>
> (Angus Hutchison, who had just begun his final shift at the last manned lighthouse in Scotland. Quoted in *The Scotsman*, 5 March 1998, p. 2.)

There are three general points to make about such a view:

- financial considerations should form only a part of an overall decision;
- accountants should only make recommendations to senior managers; and
- the ultimate decision should be taken by the senior management.

Management accountants are employed to *provide a service to managers*. This means that, as nearly all employees have some managerial responsibilities, management accountants may be in direct contact with practically all employees. Thus, irrespective of your own role within an entity, you can expect to have some contact with management accountants. This should not be regarded as an 'us and them' situation (neither by you nor by them); you are all part of a team and it can be mutually beneficial if you can work together in reasonable harmony.

What approaches, therefore, should you expect a management accountant to adopt when working with you? We would suggest that at the very least, you are entitled to expect the following:

1 *Equality.* Management accountants should treat you as an equal and they should make it obvious that your contribution is just as valuable as their own.
2 *Non-autocracy.* Management accountants should not adopt an autocratic, condescending and superior attitude when dealing with other employees.
3 *Diplomacy.* Management accountants should be courteous, patient, polite, and tactful when dealing with you.
4 *Information.* You are entitled to a detailed explanation of why, what and when some information is required and in what form it should be presented.
5 *Assistance.* Management accountants should be prepared to give you a great deal of help in providing the information that they need.
6 *Timing.* You should be given a realistic amount of time to provide any information that is required, taking into account your other responsibilities.

7 *Non-disciplinarian.* Management accountants should not imply that you may be subject to disciplinary action if you do not comply with their requests.

8 *Training.* You should receive some formal training in the operation of the various management accounting systems that reflects your particular responsibilities.

In practice, the above requirements may be somewhat idealistic. Sometimes, for example, senior managers do not encourage a participative approach and they may not always be willing to provide appropriate training courses. The management accountants in the entity then have a responsibility to point out that the planning and control systems that operate in such an environment are not likely to be particularly successful.

It must also not be forgotten that the relationship between management accountants and non-accountants is not one-sided and that non-accountants have an equal responsibility to be co-operative. Clearly, management accountants will find it difficult to work with staff who adopt a resentful or surly manner and who try to make life difficult for them.

Conclusion

This chapter has provided a framework for a more detailed study of management accounting. Management accounting is one of the five main branches of accounting. Its main purpose is to supply information to management for use in planning and controlling an entity, and in decision making. It evolved out of financial accounting towards the end of the 19th century, when basic financial accounting systems could not provide managers with sufficient timely information for use in stock control and product costing. In the early part of the 20th century, management accounting came to be recognized as a useful planning and control mechanism. More recently, it has become an integral part of overall managerial decision making. The discipline now has six main recognizable functions: planning, control, cost accounting, decision making, financial management and auditing.

There are no statutory or mandatory professional requirements that govern the practice of management accounting. None the less, management accounting techniques are now regarded as being of considerable benefit in assisting an entity to achieve its longer-term objectives. As a result, management accountants tend to hold senior positions in most entities and they may wield considerable power and influence. Even so, their work can be largely ineffective and the quality of the information that they provide poor, if they do not receive the wholehearted support of their fellow employees. Unless this is forthcoming, the eventual decisions taken by management, based on the information provided by the management accountants, may possibly lead to errors in the way the entity is run.

We will be returning to many of the points outlined in this chapter in subsequent chapters. Chapter 14 deals with costing accounting, while Chapters 15 and 16 cover some detailed aspects of short-term planning and control. Basic decision making is outlined in Chapters 17, 18 and 19. Chapter 20, the last chapter in the book, reviews some contemporary issues in management accounting.

Key points

1 Management accounting is one of the five main branches of accounting.

2 Its main purpose is to collect data and provide information for use in planning and control, and for decision making.

3 Management accounting evolved, in the second half of the 19th century, out of financial accounting because more detailed and more timely information was needed for stock control and for product costing.

4 It began to be used as a planning and control technique in the early part of the 20th century.

5 In more recent years, management accounting techniques have become incorporated into managerial decision making.

6 Six main functions of modern management accounting can be recognized: planning, control, cost accounting, decision making, financial management, and auditing.

7 Management accounting practices can have a negative impact on both the providers and the users of information if management accountants adopt an autocratic and non-participative attitude.

8 A negative approach to management accounting requirements may result in poor-quality information and erroneous decision making.

Check your learning

1 Fill in the missing blanks in each of the following statements:
   (a) Financial accounting is more concerned with reporting to parties _____ to an entity.
   (b) _____ accounting is more concerned with internal reporting.
   (c) Planning and control is essential in an entity in order to ensure that it is run _____ and _____.
   (d) Management accounting systems imposed on other managers can result in the system being ignored and a lack of _____.
   (e) _____ and control go together like debit and credit.

2 What Act of Parliament covers management accounting practice?

3 Give two reasons why 19th-century financial accounting was not useful in product costing.

4 List the six main functions of management accounting.

5 Determine whether the following statements are generally true or false:
   (a) Cost accounting is based on forecasted data.   True/False
   (b) Decision making normally incorporates only historic data.   True/False
   (c) Strategic planning involves preparing plans only for a
       short-term period.   True/False
   (d) Control means sacking managers whose actual results exceed
       their budgets.   True/False
   (e) Cost accounting is irrelevant in a service based economy.   True/False

[*The answers to these questions may be found at the back of the book.*]

Group discussion questions

13.1 Examine the usefulness of management accounting in a service based economy.

13.2 The first step in preparing a strategic plan is to specify the entity's goals.
     Formulate three possible objectives for (a) a manufacturing entity; and (b) a national
     charity involved in animal welfare.

13.3 Assess the importance of taking into behavioural considerations when operating a
     management accounting system from the point of view of (a) the management
     accountant; and (b) a senior departmental manager.

Practice questions

[*Note: The questions marked with an asterisk have answers at the back of the book.*]

13.4* Distinguish between financial accounting and management accounting.

13.5* Describe the role of a management accountant in a large manufacturing entity.

13.6 Outline the main steps involved in preparing a strategic plan.

13.7 What is the difference between 'planning' and 'control'?

13.8 'Management accountants hold an extremely powerful position in an entity, and this
     enables them to influence most of the decisions.' How far do you think that this asser-
     tion is likely to be true in practice?

No problem

Learning objectives

After preparing this case study, you should be able to:

- describe the nature and purpose of a management accounting system;
- list the benefits of such a system;
- state the problems inherent in quantifying the benefits;
- prepare a report for management on a management accounting system.

Background

Location   Yewtree Limited: the Managing Director's office

Personnel   Mark Pope: Managing Director
Alison Webster: Senior Auditor, Simey and Simey,
Chartered Accountants

Synopsis

Following the completion of the audit for the year to 30 June 2001, a meeting had been arranged between Mark Pope, the Managing Director of Yewtree Limited, and Alison Webster, a Senior Auditor in Simey and Simey, the company's auditors.

After the usual pleasantries, Mark got down to business. As befitted his army training, he did not believe in wasting time. 'Now, what was it you wanted to see me about, Alison?' he enquired.

'Well, as you will recall, Mark, we usually hold a post-audit meeting. The audit has gone very well this year, and we're quite happy with the accounts. This time, what we really wanted to do was to have a close look at the future of the company.'

Mark immediately pricked up his ears. 'You mean you think we've got problems?' he queried, the alarm registering in his voice.

'Not in the immediate future,' responded Alison, 'but there are one or two matters that we would like to advise you about.'

Mark was not easily placated. 'What on earth do you mean?' he asked somewhat aggressively. 'We seem to be doing all right. Surely there can't be a problem?'

'No real problem,' replied Alison. 'I agree that everything seems fine, but be honest now. We did an interim audit towards the end of the financial year, and you were having some problems then, weren't you?'

'Yes,' admitted a somewhat reluctant Managing Director, 'but once you pointed them out, we took immediate action.'

Alison smiled to herself. Mark had walked right into a fairly obvious trap. 'Oh yes,' she said, 'but only when the year was almost over. It's probably only because you had good results up until December that the overall results for the year appear satisfactory.'

'I don't see how you can say that,' muttered Mark. 'You can't be sure.'

'That's exactly the point I am making,' said Alison. 'You don't really know, and neither, for that matter, do we.'

'Well, we pay you to tell us these things,' Mark snapped back. 'And if I may say so, we pay you rather a lot.'

'Actually, you don't,' replied Alison. 'I mean, you don't pay us to advise on such matters. Your shareholders pay us to do the audit. Advice about the management of the company is outside the audit, and it is not strictly part of our function.'

Mark backtracked a little. 'Be that as it may, what are you trying to tell me?'

Alison consulted her notes. 'Basically, Mark, we think that you and your senior staff have found it more and more difficult in the last few years to control the company. The company has grown considerably, and now you all spend most of your time at your desks, and less time on the shop floor seeing what's going on.'

'Yes, I know,' Mark murmured. 'It certainly wasn't like that in the old days, still less so in the army, but I do my best.' He had a feeling that he was not going to like what he was about to hear.

'Of course, Mark. I appreciate that. But it does mean that you don't *really* know what's gone on until the annual accounts are ready. When the company was small, you were always wandering around the place. You knew everybody. Everybody knew you, and you could tell if something was not quite right.'

'I must admit, I preferred the old days. But what are we to do? We can't turn the clock back.'

'I'm not suggesting you should, Mark. What I think you should do now is to install what we call a "management accounting system".'

'What? Even more book-keeping?' glared a somewhat revitalized Managing Director. 'More staff. More office space. More paperwork. I thought that you had always warned us against too much administration.'

'Well, there would be an extra cost,' admitted Alison, 'although I would expect the benefits to outweigh the costs.'

'What benefits?' queried Mark.

'*Substantial* benefits, I should think,' parried Alison. 'At the moment you get most information from the annual accounts. That's a long time since some of the events took place. That means you have little idea whether anything's gone wrong until it's too late. And, even worse, you just guess when you are asked to quote a price for an order.'

'I've always been very good at that,' replied Mark, very much on the defensive.

'Yes, but you've less time for that now and, frankly, your staff are not as good at it as you were.'

Mark noted the past tense and, in his heart of hearts, he knew that Alison was right. It was not easy to take such criticism about yourself and the company that you had founded. After his army service, the company became Mark's only love, and now here was this jumped-up book-keeper daring to criticize the only thing that mattered to him.

Mark broke the silence. 'I suppose this company has prospered because I've always been willing to consider new ideas, and I'm not going to stop now. I will think about this "management accounting system" you've mentioned, but I'm not having more administration just for the sake of it. I know that there are fashions in accounting, just as there are in anything else. If I buy it, it will have to pay for itself.'

'I agree with you, Mark, although frankly it is difficult to prove on paper that such a system pays for itself.'

'Well, there you are,' said Mark. 'But I've said I would consider it, and I will. Can you look into it for me?'

'Actually, Mark, that's a bit difficult for my firm to do. You see, we are your company's auditors, and we cannot get too involved in such work. But I tell you what I can do in the meantime. I will get one of my colleagues to prepare a report for your Board. If you like it, maybe our management consultancy firm could take the project over. Would that arrangement suit you?'

Mark said that it suited him fine, and at that point, the meeting was concluded.

Required:

Assume that you are employed by Alison Webster's management consultancy firm and that you have been asked to draw up a preliminary report suitable for presentation to the Board of Directors of Yewtree Limited. Prepare such a report.

Note that before preparing your report you are advised to consult a number of management accounting textbooks in your library and to refer to issues of *Management Accounting* (the Journal of the Chartered Institute of Management Accountants) over the last 12 months. Make a note of any material that is likely to be of relevance to your report.

14 Cost accounting

Renault aims to continue scheme to reduce costs

By Tim Burt

Renault, the French automotive group, is planning a further aggressive cost-cutting drive after reducing its overheads by FFr13bn ($2.03bn, £1.98bn) in the past two years.

Pierre-Alain De Smedt, Renault's chief operating officer, said it would reduce costs by another FFr7bn this year and would seek an estimated FFr20bn of savings between 2001 and 2003.

"Our aim is to make Renault the most competitive automotive constructor in the world," he said.

The restructuring has been focused mainly on savings in component purchasing and supply chain management.

Mr De Smedt said the next tranche of cuts would affect non-manufacturing activities such as distribution and marketing.

"In the next stage we will be reducing costs associated with every part of the business from when the car leaves the factory to when it reaches the customer," he said

Financial Times, 12 January 2000. Reprinted with permission.

The control of overheads might be the key to increased profitability

In the previous chapter we gave a brief outline of the historical background of management accounting and a summary of its nature and purpose. You will recall that, following the Industrial Revolution, management accounting developed as an offshoot of financial accounting. By 1925, most of the techniques used in practice today were well established. Between 1925 and 1980 there were few new developments, but during the last 20 years or so a great many new ideas have been put into practice.

The demand for *cost accounting* information arose because the managers in the new industries of the late 19th and early 20th centuries needed information that would enable them to cost products and value stocks. The financial accounting system of the day could not cope with managers' day-to-day requirements and, over a period of time, a separate reporting and information system became established. Like their Victorian counterparts, 21st century managers of profit-making and not-for-profit entities alike still need detailed information for product costing and stock valuation purposes. Hence the collection and recording of detailed cost data is still of relevance. This function is known as 'cost accounting' and it is the subject of this chapter.

The chapter is divided into ten main sections. The first section explains why it is important for you as a non-accountant to know something about cost accounting. The next section explains what is meant by *responsibility accounting*. The third section explains how product and service costs are classified. The next four sections then deal with the elements of cost, namely *direct materials*, *direct labour*, *other direct costs*, and *production overhead*. The production overhead section is followed by a comprehensive example relating to *overhead absorption*. The remaining two sections deal with *non-production overhead* and the setting of *predetermined absorption rates*.

This is clearly a long and complicated chapter, so take your time over it. Make sure that you follow the matter covered in a particular section before you move on to the next one.

Learning objectives	**By the end of this chapter, you should be able to:** ● trace costs to particular activities; ● describe the unit cost, the first in, first out, the continuous weighted average cost, and the standard cost methods of charging direct material costs to production; ● identify direct labour costs and other direct costs; ● outline the nature of indirect production and non-production costs; ● calculate units costs using absorption costing; ● assess the usefulness of total absorption costing.

Cost accounting and the non-accountant

As a non-accountant, it is unlikely that you will be directly involved in the implementation and operation of a cost accounting system. You will, however, almost certainly be required to help the accountants by giving them some guidance over technical matters and to provide them with the information they want. They will be responsible for calculating detailed product and service costs and estimates of stock valuations. A summary of the results relating to your responsibility area will then be passed to you.

As you will not normally be involved in the preparation of the detailed figures, it might not seem important for you to know how they are compiled. This is not so. The methods that accountants use in preparing cost accounting information are based on a whole series of assumptions and estimates. This means that it is possible to arrive at different costs simply by making a different assumption or by changing a particular estimate. In order for you to be able to rely on the information presented to you, therefore, it is vital that you know just how that information has been compiled. It follows that if you are fully aware of its possible defects, you can then take them into account when assessing the reliability of the information presented to you. As a result, your decision should be more effective.

In this chapter, we are going to present you with a great many examples involving calculations. We believe that if you work your way carefully through them, you will then be in a better position to assess the importance of any cost accounting data passed to you by your management accountants.

Responsibility accounting

A cost accounting system will normally be based on a system of 'responsibility accounting'. *Responsibility accounting* contains the following features:

1 *Segments.* The entity is broken down into separate identifiable segments. Such segments are known as 'responsibility centres'. There are three main types:

(a) *Cost centre.* A cost centre manager would only be responsible for the costs for that centre, e.g. the personnel department. An income-earning centre (such as a sales region) is also known as a cost centre. There are two types of cost centres: *production cost centres*, where products are manufactured or processed (e.g. a machining department); and *service cost centres*, where a service is provided for other cost centres (including other service cost centres, such as the personnel department recruiting staff for the canteen or wages office).

(b) *Profit centre.* Profit centre managers would be responsible for both costs and revenues related to their area of responsibility, e.g. a large operational unit of a national company (such as the oil products division of a chemicals company).

(c) *Investment centre.* Investment centre managers would be responsible for costs, revenues, and investment decisions associated with their specific area of activity. Divisions of large multinational companies are usually treated as investment centres.

2 *Boundaries.* The boundaries of each segment will be clearly established.

3 *Control.* A manager will be put in charge of each separate segment.

4 *Authorisation.* Segmental managers will be given the authority to operate their segments as autonomously as possible.

By establishing clear boundaries between different segments, it is possible to identify clearly their respective costs and revenues. This means that each manager can then be expected to take charge of his costs or revenues, answer for them, and be expected to plan and control them. Furthermore, the break-down of costs and revenues on a responsibility centre basis enables product costs and services to be readily established. You will recall that this is one of the primary purposes of a cost accounting system. We explain how costs are determined in the following sections. We start with an explanation of how they are classified.

Classification of costs

We mentioned above that the establishment of a responsibility accounting system enables costs and revenues to be easily identified with various types of centres. In order to avoid tedious repetition, we will now refer to cost centres, profit centres, and investment centres generally as *cost centres*. Similarly, the term 'cost' refers equally to 'revenue'.

If a cost centre structure is in place, we should be able to identify each cost with a particular cost centre. In practice, this is not always easy because there are some costs that are so general and so basic that no one manager has con-trol over them. One example is that relating to business rates. Business rates are a form of local property tax. They are levied on the property as a whole and a manager whose cost centre occupies part of the property has no control over the rates paid in respect of his own cost centre.

Costs that are easily and economically identifiable with a particular segment are known as *direct costs*. Hence if it is possible to identify all the costs of the entity with particular cost centres, then all costs must be direct costs at the cost centre level. This will not be the case at a *product* level. In costing a particular unit, some costs will be easy to identity with that unit. These will be classed as *direct unit costs*. Some costs, however, will not be easy to identity with a particu-lar unit, e.g. the canteen or the wages department expenses. Such costs will be classed as *indirect costs* as far as any particular unit is concerned. In costing a product or service, therefore, it is necessary to devise a method for dealing with indirect costs. We return to this problem later in the chapter.

Irrespective of whether costs are classified into the direct or indirect cate-gories, we also need to have some idea of their nature. Hence management accounts usually break costs down into their elements, i.e. whether they are material costs, labour costs or other types of costs. The *elements of cost* are shown in diagrammatic form in Exhibit 14.1. This breakdown of costs into their elements is similar to that adopted in Chapter 7 when we were dealing with manufacturing accounts.

Exhibit 14.1 The elements of cost

Tutorial notes

1 Total production overhead includes those indirect production costs that cannot be easily identified with specific units or processes.

2 Administration overhead include the non-production costs of operating the entity.

3 Research expenditure includes the cost of working on new products and processes. Development expenditure will include those costs associated with trying to improve existing products, processes and production techniques.

4 Selling and distribution overhead includes the cost of promoting the entity's products and services and the cost of delivering them to its customers or clients.

5 A profit loading may be added to the total cost of sales in order to arrive at the unit's selling price.

There are two particular points to note about Exhibit 14.1. First, you should be aware that, in a competitive market, selling price can rarely be determined on a 'cost-plus' basis, i.e. total cost of sales plus a profit loading. If the entity's prices are more than its competitors, then it is not likely to sell very many units; however, if its selling price is less than its competitors, then it might sell many units but the profit on each sale may be low. The chances are, then, that if its selling prices are low its competitors will soon bring down their prices. Thus when the market largely determines selling prices, it is vital that the entity's total costs are strictly controlled and monitored so that the gap between its total sales revenue and its total cost of sales (i.e. its profit) is as wide as possible. Second, you should realize that the classification shown will not necessarily be relevant for all entities. For example, an entity in the service sector (such as insurance broker) is not likely to have any direct or indirect production costs.

Exhibit 14.1 is based on what is called *total absorption costing*. Total absorption costing is a method of costing whereby *all* costs of the entity are charged to (or absorbed into) particular products irrespective of their nature. If only production costs are absorbed into product costs, the system is referred to as *absorption costing*.

Indirect costs, however, may include some costs that do not change no matter how many units of the product are produced, i.e. they do not change with the activity level achieved during any particular period. Such costs are known as *fixed costs*. Costs that change with the activity level are known as *variable costs*. Sometimes costs are recorded on the basis of a fixed/variable classification instead of a direct/indirect one, although this is relatively uncommon. A fixed/variable classification gives rise to a form of costing known as *marginal costing*. We shall be dealing with marginal costing in Chapter 17.

We are now in a position to explain how to cost products on an absorption basis. We start by examining the costing of direct materials.

Direct materials

Materials consist of raw materials and component parts. Raw materials are those basic ingredients that are incorporated into the production of a product, such as flour, sugar, and raisins used in baking a cake. Component parts include miscellaneous ready-made goods or parts that are purchased (or manufactured specially) for insertion into a main product, e.g. a car radiator.

As we discussed earlier, a direct cost is one that can be easily and economically identified with a particular segment, such as a cost centre or a particular product. However, there is a problem when relating this definition to materials. It might be easy and economic to identify them *physically* with a particular segment, but it does not necessarily follow that it is then easy to attach a *cost* to them. There are two main problems.

First, we might, for example, be able to identify a few screws used in assembling a chair but it would not be worthwhile costing them separately because their relative value is so small. Such costs would, therefore, be classified as *indirect* material costs. Second, materials may have been purchased at different times and at different prices. Thus it might not be possible to know whether 1000 kg of material held in stock had been purchased at £1, £2, or £3 per kilo. This problem particularly applies when materials that are purchased in separate batches are stored in the same containers, e.g. grains and liquids.

In such circumstances, it is necessary to determine an appropriate pricing method. Many such methods are available. However, as the price of materials charged to production also affects any closing stock values, regard has to be had to the financial reporting requirements of the entity. In management accounting we are not bound by any statutory or mandatory professional requirements, and so we are perfectly free to adopt any stock valuation method we wish. Unfortunately, if the chosen method is not acceptable for financial reporting purposes, we would have to revalue the closing stock for the annual accounts, which may be costly both in terms of time and of effort.

Hence even in management accounting we would normally adopt a pricing method for issuing materials to production and for valuing closing stocks that is also suitable for the annual accounts. This means following the requirements contained in SSAP 9 (Stocks and Long-term Contracts). There are four preferred methods. We summarize each of them below.

1 *Unit cost*. The unit cost is the cost of purchasing identifiable units of stocks. If it is possible to identify the specific cost of materials issued to production, then no particular pricing problem arises and we would obviously opt for this method.
2 *First in, first out (FIFO)*. This method adopts the first price at which materials have been purchased. We consider it in more detail below.
3 *Average cost*. An average cost may be calculated by dividing the total value of materials in stock by the total quantity. There are a number of acceptable averaging methods, but for illustration purposes we will examine the *continuous weighted average* (CWA) cost method. More details are provided below.
4 *Standard cost*. This method involves estimating what materials are likely to cost in the future. Instead of the actual price, the *estimated* or *planned* cost is then used to charge out the cost of materials to production. The standard cost method is usually adopted as part of a standard costing system. We shall not be considering it any further in this chapter because we will be dealing with standard costing in Chapter 16.

We will now examine the FIFO method in a little more detail.

First-in, first-out (FIFO)

It is sensible to issue the oldest stock to production first, followed by the next oldest, and so on, and this should be done wherever possible. This method of storekeeping means that old stock is not kept in store for very long, thus avoiding the possibility of deterioration or obsolescence. However, as outlined above, some materials (such as grains and liquids) may be stored in such a way that they become a mixture of old and new stock, and it is then not possible to identify each separate purchase. None the less, in pricing the issue of stock to production it would still seem logical to follow the first-in, first-out procedure, and charge production with the oldest price first, followed by the next oldest price, and so on.

FIFO is a very common method used in charging out materials to production. The procedure is as follows:

1 Start with the price paid for the oldest material in stock, and charge any issues to production at that price.

2 Once all of the goods originally purchased at that price have been issued, use the next-oldest price until all of that stock has been issued.

3 The third-oldest price will be used next, then the fourth, and so on.

The prices attached to the issue of goods to production are not, of course, necessarily the same as those that were paid for the actual purchases of those goods. Indeed, they cannot be, for if it had been possible to identify specific receipts with *specific* issues, the unit cost method would have been used.

The use of the FIFO pricing method is illustrated in Exhibit 14.2.

Exhibit 14.2 The FIFO pricing method of charging direct materials to production

The following information relates to the receipts and issue of a certain material into stock during January 2001:

Date		Receipts into stores			Issue to production
	Quantity	Price	Value	Quantity	
	units	£	£	units	
1.1.01	100	10	1 000		
10.1.01	150	11	1 650		
15.1.01				125	
20.1.01	50	12	600		
31.1.01				150	

Required:
Using the FIFO (first-in, first-out) method of pricing the issue of goods to production, calculate the following:
(a) the issue prices at which goods will be charged to production; and
(b) the closing stock value at 31 January 2001.

Answer to Exhibit 14.2

(a) **The issue price of goods to production:**

Date of issue	Tutorial note	Units	Calculation	£
5.1.01	(1)	100	units × £10 =	1 000
	(2)	25	units × £11 =	275
		125		1 275
31.1.01	(3)	125	units × £11 =	1 375
	(4)	25	units × £12 =	300
		150		1 675

(b) **Closing stock:**

25 units × £12 =	300

Check:
Total receipts (£1000 + £1650 + £600)	3 250
Total issues (£1275 + £1675)	2 950
Closing stock	300

Tutorial notes

1 The goods received on 1 January 2001 are now assumed to have all been issued.
2 This leaves 125 units in stock out of the goods received on 10 January 2001.
3 All the goods purchased on 10 January 2001 are assumed to have been issued.
4 There are now 25 units left in stock out of the goods purchased on 20 January 2001.

Although Exhibit 14.2 is a simple example, it can be seen that if the amount of material issued to production includes a number of batches purchased at different prices, the FIFO method involves using a considerable number of different prices.

The advantages and disadvantages of the FIFO method may be summarized as follows.

Advantages
- The FIFO method is logical.
- It appears to match the physical issue of materials to production.
- The closing stock value is closer to the current economic value.
- The stores ledger account is arithmetically self-balancing and there are no adjustments that have to be written off to the profit and loss account.
- It meets the requirements of SSAP 9 (Stocks and Long-term Contracts).
- It is acceptable for UK tax purposes.

Disadvantages
- It is arithmetically cumbersome.
- The cost of production relates to out-of-date prices.

Continuous weighted average (CWA)

In order to avoid the detailed arithmetical calculations that are involved in using the FIFO method, it is possible to substitute an *average* pricing method. There are a number of different types, but we are going to concentrate on one called the continuous weighted average (CWA) method.

This method necessitates frequent changes to be made in calculating issue prices. Although it appears a very complicated method, it is the easiest one to use *provided* that the receipts and issues of goods are recorded in a stores ledger account. An example of a stores ledger account in shown in Figure 14.1.

You will note from Figure 14.1 that the stores ledger account shows both the quantity and the value of the stock in store at any one time. The continuous weighted average price is obtained by dividing the total value of the stock by the total quantity. A new price will be struck each time new purchases are taken into stock.

The method is illustrated in Exhibit 14.3. We use the same data that we have used in Exhibit 14.2, but we have taken the opportunity to present a little more information, so that we can explain more clearly how it is calculated.

Stores ledger account

Material: Code:
Maximum: Minimum:

Date	Receipts				Issues				Stock		
	GRN No.	Quantity	Unit price	Amount	Stores Req. No.	Quantity	Unit price	Amount	Quantity	Unit price	Amount
			£	£			£	£		£	£

Notes:
GRN = Goods received note
Stores Req. No. = Stores requisition number

Figure 14.1 Example of a stores ledger account

Exhibit 14.3 The continuous weighted average pricing method of charging direct materials to production

You are presented with the following information relating to the receipt and issue of a certain material into stock during January 2001:

Date	Receipts into stores			Issues to production			Stock balance	
	Quantity units	Price £	Value £	Quantity units	Price £	Value £	Quantity units	Value £
1.1.00	100	10	1 000				100	1 000
10.1.00	150	11	1 650				250	2 650
15.1.00				125	10.60	1 325	125	1 325
20.1.00	50	12	600				175	1 925
31.1.00				150	11.00	1 650	25	275

Note:
The company uses the continuous weighted average method of pricing the issue of goods to production.

Required:
Check that the prices of goods issued to production during January 2001 have been calculated correctly.

Answer to Exhibit 14.3

The issue prices of goods to production during January 2000 using the continuous weighted average method have been calculated as follows:

15.1.01 $\dfrac{\text{Total stock value at 10.1.01}}{\text{Total quantity in stock at 10.1.01}} = \dfrac{2\,650}{250} = \underline{\underline{£10.60}}$

25.1.01 $\dfrac{\text{Total stock value at 20.1.01}}{\text{Total quantity in stock at 20.1.01}} = \dfrac{1\,925}{175} = \underline{\underline{£11.00}}$

The main advantages and disadvantages of the CWA method are as follows.

Advantages
- The CWA is easy to calculate, especially if a stores ledger account is used.
- Prices relating to previous periods are taken into account.
- The price of goods purchased is related to the quantities purchased.
- The method results in a price that is not distorted either by low or high prices, or by small or large quantity purchases.
- A new price is calculated as recent purchases are taken into stock, and so the price is regularly being updated.

Disadvantages
- A CWA price tends to lag behind current economic prices.
- The CWA price may not relate to any actual price paid.
- It is sometimes necessary to write off any arithmetical adjustments in the stock ledger account to the profit and loss account.

We can now move on to have a look at the other main type of direct cost: labour

Direct labour

Labour costs include the cost of employees' salaries, wages, bonuses, and the employer's national insurance and pension fund contributions. Wherever it is economically viable to do so, we will want to charge labour costs to each specific unit; otherwise they will have to be treated as part of indirect costs.

The identification and pricing of direct labour is much easier than is the case with direct materials. Basically, the procedure is as follows:

1 Employees working on specific units will be required to keep a record of how many hours they spend on each unit.
2 The total hours worked on each unit will then be multiplied by their hourly rate.
3 A percentage amount will be added to the total to allow for the employer's other labour costs (e.g. national insurance, pension fund contributions, and holiday pay).
4 The total amount is then charged directly to that unit.

The procedure is illustrated in Exhibit 14.4.

Exhibit 14.4 The charging of direct labour cost to production

Alex and Will are the two employees working on Unit X. Alex is paid £10 an hour, and Will £5. Both men are required to keep an accurate record of how much time they have spent on Unit X. Alex spends 10 hours and Will 20. The employer has estimated that it costs him an extra 20 per cent on top of what he pays them to meet his contributions towards national insurance, pension contributions and holiday pay.

Required:
Calculate the direct labour cost of producing Unit X.

Answer to Exhibit 14.4

Calculation of the direct labour cost:

	Hours	Rate per hour	Total
		£	£
Alex	10	10	100
Will	20	5	100
			200
Employer's costs (20%)			40
Total direct labour cost			240

It should be made clear that, in practice, it is by no means easy to obtain an accurate estimate of the direct labour cost of one unit. We start from an assumption that, if it is very difficult to do so, then probably it will be costly and therefore not worthwhile. But even in those cases where there is no doubt that employees are working on one unit (as in Exhibit 14.4), we are dependent upon them keeping an accurate record. If you have ever had to do this in your own job, you will know that this is not easy, especially if you are frequently being switched from one job to another. It is also difficult to account for all those five minutes spent chatting in the corridor!

Notwithstanding the difficulties, however, it is important that management should emphasize to the employees just how important it is that they keep an accurate record of their time. Labour costs may form a high proportion of total cost (especially in service industries), and so tight control is important. This is particularly so, of course, if tender prices are based on total unit cost. A high cost could mean that the company fails to get a contract, whereas too low a cost diminishes profit.

Other direct costs

Apart from material and labour costs, there may be other types of costs that can be economically identified with specific units. These are, however, relatively rare because, unlike materials and labour, it is usually difficult to trace a physical link to specific units. It only occurs, therefore, in some very special cases. For example, the company may hire specialist plant for work on a specific unit. It is then easy to identify the physical link between the unit and the plant, and to identify the hire charge with the unit.

Notwithstanding the difficulties of identifying other expenses with production, it is important to do so wherever possible. Otherwise, the indirect charge becomes bigger and bigger, and that causes even more problems in building up the cost of a specific unit.

Production overhead

In the earlier part of this chapter we suggested that, if management accounting is going to be used as part of a control system, it is necessary for all costs within an entity to become the direct responsibility of a designated cost centre manager. In this section we will examine how the total production overhead eventually gets charged to specific units. It is quite a complicated procedure, and so we will take you through it in stages. These are:

- *Stage 1*: Allocate all costs to specific cost centres.
- *Stage 2*: Share out the production service cost-centre costs.
- *Stage 3*: Absorb the production overhead.

The overall flow of costs in an absorption costing system is shown in Figure 14.2 This shows how costs are absobed into one of the units (Unit 3).

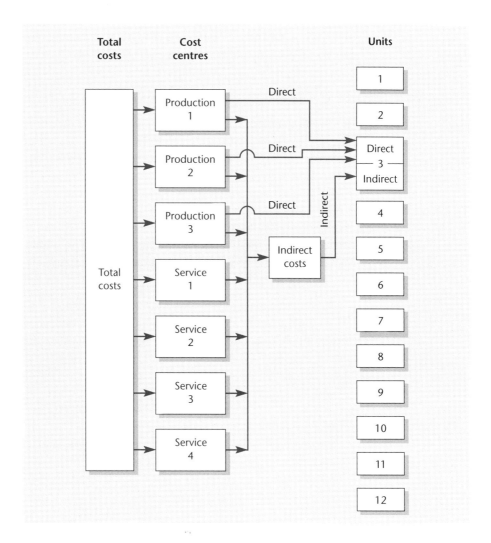

Figure 14.2
Flow of costs in an absorption costing system

Stage 1: Allocate all costs to specific cost centres

We cannot emphasize too strongly the importance of allocating all costs to specific cost centres. *Allocation* is the process of charging whole items of cost either to a cost centre or to an individual unit of production (known as a cost unit), i.e. as they can be easily identified with the cost centre or cost unit, there is no need to apportion the cost. It is not always easy to allocate every type of cost to an easily identifiable cost centre, and sometimes it is necessary to select a particular cost centre even though its manager may only be remotely responsible for the expenditure.

For control purposes, however, it will still be necessary to charge such costs to a particular cost centre, and then, at some later stage, to *apportion* (i.e. share) them among those cost centres that have benefited from the service provided. For example, most cost centres could be expected to be charged with their share of factory rates, and so they would probably be apportioned on the basis of floor space. Thus, if the rates for the factory amounted to £5000 and it had just two cost centres, one occupying 60 per cent of the total floor space and the other the remaining 40 per cent, the first cost centre would be charged with £3000 of the rates and the second cost centre with £2000.

Stage 2: Share out the production service cost-centre costs

Production service cost-centre costs will contain mainly allocated costs, but they could also include some apportioned costs (e.g. rates). By definition, service cost-centre costs are not directly related to the production of specific units, and so in relation to production units they must all be indirect costs.

The next stage in unit costing, therefore, is to share out the total service cost-centre costs among the production cost centres. This is usually done by apportioning the total cost for each service cost centre among those production cost centres that benefit from the service. The method used to apportion the service cost-centre costs may be very simple. A few of the more common methods are as follows:

- *Numbers of employees*. This method would be used for those service cost centres that provide a service to individual employees, e.g. the canteen, the personnel department, and the wages office. Costs will then be apportioned on the basis of the number of employees working in a particular production department as a proportion of the total number of employees working in all production cost centres.
- *Floor area*. This method would be used for such cost centres as cleaning and building maintenance.
- *Activity*. Examples of where this method might be used include the drawings office (on the basis of drawings made), materials handling (based on the number of requisitions processed), and the transport department (on the basis of vehicle operating hours).

A problem arises in dealing with the apportionment of service cost-centre costs when service cost centres provide a service for each other. For example, the wages office will probably provide a service for the canteen staff and, in turn, the canteen staff may provide a service for the wages staff. Before the service cost-centre costs can be apportioned among the production cost centres, therefore, it is necessary to make sure that service cost-centre costs are charged out to each other.

The problem becomes a circular one, however, because it is not possible to charge (say) some of the canteen costs to the wages office until the canteen has been charged with some of the costs of the wages office. Similarly, it is not possible to charge out the wages office costs until part of the canteen costs have been charged to the wages office. The treatment of *reciprocal service costs* (as they are called) can become an involved and time-consuming process unless a clear policy decision is taken about their treatment. There are three main ways of dealing with this problem:

1 *Ignore interdepartmental service costs.* If this method is adopted, the respective service cost-centre costs are only apportioned among the production cost centres. Any servicing that the service cost centres provide for each other is ignored.

2 *Specified order of closure.* This method requires the service cost centre costs to be closed off in some specified order and apportioned among the production cost centres and the remaining service cost centres. As the service cost centres are gradually closed off, there will eventually be only one service cost centre left. Its costs will then be apportioned among the production cost centres. Some order of closure has to be specified, and this may be quite arbitrary. It may be based, for example, on those centres that provide a service for the largest number of other service cost centres, or it could be based on the cost centres with the highest or the lowest cost in them prior to any interdepartmental servicing. It could also be based on an estimate of the benefit received by other centres.

3 *Mathematical apportionment.* Each service cost centre's total cost is apportioned among production cost centres and other service cost centres on the basis of the estimated benefit provided. The effect is that additional amounts keep being charged back to a particular service cost centre as further apportionment takes place. It can take a very long time before there is no more cost to charge out to any of the service cost centres; but when that point is reached, all the service cost centre costs will then have been charged to the production cost centres. This method involves a great deal of exhaustive arithmetical apportionment, and it is also very time-consuming, especially where there are a great many service cost centres. Although it is possible to carry out the calculations manually, it is more easily done by computer program.

In choosing one of the above methods, it should be remembered that they all depend upon an *estimate* of how much benefit one department receives from another. Such an estimate amounts to no more than an informed guess. It seems unnecessary, therefore, to build an involved arithmetical exercise on the basis of some highly questionable assumptions. We would suggest that in most circumstances interdepartmental servicing charging may be ignored.

We have covered some fairly complicated procedures in dealing with Stages 1 and 2. So, before moving on to Stage 3, we use Exhibit 14.5 to illustrate the procedure.

Exhibit 14.5 Charging overhead to cost centres

You are provided with the following indirect cost information relating to the New Manufacturing Company Limited for the year to 31 March 2005:

	£
Cost centre:	
Production 1: indirect expenses (to units)	24 000
Production 2: indirect expenses (to units)	15 000
Service cost centre A: allocated expenses	20 000
Service cost centre B: allocated expenses	8 000
Service cost centre C: allocated expenses	3 000

Additional information:
The estimated benefit provided by the three service cost centres to the other cost centres is as follows:

Service cost centre A: Production 1 50%; Production 2 30%; Service cost centre B 10%; Service cost centre C 10%.
Service cost centre B: Production 1 70%; Production 2 20%; Service cost centre C 10%.
Service cost centre C: Production 1 50%; Production 2 50%.

Required:
Calculate the total amount of overhead to be charged to cost centre units for both Production cost centre 1 and Production cost centre 2 for the year to 31 March 2005.

Answer to Exhibit 14.5

New Manufacturing Co. Ltd
Overhead distribution schedule for the year to 31 March 2005

Cost centre	Production		Service		
	1	2	A	B	C
	£	£	£	£	£
Allocated indirect expenses	24 000	15 000	20 000	8 000	3 000
Apportion service cost-centre costs:					
A (50 : 30 : 10 : 10)	10 000	6 000	(20 000)	2 000	2 000
B (70 : 20 : 0 : 10)	7 000	2 000	–	(10 000)	1 000
C (50 : 50 : 0 : 0)	3 000	3 000	–	–	(6 000)
Total overhead to be absorbed by specific units	44 000	26 000	–	–	–

Tutorial notes

1 Units passing through Production cost centre 1 will have to share total overhead expenditure amounting to £44 000. Units passing through Production cost centre 2 will have to share total overhead expenditure amounting to £26 000. Units passing through both departments may be identical: for example, they might be assembled in cost centre 1 and packed in cost centre 2.

2 The total amount of overhead to be shared amongst the units is £70 000 (44 000 + 26 000) or (15 000 + 20 000 + 8000 + 3000). The total amount of overhead originally collected in each of the five cost centres does not change.

3 This exhibit involves some interdepartmental reapportionment of service cost-centre costs. However, no problem arises because of the way in which the question requires the respective service cost-centre costs to be apportioned.

4 The objective of apportioning service cost-centre costs is to charge them out to the production cost centres so that they can be charged to specific units.

Stage 3: Absorb the production overhead

Once all the indirect costs have been collected in the production cost centres, the next step is to charge the total amount to specific units. This procedure is known as *absorption*.

The method of absorbing overhead into units is normally a simple one. Accountants recommend a single factor, preferably one that is related as closely as possible to the movement of overhead. In other words, an attempt is made to choose a factor that directly correlates with the amount of overhead expenditure incurred. Needless to say, like so much else in accounting, there is no obvious factor to choose! Indeed, if there was an obvious close relationship, it is doubtful whether it would be necessary to distinguish between direct and indirect costs.

There are six main methods that can be used for absorbing production overhead. All six methods adopt the same basic equation:

$$\text{Cost-centre overhead absorption rate} = \frac{\text{Total cost-centre overhead}}{\text{Total cost-centre activity}}$$

A different absorption rate will be calculated for each production cost centre, and so by the time that a unit has passed through various production cost centres, it may have been charged with a share of overhead from a number of production cost centres.

The six main absorption methods are as follows, and they are illustrated in Exhibit 14.6

Specific units

$$\text{Absorption rate} = \frac{\text{Total cost-centre overhead}}{\text{Number of units processed in the cost centre}}$$

This method is the simplest to operate. The same rate is applied to each unit, and thus it is only a suitable method if the units are identical.

Direct materials cost

$$\text{Absorption rate} = \frac{\text{Total cost-centre overhead}}{\text{Cost-centre total direct materials cost}} \times 100\%$$

The direct material cost of each unit is then multiplied by the absorption rate.

It is unlikely that there will normally be a strong relationship between the direct material cost and the level of overheads. There might be some special cases, but they are probably quite unusual, e.g. where a company uses a high level of precious metals and its overheads strongly reflect the cost of protecting those materials.

Direct labour cost

$$\text{Absorption rate} = \frac{\text{Total cost-centre overhead}}{\text{Cost-centre total direct labour cost}} \times 100\%$$

The direct labour cost of each unit is then multiplied by the absorption rate.

Overheads tend to relate to the amount of time that a unit spends in production, and so this method may be particularly suitable since the direct labour cost is a combination of hours worked and rates paid. It may not be appropriate, however, where the total direct labour cost consists of a relatively low level of hours worked and of a high labour rate per hour, because the cost will not then relate very closely to time spent in production.

Prime cost

$$\text{Absorption rate} = \frac{\text{Total cost-centre overhead}}{\text{Prime cost}} \times 100\%$$

The prime cost of each unit is then multiplied by the absorption rate. This method assumes that there is a close relationship between prime cost and overheads. In most cases, this is unlikely to be true.

As there is probably no close relationship between either direct materials or direct labour and overheads, then it is unlikely that there will be much of a correlation between prime cost and overheads. Hence, the prime cost method tends to combine the disadvantages of both the direct materials cost and the direct labour cost methods without having any real advantages of its own.

Direct labour hours

$$\text{Absorption rate} = \frac{\text{Total cost-centre overhead}}{\text{Cost-centre total direct labour hours}}$$

The direct labour hours of each unit are then multiplied by the absorption rate.

This method is highly acceptable, especially in those cost centres that are labour-intensive, because time spent in production is related to the cost of overhead incurred.

Machine hours

$$\text{Absorption rate} = \frac{\text{Total cost-centre overhead}}{\text{Cost-centre total machine hours}}$$

The total machine hours used by each unit is then multiplied by the absorption rate.

This is a most appropriate method to use in those departments that are machine-intensive. There is probably quite a strong correlation between the amount of machine time that a unit takes to produce and the amount of overhead incurred.

Exhibit 14.6 Calculation of overhead absorption rates

Old Limited is a manufacturing company. The following information relates to the assembling department for the year to 30 June 2004:

	Assembling department Total £000
Direct material cost incurred	400
Direct labour incurred	200
Total factory overhead incurred	100
Number of units produced	10 000
Direct labour hours worked	50 000
Machine hours used	80 000

Required:
Calculate the overhead absorption rates for the assembling department using each of the following methods:
(a) specific units;
(b) direct material cost;
(c) direct labour cost;
(d) prime cost;
(e) direct labour hours; and
(f) machine hours.

Answer to Exhibit 14.6

(a) Specific units:

$$OAR = \frac{TCCO}{Number\ of\ units} = \frac{£100\,000}{10\,000} = \underline{\underline{£10.00\ per\ unit}}$$

(b) Direct material cost:

$$OAR = \frac{TCCO}{Direct\ material\ cost} \times 100\% = \frac{£100\,000}{400\,000} \times 100\% = \underline{\underline{25\%}}$$

(c) Direct labour cost:

$$OAR = \frac{TCCO}{Direct\ labour\ cost} \times 100\% = \frac{£100\,000}{200\,000} \times 100\% = \underline{\underline{50\%}}$$

(d) Prime cost:

$$OAR = \frac{TCCO}{Prime\ cost} \times 100\% = \frac{£100\,000}{400\,000 + 200\,000} \times 100\% = \underline{\underline{16.67\%}}$$

(e) Direct labour hours:

$$OAR = \frac{TCCO}{\text{Direct labour hours}} = \frac{£100\,000}{50\,000} = £2.00 \text{ per direct labour hour}$$

(f) Machine hours:

$$OAR = \frac{TCCO}{\text{Machine hours}} = \frac{£100\,000}{80\,000} = £1.25 \text{ per machine hour}$$

Exhibit 14.6 illustrates the six absorption methods outlined in the text. You will appreciate, of course, that, in practice, only one absorption method would be chosen for each production cost centre, although different production cost centres may adopt different methods, e.g. one may choose a direct labour hour rate, and another may adopt a machine hour rate.

The most appropriate absorption rate method will depend upon individual circumstances. A careful study would have to be made of the correlation between (a) direct materials, direct labour, other direct expenses, direct labour hours, and machine hours; and (b) total overhead expenditure. However, it is generally accepted that overhead tends to move with time, so the longer a unit spends in production, the more overhead that that particular unit will generate. Thus, each individual unit ought to be charged with its share of overhead based on the *time* that it spends in production.

This argument suggests that labour-intensive cost centres should use the direct labour hour method, while machine-intensive departments should use the machine hour method.

A comprehensive example

At this stage it will be useful to illustrate overhead absorption in the form of a comprehensive example, although it will clearly be impracticable to use one that involves hundreds of cost centres. In any case, we are trying to demonstrate the principles of absorption costing, and too much data will obscure those principles. Thus, the example, given in Exhibit 14.7, contains only the most basic information.

Exhibit 14.7 Overhead absorption

Oldham Limited is a small manufacturing company producing a variety of pumps for the oil industry. It operates from one factory that is geographically separated from its head office. The components for the pumps are assembled in the assembling department; they are then passed to the finishing department, where they are painted and packed. There are three service cost centres: administration, stores and work study.

The following costs were collected for the year to 30 June 2003:

Allocated cost-centre overhead costs:	£000
Administration	70
Assembling	25
Finishing	9
Stores	8
Work study	18

Additional information:

1 The allocated cost-centre overhead costs are all considered to be indirect costs as far as specific units are concerned.
2 During the year to 30 June 2003, 35 000 machine hours were worked in the assembling department, and 60 000 direct labour hours in the finishing department.
3 The average number of employees working in each department during the year to 30 June 2003 was as follows:

Administration	15
Assembling	25
Finishing	40
Stores	2
Work study	3
	85

4 During the year to 30 June 2003, the stores received 15 000 requisitions from the assembling department, and 10 000 requisitions from the finishing department. The stores department did not provide a service for any other department.
5 The work study department carried out 2000 chargeable hours for the assembling department, and 1000 chargeable hours for the finishing department.
6 One special pump (code named MEA 6) was produced during the year to 30 June 2003. It took 10 machine hours of assembling time, and 15 direct labour hours were worked on it in the finishing department. Its total direct costs (materials and labour) amounted to £100.

Required:
(a) Calculate an appropriate absorption rate for:
   (i) the assembling department; and
   (ii) the finishing department.
(b) Calculate the total factory cost of the special MEA 6 pump.

Answer to Exhibit 14.7

(a)   **Oldham Ltd**
        Overhead distribution schedule for the year to 30 June 2003

		Production		Service		
Cost centre		Assembling	Finishing	Adminis-tration	Stores	Work study
		£000	£000	£000	£000	£000
Allocated overhead costs (1)	c/f	25	9	70	8	18

Cost centre		Production		Service		
		Assembling	Finishing	Adminis- tration	Stores	Work study
		£000	£000	£000	£000	£000
	b/f	25	9	70	8	18
Apportion administration (2):						
25 : 40 : 2 : 3		25	40	(70)	2	3
Apportion stores (3):						
3 : 2		6	4	–	(10)	–
Apportion work study:						
2 : 1		14	7	–	–	(21)
Total overhead to be absorbed		70	60	–	–	–

Tutorial notes

1 The allocated overhead costs were given in the question.
2 Administration costs have been apportioned on the basis of employees. Details were given in the question. There were 85 employees in the factory, but 15 of them were employed in the administration department. Administration costs have, therefore, been apportioned on a total of 70 employees, or £1000 per employee. The administration department is the only service department to provide a service for the other service departments, so no problem of interdepartmental servicing arises.
3 The stores costs have been apportioned on the number of requisitions made by the two production cost centres, that is 15 000 + 10 000 = 25 000, or 3 to 2.
4 The work study costs have been apportioned on the basis of chargeable hours, i.e. 2000 + 1000 = 3000, or 2 to 1.

Calculation of chargeable rates:
1 Assembling department:

$$\frac{\text{TCCO}}{\text{Total machine hours}} = \frac{£70\,000}{35\,000} = \underline{\underline{£2.00 \text{ per machine hour}}}$$

2 Finishing department:

$$\frac{\text{TCCO}}{\text{Total direct labour hours}} = \frac{£60\,000}{60\,000} = \underline{\underline{£1.00 \text{ per direct labour hour}}}$$

It would seem appropriate to absorb the assembling department's overhead on the basis of machine hours because it appears to be a machine-intensive department. The finishing department appears more labour-intensive, and so its overhead will be absorbed on that basis.

(b) MEA 6: Calculation of total factory cost

	£	£
Direct costs (as given)		100
Add: factory overhead:		
Assembling department (10 machine hours × £2.00 per MH)	20	
Finishing department (15 direct labour hours × £1.00 per DLH)	15	35
Total factory cost		135

You are now recommended to work through Exhibit 14.7 without reference to the answer.

Non-production overhead

In the previous section we concentrated on the apportionment and absorption of *production* overheads. Most companies will, however, incur expenditure on activities that are not directly connected with production activities. For example, there could be selling and distribution costs, research and development costs, and head office administrative expenses. How should these types of costs be absorbed into unit cost?

Before this question can be answered, it is necessary to find out why we should want to apportion them. There are three main reasons:

1 *Control.* The more that an entity's costs are broken down, the easier it is to monitor them. It follows that just as there is an argument for having a detailed system of responsibility accounting at cost-centre level, so there is an argument for having a similar system at unit-cost level. However, in the case of non-production expenses this argument is not a very strong one. We have seen that, in order to calculate the production cost of a unit, it is necessary to apportion a whole range of costs and then to select a number of appropriate absorption methods. The practice of absorbing fixed production overhead into specific units is a highly questionable procedure, but for control purposes the absorption of non-production fixed overheads is even more questionable.

    The relationship between units produced and non-production overhead is usually so remote that no meaningful estimate of the benefit received can be made. Consequently, the apportionment of non-production overhead is merely an arithmetical exercise, and no manager could be expected to take responsibility for such costs. From a control point of view, therefore, the exercise is not very helpful.

2 *Selling price.* In some cases, it might be necessary to add to the production cost of a specific unit a proportion of non-production overhead in order to determine a selling price that covers all costs and allows a margin for profit. This system of fixing selling prices may apply in some industries, e.g. in tendering for long-term contracts or in estimating decorating costs. In most cases, however, selling prices are determined by the market, and companies are not usually in a position to fix their selling prices based on cost with a percentage added on for profit (known as cost-plus pricing).

    Even when selling prices cannot be based on total cost, however, it may be useful to have an idea of the company's total unit costs in relation to its selling prices, but it must be clearly recognized that the calculation of such total units costs can only provide a general guide.

3 *Stock valuation.* You might think that a total unit cost will be required for stock valuation purposes, since it will be necessary to include the cost of closing stocks in the annual financial accounts. However, SSAP 9 does not permit the inclusion of non-production overhead in stock valuation. Thus, a company is unlikely to apportion non-production overhead for internal stock-valuation purposes if a different method has to be adopted when preparing the financial accounts.

It is obvious from the above summary that there are few benefits to be gained by charging a proportion of non-production overhead to specific cost units. In theory, the exercise is attractive because it would be both interesting and useful to know the *actual* (or true) cost of each unit produced. In practice, however, it is impossible to arrive at any such cost, and so it seems pointless to become engaged in spurious arithmetical exercises just for the sake of neatness.

The only real case for apportioning non-production overhead applies where selling prices can be based on cost. What can be done in those situations? There is still no magic formula, and an arbitrary estimate has still to be made. The easiest method is simply to add a percentage to the total production cost. This is bound to be a somewhat questionable method, since there can be no close relationship between production and non-production activities. It follows that the company's tendering or selling-price policy should not be too rigid if it is based on this type of cost-plus pricing.

Predetermined absorption rates

An absorption rate can, of course, be calculated on a historical basis (i.e. after the event), or it can be predetermined (i.e. calculated in advance).

As we have tried to emphasize, there is no close correlation between fixed overhead and any particular measure of activity: it can only be apportioned on what seems to be a reasonable basis. However, if we know the total actual overhead incurred, we can make sure that it is all charged to specific units, even if we are not sure of the relationship it has with any particular unit.

To do so, of course, we cannot calculate an absorption rate until we know: (a) the *actual cost of overheads*, and (b) the *actual activity level* (whether this is measured in machine hours, direct labour hours, or on some other basis). In other words, we can only make the calculation when we know what has happened.

The adoption of historical absorption rates is not usually very practicable. We have to wait until the actual period is over before an absorption rate can be calculated, the products costed and the customers invoiced. We would, therefore, normally wish to calculate an absorption rate in advance. This is known as a *predetermined absorption rate*.

In order to calculate a predetermined absorption rate, we have to estimate the overhead likely to be incurred and the direct labour hours or machine hours that are expected to be worked. If one or other of these estimates turns out to be inaccurate, then we would have either undercharged our customers (if the rate was too low), or overcharged them (if the rate was too high).

This situation could be very serious for a company. Low selling prices caused by using a low absorption rate could have made the company's products very competitive, but there is not much point in selling a lot of units if they are being sold at a loss. Similarly, a high absorption rate may result in a high selling price. Thus, each unit may make a large profit, but not enough units may be sold to enable the company to make an overall profit.

The use of predetermined absorption rates may, therefore, result in an under- or an over-recovery of overhead if the company has underestimated or overestimated the actual cost of the overhead or the actual level of activity. The difference between the actual overhead incurred and the total overhead charged to production (calculated on a predetermined basis) gives rise to what is known as a *variance*. If the actual overhead incurred is in excess of the amount charged out, the variance will be *adverse*, i.e. the profit will be less than expected. However, if the total overhead charged to production was less than was estimated, then the variance will be *favourable*. (The effect of this procedure is shown in diagrammatic form in Figure 14.3.) Other things being equal, a favourable variance gives rise to a higher profit, and an adverse variance results in a lower profit.

It is a cardinal rule in costing that variances should be written off to the profit and loss account at the end of the costing period in which they were incurred. It is not considered fair to burden the next period's accounts with the previous period's mistakes. In other words, it is as well to start off a new accounting period unburdened by the past.

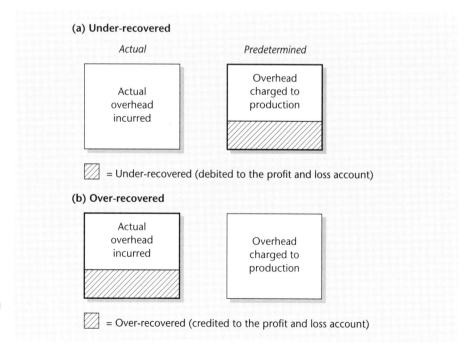

Figure 14.3
The under- and over-recovery of overhead by using predetermined rates

Throughout preceding sections we have clearly expressed many reservations about the way in which accountants have traditionally dealt with overheads. In recent years, dissatisfaction about overhead absorption has become widespread, and now a different technique called *activity-based costing* (ABC) is being advocated. ABC is examined in Chapter 20.

Conclusion

This has been a long chapter and you might have found it somewhat complicated. What we have tried to demonstrate is how management accountants build up the cost of products, processes or services. The methods described are ones that were devised towards the end of the 19th century and they have hardly changed since then.

The main purposes of cost accounting are twofold:

1 *To cost individual units of production or services.* The information obtained is fed back to cost-centre managers in order: (a) to help them plan and control their activities more effectively, efficiently and economically; (b) to assist them in decision making; and (c) to be of guidance in the determination of selling prices.

2 *To provide information for valuing closing stocks.* This is required irrespective of whether the entity's financial accounts are covered by any statutory or mandatory requirements or whether it is mainly for the purposes of managerial control.

Individual costs are usually charged to specific cost centres. Cost centres should be under the control of a designated manager. A *direct cost* is a cost that can be easily and economically identified with a particular cost centre. Some cost may then be easily and economically identified with specific units or products. Those costs that cannot be so identified are classified as *indirect costs*; the total of indirect costs is referred to as *overhead* (or *overheads*). A means has to be found of absorbing (or sharing) overhead among the units that benefit from their provision. If production overhead only is absorbed into product costs, the system is known as *absorption costing*; if non-production overhead is also absorbed into product costs it is known as *total absorption costing*.

Hence the total cost of a unit or service is made up of the following elements:

Direct materials + Direct labour + Direct expenses + Production overhead + Non-production overhead + Profit = Selling price

In theory, it should be easy to identity the quantity and cost of direct materials with a specific unit. In practice this may be difficult where batches of materials are bought at varying prices and stored collectively. It follows that, in many instances, the cost of direct materials may have to be estimated. Thus when account is taken of the arbitrary method of absorbing overheads into product costs, it will be appreciated that the total cost of a particular unit can only be an approximation.

Neither absorption costing nor total absorption costing allows for some costs being fixed irrespective of how many units are produced. As a result, the more units that are produced, the *lower* the total unit cost. Similarly, the fewer the units produced, the higher the total unit cost.

What particular relevance, therefore, is this chapter to a non-accountant? The most important point to recognize is that there is no such phenomenon as *the* cost of anything. Unit costs can only be approximations because they are based on a whole series of simple assumptions and fairly crude arithmetical apportionments. Thus you must be prepared to challenge vigorously any cost figures presented to you by your management accountants because you may not always accept the method used in calculating them.

Key points

1 Product costing has three main purposes: (a) stock valuation; (b) the planning and controlling of costs; and (c) the determination of selling prices.

2 The procedure involves isolating those costs that are easy and economic to identify with specific units. Such costs are described as *direct costs*. Those costs that are not easy or economic to identify with specific costs are known as *indirect costs*. The total of indirect costs is known as *overhead* (or *overheads*).

3 Some material costs can be physically identified with specific units and their cost easily ascertained. In cases where it is difficult to isolate the cost of material charged to production e.g. where batches of materials are purchased at different prices and where they are stored collectively, an estimated price has to be determined. There are four acceptable methods for pricing materials: (a) unit cost; (b) first in, first out: (c) average cost; and (d) standard cost. The average cost method recommended in this book is known as the *continuous weighted average* (CWA) cost method.

4 Wherever possible, labour costs should be charged directly to specific units. Employees will need to keep time sheets that record the hours that they have spent working on specific jobs. The amount charged to a particular unit will then be the time spent working on that unit multiplied by the respective hourly wage rate.

5 Some other services may also be identifiable with specific units, e.g. the hire of a machine for a particular contract. The cost of such services should be charged directly to production if it can be easily and economically determined.

6 In order to charge unit costs with a share of production overheads, *all* costs should first be identified with a specific cost centre.

7 Some cost centres provide a service to other cost centres. These are known as *service cost centres*. The various costs collected in the service

cost centres should be shared out on an apportionment basis among the other cost centres. Some costs collected in the service cost centres may be apportioned separately; otherwise, the *total service-cost centre cost* will be apportioned. An element of cross-charging arises when the service centres provide services for each other. This can be resolved either by ignoring any cross-charging, apportioning the total of the service centre costs in some specified order, or by mathematical apportionment.

8   Once the production cost centres have received their share of the service centre costs, an absorption rate for each production cost centre should be calculated. The traditional method is to take the total of each production cost centre's indirect cost (i.e. its overhead) and divide it either by the actual (or planned) direct labour hours, or by the machine hours actually worked (or planned to be worked) in that particular cost centre.

9   The absorption rate calculated for each production cost centre is used to charge each unit passing through that cost centre with a share of the production overhead. For example, if the absorption rate in Department A is £10 per direct labour hour and Unit X has five direct labour hours worked on in that department, Unit X will be charged £50 (5 × £10) of production overhead.

10 The total production cost of a particular unit can then be calculated as follows:

   direct materials cost + direct labour cost + direct expenses + share of production overhead = total production cost.

11 The absorption of non-production overhead is not recommended, except when it may be used for pricing purposes.

12 Absorption rates will normally be predetermined, i.e. they will be based on planned costs and anticipated activity levels.

13 The underabsorption or overabsorption of overhead should be written off to the profit and loss account in the period when it was incurred.

Check your learning

1 Fill in the blanks in each of the following statements:
   (a) Expenditure that can be economically identified with a specific unit is known as a _____ ___.
   (b) Overhead comprises _____ materials cost _____ labour cost, and _____ expenses.
   (c) Goods purchased for incorporation into products for sales are known as ___ _____.
   (d) Labour costs include employees' _____, bonuses, employer's national insurance and pension fund contributions.

2 What is the term used to describe a planned, or estimated, cost?

3 List four methods of pricing the cost of direct materials to production.

4 State whether each of the following statements is true or false:
   (a) When prices are rising, using current economic prices to charge
        materials to production generally results in a lower level of profit.   True/False
   (b) Some costs can be a direct departmental cost *and* an indirect cost.   True/False
   (c) All service centre costs are indirect as far as units are concerned.   True/False
   (d) Prime cost is the best method to use in a machine department
        when absorbing overhead.   True/False
   (e) Some service centre costs are included in unit costs.   True/False
   (f) The absorption of non-production overhead into production units
        is necessary in order to control costs.   True/False

5 List three methods of absorbing production overheads into specific units.

[*The answers to these questions may be found at the back of the book.*]

Group discussion questions

14.1 Examine the argument that an arbitrary pricing method used to charge direct materials cost to production is misleading in product costing.

14.2 'Arithmetical precision for precision's sake.' How far is this statement true of the traditional methods used in absorbing overheads into product costs?

14.3 Has total absorption costing any relevance in a service industry?

14.4 Some non-accountants believe that the technique of overhead absorption was devised simply to provide jobs for accountants. How far do you agree?

14.5 How should reciprocal service costs be dealt with when calculating product costs?

Practice questions

[*Note: The questions marked with an asterisk have answers at the back of the book.*]

14.6* The following stocks were taken into stores as follows:

1.1.01 1000 units @ £20 per unit.
15.1.01 500 units @ £25 per unit.

There were no opening stocks.
On 31.1.01 1250 units were issued to production.

Required:

Calculate the amount that would be charged to production on 31 January 2001 for the issue of material on that date using each of the following methods of material pricing:

1   FIFO (first-in, first-out); and
2   continuous weighted average.

14.7*   The following information relates to material ST 2:

		Units	Unit price	Value
			£	£
1.2.02	Opening stock	500	1.00	500
10.2.02	Receipts	200	1.10	220
12.2.02	Receipts	100	1.12	112
17.2.02	Issues	400	–	–
25.2.02	Receipts	300	1.15	345
27.2.02	Issues	250	–	–

Required:

Calculate the value of closing stock at 28 February 2002 assuming that the continuous weighted average method of pricing materials to production has been adopted.

14.8   You are presented with the following information for Trusty Limited:

2003	Purchases (units)	Unit cost £	Issues to production (units)
1 January	2 000	10	
31 January			1 600
1 February	2 400	11	
28 February			2 600
1 March	1 600	12	
31 March			1 000

Note: There was no opening stock.

Required:

Calculate the value of closing stock at 31 March 2003 using each of the following methods of pricing the issue of materials to production:

1   FIFO (first-in, first-out); and
2   continuous weighted average.

14.9   The following information relates to Steed Limited for the year to 31 May 2005:

	£
Sales	500 000
Purchases	440 000
Opening stock	40 000
Closing stock value using the following pricing methods:	
1 FIFO (first-in, first-out)	90 000
2 Continuous weighted average	79 950

Required:
Calculate Steed Limited's gross profit for the year to 31 May 2005 using each of the above closing stock values.

14.10   Iron Limited is a small manufacturing company. During the year to 31 December 2002 it has taken into stock and issued to production the following items of raw material, known as XY1:

Date 2002	Receipts into stock			Issues to production
	Quantity (litres)	Price per unit £	Total value £	Quantity (litres)
January	200	2.00	400	
February				100
April	500	3.00	1 500	
May				300
June	800	4.00	3 200	
July				400
October	900	5.00	4 500	
December				1 400

Notes:
1 There were no opening stocks of raw materials XY1.
2 The other costs involved in converting raw material XY1 into the finished product (marketed as Carcleen) amounted to £7000.
3 Sales of Carcleen for the year to 31 December 2002 amounted to £20 000.

Required:
(a) Illustrate the following methods of pricing the issue of materials to production:
   1 first-in, first-out (FIFO); and
   2 continuous weighted average.
(b) Calculate the gross profit for the year using each of the above methods of pricing the issue of materials to production.

14.11* Scar Limited has two production departments and one service department. The following information relates to January 2001:

	£
Allocated expenses:	
Production department: A	65 000
B	35 000
Service department	50 000

The allocated expenses shown above are all indirect expenses as far as individual units are concerned.
The benefit provided by the service department is shared amongst the production departments A and B in the proportion 60 : 40.

Required:
Calculate the amount of overhead to be charged to specific units for both production department A and production department B.

14.12* Bank Limited has several production departments. In the assembly department it has been estimated that £250 000 of overhead should be charged to that particular department. It now wants to charge a customer for a specific order. The data relevant are:

	Assembly department	Specific unit
Number of units	50 000	–
Direct material cost (£)	500 000	8.00
Direct labour cost (£)	1 000 000	30.00
Prime cost (£)	1 530 000	40.00
Direct labour hours	100 000	3.5
Machine hours	25 000	0.75

The accountant is not sure which overhead absorption rate to adopt.

Required:
Calculate the overhead to be absorbed by a specific unit passing through the assembly department using each of the following overhead absorption rate methods:

1 specific units;
2 percentage of direct material cost;
3 percentage of direct labour cost;
4 percentage of prime cost;
5 direct labour hours; and
6 machine hours.

14.13 The following information relates to the activities of the production department of Clough Limited for the month of March 2003:

	Production department	Order number 123
Direct materials consumed (£)	120 000	20
Direct wages (£)	180 000	25
Overhead chargeable (£)	150 000	
Direct labour hours worked	30 000	5
Machine hours operated	10 000	2

The company adds a margin of 50 per cent to the total production cost of specific units in order to cover administration expenses and to provide a profit.

Required:
(a) Calculate the total selling price of order number 123 if overhead is absorbed using the following methods of overhead absorption:
   1 direct labour hours;
   2 machine hours.
(b) State which of the two methods you would recommend for the production department.

14.14 Burns Limited has three production departments (processing, assembly and finishing) and two service departments (administration and work study). The following information relates to April 2004:

	£
Direct material	
Processing	100 000
Assembling	30 000
Finishing	20 000
Direct labour	
Processing (£4 × 100 000 hours)	400 000
Assembling (£5 × 30 000 hours)	150 000
Finishing (£7 × 10 000 hours) + (£5 × 10 000 hours)	120 000
Administration	65 000
Work study	33 000
Other allocated costs	
Processing	15 000
Assembling	20 000
Finishing	10 000
Administration	35 000
Work study	12 000

Apportionment of costs:

	Process	Assembling	Finishing	Work study
	%	%	%	%
Administration	50	30	15	5
Work study	70	20	10	–

Total machine hours: Processing 25 000

All units produced in the factory pass through the three production departments before they are put into stock. Overhead is absorbed in the processing department on the basis of machine hours, on the basis of direct labour hours in the assembling department, and on the basis of the direct labour cost in the finishing department.

The following details relate to unit XP6:

	£	£
Direct materials		
Processing	15	
Assembling	6	
Finishing	1	22
Direct labour		
Processing (2 hours)	8	
Assembling (1 hour)	5	
Finishing [(1 hour × £7) + (1 hour × £5)]	12	25
Prime cost		47

XP6: Number of machine hours in the processing department = 6

Required:
Calculate the total cost of producing unit XP6.

14.15 Outlane Limited's overhead budget for a certain period is as follows:

	£000
Administration	100
Depreciation of machinery	80
Employer's national insurance	10
Heating and lighting	15
Holiday pay	20
Indirect labour cost	10
Insurance: machinery	40
property	11
Machine maintenance	42
Power	230
Rent and rates	55
Supervision	50
	663

The company has four production departments: L, M, N and O. The following information relates to each department.

Department	L	M	N	O
Total number of employees	400	300	200	100
Number of indirect workers	20	15	10	5
Floor space (square metres)	2 000	1 500	1 000	1 000
Kilowatt hours' power consumption	30 000	50 000	90 000	60 000
Machine maintenance hours	500	400	300	200
Machine running hours	92 000	38 000	165 000	27 000
Capital cost of machines (£)	110 000	40 000	50 000	200 000
Depreciation rate of machines (on cost)	20%	20%	20%	20%
Cubic capacity	60 000	30 000	10 000	50 000

Previously, the company has absorbed overhead on the basis of 100 per cent of the direct labour cost. It has now decided to change to a separate machine-hour rate for each department.

The company has been involved in two main contracts during the period, the details of which are as follows:

Department	Contract 1: Direct labour hours and machine hours	Contract 2: Direct labour hours and machine hours
L	60	20
M	30	10
N	10	10
O	–	60
	100	100

Direct labour cost per hour in both departments was £3.00.

Required:
(a) Calculate the overhead to be absorbed by both contract 1 and contract 2 using the direct labour cost method.
(b) Calculate the overhead to be absorbed using a machine hour rate for each department.

15 Planning and control: budgeting

Inefficient budgeting costs companies dearly

Inefficient budgeting systems and processes are consuming an average of 20% of senior and financial manager's time, increasing to 30% in some cases, according to John Fanning of KPMG Consulting. Speaking at the ICAEW's '21st Century Budgeting Conference', sponsored by Comshare, John Fanning commented, 'The traditional budget and associated processes, such as strategic planning, forecasting, monthly reviews and reward processes, consume an enormous amount of management time. Unfortunately much of this time is being spent inefficiently and for very little reward. Companies must start to radically reassess the role of the budget and its usefulness as a management technique. Only by doing this will organisations be able to reduce the time devoted to this non-value adding activity and increase the time spent addressing the more important strategic questions confronting their business'.

Management Accounting, February 2000. Reprinted with permission.

In the previous chapter we dealt with the basic principles of cost accounting. Throughout the analysis there was an underlying assumption that much of the information was being prepared *after the event*, i.e. on a historical basis. However, managers are probably more concerned with *what might happen* in the future rather than with what did happen. A management accounting system will be even more useful, therefore, if it can also provide information about the future as well as the past.

Accountants refer to a detailed plan prepared in advance of future period as a *budget*. The preparation of a budget is a useful exercise in itself because it forces managers to look ahead, but it is even more useful if it is also used for control purposes. Control is achieved by comparing the actual results with the budgeted results: what *did* happen compared with what was *expected* to happen. Differences that were not anticipated are investigated and subsequent action is then taken either to correct or to accommodate any trends that were not expected. Such a procedure is known as *budgetary control*.

Budgeting and budgetary control form the subject of this chapter.

By the end of this chapter, you should be able to:

- describe the nature and purpose of budgeting and budgetary control;
- list the steps involved in operating a budgetary control system;
- describe the difference between fixed and flexible budgets;
- outline the behavioural consequences of a budgetary control system.

Budgeting and budgetary control

We start our analysis by establishing what we mean by a 'budget' and 'budgetary control'.

Budget

The term *budget* is usually well understood by the layman. Many people, for example, often prepare a quite sophisticated budget for their own household expenses. In fact, albeit in a very informal sense, everyone does some budgeting at some time or other, even if only by making a rough comparison between the next month's salary and the next month's expenditure. Such a budget may not be very precise, and it may not be formally written down; none the less, it contains all the ingredients of what accountants mean by a budget. The essential features of a formal budget may be summarized as follows:

1 *Policies*. A budget is based on the policies needed to fulfil the objectives of the entity.
2 *Data*. Quantitative data contained in a budget are usually translated into monetary terms.
3 *Documentation*. Details of a budget are normally contained within a formal written document.
4 *Period*. Budget details will refer to a defined future period of time.

In practice, a considerable number of budgets would be prepared. In a manufacturing entity, for example, these will include sales, production, and administration budgets. These budgets would then be combined into an overall budget known as a *master budget*, comprising (a) a budgeted profit and loss account; (b) a budgeted balance sheet; and (c) a budgeted cash flow statement.

Once a master budget had been prepared, it would be closely examined to see whether the overall plan could be accommodated. It might be the case, for example, that the sales budget indicated a large increase in sales. This may have required the production budgets to be prepared on the basis of this extra sales demand. However, the cash budget might have suggested that the entity could not meet the extra sales and production activity that would be required.

In these circumstances, additional financing arrangements may have had to be made, because obviously no organization would normally turn down the opportunity of increasing its sales.

In practice, the preparation of individual budgets can be a useful exercise even if nothing further is then done about them, since the exercise forces management to look ahead. It is a natural human tendency to be always looking back, but past experience is not always a guide for the future. If managers are asked to produce a budget, it encourages them to examine what they have done in relation to what they *could* do. None the less, the full benefits of a budgeting system are only realized when it is also used for control purposes, i.e. by the constant comparison of actual results with budgeted results, and then taking any necessary corrective action. This leads us on to consider in a little more detail what we mean by 'budgetary control'.

Budgetary control

In simple terms, *budgetary control* involves comparing the actual results for a period with the budget for that period. If there are any differences (known as *variances*) that need attention, then corrective action will be taken to ensure that future results will conform to the budget. Budgetary control has several important features. These are as follows:

1. *Responsibilities*. Managerial responsibilities are clearly defined.
2. *Action plan*. Individual budgets lay down a detailed plan of action for a particular sphere of responsibility.
3. *Adherence*. Managers have a responsibility to adhere to their budgets once the budgets have been approved.
4. *Monitoring*. The actual performance is constantly monitored and compared with the budgeted results.
5. *Correction*. Corrective action is taken if the actual results differ significantly from the budget.
6. *Approval*. Departures from budget are only permitted if they have been approved by senior management.
7. *Variances*. Variances that are unaccounted for are subject to individual investigation.

Any variance that occurs should be carefully investigated. If it is considered necessary, then the current actual performance will be immediately brought back into line with the budget. Sometimes the budget itself will be changed, e.g. if there is an unexpected increase in sales. Such changes may, of course, have an effect on the other budgets, and so it cannot be done in isolation.

Now that we have outlined the nature and purpose of budgeting and budgetary control, we are in a position to investigate how the system works.

Procedure

The budget *procedure* starts with an examination of the entity's objectives. These may be very simple. They may include, for example, an overall wish to maximize profits, to foster better relations with customers, or to improve the working conditions of employees. Once an entity has decided upon its overall objectives, it is in a position to formulate some detailed plans.

These will probably start with a *forecast*. Note that there is a technical difference between a forecast and a budget. A forecast is a prediction of what is *likely* to happen, whereas a budget is a carefully prepared plan of what *should* happen.

In order to make it easier for us to guide you through the budgeting process, we will examine each stage individually, as set out below. Note that we will assume that we will be dealing with a manufacturing entity in the private sector. The budgeting procedures for service sector entities are similar but not as involved. Budgets in the public sector (such as in local government) involve a somewhat different procedure.

The budget period

The main budget period is usually based on a calendar year. It could be shorter or longer depending upon the nature of the product cycle; for example, the fashion industry may adopt a short budget period of less than a year, while the construction industry may choose (say) a five-year period. Irrespective of the industry, however, a calendar year is usually a convenient period to choose as the base period, because it fits in with the financial accounting period.

Besides determining the main budget period, it is also necessary to prepare sub-period budgets. Sub-period budgets are required for budgetary control purposes, since the actual results have to be frequently compared with the budgeted results. The sub-budget periods for some activities may need to be very short if tight control is to be exercised over them. The cash budget, for example, may need to be compiled on a weekly basis, whereas the administration budget may only need to be prepared quarterly.

Administration

The budget procedure may be administered by a special budget committee, or it may be supervised by the accounting function. It will be necessary for the budget committee to lay down general guidelines in accordance with the entity's objectives, and to ensure that individual departments do not operate completely independently. The production department, for example, will need to know what the entity is budgeting to sell so that it can prepare its own budget on the basis of those sales. However, the detailed production budget must still remain the entire responsibility of the production manager.

This procedure is in line with the concept of responsibility accounting, which we outlined in the last chapter. If the control procedure is to work properly, managers must be given responsibility for a clearly defined area of activity, such as a cost centre. Thereafter, they are fully answerable for all that goes on there. Unless managers are given complete authority to act within clearly defined guidelines, they cannot be expected to account for something that is outside their control. This means that, as far as budgets are concerned, managers must help prepare, amend and approve their own responsibility centre's budget; otherwise, the budgetary control system will not work.

The budgeting process

The budgeting process is illustrated in Figure 15.1. Study the figure very carefully, noting how the various budgets fit together.

Later on in this chapter we shall be using a quantitative example to illustrate the budgeting process. For the moment, however, it will be sufficient to give a brief description.

In commercial organizations, the first budget to be prepared is usually the sales budget. Once the sales for the budget period (and for each sub-budget period) have been determined, the next stage is to calculate the effect on production. This will then enable an agreed level of activity to be determined. The *level of activity* may be expressed in so many units, or as a percentage of the theoretical productive capacity of the entity. Once it has been established, departmental managers can be instructed to prepare their budgets on the basis of the required level of activity.

Let us assume, for example, that 1000 units can be sold for a particular budget period. The production department manager will need this information in order to prepare his budget. This does not necessarily mean that he will budget for a production level of 1000 units, because he will also have to allow for the budgeted level of opening and closing stocks.

The budgeted production level will then be translated into how much material and labour will be required to meet that particular level. Similarly, it will be necessary to prepare overhead budgets. Much of the general overhead expenditure of the entity (such as factory administrative costs, head office costs, and research and development expenditure) will tend to be fixed, as such overheads will not be directly affected by production levels. However, in some instances a marked change in activity may lead to a change in fixed costs.

The sales and distribution overhead budget may be the one overhead budget that will not be entirely fixed in nature. An increase in the number of units sold, for example, may involve additional delivery costs.

Not all entities start the budget process with sales. A local authority usually prepares a budget on the basis of what it is likely to spend. The total budgeted expenditure is then compared with the total amount of council tax (after allowing for other income) needed to cover it. If the political cost of an increase in council tax appears too high, then the council will require a reduction in the budgeted expenditure. Once the budget has been set, and the tax has been levied on that

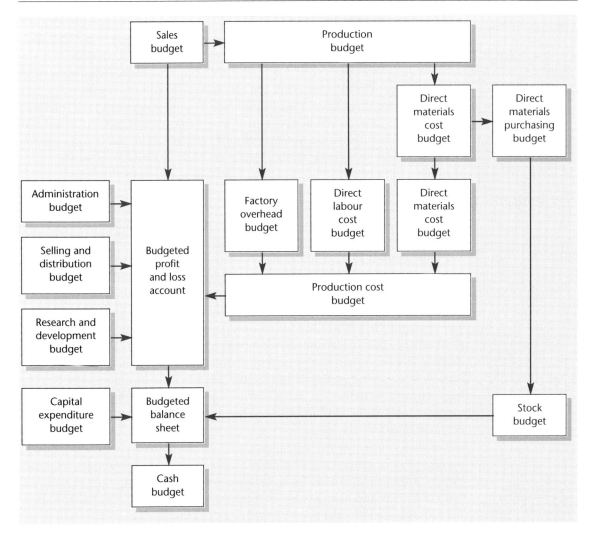

Figure 15.1 The interrelationship of budgets

basis, departments have to work within the budgets laid down. However, since the budget will have been prepared on an estimate of the actual expenditure for the last two or three months of the old financial year, account has to be taken of any a surplus or shortfall expected in the current year. If the estimate eventually proves excessive, the local authority will have overtaxed. This means that it has got some additional funds available to cushion the current year's expenditure. Of course, if it has undertaxed for any balance brought forward, departments might have to start cutting back on what they thought they could spend.

This process is quite different from the private sector, in which the budgeted sales effectively determine all the other budgets. In a local authority, it is the expenditure budgets that determine what the council tax should be, and it is only the control exercised by central government and by the local authority itself that places a ceiling on what is spent.

Functional budgets

A budget prepared for a particular department, cost centre, or other identifiable sphere of responsibility is known as a *functional budget*. All the functional budgets will then be combined into the *master budget*. The master budget is, in effect, a combined budgeted profit and loss account, a budgeted balance sheet, and a budgeted cash flow statement.

An initial draft of the master budget may not be acceptable to the senior management of the entity. This may be because the entity cannot cope with that particular budgeted level of activity, e.g. as a result of production or cash constraints. Indeed, one of the most important budgets is the *cash budget*. The cash budget translates all the other functional budgets (including that for capital expenditure) into cash terms. It will show in detail the pattern of cash inputs and outputs for the main budget period, as well as for each sub-budget period. If it shows that the entity will have difficulty in financing a particular budgeted level of activity (or if there is going to be a period when cash is exceptionally tight), the management will have an opportunity to seek out alternative sources of finance.

This latter point illustrates the importance of being aware of future commitments, so that something can be done in advance if there are likely to be constraints (irrespective of their nature). The master budget usually takes so long to prepare, however, that by the time it has been completed it will be almost impossible to make major alterations. It is then tempting for senior management to make changes to the functional budgets without referring them back to individual cost-centre managers. It is most unwise to make changes in this way, because it is then difficult to use such budgets for control purposes. If managers have not agreed to the changes, they will argue that they can hardly take responsibility for budgets that have been imposed on them.

A descriptive analysis makes it difficult to see clearly how all the functional budgets fit together, and so the procedure is illustrated in the next section by using an illustrative example.

An illustrative example

It would clearly be very difficult to observe the basic procedures involved in the preparation of functional budgets if we used an extremely detailed example, and so Exhibit 15.1 cuts out all the incidental information. As a result, it only illustrates the main procedures, but this will enable you to see how all the budgets fit together.

Exhibit 15.1 Preparation of functional budgets

Sefton Limited manufactures one product known as EC2. The following information relates to the preparation of the budget for the year to 31 March 2005:

1 Sales budget details for product EC2:
Expected selling price per unit: £100.
Expected sales in units: 10 000.
All sales are on credit terms.

2 EC2 requires 5 units of raw material E and 10 units of raw material C. E is expected to cost £3 per unit, and C £4 per unit. All goods are purchased on credit terms.

3 Two departments are involved in producing EC2: machining and assembly. The following information is relevant:

	Direct labour per unit of product (hours)	Direct labour rate per hour £
Machining	1.00	6
Assembling	0.50	8

4 The finished production overhead costs are expected to amount to £100 000.

5 At 1 April 2004, 800 units of EC2 are expected to be in stock at a value of £52 000, 4 500 units of raw material E at a value of £13 500, and 12 000 units of raw materials at a value of £48 000. Stocks of both finished goods and raw materials are planned to be 10 per cent above the expected opening stock levels as at 1 April 2004.

6 Administration, selling and distribution overhead is expected to amount to £150 000.

7 Other relevant information:
(a) Opening trade debtors are expected to be £80 000. Closing trade debtors are expected to amount to 15 per cent of the total sales for the year.
(b) Opening trade creditors are expected to be £28 000. Closing trade creditors are expected to amount to 10 per cent of the purchases for the year.
(c) All other expenses will be paid in cash during the year.
(d) Other balances at 1 April 2004 are expected to be as follows:

	£	£
(i) Share capital: ordinary shares		225 000
(ii) Retained profits		17 500
(iii) Proposed dividend		75 000
(iv) Fixed assets at cost	250 000	
Less: Accumulated depreciation	100 000	
		150 000
(v) Cash at bank and in hand		2 000

8 Capital expenditure will amount to £50 000, payable in cash on 1 April 2004.

9 Fixed assets are depreciated on a straight-line basis at a rate of 20 per cent per annum on cost.

Required:

As far as the information permits, prepare all the relevant budgets for Sefton Limited for the year to 31 March 2005.

Answer to Exhibit 15.1

Even with a much simplified budgeting exercise, there is clearly a great deal of work involved in preparing the budgets. To make it easier for you to understand what is happening, the procedure will be outlined step by step.

• Step 1: Prepare the sales budget

Units of EC2	Selling price per unit	Total sales value
	£	£
10 000	100	1 000 000

• Step 2: Prepare the production budget

	Units
Sales of EC2	10 000
Less: Opening stock	800
	9 200
Add: Desired closing stock (opening stock +10%)	880
Production required	10 080

• Step 3: Prepare the direct materials usage budget

Direct material:

E: 5 units × 10 080   50 400 units

C: 10 units × 10 080   100 800 units

• Step 4: Prepare the direct materials purchases budget

Direct materials: =	E (units)	C (units)
Usage (as per Step 3)	50 400	100 800
Less: Opening stock	4 500	12 000
	45 900	88 800
Add: Desired closing stock (opening stock+10%)	4 950	13 200
	50 850	102 000
	× £3	× £4
Direct material purchases	£152 550	£408 000

• Step 5: Prepare the direct labour budget

	Machining	Assembling
Production units (as per Step 2)	10 080	10 080
× direct labour hours required	× 1 DLH	× 0.50 DLH
	10 080 DLH	5 040 DLH
× direct labour rate per hour	× £6	× £8
Direct labour cost =	£60 480	£40 320

• Step 6: Prepare the fixed production overhead budget

Given: £100 000

● Step 7: Calculate the value of the closing raw material stock

Raw material	Closing stock* (units)	Cost per unit £	Total value £
E	4 950	3	14 850
C	13 200	4	52 800
			67 650

*Derived from Step 4.

● Step 8: Calculate the value of the closing finished stock

	£	£
Unit cost:		
Direct material E: 5 units × £3 per unit	15	
Direct material C: 10 units × £4 per unit	40	55
Direct labour for machining: 1 hour × £6 per DLH	6	
Direct labour for assembling: 0.50 hours × £8 per DLH	4	10
Total direct cost		65
× units in stock		× 880
Closing stock value =		57 200

● Step 9: Prepare the administration, selling and distribution budget

Given: £150 000

● Step 10: Prepare the capital expenditure budget

Given: £50 000

● Step 11 Calculate the cost of goods sold

	£
Opening stock (given)	52 000
Manufacturing cost:	
Production units (Step 2) × total direct cost (Step 3)	
= 10 080 × £65	655 200
	707 200
Less: Closing stock (Step 8: 880 units × £65)	57 200
Cost of goods sold (10 000 units)	650 000
(or 10 000 units × total direct costs of £65 per unit)	

● Step 12: Prepare the cash budget

	£	£
Receipts		
Cash from debtors:		
Opening debtors	80 000	
Sales	1 000 000	
	1 080 000	
Less: Closing debtors (15% × £1 000 000)	150 000	930 000

Payments	£	
Cash payments to creditors:		
Opening creditors	28 000	
Purchases [Step 4: (£152 550 + £408 000)]	560 550	
	588 550	
Less: Closing creditors (£560 550 × 10%)	56 055	532 495
Wages (Step 5: £60 480 + £40 320)		100 800
Fixed production overhead		100 000
Administration, selling and distribution overhead		150 000
Capital expenditure		50 000
Dividend paid for 2004		75 000
		1 008 295

	£
Net receipts	(78 295)
Add: Opening cash	2 000
Budgeted closing cash balance (overdrawn)	(76 295)

- Step 13: Prepare the budgeted profit and loss account

	£	£
Sales (Step 1)		1 000 000
Less: Variable cost of sales (Step 8: £10 000 × £65)		650 000
Gross margin		350 000
Less: Fixed production overhead (Step 6)	100 000	
Depreciation [(£250 000 + £50 000) × 20%]	60 000	160 000
Production margin		190 000
Less: Administration, selling and distribution overhead (Step 9)		150 000
Budgeted net profit		40 000

- Step 14: Prepare the budgeted balance sheet

	£	£	£
Fixed assets (at cost)			300 000
Less: Accumulated depreciation			160 000
			140 000
Current assets			
Raw materials (Step 7)		67 650	
Finished stock (Step 8)		57 200	
Trade debtors (15% × £1 000 000)		150 000	
		274 850	
Less: Current liabilities			
Trade creditors			
[Step 4: 10% × (£152 550 + £408 000)]	56 055		
Bank overdraft (Step 12)	76 295	132 350	142 500
			282 500
Financed by:			
Share capital			
Ordinary shares			225 000
Retained profits (£17 500 + £40 000)			57 500
			282 500

Exhibit 15.1 is a complicated example, although unnecessary detail has been avoided, e.g. it has been assumed that the company produces only one product and that the value of the opening stocks at 1 April 2004 will be the same as the budgeted costs for the year to 31 March 2005. It might be worthwhile, therefore, for you to go through the exhibit once again, and make sure that you understand how all the various budgets fit together. You can use as your guide the budgeting process shown in diagrammatic form in Figure 15.1. It would then be advisable to have yet another go at Exhibit 15.1, but this time without referring to the solution.

Fixed and flexible budgets

The master budget becomes the detailed plan for future action that everyone is expected to work towards. However, some entities only use the budgeting process as a *planning* exercise. Once the master budget has been agreed, there may be no attempt to use it as a control technique. Thus the budget may be virtually ignored, and it may not be compared with the actual results. If this is the case, then the entity is not getting the best out of the budgeting system.

As was suggested earlier, budgets are particularly useful if they are also used as a means of control. The control is achieved if the actual performance is compared with the budgeted performance. Significant variances should then be investigated and any necessary corrective action taken.

The constant comparison of the actual results with the budgeted results may be done either on a *fixed budget basis* or a *flexible budget basis*. A fixed budget basis means that the actual results for a particular period are compared with the original budgets. This is as you would expect, because the budget is a measure – you would get some very misleading results, for example, if you used an elastic ruler to measure distances. Similarly, an elastic-type budget might also give some highly unreliable results. In some cases, however, a variable measure *is* used in budgeting in order to allow for certain circumstances that might have taken place since the budgets were prepared. Accountants call this *flexing* the budget. A flexible budget is an original budget that has been amended to take account of the *actual* level of activity.

This procedure might appear somewhat strange and a little contradictory. How can a budget be changed once it has been agreed? Surely that is like using an elastic ruler to measure distances? In practice, however, even a fixed budget can be misleading.

It was explained earlier that, in order to prepare their budgets, managers (especially those directly involved in production) will need to be given the budgeted level of activity. Consequently, their budgets will be based on that level of activity. If, however, the *actual* level of activity is greater (or less) than the budgeted level, managers will have to allow for more (or less) expenditure on materials, labour, and other expenses.

Suppose, for example, that a manager has prepared his budget on the basis of an anticipated level of activity of 70 per cent of the plant capacity. Suppose that the company turns out to be much busier than it expected, and it achieves an actual level of activity of 80 per cent. The production manager is likely to have spent more on materials, labour, and other expenses than he had originally budgeted. If the actual performance is then compared with the budget (i.e. on a fixed budget basis), it will appear as though he had greatly exceeded what he thought he would spend. No doubt he would then argue that the differences had arisen as a result of a greatly increased level of activity (which may be outside his control). While this may be true, there is no certainty that all of the variances are as a result of the increased activity.

Hence, the need to flex the budget, i.e. it needs to be revised on the basis of what it would have been if the manager had budgeted for an activity of 80 per cent instead of 70 per cent. The other assumptions and calculations made at the time the budget was prepared (such as material prices and wage rates) should not be amended.

If the entity operates a flexible budget system, the original budgets may be prepared on the basis of a wide range of possible activity levels. This method, however, is very time-consuming, and managers will be very lucky if they prepare one that is identical to the actual level of activity. The best method is to wait until the actual level of activity is known, and then amend the budget on that basis.

This procedure might appear fairly complicated, and so it is best if it is illustrated with an example. This is done in Exhibit 15.2.

Exhibit 15.2 Flexible budget procedure

The following information had been prepared for Carp Limited for the year to 30 June 2005.

Level of activity	Budget 50%	Actual 60%
	£	£
Costs:		
Direct materials	50 000	61 000
Direct labour	100 000	118 000
Variable overhead	10 000	14 000
Total variable cost	160 000	193 000
Fixed overhead	40 000	42 000
Total costs	200 000	235 000

Required:
Prepare a flexed budget operating statement for Carp Limited for the year to 30 June 2005.

Answer to Exhibit 15.2

Carp Ltd
Flexed budget operating statement for the year 30 June 2005

Activity level	Fixed budget 50% Note 1 £	Flexed budget 60% Note 2 £	Actual costs 60% Note 3 £	Variance (col. 2 less col. 3) favourable/ (adverse) Note 4 £
Direct materials (1)	50 000	60 000	61 000	(1 000)
Direct labour (1)	100 000	120 000	118 000	2 000
Variable overhead (1)	10 000	12 000	14 000	(2 000)
Total variable costs	160 000	192 000	193 000	(1 000)
Fixed overhead (2)	40 000	40 000	42 000	(2 000)
Total costs (3)	200 000	232 000	235 000	(3 000)

Tutorial notes

1 All the budgeted *variable* costs have been flexed by 20% because the actual activity was 60% compared with a budgeted level of 50%, i.e. a 20% increase $\left(\dfrac{60\% - 50\%}{50\%} \times 100\right)$.

2 The budgeted fixed costs are not flexed because by definition they should not change with activity.

3 Instead of using the total fixed budget cost of £200 000, the total flexed budget costs of £232 000 can be compared more fairly with the total actual cost of £235 000.

4 Note that the terms 'favourable' and 'adverse' (as applied to variances) mean favourable or adverse to profit. In other words, profit will be either greater (if a variance is favourable) or less (if it is adverse) than the budgeted profit.

5 The reasons for the variances between the actual costs and the flexed budget will need to be investigated. The flexed budget shows that even allowing for the increased activity, the actual costs were in excess of the budget allowance.

6 Similarly, it will be necessary to investigate why the actual activity was higher than the budgeted activity. It could have been caused by inefficient budgeting, or by quite an unexpected increase in sales activity. While this would normally be welcome, it might place a strain on the productive and financial resources of the entity. If the increase is likely to be permanent, management will need to make immediate arrangements to accommodate the new level of activity.

The primary purpose of a budgetary control system is to control as closely as possible the activities of the entity. There will invariably be differences between the actual and the budgeted results, no matter how carefully the budgets are prepared. This does not matter unduly, as long as it is possible to find out why there were differences, and to take action before it is too late to do anything about them.

Behavioural consequences

Budgeting and budgetary control systems are not neutral. They have an impact on people so that they react favourably, unfavourably or with indifference.

If managers react favourably, then the data that they supply are likely to be accurate and relevant. Similarly, any information supplied to them will be received with interest and it will be taken seriously. As a result, any necessary corrective action that is required will be pursued with some vigour.

Managers who react unfavourably or with indifference may supply data that are inaccurate or irrelevant, and they may do so only under protest. Obviously, such managers are not likely to take seriously any subsequent information they receive that is based on data that they know to be suspect. Furthermore they will be unlikely to take any apparent necessary 'corrective action' unless they are forced to do so.

All of this means that, for budgeting and budgetary control systems to work effectively and efficiently, a number of important elements must be present. These are as follows:

1 *Consultation*. Managers must be consulted about any proposal to install a budgeting or a budgetary control system.
2 *Education and training*. Managers must undergo some education and training so that they are fully conversant with the relevance and importance of budgeting and budgetary control systems and the part that the managers are expected to play in them.
3 *Involvement*. Managers must be directly involved in the installation of the systems, at least in so far as their own sphere of responsibility is concerned.
4 *Participative*. Ideally, managers should prepare their own budgets (subject to some general guidelines) rather than having budgets imposed on them. *Imposed* budgets (as they are called) usually mean that managers do not take them seriously and they will then disclaim responsibility for any variances that may have occurred.
5 *Disciplinary action*. Managers should not be disciplined for any variances (especially if a budget has been imposed on them) unless they are obviously guilty of gross mismanagement. Budgetary control is a means of finding out *why* a variance occurred. It is not supposed to be a means of catching managers out so that they can be disciplined.

As far as the last point is concerned, if managers believe that the budgeting or budgetary control system operates against them rather than for them, they are likely to undermine it. This may take the form of *dysfunctional behaviour*, i.e. behaviour that may be in their own interest but not in the best interests of the company. They may, for example, act aggressively, become unco-operative, blame other managers, build a great deal of slack (i.e. tolerance) into their budgets, take decisions on a short-term basis or avoid taking them altogether, and spend money unnecessarily up to the budget level imposed upon them.

All of these points emphasize the importance of consulting managers and involving them fully both in the installation and operation of budgeting and budgetary control systems. If this is not the case, experience suggests that such systems will not work.

Conclusion

It has been suggested in this chapter that the full benefits of budgeting can best be gained if it is combined with a budgetary control system. The preparation of budgets is a valuable exercise in itself because it forces management to look ahead to what *might* happen, rather than to look back to what *did* happen. However, it is even more valuable if it is also used as a form of control.

Budgetary control enables actual results to be measured frequently against an agreed budget (or plan). Departures from that budget can then be quickly spotted, and steps can be taken to correct any unwelcome trends. However, the comparison of actual results with a fixed budget may not be particularly helpful if the actual level of activity is different from that budgeted. It is advisable, therefore, to compare actual results with a flexed budget.

As so many of the functional budgets are based upon the budgeted level of activity, it is vital that it is calculated as accurately as possible, since an error in estimating the level of activity could affect all of the company's financial and operational activities. Thus it is important that any difference between the actual and the budgeted level of activity is carefully investigated.

Budgeting and budgetary control systems may be resented by managers. Thus the managers might react to the systems in such a way that their own position is protected. This may not be of benefit to the entity as a whole.

Key points

1 A budget is a plan.

2 Budgetary control is a cost control method that enables actual results to be compared with the budget, thereby enabling any necessary corrective action to be taken.

3 The preparation of budgets will be undertaken by a budget team.

4 Managers must be responsible for producing their own functional budgets.

5 Functional budgets are combined to form a master budget.

6 A fixed budget system compares actual results with the original budgets.

7 A flexible budget system compares actual results with the original budget that is subsequently flexed (or amended) to allow for any difference between the actual level of activity and the budgeted level.

8 A budgeting and budgetary control system is not neutral. It may cause managers to act in a way that is not in the best interests of the entity.

Check your learning

1 Fill in the missing words in each of the following sentences:
  (a) A budget is a _____ expressed in monetary terms.
  (b) The continual comparison of actual with budgeted results is known as _____
    _____ .
  (c) A _____ budget is one that recognizes different cost behaviour patterns.

2 Over what period of time might a budget normally be prepared?
  (a) three months (b) a year (c) two years (d) five years (e) none of these.

3 What is the term normally given to the overall budgeted profit and loss account, budgeted balance sheet, and budgeted cash flow statement?

4 (a) In a manufacturing entity, which budget will normally be prepared first?
  (b) What is the main determinant of a local authority's budget?

[The answers to these questions may be found at the back of the book.]

Group discussion questions

15.1 The Head of Department of Business and Management at Birch College has been told by the Vice Principal (Resources) that his departmental budget for the next academic year is £150 000. What comment would you make about the system of budgeting used at Birch College?

15.2 Suppose that when all the individual budgets at Sparks plc are put together there is a shortfall of resources needed to support them. The Board suggests that all departmental budgets should be reduced by 15 per cent. As the company's Chief Accountant, how would you respond to the Board's suggestion?

15.3 Does a fixed budget serve any useful purpose?

15.4 'It is impossible to introduce a budgetary control system into a hospital because, if someone's life needs saving, it has to be saved irrespective of the cost.' How far do you agree with this statement?

Practice questions

[Note: The questions marked with an asterisk have answers at the back of the book.]

15.5* The following information has been prepared for Tom Limited for the six months to 30 September 2004:

Budgeted production levels for product X

	Units
April	140
May	280
June	700
July	380
August	300
September	240

Product X uses two units of component A6 and three units of component B9. At 1 April 2004 there were expected to be 100 units of A6 in stock, and 200 units of B9. The desired closing stock levels of each component were as follows:

Month end 2004	A6 (units)	B9 (units)
30 April	110	250
31 May	220	630
30 June	560	340
31 July	300	300
31 August	240	200
30 September	200	180

During the six months to 30 September 2004, component A6 was expected to be purchased at a cost of £5 per unit, and component B9 at a cost of £10 per unit.

Required:
Prepare the following budgets for each of the six months to 30 September 2004:
1 direct materials usage budget; and
2 direct materials purchase budget.

15.6* Don Limited has one major product that requires two types of direct labour to produce it. The following data refer to certain budget proposals for the three months to 31 August 2005:

Month	Production units
30.6.05	600
31.7.05	700
31.8.05	650

Direct labour hours required per unit:

	Hours	Budgeted rate per hour £
Production	3	4
Finishing	2	8

Required:
Prepare the direct labour cost budget for each of the three months to 31 August 2005.

15.7 Gorse Limited manufactures one product. The budgeted sales for period 6 are for 10 000 units at a selling price of £100 per unit. Other details are as follows:

1 Two components are used in the manufacture of each unit:

Component	Number	Unit cost of each component £
XY	5	1
WZ	3	0.50

2 Stocks at the beginning of the period are expected to be as follows:
   (a) 4000 units of finished goods at a unit cost of £52.50.
   (b) Component XY: 16 000 units at a unit cost of £1.
      Component WZ: 9600 units at a unit cost of £0.50.

3 Two grades of employees are used in the manufacture of each unit:

Employee	Hours per unit	Labour rate per hour £
Production	4	5
Finishing	2	7

4 Factory overhead is absorbed into unit costs on the basis of direct labour hours. The budgeted factory overhead for the period is estimated to be £96 000.

5 The administration, selling and distribution overhead for the period has been budgeted at £275 000.

6 The company plans a reduction of 50 per cent in the quantity of finished stock at the end of period 6, and an increase of 25 per cent in the quantity of each component.

Required:

Prepare the following budgets for period 6:

1 sales;

2 production quantity;

3 materials usage;

4 materials purchase;

5 direct labour;

6 the budgeted profit and loss account.

15.8 Avsar Limited has extracted the following budgeting details for the year to 30 September 2009:

1 Sales: 4000 units of V at £500 per unit

7000 units of R at £300 per unit

2 Materials usage (units):

	Raw material		
	O1	I2	L3
V	11	9	12
R	15	1	10

3 Raw material costs (per unit):

	£
O1	8
I2	6
L3	3

4 Raw material stocks:

	Units		
	O1	I2	L3
At 1 October 2008	1300	1400	400
At 30 September 2009	1400	1000	200

5 Finished stocks:

	Units	
	V	R
At 1 October 2008	110	90
At 30 September 2009	120	150

6 Direct labour:

	Product	
	V	*R*
Budgeted hours per unit	10	8
Budgeted hourly rate (£)	12	6

7 Variable overhead:

	Product	
	V	*R*
Budgeted hourly rate (£)	10	5

8 Fixed overhead: £193 160 (to be absorbed on the basis of direct labour hours).

Required:
(a) Prepare the following budgets:
   (i)   sales;
   (ii) production units;
   (iii) materials usage;
   (iv) materials purchase; and
   (v)   production cost.
(b) Calculate the total budgeted profit for the year to 30 September 2009.

15.9 The following budget information relates to Flossy Limited for the three months to 31 March 2007:

1 Budgeted profit and loss accounts:

Month	31.1.06	28.2.07	31.3.07
	£000	£000	£000
Sales (all on credit)	2 000	3 000	2 500
Cost of sales	1 200	1 800	1 500
Gross profit	800	1 200	1 000
Depreciation	(100)	(100)	(100)
Other expenses	(450)	(500)	(600)
	(550)	(600)	(700)
Net profit	250	600	300

2 Budgeted balance sheets:

Budgeted balances	31.12.06	31.1.07	28.2.07	31.3.07
	£000	£000	£000	£000
Current assets:				
Stocks	100	120	150	150
Debtors	200	300	350	400
Short-term investments	60	–	40	30
Current liabilities:				
Trade creditors	110	180	160	150
Other creditors	50	50	50	50
Taxation	150	–	–	–
Dividends	200	–	–	–

3 Capital expenditure to be incurred on 20 February 2007 is expected to amount to £470 000.

4 Sales of plant and equipment on 15 March 2007 is expected to raise £30 000 in cash.

5 The cash at bank and in hand on 1 January 2007 is expected to be £15 000.

Required:
Prepare Flossy Limited's cash budget for each of the three months during the quarter ending 31 March 2007.

15.10 Chimes Limited has prepared a flexible budget for one of its factories for the year to 30 June 2008. The details are as follows:

% of production capacity	30%	40%	50%	60%
	£000	£000	£000	£000
Direct materials	42	56	70	84
Direct labour	18	24	30	36
Factory overhead	22	26	30	34
Administration overhead	17	20	23	26
Selling and distribution overhead	12	14	16	18
	111	140	169	198

Additional information:
1 The company only expects to operate at a capacity of 45%. At that capacity, the sales revenue has been budgeted at a level of £135 500.
2 Variable costs per unit are not expected to change, irrespective of the level of activity.
3 Fixed costs are also not likely to change, irrespective of the level of activity.

Required:
Prepare a flexible budget for the year to 30 June 2008 based on an activity level of 45%.

16 Planning and control: standard costing

Cost cutting lifts bearings group

By Christopher Brown-Humes

SKF, the world's leading maker of rolling bearings, said yesterday it expected stronger demand this year as it reported better-than-expected profits for 1999 on the back of restructuring.

Pre-tax profits of SKr1.77bn ($208m) turned round a loss of SKr2.06bn in 1998 when the Swedish group's figures were hit heavily by restructuring costs. Analysts had expected profits of about sKR1.57bn.

Sune Carlsson, chief executive, said cost-cutting, increased efficiency, and better prices had contributed to turn-around. He said the group's performance had improved throughout the year, culminating in a fourth quarter profit of SKr693m after losses of SKr1.8bn a year earlier.

The group deliberately held back production to reduce inventory levels for much of the year, resulting in a 2.6 per cent fall in sales to SKr36.7bn.

However, it said it was now stepping up production to meet improved demand.

Financial Times, 27 January 2000. Reprinted with permission.

In the previous chapter we dealt with budgeting and budgetary control systems. A *budget* is a short-term detailed plan formulated in monetary terms. *Budgetary control* is a control mechanism whereby the actual results for a particular period are compared with the budgeted results for the same period. If there are any significant variances (i.e. differences) between the two results, then managerial action is taken to correct or accommodate any unexpected trends.

In this chapter we are going to deal with what is called *standard costing*. Standard costing is similar to budgeting except that detailed budgets are prepared for units of production as well as for individual departments. Action is then taken to correct any unexpected trends if the actual cost of producing the units differs from their standard (or budgeted) cost. The same procedure may also be applied to sales.

The chapter falls broadly into two main parts. The first part deals with the operation of a standard costing system. The second part examines how variances are calculated.

By the end of this chapter, you should be able to:

- describe the nature and purpose of standard costing;
- identify the main steps involved in implementing and operating a standard costing system;
- calculate three standard costing performance measures;
- calculate variances relating to sales, direct materials, direct labour, variable overheads and fixed overheads;
- describe the importance of standard costing and variance analysis.

Operation

Definitions

It would be helpful if we first define four terms that will be occurring throughout this chapter. These are as follows:

1 *Standard*: the amount or level set for the performance of a particular activity.
2 *Standard cost*: the planned cost for a particular level of activity.
3 *Variance*: the difference the between the standard (or planned) cost and the actual cost.
4 *Variance analysis*: an investigation into and an explanation of why variances occurred.

Types of entities

Standard costing is only appropriate for certain types of entities. Its main features are particularly suitable for incorporation into those manufacturing entities where it is possible to analyze the cost of particular units or processes into materials, labour and overheads. Standard costing is probably only cost-effective in larger entities, since it can be a fairly expensive system both to install and to operate; it is certainly a time-consuming control technique.

The non-accountant's role

The overall responsibility for administering a standard costing system would normally be delegated either to a special budget committee or left to the accounting function. Thus it is unlikely that many non-accountants would be involved in detailed standard costing operations. They will, however, almost certainly be required to help prepare standard costs for their own cost centres and to investigate any variances that may have arisen.

It follows that if the standard costing system is going to help non-accountants carry out their managerial functions more effectively and efficiently, then those non-accountants need to be familiar with the nature and purpose of standard costing. In particular, they need to know how the variances have been calculated; otherwise, they may take unnecessary corrective action.

The standard costing period

The standard costing period will usually be the same as that for the main budget and sub-budget periods. Short periods are preferable so that the actual results can be compared frequently with the standard results. Corrective action can then be taken quickly before it is too late to do anything about any unexpected trends. Short standard costing periods may also be necessary where market or production conditions are subject to frequent changes or where it is particularly difficult to prepare long-term plans, e.g. in the fashion industry.

Types of standard

The preparation of standard costs requires great care and attention. As each element of cost is subject to detailed arithmetical analysis, it is important that the initial information is accurate. Indeed, the information produced by a standard costing system will be virtually worthless if subsequent analyses reveal that variances were caused by inefficient budgeting or standard setting.

In preparing standard costs, management will need to be informed of the level of activity to be used in preparing the standard costs, i.e. whether the entity will need to operate at say 80 per cent or 90 per cent of its theoretical capacity. An activity level should be chosen that is capable of being achieved. It would be possible to choose a standard that was *ideal*, i.e. one that represented a performance that could be achieved only under the most favourable of conditions. Such a standard would, however, be unrealistic, because it is rare for ideal conditions to prevail. An ideal standard is a standard that is attainable under the most favourable conditions and where no allowance is made for normal losses, waste and machine downtime.

A much more realistic standard is called an *attainable standard*. An attainable standard is one that the entity can expect to achieve in reasonably efficient working conditions. In other words, it is accepted that some delays and inefficiencies (such as normal losses, waste and machine downtime) will occur, but it is also assumed that management will attempt to minimize them.

You may also come across the term *basic* cost standards. These are standards that are left unchanged over long periods of time. This enables some consistency to be achieved in comparing actual results with the same standards over a substantial period of time, but the standards may become so out of date that meaningful comparisons are not possible.

Information required

Standard costing is a sophisticated means of planning and controlling an entity's operations. Standard costs are time-consuming to prepare, costly to produce and the entire system is expensive to operate. The technique requires so much detailed information that most employees need to be convinced of its value if it is to work properly, since it also calls for considerable teamwork.

There is no point in having a standard costing system if those who are supposed to benefit do not want it. If standard costing is to operate effectively, its purpose must be understood by the employees because they will have to provide the basic information. If this is done ineffectively or inefficiently, then any decision based upon it will be questionable.

The basic information required to produce standard costs may be summarized as follows:

1 *Direct materials*: types, quantities and price.
2 *Direct labour*: grades, numbers and rates of pay.
3 *Variable overhead*: the total variable overhead cost analyzed into various categories, such as employee and general support costs.
4 *Fixed overhead*: the total fixed overhead, also analyzed into various categories such as employee costs, building costs and general administration expenses.

From the above information, it can be seen that the standard cost of a particular unit comprises four main elements: (a) direct materials; (b) direct labour; (c) variable overhead; and (d) fixed overhead. In turn, each element comprises two factors, namely quantity and price. The total standard cost of a specific unit may be built up as shown in Exhibit 16.1. The exhibit is based on some fictitious data.

Exhibit 16.1 Calculation of the total standard cost of a specific unit using absorption costing

	£
1 Direct materials	
Quantity × price (2 units × £5)	10
2 Direct labour	
Hours × hourly rate (5 hours × £10)	50
3 Variable overhead	
Hours × variable overhead absorption rate per hour	
(5 hours × £6)	30
4 Fixed overhead	
Hours × fixed overhead absorption rate per hour	
(5 hours × £3)	15
Total standard cost per unit	105

Note: The exhibit assumes that the unit cost is calculated on the basis of standard *absorption* costing. This is the most common method of standard costing, although it is possible to adopt a system of standard *marginal* costing.

Standard hours and the absorption of overhead

For standard costs prepared on the basis of absorption costing, overhead will be absorbed on the basis of *standard* hours. You will recall that in a non-standard costing system overhead is absorbed on the basis of actual hours. A standard hour represents the amount of work that should be performed in an hour, given that it is produced in standard conditions, i.e. in *planned* conditions. Each unit is given a standard time of so many hours in which the work should be produced. It is against that standard that the actual hours will be compared.

In order to calculate the standard overhead cost of a unit, the standard overhead absorption rate for the period is multiplied by the number of *standard* (not actual) hours that the unit should have taken to produce. The absorption of overhead by multiplying the standard absorption rate by the standard hours is a significant departure from that approach adopted in a non-standard costing system. This is a most important point, and we will return to it a little later on in the chapter.

Sales variances

Some companies also prepare standard costings for sales, although they are not as common as cost variances. If sales variances are required, the difference between the actual sales revenue and the standard revenue is analyzed into a number of sub-variances, such as price and quantity. A detailed analysis of the budgeted sales will be needed in order to obtain the following information:

1 the range and number of each product to be sold;
2 the selling price of each product;
3 the respective periods in which sales are to take place;
4 the geographical areas in which they are to be sold.

Performance measures

Management may find it useful if some performance measures are extracted from the standard costing data. There are three particularly important ones. They assist in informing managers about the level of efficiency of the entity, help them to spot unfavourable trends and enable them to take immediate corrective action.

Before these performance measures are examined, we must emphasize once again that, in standard costing, actual costs are compared with the *standard* cost for the *actual* level of activity. It is tempting to compare the actual cost with the budgeted cost, but it is not customary to do so in standard costing. By comparing the actual cost with the standard cost for the actual production, the budget is, in effect, being flexed. This means that any variances that do then arise can be more realistically assessed, as the same level of activity is being used to measure the actual costs against the budgeted costs. The relationship between actual, budgeted and standard hours is shown in diagrammatic form in Figure 16.1.

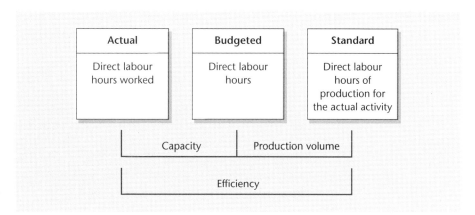

**Figure 16.1
The constituent
elements of three
capacity ratios**

With reference to Figure 16.1, the actual hours are those direct labour hours actually worked. The budgeted direct labour hours are those that were expected or planned to be worked. The standard direct labour hours of production for the actual activity measure the output produced in standard direct labour hours. For example, if each unit produced *should have* taken five hours each and 100 units were produced, the total standard direct labour hours for the actual activity would be 500 (5 DLH × 100). The budget might have been planned on the basis of 120 units, in which case the total budgeted labour hours would have been 600 (5 DLH × 120).

The three performance measures are as follows:

The efficiency ratio

This ratio compares the total standard (or allowed) hours of units produced with the total actual hours taken to produce those units. It is calculated as follows:

$$\frac{\text{Standard hours produced}}{\text{Actual direct labour hours worked}} \times 100\%$$

With respect to this formula, the standard hours produced = the standard direct labour hours of production for the actual activity.

The efficiency ratio enables management to check whether the company has produced the units in more or less time than had been allowed.

The capacity ratio

The capacity ratio compares the total actual hours worked with the total budgeted hours. It is calculated as follows:

$$\frac{\text{Actual direct labour hours worked}}{\text{Budgeted direct labour hours}} \times 100\%$$

This ratio enables management to ascertain whether all of the budgeted hours were used to produce the actual units.

The production volume ratio

This ratio compares the total allowed hours for the work actually produced with the total budgeted hours. It is calculated as follows:

$$\frac{\text{Standard hours produced}}{\text{Budgeted direct labour hours}} \times 100\%$$

With respect to this formula, the standard hours produced = the standard direct labour hours of production for the actual activity.

The production volume ratio enables management to compare the work produced (measured in terms of standard hours) with the budgeted hours of work. This ratio gives management some information about how effective the company has been in using the budgeted hours.

Note that machine hours may be substituted for direct labour hours.

The calculation of efficiency, capacity and production volume ratios are illustrated in Exhibit 16.2.

Exhibit 16.2 Calculation of efficiency, capacity and production volume ratios

The following information relates to the Frost Production Company Limited for the year to 31 March 2004:
1 Budgeted direct labour hours: 1 000.
2 Budgeted units: 100.
3 Actual direct labour hours worked: 800.
4 Actual units produced: 90.

Required:
Calculate the following performance ratios:
(a) the efficiency ratio;
(b) the capacity ratio; and
(c) the production volume ratio.

Answer to Exhibit 16.3

(a) The efficiency ratio:

$$\frac{\text{Standard hours produced}}{\text{Actual direct labour hours worked}} \times 100\% = \frac{900^*}{800} \times 100\% = \underline{112.5\%}$$

* Each unit is allowed 10 standard hours (1000 hours/100 units). Since 90 units were produced, the total standard hours of production must equal 900.

It would appear that the company has been more efficient in producing the goods than was expected. It was allowed 900 hours to do so, but it produced them in only 800 hours.

(b) The capacity ratio:

$$\frac{\text{Actual direct labour hours worked}}{\text{Budgeted hours}} \times 100\% = \frac{800}{1000} \times 100\% = \underline{80\%}$$

All of the time planned to be available (the capacity) was not utilized, either because it was not possible to work 1000 direct labour hours, or because the company did not undertake as much work as it could have done.

(c) The production volume ratio:

$$\frac{\text{Standard hours produced}}{\text{Budgeted hours}} \times 100\% = \frac{900^*}{1000} \times 100\% = \underline{\underline{90\%}}$$

* As calculated for the efficiency ratio.

It appears that if 90 units had been produced in standard conditions, another 100 hours would have been available (10 units × 10 hours). In fact, since the 90 units only took 800 hours to produce, at least another 20 units could have been produced in standard conditions.

$$\frac{1000 - 800}{10} = \underline{\underline{20 \text{ units}}}$$

Comments on the results

The budget allowed for 100 units to be produced and each unit was expected to take 10 direct labour hours to complete, a total budgeted activity of 1000 direct labour hours. However, only 90 units were actually produced. If these units had been produced in standard time, they should have taken 900 hours (90 units × 10 direct labour hours). These are the standard hours produced. The 90 units were completed in 800 actual hours. It appears, therefore, that the units were produced more efficiently than had been expected. The management will still need, of course, to investigate why only 90 units were produced and not the 100 expected in the budget.

The operation of a standard costing system has now been covered. In the next section we will examine how standard cost variances may be ascertained and whether they may be viewed as being either favourable or unfavourable.

Variances

Structure

The difference between actual costs and standard costs consists of two main variances: price and quantity. These variances may either be favourable (F) to profit, or adverse (A). This means that the actual prices paid or costs incurred can be more than was anticipated (adverse to profit), or less than anticipated (favourable to profit). Similarly, the quantities used in production can result in more being used (adverse to profit) or less than expected (favourable to profit).

Each element of cost can be analyzed into price and quantity variances (although different terms may be used). The main standard production cost variances are shown in diagrammatic form in Figure 16.2. The main cost variances are also summarized below; sales variances will be dealt with later in the chapter. Thus:

1 *Direct material*: Total = Price + Usage.
2 *Direct labour*: Total = Rate + Efficiency.
3 *Variable production overhead*: Total = Expenditure + Efficiency.
4 *Fixed production overhead*: Total = Expenditure + Volume.

In an absorption costing system the fixed production overhead volume variance may be subanalyzed into a capacity and an efficiency variance. In a marginal costing system (a topic we consider in the next chapter), only an expenditure variance will be calculated. Our analysis in this section assumes that we are dealing with an absorption costing system.

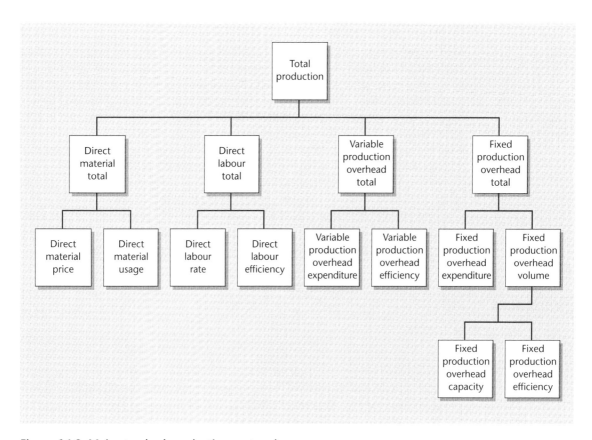

Figure 16.2 Main standard production cost variances

Variance analysis formulae

Before we explain how to calculate cost variances, it would be useful if we were first to summarize the basic formulae. You will then find it convenient to refer back to this summary when dealing with later exhibits.

The formulae used in calculating the main standard cost variances are as follows:

Direct materials

1 Total = (Actual cost per unit × Actual quantity used) – (Standard cost per unit × Standard quantity for actual production).

2 Price = (Actual cost per unit – Standard cost per unit) × Total actual quantity used.

3 Usage = (Total actual quantity used – Standard quantity for actual production) × Standard cost.

These relationships are shown in Figure 16.3.

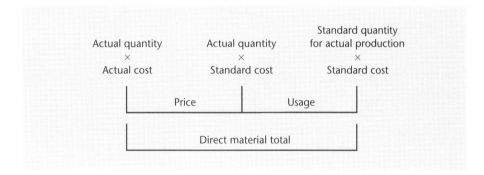

Figure 16.3 Calculation of direct material variances

Direct labour

1 Total = (Actual hourly rate × Actual hours) – (Standard hourly rate × Standard hours for actual production).

2 Rate = (Actual hourly rate – Standard hourly rate) × Actual hours worked.

3 Efficiency = (Actual hours worked – Standard hours for actual production) × Standard hourly rate.

These relationships are shown in Figure 16.4.

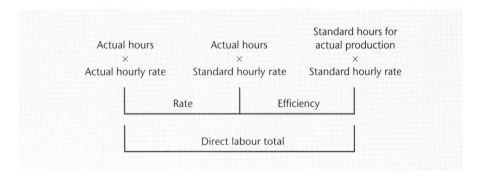

Figure 16.4 Calculation of direct labour variances

Variable production overhead

1 Total = Actual variable overhead – [Standard hours for actual production × Variable production overhead absorption rate (V.OAR)]

2 Expenditure = Actual variable overhead – (Actual hours worked × V.OAR)

3 Efficiency = (Standard hours for actual production – Actual hours worked) × V.OAR

These relationships are shown in Figure 16.5.

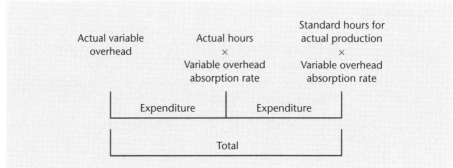

Figure 16.5 Calculation of variable production overhead variances

Fixed production overhead

1 Total = Actual fixed overhead – [Standard hours of production × Fixed overhead absorption rate (FOAR)].

2 Expenditure = Actual fixed overhead – Budgeted fixed expenditure.

3 Capacity = Budgeted fixed overhead – (Actual hours worked × FOAR).

4 Efficiency = (Actual hours worked – Standard hours for actual production) × FOAR.

5 Volume = Budgeted fixed overhead expenditure – (Standard hours for actual production × FOAR).

Note: Volume = Capacity + Efficiency

These variances are shown in Figure 16.6.

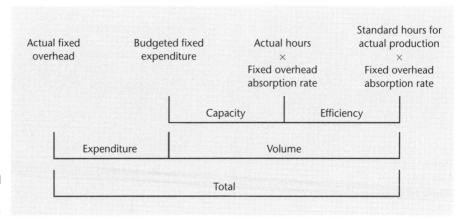

Figure 16.6 Calculation of fixed production overhead variances

A comprehensive example

We will now use a comprehensive example to illustrate the main cost variances. The details are contained in Exhibit 16.3.

Exhibit 16.3 Calculation of the main cost variances

The following information has been extracted from the records of the Frost Production Company Limited for the year to 31 March 2004:

Budgeted costs per unit:	£
Direct materials (15 kilograms × £2 per kilogram)	30
Direct labour (10 hours × £4 per direct labour hour)	40
Variable overhead (10 hours × £1 per direct labour hour)	10
Fixed overhead (10 hours × £2 per direct labour hour)	20
Total budgeted cost per unit	100

The following budgeted data are also relevant:
1 The budgeted production level was 100 units.
2 The total standard direct labour hours amounted to 1000.
3 The total budgeted variable overhead was estimated to be £1000.
4 The total budgeted fixed overhead was £2000.
5 The company absorbs both fixed and variable overhead on the basis of direct labour hours.

Actual costs:	£
Direct materials	2 100
Direct labour	4 000
Variable overhead	1 000
Fixed overhead	1 600
Total actual costs	8 700

Note: 90 units were produced in 800 actual hours, and the total actual quantity of direct materials consumed was 1400 kilograms.

Required:
Calculate the direct materials, direct labour, variable production overhead and fixed production overhead cost variances.

Answers to Exhibit 16.3

In answering this question we will first summarize the total variance for each element of cost for the Frost Production Company Ltd for the actual 90 units produced:

	Actual costs	Total standard cost for actual production	Variance
	£	£	£
Direct materials	2 100	2 700 (1)	600 (F)
Direct labour	4 000	3 600 (2)	400 (A)
Variable production overhead	1 000	900 (3)	100 (A)
Fixed production overhead	1 600	1 800 (4)	200 (F)
Total	8 700	9 000	300 (F)

Notes:

(a) F = favourable to profit; A = adverse to profit.

(b) The numbers in brackets refer to the tutorial notes below.

Tutorial notes

1 The standard cost of direct material for actual production = the actual units produced × the standard direct material cost per unit, i.e. 90 × £30 = £2700.
2 The standard cost of direct labour for actual production = the actual units produced × standard direct labour cost per unit, i.e. 90 × £40 = £3600.
3 The standard variable cost for actual performance = the actual units produced × variable overhead absorption rate per unit, i.e. 90 × £10 = £900.
4 The fixed overhead cost for the actual performance = the actual units produced × fixed overhead absorption rate, i.e. 90 × £20 = £1800.

As can be seen from the above summary, the total actual cost of producing the 90 units was £300 less than the budget allowance. An investigation would need to be made in order to find out why only 90 units were produced when the company had budgeted for 100. Furthermore, although the 90 units have cost £300 less than might have been expected, a number of other variances have contributed to the total variance. Assuming that these variances are considered significant, they would need to be carefully investigated in order to find out what caused them. Both the direct materials and the fixed production overhead, for example, cost respectively £600 and £200 less than the budget allowance, while the direct labour cost £400 and the variable production overhead £100 more than might have been expected.

As a result of calculating variances for each element of cost, it would now be much easier for management to investigate why the actual production cost was £300 less than might have been expected. However, by analyzing the variances into their major causes, the accountant can provide even greater guidance. In order to explain how this is done, each element of cost and its constituent variances will be examined. A brief explanation will then be given of the possible causes.

Direct materials

1 Price = (actual cost per unit – standard cost per unit) × total actual quantity used. Thus:

$$\text{The price variance} = (£1.50 - 2.00) \times 1400 \text{ (kg)} = £700 \text{ (F)}$$

The actual price per unit was £1.50 (£2100/1400) and the standard price was £2.00 per unit. There was, therefore, a total saving (as far as the price of the materials was concerned) of £700 (£0.50 × 1400). This was favourable (F) to profit.

2 Usage = (total actual quantity used – standard quantity for actual production) × standard cost. Thus:

$$\text{The usage variance} = (1400 - 1350) \times £2.00 = \underline{£100 \text{ (A)}}$$

In producing 90 units, Frost should have used 1350 kilograms (90 × 15 kg), instead of the 1400 kilograms actually used. If this extra usage is valued at the standard cost (the difference between the actual price and the standard cost has already been allowed for), there is an adverse usage variance of £100 (50 (kg) × £2.00).

3 Total = price + usage:

$$= £700 \text{ (F)} + £100 \text{ (A)} = \underline{\underline{£600 \text{ (F)}}}$$

The £600 favourable total variance was shown earlier in the cost summary in Exhibit 16.3. This variance might have arisen because Frost purchased cheaper materials. If this were the case, then it probably resulted in a greater wastage of materials, perhaps because the materials were of an inferior quality.

Direct labour

1 Rate = (actual hourly rate – standard hourly rate) × actual hours worked. Thus:

$$\text{The rate variance} = (£5.00 - £4.00) \times 800 \text{ DLH} = \underline{\underline{£800 \text{ (A)}}}$$

The actual hourly rate is £5.00 per direct labour hour (£4000/800) compared with the standard rate per hour of £4. Every extra actual hour worked, therefore, resulted in an adverse variance of £1, or £800 in total (£1 × 800).

2 Efficiency = (actual hours worked – standard hours for actual production) × standard hourly rate. Thus:

$$\text{The efficiency variance} = (800 - 900) \times £4.00 = \underline{\underline{£400 \text{ (F)}}}$$

The actual hours worked were 800. However, 900 hours would be the allowance for the 90 units actually produced (90 × 10 DLH). If these hours were valued at the standard hourly rate (differences between the actual rate and the standard rate having already been allowed for when calculating the rate variance), a favourable variance of £400 arises. The favourable efficiency variance has arisen because the 90 units took less time to produce than the budget allowed for.

3 Total = rate + efficiency:

$$£800 \text{ (A)} + £400 \text{ (F)} = \underline{\underline{£400 \text{ (A)}}}$$

The £400 adverse variance was shown earlier in the cost summary in Exhibit 16.3. It arises because the company paid more per direct labour hour than had been budgeted, although this was offset to some extent by the units being produced in less time than the budgeted allowance. This variance could have been caused by using a higher grade of labour than had been intended. Unfortunately, the higher labour rate per hour was not completely offset by greater efficiency.

Variable production overhead

1 Expenditure = actual variable overhead − (actual hours worked × variable production overhead absorption rate). Thus:

$$\text{Expenditure variance} = £1000 - (800 \times £1.00) = \underline{£200\ (A)}$$

2 Efficiency = (standard hours for actual production − actual hours worked) × variable production overhead absorption rate. Thus:

$$\text{Efficiency variance} = (900 - 800) \times £1.00 = \underline{£100\ (F)}$$

3 Total = expenditure + efficiency:

$$= £200\ (A) + £100\ (F) = \underline{£100\ (A)}$$

The adverse variance of £100 (A) arises because the variable overhead absorption rate was calculated on the basis of a budgeted cost of £10 per unit. In fact the absorption rate ought to have been £11.11 per unit (£1000/90), because the total actual variable cost was £1000. There would, of course, be no variable production overhead cost for the ten units that were not produced.

Fixed production overhead

1 Expenditure = actual fixed overhead − budgeted fixed expenditure Thus:

$$\text{Expenditure variance} = £1600 - £2000 = \underline{£400\ (F)}$$

The actual expenditure was £400 less than the budgeted expenditure. This means that the fixed production overhead absorption rate was £400 higher than it needed to have been if there had not been any other fixed overhead variances.

2 Volume = budgeted fixed overhead − (standard hours of production × fixed production overhead absorption rate). Thus:

$$\text{Volume variance} = £2000 - (900 \times £2.00) = \underline{£200\ (A)}$$

As a result of producing fewer units than expected, £200 less overhead has been absorbed into production.

3 Capacity = budgeted fixed overhead − (actual hours worked × fixed production overhead absorption rate). Thus:

$$\text{Capacity variance} = £2000 - (800 \times £2.00) = \underline{£400\ (A)}$$

The capacity variance shows that the actual hours worked were less than the budgeted hours. Other things being equal, therefore, not enough overhead would have been absorbed into production. It should be noted that the capacity variance will be favourable when the actual hours are in excess of the budgeted hours. This might seem odd, but it means that the company has been able to use more hours than it had originally budgeted. As a result, it should have been able to produce more units, thereby absorbing more overhead into production. This variance links with the capacity ratio calculated earlier in the chapter. The capacity ratio showed that only 80 per cent of the budgeted capacity had been utilized, and so probably not as much overhead was absorbed into production as had been originally expected.

4 Efficiency = (actual hours worked – standard hours for actual production) × fixed production overhead absorption rate. Thus:

$$\text{Efficiency variance} = (800 - 900) \times £2.00 = \underline{£200 \text{ (F)}}$$

This variance shows the difference between the 900 standard hours that the work is worth ($90 \times 10 = 900$ hours), compared with the amount of time that it took to produce those units (i.e. 800 hours). Thus the factory has been more efficient in producing the goods than might have been expected. This variance complements the efficiency ratio of 112.5 per cent that was illustrated earlier in the chapter in Exhibit 16.2.

Remember that the capacity variance + the efficiency variance = the volume variance. Thus:

$$\text{Volume variance} = £400 \text{ (A)} + £200 \text{ (F)} = \underline{£200 \text{ (A)}}$$
(see also 2 above).

5 Fixed production overhead total variance was calculated earlier (shown on the summary of variances in Exhibit 16.3). The simplified formula is as follows:

$$\text{Total} = \text{expenditure} + \text{volume:}$$
$$= £400 \text{ (F)} + £200 \text{ (A)} = \underline{£200 \text{ (F)}}$$

As the actual activity was less than the budgeted activity, only £1800 of fixed overhead was absorbed into production instead of the £2000 expected in the budget. However, the *actual* expenditure was only £1600. The overestimate of expenditure, therefore, compensated for the overestimate of activity.

A considerable number of variances have now been illustrated. You are now recommended to attempt Exhibit 16.3 without reference to the solution.

Sales variances

Apart from calculating cost variances, it is also possible to do the same for sales. In an absorption costing system, a total sales variance would be classified into a selling price variance and a sales volume profit variance (see Figure 16.7).

The sales variance formulae are as follows:

1 Total sales variance = [Actual sales revenue – (Actual sales quantity × Standard cost per unit)] – (Budgeted quantity × Standard profit per unit).
2 Selling price variance = (Actual selling price per unit – Standard selling price per unit) × Actual sales quantity.
3 Sales volume profit variance = (Actual quantity – Budgeted quantity) × Standard profit per unit.

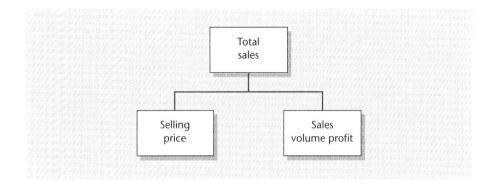

Figure 16.7
Main sales
variances

The above variances are shown diagramatically in Figure 16.8.

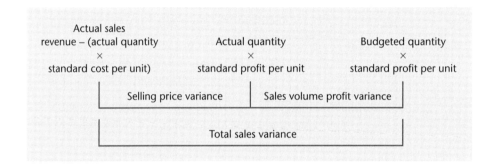

Figure 16.8
Calculation of
sales variances
based on profit

These formulae are further illustrated in Exhibit 16.4.

Exhibit 16.4 Calculating sales variances

The following data relate to Frozen Limited for the year to 31 July 2004:

	Budget/standard	Actual
Sales (units)	100	90
Selling price per unit	£10	£10.50
Standard cost per unit	£7	–

Required:
Calculate the sales variances.

Answer to Exhibit 16.4

(a) Selling price variance = (actual selling price per unit – standard selling price per unit) × actual sales quantity

$$= (£10.50 - 10.00) \times 90 \text{ units} = \underline{\underline{£45 \text{ (F)}}}$$

The actual selling price per unit was £0.50 (£10.50 – 10.00) more than the standard selling price, and so the variance is favourable. Other things being equal, the profit would be £45 higher than budgeted *for the actual number of units sold*.

(b) Sales volume profit variance = actual quantity – budgeted quantity) × standard profit per unit.
The standard profit is £3 per unit (£10 – 7). Thus:

$$(90 \text{ units} - 100 \text{ units}) = 10 \times £3 = \underline{\underline{£30 \text{ (A)}}}$$

The sales volume profit variance is £30 adverse because only 90 units were sold instead of the budgeted amount of 100 units. As a result, £30 less profit was made.

(c) Total sales variance = [actual sales revenue – (actual sales quantity × standard cost per unit)] – (budgeted quantity × standard profit per unit).
The actual sales revenue = £945 (90 units × £10.50). Thus:

$$[£945 - (90 \text{ units} \times £7)] - (100 \text{ units} \times £3)$$
$$= (£945 - 630) - £300 = \underline{\underline{£15 \text{ (F)}}}$$

When the £45 favourable selling price is set off against the £30 adverse sales volume profit variance, there is a favourable sales variance of £15 (£45 – 30).

You are now recommended to work through Exhibit 16.4 without reference to the solution.

Operating statements

As has been seen, the calculation of standard cost variances is a complex arithmetical process. The process can become more complicated if the variances outlined in the preceding sections are analyzed into subvariances (e.g. sales mix and sales quantity, and direct material mix and direct material yield). Fortunately, as a non-accountant, it is unlikely that you will ever have to calculate such variances for yourself. However, it is important for you to have some knowledge of how variances are calculated, so that you are in a better position to investigate how they may have occurred. Indeed, your main role will probably be to carry out a detailed investigation of the causes of variances, and then to take any necessary corrective action.

It is very difficult to carry out a meaningful variance analysis if you have no idea what you are supposed to be investigating. Hence, you will find it helpful if you can define the main variances and have some knowledge of how they have been calculated. You will then know where to begin looking for any discrepancies.

Once all the variances have been calculated, they may usefully be summarized in the form of an operating statement. There is no standardized format for such a statement but the one shown in Exhibit 16.5 is adequate for demonstration purposes.

Exhibit 16.5 Preparation of a standard cost operating statement

Exhibit 16.3 gave some information relating to the Frost Production Company Limited for the year to 31 March 2004. The cost data used in that exhibit will now be used in this Exhibit, but some additional information is required.

Additional information:
1 Assume that the budgeted sales were 100 units at a selling price of £150 per unit.
2 90 units were sold at £160 per unit.

Required:
Prepare a standard cost operating statement for the year to 31 March 2004.

Answer to Exhibit 16.5

Frost Production Company Limited. Standard cost operating statement for the year to 31 March 2004:

	(F)	(A)	£
Budgeted sales (100 × £150)			15 000
Budgeted cost of sales (100 × £100)			10 000
Budgeted profit			5 000
Sales volume profit variance (1)			(500)
Budgeted profit from actual sales			4 500
Variances: (2)	£	£	
Sales price (3)	900		
Direct materials usage		100	
Direct materials price	700		
Direct labour efficiency	400		
Direct labour rates		800	
Variable overhead efficiency	100		
Variable overhead expenditure		200	
Fixed overhead			
Fixed overhead capacity		400	
Fixed overhead efficiency	200		
Fixed overhead expenditure	400		
	2 700	1 500	1 200
Actual profit			5 700

Tutorial notes

1 Sales volume profit variance
   = (actual quantity – budgeted quantity) × standard profit per unit
   = (90 – 100) × £50 = £500 (A)

2 Details of the cost variances were shown in the answer to Exhibit 16.3.
3 Selling price variance
   = (actual selling price per unit – standard selling price per unit) × actual sales quantity
   = (£160 – £150) × 90 = £900 (F)

The format used in Exhibit 16.5 is particularly helpful because it shows the link between the budgeted profit and the actual profit. Thus, management can trace the main causes of sales and cost variances. In practice, the statement would also show the details for each product.

The operating profit statement will help management decide where to begin an investigation into the causes of the respective variances. It is unlikely that they will all need to be investigated. It may be company policy, for example, to investigate only those variances that are particularly significant, irrespective of whether they are favourable or adverse. In other words, only *exceptional* variances would be investigated. A policy decision would then have to be taken on what was meant by 'exceptional'.

Conclusion

We have now come to the end of a long and complex chapter. You may have found that it has been extremely difficult to understand just how standard cost variances are calculated. Fortunately, it is unlikely that, as a non-accountant, you will ever have to calculate variances for yourself. It is sufficient for your purposes to understand their meaning and to have some idea of the arithmetical foundation on which they are based.

Your job will largely be to investigate the causes of the variances, and to take necessary action. A standard costing system is supposed to help management plan and control the entity much more tightly than can be achieved in the absence of such a system. However, it can only be of real benefit if it is welcomed by those managers whom it is supposed to help; it can hardly be of help if it just produces a great deal of incomprehensible data. After reading this chapter, it is hoped that the data will now mean something to you.

In the next chapter we move on to another function of management accounting, namely decision making. Before you do move on, however you would be well advised to work your way through this chapter once again.

Key points

1 A standard cost is the planned cost of a particular unit or process.

2 Standard costs are usually based on what is reasonably attainable.

3 Actual costs are compared with standard costs.

4 Corrective action is taken if there are any unplanned trends.

5 Three performance measures used in standard costing are: the efficiency ratio, the capacity ratio, and the production volume ratio.

6 Variance analysis is an arithmetical exercise that enables differences between actual and standard costs to be broken down into the elements of cost.

7 The degree of analysis will vary, but usually a total cost variance will be analyzed into direct material, direct labour, variable overhead and fixed overhead variances. In turn, these will be analyzed into quantity and expenditure variances. An even more detailed analysis is possible.

8 Sales variances may also be calculated. Like cost variances, sales variances may also be analyzed in greater detail, e.g. into a selling price variance and a sales volume profit variance.

9 The variances help in tracing the main causes of differences between actual and budgeted results, but they do not explain what has actually happened.

Check your learning

1 What is a standard?

2 List four main steps in setting up a standard costing system.

3 Name three performance measures used in standard costing.

4 Complete the following equations:
   (a) _____ = direct material price + direct labour usage.
   (b) Direct labour total = _____ + direct labour efficiency.
   (c) Variable production overhead total = variable production expenditure + _____ .
   (d) Fixed production overhead total = fixed production overhead expenditure + _____ + fixed efficiency volume.
   (e) Sales variances = _____ + sales volume profit.

[*The answers to these questions may be found at the back of the book.*]

Group discussion questions

16.1 Is it likely that a standard costing system is of any relevance in a service industry?

16.2 'Standard costing is all about number crunching, and for someone on the shop floor it has absolutely no relevance.' Do you agree with this statement?

16.3 'Sales variance calculations are just another example of accountants playing around with numbers.' Discuss.

[*Note: The questions marked with an asterisk have answers at the back of the book.*]

16.4* You are presented with the following information for X Limited:
Standard price per unit: £10.
Standard quantity for actual production: 5 units.
Actual price per unit: £12.
Actual quantity: 6 units.

Required:
Calculate the following variances:
1 direct material total variance;
2 direct material price variance; and
3 direct material usage variance.

16.5 The following information relates to Malcolm Limited:
Budgeted production: 100 units.
Unit specification (direct materials): 50 kilograms × £5 per kilogram = £250.
Actual production: 120 units.
Direct materials used: 5400 kilograms at a total cost of £32 400.

Required:
Calculate the following variances:
1 direct material total;
2 direct material price; and
3 direct material usage.

16.6* The following information relates to Bruce Limited:
Actual hours: 1000.
Actual wage rate per hour: £6.50.
Standard hours for actual production: 900.
Standard wage rate per hour: £6.00.

Required:
Calculate the following variances:
1 direct labour total;
2 direct labour rate; and
3 direct labour efficiency.

16.7 You are presented with the following information for Duncan Limited:
Budgeted production: 1000 units.
Actual production: 1200 units.
Standard specification for one unit: 10 hours at £8 per direct labour hour.
Actual direct labour cost: £97 200 in 10 800 actual hours.

Required:
Calculate the following variances:
1 direct labour total;
2 direct labour rate; and
3 direct labour efficiency.

16.8* The following overhead budget has been prepared for Anthea Limited:
Actual fixed overhead: £150 000.
Budgeted fixed overhead: £135 000.
Fixed overhead absorption rate per hour: £15.
Actual hours worked: 10 000.
Standard hours of production: 8000.

Required:
Calculate the following fixed production overhead variances:
1 total;
2 expenditure;
3 volume;
4 capacity; and
5 efficiency.

16.9* Using the data contained in the previous question, calculate the following performance measures:
1 efficiency ratio;
2 capacity ratio; and
3 production volume ratio.

16.10 The following information relates to Osprey Limited:
Budgeted production: 500 units.
Standard hours per unit: 10.
Actual production: 600 units.
Budgeted fixed overhead: £125 000.
Actual fixed overhead: £120 000.
Actual hours worked: 4900.

Required:
Calculate the following fixed production overhead variances:
1 total;
2 expenditure;
3 volume;
4 capacity; and
5 efficiency.

16.11 Using the data from the previous question, calculate the following performance measures:
1 efficiency ratio;
2 capacity ratio; and
3 production volume ratio.

16.12* Milton Limited has produced the following information:
Total actual sales: £99 000.
Actual quantity sold: 9000 units.
Budgeted selling price per unit: £10.
Standard cost per unit: £7.
Total budgeted units: 10 000 units.

Required:
Calculate the selling price variance, the sales volume profit variance, and the sales variance in total.

16.13 You are presented with the following budgeted information for Doe Limited:

Sales units	*100*
Per unit:	*£*
Selling price	30
Cost	(20)
Profit	10
Actual sales	120 units
Actual selling price per unit	£28

·*Required*:
Calculate the sales variances.

16.14 The budgeted selling price and standard cost of a unit manufactured by Smillie Limited is as follows:

	£
Selling price	30
Direct materials (2.5 kilos)	5
Direct labour (2 hours)	12
Fixed production overhead	8
	25
Budgeted profit	5

Total budgeted sales: 400 units

During the period to 31 December 2002, the actual sales and production details for Smillie were as follows:

	£
Sales (420 units)	13 440
Direct materials (1260 kilos)	2 268
Direct labour (800 hours)	5 200
Fixed production overhead	3 300
	10 768
Profit	2 672

Required:
Prepare a standard cost operating statement for the period to 31 December 2002 incorporating as many variances as the data permit.

16.15 Mean Limited manufactures a single product, and the following information relates to the actual selling price and actual cost of the product for the four weeks to 31 March 2003:

	£000
Sales (50 000 units)	2 250
Direct materials (240 000 litres)	528
Direct labour (250 000 hours)	1 375
Variable production overhead	245
Fixed production overhead	650
	2 798
Loss	(548)

The budgeted selling price and standard cost of each unit was as follows:

	£
Selling price	55
Direct materials (5 litres)	10
Direct labour (4 hours)	20
Variable production overhead	5
Fixed production overhead	15
	50
Budgeted profit	5

Total budgeted production: 40 000 units.

Required:
Prepare a standard cost operating statement for the four weeks to 31 March 2003 incorporating as many variances as the data permit.

17 Decision making: contribution analysis

Nokia

FT

Nice business if you can get it: as Nokia's share of the mobile phone market has soared over the past three years, so its operating margins have swelled – to a fat 23.5 per cent last year. The figure may have been helped by circumstances: a components shortage and a supply/demand imbalance. But it underscores the economies of scale that can be achieved by a nimble market leader.

Size cuts unit costs and can help twist suppliers' arms - useful when components are in short supply. It also plays to Nokia's ability to segment the market, to win brand loyalty through marketing and to introduce a strong stream of new products, supported by a research and development budget that was 9 per cent of group sales last year. Handset sales have got off to a cracking start this year, like those of rivals Motorola and Ericsson, with first quarter figures expected to be even higher than the fourth. But while Nokia is going after market share, margins are likely to be trimmed as supply and demand move more into equilibrium.

Financial Times, 2 February 2000. Reprinted with permission.

More units sold means a lower unit cost and increased profitability

In the previous two chapters we have been concerned with the planning and control functions of management accounting. We now turn our attention to another important function of management accounting: decision making. In this chapter we explore a basic technique of decision making known as *contribution analysis*. In the next chapter we will demonstrate how the technique may be used to deal with a number of problem-solving issues.

Learning objectives

By the end of this chapter, you should be able to:

- **explain why absorption costing may be inappropriate in decision making;**
- **describe the difference between a fixed cost and a variable cost;**
- **apply contribution analysis to managerial decision-making problems;**
- **assess the usefulness of contribution analysis in problem solving.**

Background

Chapter 14 dealt with cost accounting. The costing method described in some detail in that chapter is known as *absorption costing*. The ultimate aim of absorption costing is to charge out all the costs of an entity to individual units of production. The method involves identifying the *direct costs* of specific units and then absorbing a share of the *indirect costs* into each unit. Indirect costs are normally absorbed on the basis of direct labour hours or machine hours. Assuming that an overhead absorption rate is predetermined, i.e. calculated in advance, this method involves estimating (a) the total amount of overhead likely to be incurred; and (b) the total amount of direct labour hours or machine hours expected to be worked. Hence the absorption rate could be affected by: (1) the total cost of the overhead; (2) the hours worked; or (3) by a combination of cost and hours.

The total of the indirect costs (overhead) is, however, likely to be made up of a combination of costs that change with how many units a department produces and those costs that are not likely to change with the number of units produced. Costs that change with activity are known as *variable costs*. It is usually assumed that variable costs vary directly with activity, e.g. if 1 kg costs £1, then 2 kg will cost £2, 3 kg will cost £3, and so on. Those costs that do not change with activity are known as *fixed costs*.

As we indicated in Chapter 14, if we are attempting to work out the total cost of manufacturing particular units, or if we want to value our stocks, it is appropriate to use absorption costing. Indeed, most cost book-keeping systems are based on this method of costing. Absorption costing is not, however, normally appropriate in decision making.

Decision making is a major part of most managers' jobs. They are constantly faced with having to take many decisions, both on a day-to day basis and for the longer term, e.g. *'Can we quote a special price for this job'*, *'Are we prepared to offer a special discount for a large order?'*, *'Is it possible to increase the output of this machine?'*, *'Are there cheaper ways of making this unit?'* or *'Should we close this production line down?'* All of these questions involve taking various decisions. As part of the decision-making process, managers will have to take into account the cost and revenue implications. Decisions based on absorption costing may not always be appropriate, however, as the fixed element inherent in many costs may not be affected by that particular decision. In order to illustrate this point, let us use an example.

Suppose that a manager is costing a particular journey that a member of his staff is proposing to make to visit a client. The staff member has a car that is already taxed and insured. Thus the main cost of the journey will be for petrol, although the car may depreciate slightly more quickly and it may require a service sooner. The tax and insurance costs will not be affected by one particular journey: they are *fixed costs*, no matter how many extra journeys are undertaken. The manager is, therefore, only interested in the *extra* cost of using the car to visit the client. He can then compare the cost of using the car with the cost of the bus, the train, or going by air. Note that cost alone would not necessarily be the determining factor in practice; non-quantifiable factors such as comfort, convenience, fatigue and time would also be important considerations.

The extra cost of making the journey is sometimes described as the *marginal cost*. Hence the technique used in the above example is commonly referred to as *marginal costing*. Economists also use the term 'marginal cost' to describe the extra cost of making an additional unit (as with the extra cost of a particular journey). When dealing with production activities, however, units are more likely to be produced in batches. It is perhaps more appropriate to substitute the term *incremental costing* and refer to the *incremental cost*, meaning the extra cost of producing a batch of units. The terms 'marginal costing' and 'marginal cost' are, however, still in frequent use.

The application of marginal (or incremental) costing revolves round the concept of what is known as *contribution*. We explore this concept in the next section.

Contribution

In order to illustrate what is meant by 'contribution' we will use a series of equations. The first equation is straightforward:

$$\text{Sales revenue} - \text{Total costs} = \text{Profit (or loss)} \qquad (1)$$

The second equation is based on the assumption that total costs can be analyzed into variable costs and fixed costs:

$$\text{Total costs} = \text{Variable costs} + \text{Fixed costs} \qquad (2)$$

By substituting Equation 2 into Equation 1 we can derive Equation 3:

$$\text{Sales revenue} - (\text{Variable costs} + \text{Fixed costs}) = \text{Profit (or loss)} \qquad (3)$$

By rearranging Equation 3 we can derive the following equation:

$$\text{Sales revenue} - \text{Variable costs} = \text{Fixed costs} + \text{Profit} \qquad (4)$$

Equation 4 is known as the *marginal cost equation*. Let us simplify it and substitute symbols for words, namely Sales revenue = S, Variable costs = V, Fixed costs = F, and Profit = P (or loss = L). The equation now reads as follows:

$$S - V = F + P \qquad (5)$$

But where does contribution fit into all of this? Contribution (C) is *the difference between the sales revenue and the variable costs of that sales revenue*. Hence, in equation form:

$$S - V = C \qquad (6)$$

Contribution can also be looked at from another point of view. If we substitute C for $(S - V)$ in Equation 5, the result will be:

$$C = F + P \qquad (7)$$

In other words, contribution can be regarded as being either the difference between the sales revenue and the variable costs of that sales revenue, or the total of fixed cost plus profit.

What do these relationships mean in practice and what is their importance? The meaning is reasonably straightforward. If an entity makes a contribution, it means that it has generated a certain amount of sales revenue and the variable cost of making those sales is less than the total sales revenue $(S - V = C)$. Hence there is a balance left over that can go towards contributing towards the fixed costs $(C - F)$; any remaining balance must be the profit $(C - F = P)$. Alternatively, if the contribution is insufficient to cover the fixed costs, the entity will have made a loss: $C - F = L$.

The importance of the relationships described above in equation format is important for two main reasons. First, fixed costs can often be ignored when taking a particular decision because, by definition, fixed costs will not change irrespective of whatever decision is taken. This means that any cost and revenue analysis is made much simpler. Second, managers can concentrate on decisions that will maximize the contribution, since every additional £1 of contribution is an extra amount that goes toward covering the fixed costs. Once the fixed costs have been covered, every extra £1 of contribution is an extra £1 of profit.

Assumptions

The marginal cost technique used in contribution analysis is, of course, based on a number of assumptions. At this stage it would be convenient to summarize them for you. They are as follows:

- Total costs can be split between fixed costs and variable costs.
- Fixed costs remain constant irrespective of the level of activity.
- Fixed costs do not bear any relationship to specific units.
- Variable costs vary in direct proportion to activity.

The reliability of the technique depends very heavily on being able to distinguish between fixed and variable costs. Some costs may be semivariable, i.e. they may consist of both a fixed and variable element. Electricity costs and telephone charges, for example, both contain a fixed rental element plus a variable charge; the variable charge depends upon the units consumed or the number of telephone calls made. Such costs are relatively easy to analyze into their fixed and variable elements.

In practice, it may be difficult to split other costs into their fixed and variable components. The management accountants may need the help of engineers and work study specialists in determining whether a particular cost is fixed or variable. They may also have to draw upon a number of graphical and statistical techniques. These techniques are somewhat advanced and beyond this book, and so we will assume that, for our purposes, it is relatively easy to analyze costs into their fixed and variable components.

Format

In applying the marginal cost technique, the cost data are usually arranged in a vertical format on a line-by-line basis. The order of the data reflects the marginal cost equation $(S - V = F + P)$. This format enables the attention of managers to be directed towards the contribution that may arise from any particular decision. In modern parlance, this is called *contribution analysis*. The basic procedure is illustrated in Exhibit 17.1.

Exhibit 17.1 A typical marginal cost statement

	Symbol	Product A £000	B £000	C £000	Total £000
Sales revenue (1)	S	100	70	20	190
Less: variable costs of sales (2)	V	30	32	18	80
Contribution (3)	C	70	38	2	110
Less: fixed costs (4)	F				60
Profit (5)	P				50

Notes:
1 The number in brackets after each item description refers to the tutorial notes below.
2 The marginal cost equation is represented in the 'symbol' column, i.e. $S - V = C$; $C = F + P$; and thereby $S - V = F + P$.

Tutorial notes

1 The total sales revenue would normally be analyzed into different product groupings. In this Exhibit there are three products: A, B, and C.
2 The variable costs include direct materials, direct labour costs, other direct costs, and variable overheads. Variable costs are assumed to vary *in direct proportion* to activity. Direct costs will normally be the same as variable costs, but in some cases, this will not be so. A machine operator's salary, for example, may be fixed under a guaranteed annual wage agreement. It is a direct cost in respect of the machine but it is also a fixed cost because it will not vary with the number of units produced.
3 As stated above, the term *contribution* is used to describe the difference between the sales revenue and the variable cost of those sales. A positive contribution helps to pay for the fixed costs.
4 The fixed costs include all the other costs that do not vary in direct proportion to the sales revenue. Fixed costs are assumed to remain constant over a period of time.

They do not bear any relationship to the units produced or the sales achieved. Consequently, it is not possible to apportion them to individual products. The *total* of the fixed costs can only be deducted from the *total contribution*.

5 The total contribution less the fixed costs gives the profit (if the balance is positive) or a loss (if the balance is negative).

Managers supplied with information similar to that contained in Exhibit 17.1 may subject the information to a series of 'What if?' possibilities. The following are some of the questions that they might pose:

- What would the profit be if we increased the selling price of Product A, B or C?
- What would be the effect if we reduced the selling price of Product A, B or C?
- What would be the effect if we eliminated one or more of the products?
- What would happen if we changed the quality of any of the products, thereby increasing (or otherwise) the variable cost of each product?
- Would any of the above decisions have an impact on fixed costs?

We will now examine the application of the marginal cost technique in a little more detail. We do so in the next section.

Application

As we have seen, the basic assumptions used in marginal costing are somewhat simplistic. In practice, they would probably only be regarded as appropriate when a particular decision was first considered. Thereafter, each of the various assumptions would be rigorously tested and they would be subject to a number of searching questions, such as: *'If we change the selling price of this product, will it affect the sales of the other products?'*, *'Will variable costs always remain in direct proportion to activity?'* or *'Will fixed costs remain fixed irrespective of the level of activity?'*

We will now use a simple example to illustrate the application of the technique. The details are shown in Exhibit 17.2. The Exhibit illustrates the effect of a change in variable costs on contribution.

Exhibit 17.2 Changes in the variable cost

	One unit	Proportion	100 units	1000 units
	£	%	£	£
Sales revenue	10	100	1000	10 000
Less: variable costs	5	50	500	5 000
Contribution	5	50	500	5 000

Tutorial notes

1 The selling price per unit is £10, and the variable cost per unit is £5 (50 per cent of the selling price). The contribution, therefore, is also £5 per unit (50 per cent of the selling price).

2 These relationships are assumed to hold good no matter how many units are sold. Hence, if 100 units are sold the contribution will be £500; if 1000 units are sold there will be a contribution of £5000, i.e. the contribution is assumed to remain at 50 per cent of the sales revenue.

3 The fixed costs are ignored because it is assumed that they will *not* change as the level of activity changes.

Every extra unit sold will increase the profit by £5 per unit *once the fixed costs have been covered* – an important qualification. This point is illustrated in Exhibit 17.3.

Exhibit 17.3 Changes in profit at varying levels of activity

Activity (units)	1000	2000	3000	4000	5000
	£	£	£	£	£
Sales	10 000	20 000	30 000	40 000	50 000
Less: variable costs	5 000	10 000	15 000	20 000	25 000
Contribution	5 000	10 000	15 000	20 000	25 000
Less: fixed costs	10 000	10 000	10 000	10 000	10 000
Profit/(Loss)	(5 000)	–	5 000	10 000	15 000

Tutorial notes

1 The exhibit illustrates five levels of activity: 1000 units, 2000 units, 3000 units, 4000 units, and 5000 units.

2 The variable costs remain directly proportional to activity at all levels, i.e. 50 per cent. The contribution is, therefore, 50 per cent (100% – 50%). The contribution per unit may be obtained by dividing the contribution at any level of activity level by the activity at that level, e.g. at an activity level of 1000 units the contribution per unit is £5 (£5000 ÷ 1000).

3 The fixed costs do not change, irrespective of the level of activity.

4 The contribution needed to cover the fixed costs is £10 000. As each unit makes a contribution of £5, the total number of units needed to be sold in order to break even (i.e. to reach a point where sales revenue equals the total of both the variable and the fixed costs) will be 2000 (£10 000 ÷ £5).

5 When *more than* 2000 are sold, the increased contribution results in an increase in profit. Thus, for instance when 3000 units are sold instead of 2000, the increased

contribution is £5000 (£15 000 – 10 000); the increased profit is also £5000 (£5000 – 0). Similarly, when 4000 units are sold instead of 3000, the increased contribution is another £5000 (£20 000 – 15 000) and the increased profit is also £5000 (£10 000 – 5000). Finally, when 5000 units are sold instead of 4000 units, the increased contribution is once more £5000 (£25 000 – 20 000), as is the increased profit (£15 000 – 10 000).

6 The relationship between contribution and sales is known (rather confusingly) as the *profit/volume* (or P/V) ratio. Note that it does not mean *profit* in relationship to sales but the *contribution* in relationship to sales.

7 Assuming that the P/V ratio does not change, we can quickly calculate the profit at any level of sales. All we need to do is to multiply the P/V ratio by the sales revenue and then deduct the fixed costs. The balance will then equal the profit at that level of sales. It is also easy to accommodate any possible change in fixed costs as the activity level moves above or below a certain range.

While Exhibit 17.2 and Exhibit 17.3 are simple examples, we hope that they demonstrate just how useful contribution analysis can be in managerial decision making. While the basic assumptions may be somewhat simplistic, they can readily be adapted to suit more complex problems.

Charts and graphs

Contribution analysis lends itself to the presentation of information in a pictorial format. Indeed, the $S - V = F + P$ relationship is often easier to appreciate when it is reported to managers in this way.

The most common format is in the form of what is called a *break-even chart*. A break-even chart is illustrated in Exhibit 17.4. The chart is based on the data used in Exhibit 17.3.

Exhibit 17.4 shows quite clearly the relationships that are assumed to exist when the marginal costing technique is adopted. Sales revenue, total costs and fixed costs are all assumed to be linear, so that they are all drawn as straight lines. Note also the following points:

1 When no units are sold, the sales revenue line runs from the origin up to £50 000 when 5000 units are sold. It may then continue as a straight line beyond that point.

2 The total cost line is made up of both the fixed costs and the variable costs. When there is no activity, the total costs will be equal to the fixed costs, so the total cost line runs from the fixed cost point of £10 000 up to £35 000 when 5000 units are sold. It may then continue beyond that point.

3 The fixed cost line is drawn from the £10 000 point as a straight line parallel to the x axis irrespective of the number of units sold.

Exhibit 17.4 A break-even chart

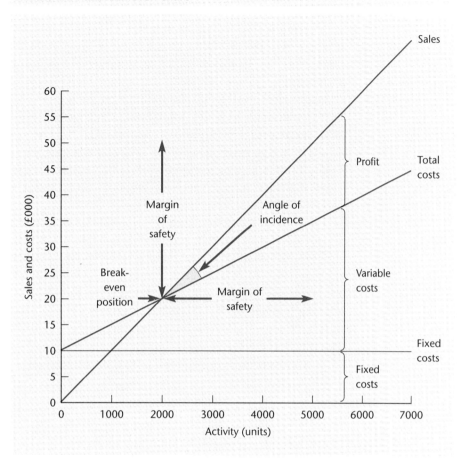

Tutorial notes

1 The total costs line is a combination of the fixed costs and the variable costs. It thus ranges from a total cost of £10 000 (fixed costs only) at a nil level of activity, to £35 000 when the activity level is 5000 units (fixed costs of £10 000 + variable costs of £25 000).

2 The angle of incidence is the angle formed between the sales line and the total cost line. The wider the angle, the greater the amount of profit. A wide angel of incidence and a wide margin of safety (see 3 below) indicates a highly profitable position.

3 The margin of safety is the distance between the sales achieved and the sales level needed to break even. It can be measured either in units (along the x axis of the graph) or in sales revenue terms (along the y axis).

4 Activity (measured along the x axis) may be measured either in units, or as a percentage of the theoretical maximum level of activity, or in terms of sales revenue.

In practice, the above relationships are not likely to hold good over the range of activity indicated in the Exhibit. They are usually assumed to remain valid over only a small range of activity. This is known as the *relevant range*. In this Exhibit the relevant range may be from (say) 1000 to 3000 units; above or below these levels, the selling prices, the variable costs and the fixed costs may all change.

While this point might appear to create some difficulty, it should be appreciated that wide fluctuations in activity are not normally experienced. It is usually quite reasonable to assume that the entity will be operating in a fairly narrow range of activity and that the various relationships will be linear. It must also be remembered that the information is meant to be only a *guide* to managerial decision making and that it is impossible to be absolutely precise.

You will see that the break-even chart shown in Exhibit 17.4 does not show a separate variable cost line. This may be somewhat confusing, and so sometimes the information is presented in the form of a *contribution graph*. Based on the same data as in Exhibit 17.4 a contribution graph is illustrated in Figure 17.1. You are recommended to compare the two exhibits and see if you can spot the differences.

If you have studied the two exhibits closely, you will have observed that Exhibit 17.4 (the break-even chart) is very similar to Figure 17.1 (the contribution graph), although there are some differences. The main ones are as follows:

1 The contribution graph shows the variable cost line ranging from the origin when there is no activity to £25000 when 5000 units are sold. It then continues beyond that point in a straight line.
2 The fixed cost line is drawn parallel to the variable cost line, i.e. higher up the *y* axis. As the fixed costs are assumed to remain fixed irrespective of the level of activity, the fixed cost line runs from £10000 when there is no activity to £35000 when 5000 units are sold. It is then continued as a straight line beyond that point.
3 The fixed cost line also serves as the total cost line.

Apart from the above differences, the break-even chart and the contribution graph are identical. Which one should you adopt? There is no specific guidance that we can give you since the decision is one largely of personal preference. The break-even chart is more common, but the contribution chart is probably more helpful since the fixed and the variable cost lines are shown separately.

You will have noticed that both the break-even chart and the contribution graph do not show the *actual amount of profit or loss* at varying levels of activity. Thus, if you wanted to know what the profit was when (say) 4000 units were sold, you would have to use a ruler to measure the distance between the sales line and the total cost line. This is not very satisfactory. In order to avoid this

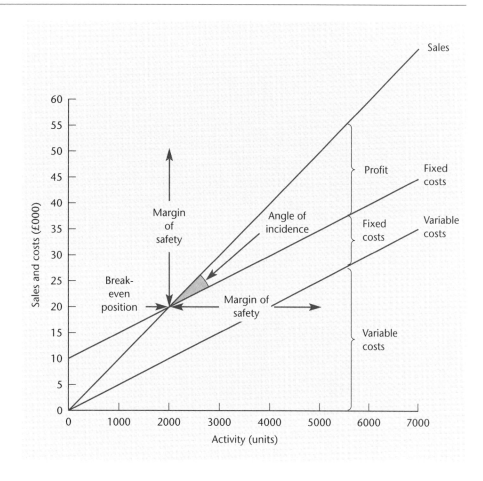

Figure 17.1
A contribution
graph

problem, the information may be displayed in the form of a profit/volume chart (or graph).

A profit/volume chart shows the effect of a change in activity on profit. An example of such a chart is shown in Exhibit 17.5. It is based on the data used in Exhibit 17.3.

Throughout the chapter we have been at pains to stress that, while contribution analysis is extremely useful as an aid to managerial decision making, there are many criticisms that can be levelled at it. We summarize them in the next section.

Exhibit 17.5 A profit/volume chart

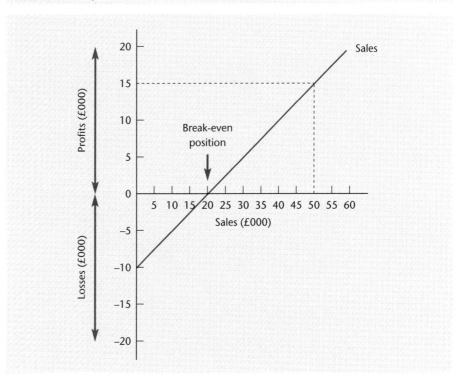

Tutorial notes

1 The *x* axis can be represented either in terms of units, as a percentage of the activity level, or in terms of sales revenue.
2 The *y* axis represents profits (positive amounts) or losses (negative amounts).
3 With sales at a level of £50 000, the profit is £15 000. The sales line cuts the *x* axis at the break-even position of £20 000 sales. If there are no sales, the loss equals the fixed costs of £10 000.

Criticisms

The assumptions adopted in preparing marginal cost statements and their use in contribution analysis lead to a number of important reservations about the technique. The main ones are as follows:

1 *Cost classification.* Costs cannot be easily divided into fixed and variable categories.
2 *Variable costs.* Variable costs do not necessarily vary in direct proportion to sales revenue at all levels of activity. The cost of direct materials, for example, may change if supplies are limited in availability or if they are bought in bulk. It is also questionable whether direct labour should be treated as a

variable cost (as is often the case) since current legislative practice makes it difficult to dismiss employees at short notice.

3 *Fixed costs*. Fixed costs are unlikely to remain constant over a wide range of activity. There is a good chance that they will change both beyond and below a fairly narrow range. They may perhaps move in 'steps', so that between an activity level of 0 and 999 units, for example, the fixed costs may be £10 000, be £12 000 between an activity level of 1000 and 2999 units, be £15 000 between an activity level of 3000 and 5000 units, and so on.

4 *Time period*. The determination of the time period over which the relationship between the fixed and variable costs may hold good is difficult to determine. In the very short term (say a day), all costs may be fixed. In the long term (say five years), all cost may be variable as the entity could go out of business.

5 *Complementary products*. A specific decision affecting one product may affect other products. For example, a garage sells both petrol and oil. A decision to stop selling oil may affect sales of petrol.

6 *Cost recovery*. It may be unwise to exclude fixed costs altogether from the analysis. In the medium-to-long term, an entity must recover all of its costs. Decisions cannot be taken purely in terms of the impact that they may have on contribution.

7 *Diagrammatic presentations*. Break-even charts, contribution graphs and profit/volume charts are somewhat simplistic. The sales of individual products are considered in total and it is assumed that any change made to one product will have a proportionate effect on all the other products.

8 *Non-cost factors*. Decisions cannot be taken purely on the basis of cost. Sometimes factors that cannot be easily quantified and costed are more important – for instance comfort, convenience, loyalty, reliability or speed.

9 *Behavioural factors*. In practice, behavioural factors also have to be considered. Individuals do not always act rationally and an actual behaviour pattern may be quite different from what was expected. A decrease in the selling price of a product, for example, may reduce the quantity of good purchased because it is *perceived* to be of poor quality.

The factors listed above are all fairly severe criticisms of the marginal costing technique and its use in contribution analysis. None the less, experience suggests that it has still a useful part to play in managerial decision making, provided that: (1) the basis upon which the information is built is understood; (2) its apparent arithmetical precision is not regarded as a guarantee of absolute certainty; and (3) non-cost factors are also taken into account.

With these reservations in mind, we can now move on to look at the technique in a little more detail. Before we do so, however, it would be useful to summarize the main formulae so that it will be easier for you to refer back to them when dealing with the various exhibits and examples.

Formulae

Earlier in the chapter we explained that marginal costing revolves around the assumption that total costs can be classified into fixed and variable costs. This then led us on to an explanation of what we called the *marginal cost equation*, i.e. $S - V = F + P$. This equation can be used as the basis for a number of other simple equations that are useful in contribution analysis. The main ones are summarized below.

1 Sales – Variable cost of sales = Contribution $\qquad\qquad$ $S - V = C$

2 Contribution – Fixed costs = Profit/(Loss) $\qquad\qquad$ $C - F = P/(L)$

3 Break-even (B/E) point = Contribution – Fixed costs $\qquad$ $C - F$

4 B/E in sales value terms = $\dfrac{\text{Fixed costs} \times \text{Sales}}{\text{Contribution}}$ $\qquad$ $\dfrac{F \times S}{C}$

5 B/E in units = $\dfrac{\text{Fixed costs}}{\text{Contribution per unit}}$ $\qquad$ $\dfrac{F}{C \text{ per unit}}$

6 Margin of safety (M/S) in sales value terms =
$\dfrac{\text{Profit} \times \text{Sales}}{\text{Contribution}}$ $\qquad$ $\dfrac{P \times S}{C}$

7 M/S in units = $\dfrac{\text{Profit}}{\text{Contribution per unit}}$ $\qquad$ $\dfrac{P}{C \text{ per unit}}$

Exhibit 17.6 examines the use of some of these formulae.

Exhibit 17.6 Example showing the use of the marginal cost formulae

The following information relates to Happy Limited for the year to 30 June 2001:

Number of units sold: 10 000

	Per unit £	Total £000
Sales	30	300
Less: Variable costs	18	180
Contribution	12	120
Less: Fixed costs		24
Profit		96

Required:
In value and unit terms, calculate the following:
(a) the break-even position; and
(b) the margin of safety.

Answer to Exhibit 17.6

(a) Break-even position in value terms:

$$\frac{F \times S}{C} = \frac{£24\,000 \times 300\,000}{120\,000} = \underline{\underline{£60\,000}}$$

Break-even in units:

$$\frac{F}{C\ per\ unit} = \frac{£24\,000}{12} = \underline{\underline{2000\ units}}$$

(b) Margin of safety in value terms:

$$\frac{P \times S}{C} = \frac{£96\,000 \times 300\,000}{120\,000} = \underline{\underline{£240\,000}}$$

Margin of safety in units:

$$\frac{P}{C\ per\ unit} = \frac{£96\,000}{12} = \underline{\underline{8000\ units}}$$

Check that you understand the significance of the answer to Exhibit 17.6. You might also use the data to practice preparing a break-even chart and a profit/volume chart.

An illustrative example

It would now be helpful to incorporate the principles behind contribution analysis into a simple example. Exhibit 17.7 outlines a typical problem which a board of directors might well face.

Exhibit 17.7 Marginal costing example

Looking ahead to the financial year ending 31 March 2005, the directors of Problems Limited are faced with a budgeted loss of £10 000. This is based on the following data:

Budgeted number of units	10 000
	£000
Sales revenue	100
Less: Variable costs	80
Contribution	20
Less: Fixed costs	30
Budgeted loss	(10)

The directors would like to aim for a profit of £20 000 for the year to 31 March 2005. Various proposals have been put forward, none of which require a change in the budgeted level of fixed costs. These proposals are as follows:

1 Reduce the selling price of each unit by 10 per cent.
2 Increase the selling price of each unit by 10 per cent.
3 Stimulate sales by improving the quality of the product, which would increase the variable cost of the unit by £1.50 per unit.

Required:
(a) For each proposal calculate:
    (i)   the break-even position in units in value terms;
    (ii) the number of units required to be sold in order to meet the profit target.
(b) State which proposal you think should be adopted.

Answer to Exhibit 17.7

Problems Limited
(a) (i) and (ii)

Workings:	£
Profit target	20 000
Fixed costs	30 000
Total contribution required	50 000

The budgeted selling price per unit is £10 (£100 000/10 000). The budgeted variable cost per unit is £8 (£80 000/10 000).

The budgeted outlook compared with each proposal may be summarized as follows:

Per unit:	*Budgeted position*	*Proposal 1*	*Proposal 2*	*Proposal 3*
	£	£	£	£
Selling price	10	9	11	10.00
Less: Variable costs	8	8	8	9.50
(a) Unit contribution	2	1	3	0.50
(b) Total contribution required to break even (= fixed costs)	£30 000	£30 000	£30 000	£30 000
(c) Total contribution required to meet the profit target	£50 000	£50 000	£50 000	£50 000
Number of units to break even [(b)/(a)]	15 000	30 000	10 000	60 000
Number of units to meet the profit target [(c)/(a)]	25 000	50 000	16 667	100 000

(b)

Comments:

1 By continuing with the present budget proposals, the company would need to sell 15 000 units to break even, or 25 000 units to meet the profit target. Thus in order to break even the company needs to increase its unit sales by 50%

$$\left(\frac{£15\,000 - 10\,000}{10\,000} \times 100\% \right) \text{ or by 150\% } \left(\frac{£25\,000 - 10\,000}{10\,000} \times 100\% \right) \text{ to meet the }$$

profit target.

2 A reduction in selling price of 10% per unit would require unit sales to increase by 200%

$$\left(\frac{£30\,000 - 10\,000}{10\,000} \times 100\% \right) \text{ in order to break even, or by 400\% }$$

$$\left(\frac{£50\,000 - 10\,000}{10\,000} \times 100\% \right) \text{ to meet the profit target.}$$

3 By increasing the selling price of each unit by 10%, the company would only have to sell at the budgeted level to break even, but its unit sales would have to increase by

66.7% $\left(\frac{£16\,667 - 10\,000}{10\,000} \times 100\% \right)$ to meet the profit target.

4 By improving the product at an increased variable cost of £1.50 per unit, the company would require a 500% $\left(\frac{£60\,000 - 10\,000}{10\,000} \times 100\% \right)$ increase in unit sales to

break even, or a 900% $\left(\frac{£100\,000 - 10\,000}{10\,000} \times 100\% \right)$ to meet the profit target.

Conclusion:

It would appear that increasing the selling price by 10% would be a more practical solution for the company to adopt. In the short run at least, it will break even, and there is the possibility that sales could be sufficient to make a small profit. In the long run this proposal has a much better chance of meeting the profit target than do the others. Some extra stimulus would be needed, however, to lift sales to this level over such a relatively short period of time. It is not clear, why an increase in price would increase sales, unless the product is one that only sells at a comparatively high price, such as cosmetics and patent medicines. It must also be questioned whether the cost relationships will remain as indicated in the exhibit over such a large increase in activity. In particular, it is unlikely that the fixed costs will remain entirely fixed if there were to be a 66.7% increase in sales.

Limiting factors

When optional decisions are being considered, the aim will always be to maximize contribution, because the greater the contribution, the more chance there is of covering the fixed costs and hence of making a profit. When managers are faced with a choice, therefore, between (say) producing product A at a contribution of £10 per unit, or of producing product B at a contribution of £20 per unit, they would normally choose product B. Sometimes, however, it may not be possible to produce unlimited quantities of product B because there could be a limit on how many units could either be sold or produced. Such limits are known as *limiting factors* (or *key factors*).

Limiting factors may arise for a number of reasons. It may not be possible, for example, to sell more than a certain number of units; there may be production restraints (such as shortages of raw materials, skilled labour, or factory space), or the company may not be able to finance the anticipated rate of expansion.

If there is a product that cannot be produced and sold in unlimited quantities, then it is necessary to follow a simple rule in order to decide which product to concentrate on producing. The rule can be summarized as follows:

Choose the work that provides the maximum contribution per unit of limiting factor employed.

This sounds very complicated, but it is quite simple to use. The procedure is illustrated below:

1. Assumption: direct labour hours are in short supply.
2. Calculate the contribution made by each product.
3. Divide the contribution that each product makes by the number of direct labour hours used in making each product.
4. The solution = the contribution per direct labour hour employed (i.e. the limiting factor).

Thus if we had to choose between two jobs, (say) A and B, we would convert A's contribution and B's contribution into the amount of contribution earned for every direct labour hour worked on A and on B, respectively. We would then opt for the job that earned the most contribution per direct labour hour. The technique is illustrated in Exhibit 17.8.

Exhibit 17.8 Application of key factors

Quays Limited manufactures a product for which there is a shortage of the raw material known as PX. During the year to 31 March 2004, only 1000 kilograms of PX will be available. PX is used by Quays in manufacturing both product 8 and product 9. The following information is relevant:

Per unit:	Product 8	Product 9
	£	£
Selling price	300	150
Less: Variable costs	200	100
Contribution	100	50
P/V ratio $\left(\dfrac{£100}{300} \times 100\%\right) ; \left(\dfrac{£50}{150} \times 100\%\right)$	$33\frac{1}{3}$	$33\frac{1}{3}$
Kilograms of PX required	5	2

Required:
State which product Quays Limited should concentrate on producing.

Answer to Exhibit 17.8

	Product 8	Product 9
	£	£
Contribution per unit	100	50
Limiting factor per unit (kg)	5	2
Contribution per kilogram	20	25

Decision:
Quays should concentrate on product 9 because it gives the highest contribution per unit of limiting factor.

Check:
Maximum contribution of product 8:

200 units (1000kg/5) × contribution per unit = 200 × £100 = £20 000

Maximum contribution of product 9:

500 units (1000kg/2) × contribution per unit = 500 × £50 = £25 000

In Exhibit 17.8 it was assumed that this was only one limiting factor, but there could be many more. This situation is illustrated in Exhibit 17.9. The basic data are the same as for Exhibit 17.8.

Exhibit 17.9 Example of marginal costing using two key factors

Information:
1 Assume now that it is not possible for Quays Limited to sell more than 400 units of product 9.
2 The company would aim to sell all of the 400 units because product 9's contribution per unit is greater than product 8's. The total contribution would then be £20 000 (400 × £50).
3 The 400 units would consume 800 units of raw materials (400 × 2 kilograms), leaving 200 (1000 – 800) kilograms for use in producing product 8.
4 Product 8 requires 5 kilograms per unit of raw materials, so 40 units (200kg ÷ 5kg) could be completed at a total contribution of £4000 (40 × £100).

Summary of the position:

	Product 8	Product 9	Total
Units sold	40	400	
Raw materials (kilograms used)	200	800	1 000
Contribution per unit (£)	100	50	
Total contribution (£)	4 000	20 000	24 000

Note: The £24 000 total contribution compares with the contribution of £25 000 that the company could have made if there were no limiting factors affecting the sales of product 9.

Conclusion

Contribution analysis is particularly useful in short-term decision making, but it is of less value when decisions have to be viewed over the long term. The system revolves around two main assumptions:

1 some costs remain fixed, irrespective of the level of activity;
2 other costs vary in direct proportion to sales.

These assumptions are not valid over the long term but, provided that they are used with caution, they can be usefully adopted in the short term.

It should also be remembered that the technique is only a *guide* to decision making, and that other non-cost factors have to be taken into account.

In the next chapter we use contribution analysis to deal with other managerial problems.

Key points

1 Total cost can be analyzed into fixed costs and variable costs.

2 Fixed costs are assumed to be unrelated to activity. They may be ignored in making short-term managerial decisions.

3 A company will aim to maximize the *contribution* that each unit makes to profit.

4 The various relationships between costs can be expressed in the form of an equation: $S - V = F + P$, where S = sales, V = variable costs, F = fixed costs, and P = profit.

5 It may not always be possible to maximize unit contribution, because materials, labour, finance or other factors may be in short supply.

6 In the long run, fixed costs cannot be ignored.

Check your learning

1 Fill in the missing blanks in each of the following sentences:
  (a) A _____ _____ is a cost that is incurred for a period, and that within certain outputs and turnover limits, tends to be unaffected by fluctuations in the levels of activity.
  (b) Costs that tend to vary with the level of activity are known as _____ _____ .

2 Complete the following equations:
  (a) Sales revenue – _____ = Contribution.
  (b) Contribution – Fixed costs = _____ .
  (c) Break-even point = _____ – _____ .
  (d) Break-even point in units = $\dfrac{\text{Fixed costs}}{\rule{3cm}{0.4pt}}$.
  (e) $\dfrac{\text{Profit} \times \text{Sales}}{\text{Contribution}} = $ _____ .

3 What term is used to describe anything that restricts the level of activity of an entity?

[*The answers to these questions may be found at the back of the book.*]

Group discussion questions

17.1 'It has been suggested that although contribution analysis is fine in theory, fixed costs cannot be ignored in practice.' Discuss this statement.

17.2 'Contribution analysis described in text books is too simplistic and is of little relevance to management.' How far do you agree with this statement?

17.3 Do break-even charts and profit graphs help management to take more meaningful decisions?

Practice questions

[*Note: The questions marked with an asterisk have answers at the back of the book.*]

17.4* The following information relates to Pole Limited for the year to 31 January 2002.

	£000
Administration expenses:	
Fixed	30
Variable	7
Semi-variable (fixed 80%, variable 20%)	20
Materials:	
Direct	60
Indirect	5
Production overhead (all fixed)	40
Research and development expenditure:	
Fixed	60
Variable	15
Semi-variable (fixed 50%, variable 50%)	10
Sales	450
Selling and distribution expenditure:	
Fixed	80
Variable	4
Semi-variable (fixed 70%, variable 30%)	30
Wages:	
Direct	26
Indirect	13

Required:

Using the above information, compile a contribution analysis statement for Pole Limited for the year to 31 January 2002.

17.5* You are presented with the following information for Giles Limited for the year to 28 February 2002:

	£000
Fixed costs	150
Variable costs	300
Sales (50 000 units)	500

Required:
(a) Calculate the following:
(i) the break-even point in value terms and in units; and
(ii) the margin of safety in value terms and in units.
(b) Prepare a break-even chart.

17.6 The following information applies to Ayre Limited for the two years to 31 March 2002 and 2003, respectively:

Year	Sales	Profits
	£000	£000
31.3.2002	750	100
31.3.2003	1 000	250

Required:
Assuming that the cost relationships had remained as given in the question, calculate the company's profit if the sales for the year to 31 March 2003 had reached the bud-geted level of £1 200 000.

17.7 The following information relates to Carter Limited for the year to 30 April 2003:

Units sold	50 000
Selling price per unit	£40
Net profit per unit	£9
Profit/volume ratio	40%

During 2004 the company would like to increase its sales substantially, but to do so it would have to reduce the selling price per unit by 20 per cent. The variable cost per unit will not change, but because of the increased activity, the company will have to invest in new machinery which will increase the fixed costs by £30 000 per annum.

Required:
Given the new conditions, calculate how many units the company will need to sell in 2004 in order to make the same amount of profit as it did in 2003.

17.8 Puzzled Limited would like to increase its sales during the year to 3l May 2005. To do so, it has several mutually exclusive options open to it:

1 reduce the selling price per unit by 15 per cent;
2 improve the product resulting in an increase in the variable cost per unit of £l.30;
3 spend £15 000 on an advertising campaign;
4 improve factory efficiency by purchasing more machinery at a fixed extra annual cost of £22 500.

During the year to 31 May 2004, the company sold 20 000 units. The cost details were as follows:

	£000
Sales	200
Variable costs	150
Contribution	50
Fixed costs	40
Profit	10

These cost relationships are expected to hold in 2005.

Required:
State which option you would recommend and why.

17.9 The following information relates to Mere's budget for the year to 31 December 2007:

Product	K	L	M	Total
	£000	£000	£000	£000
Sales	700	400	250	1350
Direct materials	210	60	30	300
Direct labour	100	200	200	500
Variable overhead	90	60	50	200
Fixed overhead	20	40	40	100
	420	360	320	1100
Profit/(loss)	280	40	(70)	250
Budgeted sales (units)	140	20	25	

Note:
Fixed overheads are apportioned on the basis of direct labour hours.

The directors are worried about the loss that product M is budgeted to make, and various suggestions have been made to counteract the loss, viz.:
1 stop selling product M;
2 increase M's selling price by 20 per cent;
3 reduce M's selling price by 10 per cent;
4 reduce its costs by purchasing a new machine costing £350 000, thereby decreasing the direct labour cost by £100 000 (the machine would have a life of five years; its residual value would be nil).

Required:
Evaluate each of these proposals.

18 Decision making: specific decisions

Severfield-Rowen close to sale of glove business

By Gautam Malkani

Shares in Severfield-Rowen jumped 40 per cent yesterday after the structural steelwork company said it was close to selling its steel glove business and issued a positive trading statement.

Manabo, which makes protective chainmail gloves for abattoir workers, failed to break even as was predicted last year. But the company confirmed it was in advanced negotiations to sell the subsidiary to a US-based food and hygiene company. Analysts said it could fetch between £2m and £2.5m. The shares gained 77.5p to 270p. The company said order books were at more than £70m, equivalent to more than 60,000 tonnes of steel.

Financial Times, 7 January 2000. Reprinted with permission.

Closing a business is a major managerial decision

In this chapter we are going to explain how management accounting may help managers come to a decision about various problems. The guidance that management accountants may provide will normally be primarily – although not exclusively – of a financial nature. In arriving at a particular decision, however, managers will also have to take into account other factors, such as technical requirements, material and labour availability, and labour relations. Hence some decisions could be based mainly on non-quantifiable and non-financial factors and cost may not always be an overriding consideration.

The chapter is divided into six main sections. In the first section we deal with the nature of decision-making. The second section examines the ways in which costs may be classified for decision-making purposes. The sections thereafter examine four specific types of decisions, namely closure and shutdown decisions, make or buy decisions, pricing decisions and special-order decisions. The replacement of fixed assets is another decision that managers have also to take, but this topic is left to the next chapter.

Learning objectives

By the end of this chapter, you should be able to:

- outline the nature of decision making;

- list six ways of classifying costs for decision-making purposes;

- incorporate cost and financial data into managerial problems involving closure and shut-down decisions, make or buy decisions, pricing decisions and special-order decisions.

The nature of decision making

We start our examination of some specific decision-making problems by considering what is involved in decision making.

The term *decision* will be familiar to you in your everyday life. It means coming to a conclusion about a particular issue – for example, determining (i.e. deciding) when to get up in the morning, whether to have tea or coffee for breakfast, or choosing between a holiday and buying some new clothes. Similarly, in a managerial context, decisions have to be taken about whether or not to sell in particular markets, buy some new machinery or spend more money on research.

Management accountants will be involved in collecting data and supplying information for such decisions. While the information that the management accountants supply will be primarily of a financial nature, they will highlight other considerations that need to be taken into account before a decision is made. The eventual decision will rest with the cost centre manager concerned, and it may well be that non-cost factors turn out to be more important than measurable financial considerations. Instead of manufacturing components for its products, for example, it may be cheaper for an entity to purchase them from an external supplier. But that supplier could be unreliable, and so it might be worth the extra cost of manufacturing the components internally in order to avoid the risk of any disruption to the entity's normal production processes.

The data required for decision-making purposes tend to be more wide-ranging and less constrained than those used in cost accounting. Their main characteristics may be summarized as follows:

1 *Forward looking*. While historical data may be used as a guide, information for decision making is much more concerned with what *will* happen rather than with what *did* happen. So because much of the information required is concerned with the future, considerable initiative and intuitive judgement is required in being able to obtain it.

2 *One-off decisions*. Decision making often involves dealing with a problem that is unique. Thus a solution has to be specially designed to deal with that particular problem.

3 *Data availability*. While some of the data required for decision making may be extracted from the cost accounting system, much of what is required may have to be specially obtained.

4 *Net cash flow approach.* Managers will be concerned with the impact that a decision may have on the expected net cash flow of a particular project (i.e. future cash receipts less future cash expenditure). The calculation of periodic profit and loss account based on accruals and prepayments will be largely irrelevant.

5 *Relevant costs.* Costs and revenues that are not affected by a decision are excluded from the analysis. Thus fixed costs, for example, that are not likely to change as a result of taking a particular decision will be ignored.

6 *Opportunity costs.* Those benefits that would be foregone or lost as a result of taking a particular decision are known as opportunity costs. They should form part of any decision-making analysis. You may decide, for example, to look after your own garden yourself instead of doing some paid overtime. The opportunity cost would be the wages you lose by not working overtime less the amount you save by not employing a gardener. Opportunity costs are not usually stored in the cost accounting system and it may not be easy to determine them.

7 *Probability testing.* Much of the information used in problem solving is speculative because it relates to the future and so it is advisable to carry out some probability testing. This is a complex area and it goes beyond this book. Essentially, probability testing involves calculating the *expected value* of a particular project or proposal. The basic idea is exemplified in Exhibit 18.1.

Exhibit 18.1 Probability testing

Company X sells one product codenamed A1. The marketing department has estimated that the sales of A1 for a forthcoming budget period could be £1000, £1500, or £2000. Upon further investigation, it would appear that there is a 70 per cent chance that the sales will be £1000, a 20 per cent chance that the sales will be £1500, and a 10 per cent chance that the sales will be £2000.

Required:
Calculate the expected value of sales for product A1 during the forthcoming budget period.

Answer to Exhibit 18.1

The question requires us to calculate the expected value of the sales of A1 for the forthcoming period. It might be easier for you to think of the expected value as the *weighted average*, which perhaps provides a clue to what is required. In order to calculate the expected values the budgeted sales figures are multiplied by their respective chances or probabilities. Thus:

Budgeted sales	Probability		Expected value
(1)	(2)		(3)
£	%		£
1 000	70		700
1 500	20		300
2 000	10		200
Expected value	100	Total expected value	1 200

Tutorial notes

1 The expected value (or weighted average) of the sales for the forthcoming budget period is £1200 as per Column (3).

2 The answer has been obtained by multiplying the three estimated level of sales by their respective probabilities (Column (1) multiplied by Column (2)).

3 In this exhibit, the probabilities are expressed in percentage terms. When combined they should always total 100 per cent. Note that sometimes they are expressed in decimal terms; they should then total 1.0, i.e. (in our example) 0.7 + 0.2 + 0.1 = 1.0.

4 The probabilities are estimates. They may be made partly on past experience, partly on an investigation of the market and partly on instinct. Hence they might be better described as 'guesstimates'.

5 Does the solution make sense? The expected value is £1200; this is £200 more than the lowest level of sales of £1000; the probability of this level being achieved is 70 per cent. Thus the chances of the sales being at least £1000 is quite high. By contrast, there is only a 20 per cent probability that the sales could be as high as £1500 and only a 10 per cent chance that they could reach £2000. It seems reasonable to assume, therefore, that the sales are likely to be nearer £1000 than £1500. Thus £1200 appears to be a reasonable compromise.

Before we examine some specific decision-making situations, it would be useful to examine some common cost terms used in decision making. We do so in the next section.

Cost classification

As we saw in Chapter 14, costs (and revenues) may be classified into various categories depending upon the purpose for which they are going to be used. In cost accounting, information is required mainly for product costing and stock valuation purposes, and so the most important category is the distinction between direct costs and indirect ones.

A direct/indirect cost classification is not normally appropriate in decision making. The preferred classification is that relating to fixed and variable costs, but other cost classifications are also used. We summarize the main ones used in decision making below.

Fixed and variable costs

As we saw in the last chapter, fixed costs are those costs that are likely to remain unchanged irrespective of the level of activity. Variable costs are those that move directly proportional to activity (one unit results in £1 of variable cost, two units results in £2 of variable cost, three units in £3 of variable cost, and so on).

In theory, those costs classified as 'fixed' will remain payable irrespective of whether the entity is completely inactive or if it is operating at full capacity. In practice, fixed costs tend to remain fixed only over a relatively small range of activity range and only in the short term.

The assumption that some costs remain unchanged means that, in a decision-making exercise, fixed costs do not normally need to be taken into account. In other words, fixed costs can be ignored, because they will not be affected by the decision and are not therefore relevant to a consideration of the issues.

Relevant and non-relevant costs

Relevant costs are those future costs that are likely to be affected by a particular decision. It follows that non-relevant costs are those that are *not* likely to be affected by the decision. This means that non-relevant costs (e.g. those fixed costs not affected by the decision) can be excluded from any cost analysis.

Avoidable and non-avoidable costs

Avoidable costs are those costs that may be saved by not taking a particular decision. Non-avoidable costs will still be incurred if the decision is taken. Avoidable and non-avoidable costs are very similar to relevant and non-relevant costs. Indeed, sometimes the terms are used synonymously.

Sunk costs

Sunk costs are those costs that have already been incurred as a result of a previous decision. Hence they are not relevant as far as future decisions are concerned and they can be excluded from any decision-making analysis.

Committed costs

A committed cost arises out of a decision that has previously been taken, although the event has not yet taken place. For example, a proposal to increase the capacity of a factory from 1000 to 1500 units per annum will result in increased capital expenditure. A decision to accept the proposal means that certain costs are *committed*, and it only becomes a matter of timing before there is a cash outflow. Once the proposal has gone ahead and it has been paid for, the costs become *sunk* costs. Committed costs (like sunk costs) are not relevant as far as *future* decisions are concerned.

Opportunity costs

We referred to opportunity costs in the previous section of this chapter. Just to remind you, an opportunity cost is a measure of the net benefit that would be lost if one decision is taken instead of another decision. Such costs are rarely recorded in the cost accounting system and they usually require to be calculated separately.

We can now turn to some specific decisions that managers may face and the type of management accounting information that can help them arrive at an appropriate solution.

Closure and shutdown decisions

A common problem that managers may face from time to time is whether to close some segment of the enterprise, such as a product, a service, a department, or even an entire factory. This is a *closure* decision; the assumption behind it is that the closure would be permanent. A similar decision may have to be taken in respect of a temporary closure. This is known as a *shutdown* decision.

A closure decision sometimes needs to be taken because a segment within the overall entity may perhaps have become unprofitable, out of date or unfashionable, and therefore no future is seen for it. A decision to close a segment of an entity temporarily would be taken when the segment's problems are likely to be overcome in the near future. Thus a segment may be unprofitable at the moment but is expected to recover in (say) 12 months' time.

Closure and shutdown decisions are often required because a section is regarded as being 'unprofitable'. The definition of 'unprofitable' has to be looked at very closely. A product, for example, may not be making a *profit* but it may be making a *contribution* towards the fixed costs of the company. Should it be abandoned? Great care would need to be taken before such a decision was taken. The abandonment of one product may have an impact on the sales of other products in such circumstances, it may even be beneficial to sell the product below its variable cost (at least in the short term).

Closure and shutdown decisions are not easy to make. They cannot be determined purely on narrow cost grounds, as other wide-ranging factors may need to be considered. We illustrate a relatively straightforward closure decision in Exhibit 18.2

Exhibit 18.2 A closure decision

Vera Limited has three main product lines: 1, 2, and 3. The company uses an absorption costing system, and the following information relates to the budget for the year 2002.

Product line	1	2	3	Total
Budgeted sales (units)	10 000	4 000	6 000	
	£000	£000	£000	£000
Sales revenue	300	200	150	650
Direct materials	100	40	60	200
Direct labour	50	70	80	200
Production overhead	75	30	35	140
Non-production overhead	15	10	5	30
	240	150	180	570
Profit (Loss)	60	50	(30)	80

Additional information:
1   Both direct materials and direct labour are considered to be variable costs.
2   The total production overhead of £140 000 consists of £40 000 variable costs and £100 000 fixed costs. Variable production overheads are absorbed on the basis of 20 per cent of the direct labour costs.
3   The non-production overhead of £30 000 is entirely fixed.
4   Assume that there will be no opening or closing stock.

Required:
Determine whether Product line 3 should be closed.

Answer to Exhibit 18.2

Points:
1   The first step in determining whether to recommend a closure of Product line 3 is to calculate the *contribution* that each product line makes.
2   To do this, it is necessary to rearrange the data given in the question in a marginal cost format, i.e. separate the fixed costs from the variable costs.
3   If Product line 3 makes a contribution, then other factors will have to be taken into account before an eventual decision can be made.

Calculations:

Product line	1	2	3	Total
Budgeted sales (units)	10 000	4 000	6 000	
	£000	£000	£000	£000
Sales revenue	300	200	150	650
Less: Variable costs:				
Direct materials	100	40	60	200
Direct labour	50	70	80	200
Variable production overhead (Question Note 2: 20% of direct labour cost)	10	14	16	40
	160	124	156	440
Contribution	140	76	(6)	210
Less: Fixed costs:				
Production overheads (£140 – 40)				(100)
Non-production overheads (See Note 3)				(30)
Profit				80

Observations:
It would appear that Product line 3 neither makes a profit nor contributes towards the fixed costs. Should it be closed? Before such a decision is taken a number of other factors would have to be considered. These are as follows.

1 Are the budgeted figures accurate? Have they been checked? How reliable are the budgeted data?
2 What method has been used for identifying the direct material costs that each product line uses? Is it appropriate for all three product lines?
3 The question states that direct labour is a variable cost. Is direct labour really a variable cost? Is the assessment of its cost accurate and realistic?
4 Variable production overheads are absorbed on a very broad basis related to direct labour costs. Does this method fairly reflect Product line 3's use of variable overheads?
5 Product line 3's appears to result in only a small negative contribution. Can this be made positive by perhaps a small increase in the unit selling price or by the more efficient use of direct materials and direct labour?
6 Assuming that the cost data supplied are both fair and accurate, would the closure of Product line 3 affect (a) sales for the other two product lines; or (b) the overall variable costs?
7 If closure of Product line 3 is recommended, should it be closed permanently or temporarily? More information, is needed of its prospects beyond 2002.

The decision:
Clearly, without more information it is impossible to come to a firm conclusion. Assuming that the cost accounting procedures are both accurate and fair, it would appear that *on purely financial grounds*, Product line 3 should be closed. However, there are too many unknown factors to put this forward as a conclusive recommendation.

Make or buy decisions

Make or buy decisions require management to determine whether to manufacture internally or purchase externally. For example, should a car company manufacture its own components or purchase them from a specialist supplier? Similarly, should a glass manufacturer concentrate on producing glass and purchase all its other requirements (e.g. safety equipment and containers for the glass) externally? In local government, should a housing department employ its own joiners or contract outside firms to do the necessary work?

The theory beyond make or buy decisions revolves round the argument that entities should do what they are best at doing and employ others to undertake the peripheral activities. In other words, they should concentrate on their main objective and contract out (or 'privatize', in the case of governmental activities) all other essential activities.

A decision to contract out will often be taken on a purely financial basis (*'Is it cheaper to buy in this service?'*). This may be unwise. There could be important non-financial and non-quantifiable factors that should be taken into account. If a supplier has labour relations' problems, for example, deliveries may be uncertain and production could be disrupted. This could then cause problems with the entity's own customers. It would be extremely difficult to estimate an accurate cost of such a possible outcome. None the less, a make or buy decision will be based partly on cost and partly on other such factors, including an assessment of any opportunity costs.

A simple make or buy decision is illustrated in Exhibit 18.3.

Exhibit 18.3 A make or buy decision

Zam Limited uses an important component in one of its products. An estimate of the cost of making one unit of the component internally is as follows.

	£
Direct materials	5
Direct labour	4
Variable overhead	3
Total variable cost	12

Additional information:

1 Fixed costs specifically associated with manufacturing the components are estimated to be £8000 per month.

2 The number of components normally required is 1000 per month.

An outside manufacturer has offered to supply the components at a cost of £18 per component. Should the components be manufactured internally or purchased externally?

Required:

Determine whether Zam Limited should purchase the components from the outside supplier.

Answer to Exhibit 18.3

Points:

Assuming that the cost data given in the question are accurate, the first step in answering the question is to calculate the cost of manufacturing the components internally. Although the variable cost of each unit is given, there are some fixed costs directly associated with manufacturing internally and these have to be taken into account.

The fixed costs cause us a problem because the monthly activity levels may vary. However, we can only work on the data given in the question, i.e. 1000 units per month.

Calculations:

Total cost of manufacturing internally 1000 units per month of the component:

	£
Total variable cost (1000 units × £12)	12 000
Associated fixed costs	8 000
Total cost	20 000
Total unit cost (£20 000 ÷ 1000) =	£20

Tutorial notes

1 Assuming that Zam Limited requires 1000 units per month, it would be cheaper to obtain them from the external supplier (£20 compared with £18 per component).

2 The above assumption is based on purchases of 1000 units. The more units required, the cheaper they would be to manufacture internally. In order to match the external price, the fixed costs can be no more than £6 per unit (the external purchase price of £18 less the internal variable cost of £12 per unit). If the fixed costs were to be limited to £6 per unit, the company would need to manufacture 133 units (£8000 ÷ £6). The cost would then be the same as the external price, of course, but it would involve a one-third increase in the activity level.

3 The cost data should be carefully checked (especially the estimated associated fixed costs) and the monthly activity level reviewed. It might then be possible to put forward a tentative recommendation.

The decision:

Given the data provided in the question, it would be cheaper to purchase the components externally. This would free some resources within Zam Limited, enabling it to concentrate on manufacturing its main product.

However, there are a number of other considerations that need to be taken into account. In particular the following questions would require some answers.

1 How accurate are the cost data?
2 How variable is the monthly activity level?
3 Is the external supplier's component exactly suited to the company's purposes?
4 How reliable is the proposed supplier?
5 Are there other suppliers who could be used in an emergency and, if so, at what cost?
6 What control could be exercised over the quality of the components received?
7 How firm is the price quoted of £18 per component, and for what period will that prize be maintained?
8 How easy would it be to switch back to internal manufacturing if the supplier proved unreliable?

It follows that much more information (largely of a non-cost nature) would be required before a conclusive decision could be taken.

Pricing decisions

A very important decision that managers in both the profit-making sector and the not-for-profit sector have to take is that relating to pricing. Supermarkets, for example, have to decide what to charge their customers, while local authorities have similar decisions to take in respect of charges for various services, such as adult education fees, leisure centres, and meals on wheels.

Two types of pricing decisions can be distinguished. The first type relates to the prices charged to customers or clients external to the entity. We will refer to this type as *external pricing*. The second type relates to prices charged by one part of an entity to another part, such as when components are supplied by one segment to another segment. This type of pricing is known as *transfer pricing*. We will deal with each type separately, although it should be borne in mind that pricing is a complicated subject and we have only the space to go into it very briefly.

External pricing

There are two basic ways of determining external selling prices, meaning the price to be charged for goods and services offered to parties *outside* an organization. External selling prices may be based either on market prices or on cost. We will deal first with market-based prices.

Market-based pricing

Many goods and services are sold in highly competitive markets. This means that there may be many suppliers offering identical or near-identical products, and they will be competing fiercely in respect of price, quality, reliability and service. If the demand for a product is *elastic*, then the lower the price the more units that will be sold. The opposite also applies, and higher prices will result in fewer goods being sold. The demand for most everyday items of food, for example, is elastic in the manner described.

It follows that when demand is elastic it is unlikely that individual sellers can determine their own selling prices. Hence within narrow limits they will have to base their selling prices on what is being charged in the market. Otherwise, if they charge more than the market price, their sales will be reduced. If they charge less than the market, then their sales will increase but the market will quickly adjust to a lower level of selling prices.

Where market conditions largely determine a supplier's selling prices, it is particularly important to ensure that tight control is exercised over costs. Otherwise, the gap between total sales revenue and total costs (i.e. the profit) will be insufficient to ensure an adequate return on capital employed.

The demand for some goods, in contrast, is *inelastic* – i.e. price has little or no effect on the number of units sold. The demand for writing paper and stationery, for example, tends to be inelastic, probably because it is an infrequent purchase and it is not a significant element in most people's budgets. Thus when the demand for goods is inelastic, suppliers have much more freedom in determining their own selling prices. In such circumstance they may then base them on cost.

Cost-based pricing

There are a number of cost-based pricing methods. We summarize the main ones below and the circumstances in which they are most likely to be used.

1 *Below variable cost.* This price would be used (1) when an entity was trying to establish a new product on the market; (2) when an attempt was being made to drive out competitors; and (3) as a loss leader (i.e. to encourage other goods to be bought). A price at this level could only be sustained for a very short period (unless it is used as a loss leader) since each unit sold would not be covering its variable cost.

2 *At variable cost*. Variable cost prices may be used (1) to launch a new product; (2) to drive out competition; (3) in difficult trading conditions; and (4) as a loss leader. Price could be held for some time but ultimately some contribution will be needed to cover the fixed costs.

3 *At total production cost*. The total production cost will include the unit's direct costs and a share of the production overheads. Prices at this level could be held for some time (perhaps when demand is low) but eventually the entity would need to cover its non-production overheads and to make a profit.

4 *At total cost*. The total cost of a unit will include the direct cost and a share of both the production and non-production overheads. Again, such prices could be held for a very long period, perhaps during a long recession. Eventually, however, some profit would need to be earned.

5 *At cost plus*. The cost-plus method would either relate to total production cost or to total cost. The 'plus' element would be an addition to the cost to allow for non-production overhead and profit (in the case of total production cost) and for profit alone (in the case of total cost). In the long run, cost-plus prices are the only option for a profit-making entity. However, if prices are based on cost, inefficiencies may be automatically built into the costing system and this could lead to uncompetiveness.

As far as external price determination is concerned, we can generalize by arguing that prices tend to be governed by the market. Hence it is important to ensure that tight control is exercised over costs since there will normally be little opportunity to raise selling prices.

Transfer pricing

In large entities it is quite common for one segment to trade with another segment. Thus what is 'revenue' to one segment will be 'expenditure' to a fellow segment. This means that when the results of all the various segments are consolidated (meaning added together), the revenue recorded in one segment's books of account will cancel out the expenditure in the other segment's books. Does it matter, therefore, what prices are charged for internal transfers?

The answer is 'Yes it does', because some segments (particularly if they are divisions of companies) are given a great deal of autonomy. They may have the authority, for example, to purchase the goods and services that they need from outside the entity. They almost certainly will do so if the price and service offered externally appears superior to any internal offer. Thus it may cause them to suboptimize, i.e. to act in their own best interest although it may not be in the best interests of the entity as a whole.

Let us suppose that Segment A fixes its transfer price on a cost-plus basis, say at £10 per unit. Segment B finds it can purchase an identical unit externally at £8 per unit. Segment B is very likely to accept the external offer. But Segment A's costs may be based on *absorbed costs*. The *extra cost* (i.e. the variable cost) of meeting Segment B's order may be much less the external price of

£8 per unit. Thus it may not be beneficial for the *entity as a whole* for Segment B to purchase the units from an outside supplier.

Do you follow the above argument? It is somewhat complicated, so read it again if you do not follow the point. When you do, read on.

It follows from what has been said that a transfer price has to be set at a level that will encourage a supplying segment to trade internally and to discourage a receiving segment to purchase its requirements in the external market. Within this broad overall aim, a number of different transfer-pricing methods can be distinguished. The main ones are itemized below.

1 *At market prices.* If there are identical or similar goods and services offered externally, transfer prices based on market prices will neither encourage nor discourage supplying or receiving segments to trade externally.
2 *At adjusted market prices.* Transfer prices based at market levels do not encourage segments to deal with each other. Market prices may be reduced in order to act as an incentive for segments to trade internally. This approach also gives some recognition to lower costs normally attached to internal trading, e.g. advertising, administration, and financing.
3 *At total cost or total cost plus.* A transfer price based on total cost will include the direct costs plus a share of both production and non-production overhead. Total cost-plus methods allow for some profit. The main problems attached to the total cost methods is that they build inefficiencies into the transfer price (as there is no incentive to control costs) and they therefore encourage suboptimization.
4 *At variable cost or variable cost plus.* The variable cost method does not encourage a supplying segment to trade internally as no incentive is built into the transfer price. A percentage addition may provide some incentive since it enables some contribution to be made towards fixed costs. Transfer prices based on variable costs may be very attractive to receiving segments as they normally compare favourably with external prices.
5 *Negotiated prices.* This method involves striking a bargain between the supplying and the receiving segments based on a combination of market price and costs. As long as the discussions are mutually determined, this method can be a highly successful one.
6 *Opportunity costs.* This method may be somewhat impractical, but if it can be determined it is the ideal one to adopt. A transfer price based on the opportunity cost comprises two elements: first, the standard variable cost in the supplying segment; and second, the entity's opportunity cost resulting from the transaction. It is the second element that is the hardest to determine.

As you have no doubt gathered, pricing decisions are extremely complex. The main role of management accounting (as always) is to supply relevant data and to provide advice. The eventual decision ranges far beyond the remit of the management accountant. Besides incorporating basic cost and financial data, it also incorporates a great many other internal and external considerations, including macro-economic, environmental, financial, political and social factors.

Special orders

On some occasions an entity may be asked to undertake an order beyond its normal trading arrangement and to quote a price for it. Such arrangements are known as *special orders*. The potential customer or client would normally expect to pay a lower price than the entity ordinarily charges and possibly to receive some favourable treatment. What pricing policy should the entity adopt when faced with such demands?

Much will depend upon whether the entity has some surplus capacity. If this is the case, it may be prepared to quote a price below variable cost if it wants to avoid a possible shutdown problem. However, the minimum price that it would normally be willing to accept would be equal to the incremental (or extra) cost of fulfilling the order.

The extra cost involved may be the equivalent of the variable cost. Prices based at or below the variable cost would be extremely competitive, thereby helping to ensure that the customer accepted the quotation. The work gained would then absorb some of the entity's surplus capacity and help to keep its workforce occupied. There is also the possibility that the customer may place future orders at prices that would enable the entity to make a profit on them. However, there is the danger that in the meantime more profitable work has to be rejected because the entity cannot cope with both the special order and additional work.

A price in excess of the variable cost would make a contribution towards fixed costs and this would clearly be the preferred option. The quoted price would have to be judged very finely because the higher the price the greater the risk that the customer would reject the quotation. Hence the decision would involve trying to determine what other suppliers are likely to charge and the other terms that they may offer.

An indication of the difficulties associated with determining whether a special order should be accepted is demonstrated in Exhibit 18.4. Although the exhibit is a highly simplified one, it illustrates the basic approach to decision making when faced with such an issue.

Exhibit 18.4 A special order

Amber Limited has been asked by a customer to supply a specially designed product. The customer has indicated that he would be willing to pay a maximum price of £100 per unit. The cost details are as follows.

Unit cost	£	£
Contract price		100
Less: Variable costs		
Direct materials	40	
Direct labour (2 hours)	30	
Variable overhead	10	80
Contribution		20

At a contract price of £100 per unit, each unit would make a contribution of £20. The customer is prepared to take 400 units, and so the total contribution towards fixed costs would be £8000 (400 units × £20). However, Amber has a shortage of direct labour, and some of the staff would have to be switched from other orders to work on the special order. This would mean an average loss in contribution of £8 for every direct labour hour worked on the special order.

Required:
Determine whether Amber Limited should accept the special order.

Answer to Exhibit 18.4

In order to determine whether Amber Limited should accept the special order, the extra contribution should be compared with the loss of contribution by having to switch the workforce from other orders. The calculations are as follows.

	£
Total contribution from the special order (400 units × £20 per unit)	8 000
Less: the opportunity cost of the normal contribution foregone	
[800 direct labour hours (400 units × 2 DLH) × £8 per unit]	6 400
Extra contribution	1 600

Tutorial notes

Before coming to a decision, the following points should also be considered. You will see that they range well beyond simple cost factors.
1 The costings relating to the special order should be carefully checked.
2 The customer should be asked to confirm in writing that it would be willing to pay a selling price of £100 per unit.
3 Determine whether the customer is likely to place additional orders for the product.
4 Check that the *average* contribution of £8 per direct labour hour, obtained from other orders, applies to the workforce that would be switched to the special order, i.e. is the contribution from the other orders that would be lost more or less than £8 per direct labour hour?
5 Is it possible that new staff could be recruited to work on the special order?
6 Is more profitable work likely to come along in the meantime? Would it mean that it could not be accepted during the progress of the order?

Recommendation:
Assuming that the points raised in the above notes are satisfied, then the recommendation would be to accept the special order at a price of £100 per unit. This would mean that Amber's total contribution would be increased by £1600.

The management accountant's main role in dealing with special orders would be to supply historical and projected cost data of the financial consequences of particular options. The eventual decision would be taken by senior management using a wide range of quantitative and qualitative information. The type of questions asked would be similar to some of the issues covered in the tutorial notes in the solution to Exhibit 18.4.

Conclusion

An important function of the modern management accountant is to assist in managerial decision making. In such a role, the primary task of the management accountant is to provide managers with financial and non-financial information in order to help them take more effective decisions. Although the information provided may include much historical data, decision making often means dealing with future events. Thus the information provided consists of a great deal of speculative material. This means that the management accountant needs to exercise considerable skill and judgement in collecting information that is relevant for a particular purpose. In particular, non-relevant information can be ignored as it only obscures the broader picture.

The significance of including only relevant data is seen when managers have to take special decisions, such as whether to close or shut down a segment of an entity, make or provide internally goods and services instead of obtaining them from an outside supplier, determine a selling price for the entity's goods and services, or whether to accept a special order and at what price. These are all-important and complex decisions and managers need reliable information before they can take them.

There is one other area that involves the collection and analysis of some highly complex data before a decision can be taken. Managers face a continual dilemma in determining whether to replace fixed assets and how their replacement should be financed. This is such an important topic that the next chapter is entirely devoted to it.

Key points

1 Decision making involves having to resolve an outcome for a specific problem.

2 The information required for helping to resolve a particular problem tends to relate to the future, it is specific to the problem, it may have to be collected specially for the task and it is geared towards estimating the future net cash flows of particular outcomes.

3 The information provided to management should include only relevant costs and revenues, including an estimate of any opportunity costs.

4 The data used in a management accounting information report should be subject to some probability testing.

5 The terms 'fixed and variable costs', 'relevant and non-relevant costs', 'avoidable and non-avoidable costs', 'sunk costs', 'committed costs' and 'opportunity costs' are all of special significance in decision making.

6 Closure and shutdown decisions should be based on the contribution earned or likely to be earned on the segment under consideration and compared with the likely closure or shutdown costs.

7 Generally, it is more profitable to make goods or to provide services internally than to obtain them externally if their variable cost is less than or equal to external prices.

8 The pricing goods and services for selling externally will normally be determined by the market price for similar goods and services. In some cases, however, selling prices can be based on cost. Depending on market conditions, the cost could be at or below variable cost, the absorbed or the total absorbed cost and with or without an addition for profit.

9 The internal transfer of goods and services should be based on market price or adjusted market price. Where this is not possible, any price at or in excess of the variable cost should be acceptable.

10 The ideal transfer price is that based on the standard variable cost in the supplying segment plus the entity's opportunity cost resulting from the transaction.

11 Special orders should be priced so that they cover their variable cost. There may be some circumstances when it is acceptable to price them below variable cost but this can only be a short-term solution. Any price in excess of variable costs helps to cover the entity's fixed costs.

12 Cost and financial factors form only one part of decision making. There are other factors of a non-financial and non-quantifiable nature (such as behavioural factors) that must be taken into account.

Check your learning

1 Fill in the blank in each of the following statements:
   (a) A relevant cost is a cost that is _____ by a decision.
   (b) An _____ cost is a cost that is lost or foregone as a result of taking a particular decision.
   (c) A cost that remains unchanged irrespective of the level of activity is called a _____ cost.
   (d) An avoidable cost is the same as a _____ cost.
   (e) A cost incurred as a result of taking a previous decision is called a _____ cost.

2 Describe in one sentence each of the following terms used in decision making:
   (a) closure;
   (b) shutdown;
   (c) make or buy;
   (d) external pricing;
   (e) transfer pricing;
   (f) special order.

3 State whether each of the following statements would be generally true or false:

(a) A factory would always be shut down if its contribution was negative.   True/False

(b) An unprofitable production line may be kept open as a loss leader.   True/False

(c) Components would always be purchased externally if they cost more to make internally.   True/False

(d) External selling prices must be at a level to recover some of their fixed cost.   True/False

(e) The prices at which services are transferred internally are of no relevance to segmental managers.   True/False

(f) A manager may sometimes accept a selling price for a particular unit even if it is below its variable cost.   True/False

[*The answers to these questions may be found at the back of the book.*]

Group discussion questions

18.1 This chapter has emphasized that it is managers that take decisions and not management accountants. How far do you agree with this assertion?

18.2 Many of the solutions to the problems posed in this chapter depend upon being able to isolate the variable cost associated with a particular decision. In practice, is it realistic to expect that such costs can be readily identified and measured?

18.3 Assume that you were an IT manager in a large entity, and that the services that you provide are made available to both internal and external parties. Specify how you would go about negotiating an appropriate fee for services sought by other departments within the entity.

Practice questions

[*Note: The questions marked with an asterisk have answers at the back of the book.*]

18.4* Micro Limited has some spare capacity. It is now considering whether it should accept a special contract to use some of the spare capacity. However, this contract will use some specialist direct labour that is in short supply. The following details relate to the proposed contract:

	£000
Contract price	50
Variable costs:	
Direct materials	10
Direct labour	30

In order to complete the contract, 4000 direct labour hours would be required. The company's budget for the year during which the contract would be undertaken is as follows:

	£000
Sales	750
Variable costs	(500)
Contribution	250
Fixed costs	(230)
Profit	20

There would be 50 000 direct labour hours available during the year.

Required:
Determine whether the special contract should be accepted.

18.5* Temple Limited has been offered two new contracts, the details of which are as follows:

Contract	(1)	(2)
	£000	£000
Contract price	1 000	2 100
Direct materials	300	600
Direct labour	300	750
Variable overhead	100	250
Fixed overhead	100	200
	800	1 800
Profit	200	300
Direct materials required (kilos)	50 000	100 000
Direct labour hours required	10 000	25 000

Note:
The fixed overhead has been apportioned on the basis of direct labour cost. Temple is a one-product firm. Its budgeted cost per unit for its normal work for the year to 31 December 2002 is summarized below.

	£
Sales	6 000
Direct materials (100 kilos)	700
Direct labour (200 hours)	3 000
Variable overhead	300
Fixed overhead	1 000
	5 000
Profit	1 000

The company would only have the capacity to accept one of the new contracts. Unfortunately, materials suitable for use in all of its work are in short supply and the company has estimated that only 200 000 kilos would be available during the year to December 2002. Even more worrying is the shortage of skilled labour; only 100 000 direct labour hours are expected to be available during the year. The good news is that there may be an upturn in the market for its normal contract work.

Required:
Calculate:
(1) the contribution per unit of each limiting factor for
    (a) the company's normal work;
    (b) Contract 1; and
    (c) Contract 2.
(2) the company's maximum contribution for the year to 31 December 2002, assuming that it accepts either Contract 1 or Contract 2.

18.6 Agra Limited has been asked to quote a price for a special contract. The details are as follows:
1 Agra asked to quote for an order of 100 000 units.
2 The direct costs per unit for the order would be: materials £3; labour £15; distribution £12.
3 Additional production and non-production overhead would amount to £500 000, although £100 000 could be saved if the order was for less than 100 000 units.
4 Agra's normal profit margin is 20 per cent of total cost.

Required:
Recommend a minimum selling price if the order was for (a) 100 000 units; and (b) 80 000 units.

18.7 Foo Limited has been asked to quote for a special order. The details are as follows:
1 Prices are to be quoted at order levels of 50 000, 100 000 and 150 000 units respectively. Foo has some surplus capacity and it could deal with up to 160 000 units.
2 Each unit would cost £2 for direct materials, and £12 for direct labour.
3 Foo normally absorbs production and non-production overhead on the basis of 200 per cent and 100 per cent respectively of the direct labour cost.
4 Distribution costs are expected to be £10 per unit.
5 Foo's normal profit margin is 20 per cent of the total cost. However, it is prepared to reduce this margin to 15 per cent if the order is for 100 000 units, and to 10 per cent for an order of 150 000 units.
6 The additional non-production overhead associated with this contract would be £200 000, although this would be cut by £25 000 if the output dropped below 100 000 units.

Required:
Calculate (a) the selling price per unit that Foo Limited would normally charge if the contract was for 50 000, 100 000, and 150 000 units respectively; and (b) the profit that it could expect to make at these levels.

18.8 Bamboo Limited is a highly specialist firm of central heating suppliers operating exclusively in the textiles industry. It has recently been asked to tender for a contract for a prospective customer. The following details relate to the proposed contract.

1 Materials:
   (a) £20 000 of materials would need to be purchased.
   (b) £10 000 of materials would need to be transferred from another contract (and these materials would need to be replaced).
   (c) Some obsolete stock would be used. The stock had originally cost £18 000. Its current disposable value is £4 000.

2 The contract would involve labour costs of £60 000, of which £30 000 would be incurred regardless of whether the contract was undertaken.

3 The production manager will have to work several evenings a week during the progress of the contract. He is paid a salary of £30 000 per year, and on successful completion of the contract he would receive a bonus of £5 000.

4 Additional administrative expenses incurred in undertaking the contract are estimated to be £1 000.

5 The company absorbs its fixed overheads at a rate of £10 per machine hour. The contract will require 2 000 machine hours.

Required:
Calculate the minimum contract price that would be acceptable to Bamboo Limited.

18.9 Dynasty Limited has been involved in a research project (code named DNY) for a number of months. There is some doubt as to whether the project should be completed. If it is, then it is expected that DNY will require another 12 months' work. The following information relates to the project.

1 Costs incurred to date: £500 000.

2 Sales proceeds if the project continues: £600 000.

3 Direct material costs amount to £200 000. The type of material required for DNY had already been purchased for another project, and it would cost £20 000 to dispose of it.

4 Direct labour costs have come to £150 000. The direct labour used on DNY is highly skilled and it is not easy to recruit the type of staff required. In order to undertake DNY, some staff would have to be transferred from other projects. This would mean that there was a total loss in contribution from such projects of £350 000.

5 Research staff costs amount to £200 000. The staff would be made redundant at the end of project DNY at a cost of £115 000. If they were to be made redundant now, there would be a cost of £100 000.

6 The company can invest surplus cash at a rate of return of 10% per annum.

7 Non-production overhead that is budgeted to be apportioned to DNY for the forthcoming 12 months amounts to £60 000.

Required:
Determine whether or not the project DNY should continue.

CASE STUDY

A special order

<table>
<tr>
<td>Learning
objectives</td>
<td colspan="2">After working through this case study, you should be able to:
• describe the circumstances in which total absorption costing may be used as a means of pricing;
• outline the technique of contribution analysis;
• prepare a report suitable for presentation to management containing data based on contribution analysis.</td>
</tr>
<tr>
<td>Background</td>
<td>Location</td>
<td>Fast Clean Products Limited: the Managing Director's office</td>
</tr>
<tr>
<td></td>
<td>Personnel</td>
<td>Stanley Newton: Managing Director
Omar Khan: Mini-supermarket owner
Ralph Timmins: Production Manager
Su Yamamoto: Distribution Manager
Gerald White: Chief Accountant</td>
</tr>
</table>

Synopsis

Fast Clean Products Limited manufactures household cleaning products, operating from a small factory on the outskirts of Leeds. The company has always been reasonably profitable, although for the last two years it has been producing well under capacity, largely as a result of a general reduction in consumer spending.

Stanley Newton, the Managing Director of the company, has been assiduously reading the financial press, and he has come to the conclusion that there is not likely to be an upturn in the market for at least the next 12 months. He assumes, therefore, that Fast Clean Products is also unlikely to see a revival in its fortunes for at least that time.

Stanley spends a lot of time playing golf. Some months ago he had got talking to a new member of the golf club, Omar Khan, who told him that he owned a chain of mini-supermarkets. The other day, Stanley was going through his morning mail and, rather to his surprise, he found a letter from Omar asking him to quote for a special order.

'Who said that golf was a waste of time?' Stanley asked himself.

He immediately called in his team of senior managers to tell them about the request. 'Can we do it?' he asked each one of them in turn.

Ralph Timmins, the Production Manager, was the first to speak. 'Well, Stanley, we have the capacity at the moment, although we might have to take on more staff. But what happens if trade revives? We certainly could not do this order and satisfy our ordinary trade outlets.'

'As far as I can gather, Ralph, this is a one-off request,' replied Stanley. 'Omar has been let down by his ordinary supplier, and he cannot promise us anything beyond this order.'

He then turned to his Distribution Manager, 'I assume that you will not have any problems in dealing with this order if we take it on?' he queried.

'None whatsoever, Stanley,' replied Su. 'As you know, we have not laid-off any of the distribution staff. And, to be quite honest, most of them have forgotten what it's like to work hard.'

Stanley made a mental note that, order or no order, he must take up this point with Su. 'What on earth are we doing with underemployed staff?' he asked himself.

Su continued, 'And it's also highly unlikely that we would need any more vehicles, although some of the present ones are getting very old.'

'Yes, yes,' intervened Stanley hastily. 'We won't go into that this morning.'

For some time Su had been campaigning for a greater allocation of the capital expenditure budget for the replacement of distribution vehicles.

'So, it seems that we don't anticipate any great problems if we take on this order,' stated Stanley.

'Excuse me, Stanley,' interjected a quiet voice. 'You haven't asked about the cost-ings.' The voice belonged to Gerald White, the company's Chief Accountant. Gerald was a highly self-effacing member of the management team. He was precise and pedantic, but he was usually right.

'Oh! I don't think that there is any problem there, Gerald,' Stanley replied. 'We shall just cost the job as we normally do and then charge accordingly.'

Some time ago, Gerald had persuaded Stanley to introduce a management accounting system into the company. Stanley was largely a marketing man, and he was not really interested in accounting. However, like most converts, he was all for an idea once he had accepted it.

'I shall expect you to cost the product on the normal absorption costing lines. I will have a word with you about the precise profit percentage to be added once you have got the details,' said Stanley firmly.

'That may not be wise, Stanley,' responded Gerald, somewhat equivocally.

The others laughed just in case Gerald was joking. However, he obviously was in earnest because he carried on regardless.

'These chains of supermarkets are very competitive. You can, I beg your pardon, *one* can guarantee that Mr Khan will have asked other companies to tender and, unless Fast Clean Products is competitive, the order will go elsewhere.'

The room went quiet. Some of the excitement and elation felt by all members of the management team began to evaporate.

'That's just like all you accountants,' interposed Su, who besides looking after dis-tribution also had an interest in sales. 'Gloom, gloom and yet more gloom. You're always looking on the black side. Here we are: for the first time for months we've got the chance of a large new order, and you want to put the brake on it.'

'I am afraid that you have misunderstood me, Su,' Gerald replied quietly. 'Far from wanting to reject the order, I want to ensure that the company is successful. All I meant was that the company's normal accounting procedures may not be appropri-ate in the case of a 'one-off' order, as some people call it. A total absorbed cost may not, in fact, be the most suitable basis to adopt in the case of a special order.'

'But you've always been going on at me,' interjected Su, rather angrily, 'that it's no use making sales if we don't make a profit on them.'

'That's quite correct, but only in the long run. Over a period of time, the company must, of course, cover all of its costs. For a special order, however, it may be profitable to accept that order, provided that the extra costs incurred by undertaking it are less than the amount received from the customer.'

By now, everyone at the meeting had gone *unusually* quiet. 'I'm not quite sure that I understand you,' said Stanley. 'You seem to be suggesting that we undercut our normal prices, and I don't like the idea of that. But in any case, how do you work out the "extra" costs of an order?'

'Ah, Stanley, that is an accounting problem of some complexity,' responded Gerald with some satisfaction. 'But I shall be glad to discuss it with you when the accounting team has derived some appropriate costings.'

'Please do,' said Stanley with heavy irony. 'I would like the costings in the morning, *if* you please.'

'Certainly, Stanley. I shall arrange for that. You will have them on your desk at eight o'clock tomorrow morning.'

Stanley realized that he should have known better. Nothing seemed to ruffle the calm of his Chief Accountant. 'Suppose I had asked for them at eight o'clock this evening,' he thought, 'would he have replied, "Certainly, Stanley. I shall arrange for that"?' He answered his own question. 'Probably,' he muttered rather gloomily. 'One of these days I shall put it to the test.'

Required:

1 Prepare a critical appraisal of contribution analysis. Be careful to explain why the total absorbed cost of a product may not be an appropriate method of determining the selling price of a special order.

2 Assume that you are Gerald White. Using the information listed in the Appendix, to this Case Study prepare a report suitable for presentation to Stanley Newton.

Appendix

Fast Clean Products Ltd
Miscellaneous data for the year to 30 June 2005

1 Abridged profit and loss account

	£000	£000	£000
Sales			3 260
Less: Cost of goods sold			
Direct materials	560		
Direct labour	1 660	2 220	
Factory overhead		400	
Factory cost of production		2 620	
Administration overhead		250	
Selling and distribution overhead		300	
Total operating cost			3 170
Operating profit			90

2 The company uses a total absorption costing system. The selling price of its goods is determined on a cost-plus price basis. A 20 per cent loading for non-manufacturing overhead is added to the total factory cost, to which is added a further 10 per cent for profit. Factory overheads are absorbed into product costs on the basis of machine hours. The machine hour absorption rate for the year to 30 June 2005 was £2 per hour.

3 Gerald White's team had available to them the following breakdown of overheads for the year to 30 June 2005:

	Factory %	Administration %	Selling and Distribution %
Fixed	80	90	60
Variable	20	10	40
Total	100	100	100

4 From the preliminary investigation made, it is expected that Omar Khan's special order would require £75 000 of direct materials. The direct labour cost would be £200 000, and the variable overhead cost £25 000. The order would involve 40 000 machine hours.

5 Although it is anticipated that prices will rise during the year to 30 June 2006, Gerald White has decided to base his initial costings on the financial results for the year to 30 June 2005.

19 Decision making: capital investment

Baan starts hunt for finance

By Ian Bickerton in Amsterdam

Baan, the Dutch business software company, said yesterday it had recruited Lazard, the investment bank, to help it hunt for badly needed finance and investigate the possibility of alliances.

The Dutch group said it had retained two of the bank's senior partners to "assist in raising additional equity and evaluating long-term strategic alternatives".

Baan said it was too early to say what those alternatives were but it would not rule out alliances.

International Business Machines has built a range of products around Baan systems and Microsoft has a licensing agreement with the Dutch group.

Analysts doubted competitors would be interested.

The Dutch group said raising equity was its priority. "This is the issue that we need to address and we are not going to hide from that," it said. "It is not a crisis, we have $197m in the bank."

Financial Times, 4 February 2000. Reprinted with permission.

Finding the necessary finance is not always easy

As we saw in Chapter 15, the budgetary process usually starts with the preparation of the sales forecast. The forecast then enables the production manager to assess whether he is likely to have the productive capacity to meet it. If the capacity is not available, the sales budgets will have to be prepared on what *can* be produced. In the long run, of course, the entity will want to maximize its sales. If the forecasts suggest a sustained growth in sales, therefore, additional capital expenditure may be required, such as for new factories, plant, and equipment. Expenditure on such proposals is known as *capital investment* (CI), and accountants refer to the process of investigating them as *capital investment appraisal*.

Capital investment may be considered to be part of the capital budgeting process. It involves both the selection of long-term investments and the financing of them, and these are the matters that are going to be considered in this chapter. We are only going to deal with them briefly, however, as the detailed considerations are well outside the scope of this book. The main purpose is to give you an overall appreciation of what is involved in capital investment appraisal, because it is unlikely that as a non-accountant you will have to deal with the involved arithmetical calculations. We intend to use only simple examples, but these should enable you to grasp the main principles behind the technique.

The chapter is divided into three main sections. In the first section, we outline the background to CI appraisal. The following section examines the main accounting techniques used in selecting individual projects. The final section summarizes the main sources of finance available for capital investment.

Learning objectives

By the end of this chapter, you should be able to:

- **describe what is meant by capital investment appraisal;**
- **identify five capital-investment appraisal techniques;**
- **recognize the significance of such techniques;**
- **list the main sources of financing capital-investment projects.**

Background

We explained in Chapter 4 that accountants distinguish between capital expenditure and revenue expenditure (the same distinction also applies to income). The borderline between capital and revenue expenditure is somewhat imprecise. Generally, expenditure that is likely to be of benefit in more than one accounting period is classed as capital.

However, expenditure that is classed as capital would normally have other significant characteristics. These can be summarized as follows:

1 it will probably involve substantial expenditure;
2 the benefits may be spread over very many years;
3 it is difficult to predict what the benefits will be;
4 it will help the entity to achieve its organizational objectives;
5 it will have some impact on the entity's employees.

Indeed, if the entity is to survive and especially if it wants to grow, it will need to invest continually in capital projects. Existing fixed assets will begin to wear out, and more efficient ones will become available. Furthermore, capital expenditure may be required not just in the administration, production and stores departments but also on social and recreational facilities. In the public sector also, universities and colleges may be faced with capital expenditure decisions that go beyond providing lecture halls and tutorial rooms, e.g. student accommodation and union facilities.

Irrespective of where the demand for capital expenditure arises, however, all entities face two common problems: (a) the priority to be given to individual projects; and (b) how they can be financed. Hence, competing projects will need to be ranked according to either their importance or their potential profitability. In the next section we examine how this may be done.

Selecting projects

We will assume that we are dealing with a profit-making entity. There is little point in investing in a project unless it is likely to make a profit. The exceptions are those projects that are necessary on health, social and welfare grounds, and these are particularly difficult to assess. There are five main techniques that accountants can use in CI appraisal. They are shown in diagrammatic form in Figure 19.1 and examined in each of the following subsections.

Payback

The payback method is an attempt to estimate how long it would take before a project begins to pay for itself. For example, if a company was going to spend £300 000 on purchasing some new plant, the accountant would calculate how many years it would take before £300 000 had been received back in cash. The recovery of an investment in a project is usually measured in terms of *net cash flow*. Net cash flow is the difference between cash received and cash paid

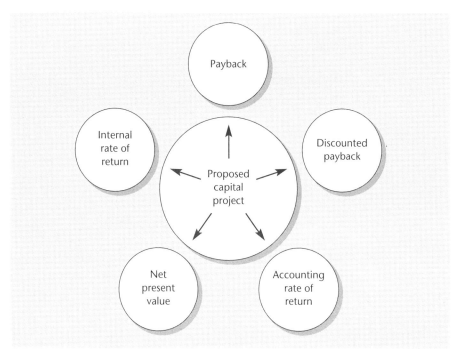

Figure 19.1
Methods of capital investment appraisal

during a defined period of time. In order to adopt this method, therefore, the following information is required:

1 the total cost of the investment;
2 the amount of cash instalments to be paid back on the investment;
3 the accounting periods in which the instalments will be paid;
4 the cash receipts and any other cash payments connected with the project;
5 the accounting periods in which they fall.

As the payback measures the rate of recovery of the original investment in terms of net cash flow, it follows that non-cash items (such as depreciation, and profits and losses on sales of fixed assets) are not taken into account.

The payback method is illustrated in Exhibit 19.1.

Exhibit 19.1 The payback method

Miln Limited is considering investing in some new machinery. The following information has been prepared to support the project:

	£000	£000
Cost of machinery		20
Expected net cash flow:		
Year 1	1	
2	4	
3	5	
4	10	
5	10	30
Net profitability		10

Required:
Calculate the prospective investment's payback period.

Answer to Exhibit 19.1

The payback period is as follows:

	£000
Cumulative net cash flow:	
Year 1	1
2 (£1 000 + £4 000)	5
3 (£5 000 + £5 000)	10
4 (£10 000 + £10 000)	20
5 (£20 000 + £10 000)	30

Thus, the investment will have paid for itself at the end of the fourth year. At that stage £20 000 will have been received back from the project in terms of net cash flow and that sum would be equal to the original cost of the project.

As can be seen from Exhibit 19.1 the payback method is a fairly straightforward technique, but it does have several disadvantages. These are as follows:

1 An estimate has to be made of the amount and the timing of cash instalments due to be paid on an original investment.
2 It is difficult to calculate the net cash flows and the period in which they will be received.
3 There is a danger that projects with the shortest payback periods may be chosen even if they are less profitable than projects that have a longer payback period. The method only measures cash flow; it does not measure profitability.
4 The total amount of the overall investment is ignored and comparisons made between different projects may result in a misleading conclusion. Thus a project with an initial investment of £10 000 may have a shorter payback period than one with an initial investment of £100 000, although in the long run the larger investment may prove more profitable.
5 The technique ignores any net cash flows received after the payback period.
6 The timing of the cash flows is not taken into account: £1 received now is preferable to £1 received in five years' time. Thus, a project with a short payback period may recover most of its investment towards the end of its payback period while another project with a longer payback period may recover most of the original investment in the first few years. There is clearly less risk in accepting a project that recovers most of its cost very quickly than there is in accepting one where the benefits are deferred.

Notwithstanding these disadvantages, the payback method has something to be said for it. While it may appear to be rather simplistic, it does help managers to compare projects and to think in terms of how long it takes before a project has recovered its original cost. The timing problem can also be overcome by adopting what is called the *discounted payback method*.

Discounted payback

As was explained above, the simple payback method ignores the timing of net cash receipts. This problem can be overcome by *discounting* the net cash receipts. You will probably be familiar with discounting in your everyday life. You know, for example, that if you put £91 into the building society, and the rate of interest is 10% per annum, your original investment will be worth about £100 [£91 + £9 (10% × £91)] at the end of the year. We could look at this example from another point of view. Assuming a rate of interest of 10% per annum, what amount of money do you have to invest in the building society in order to have £100 at the end of the year? The answer is, of course, £91 (ignoring the odd 10p). In other words, £91 received now is about the same as £100 received in a year's time. This is what is meant by *discounting*. The procedure is as follows:

1 Calculate the future net cash flows.
2 Estimate an appropriate rate of interest.
3 Multiply the net cash flows by a discount factor.

The discount factor will depend on the cost of borrowing money. In the case of the building society example above, the discount factor is based on a rate of interest of 10%. The factor itself is 0.9091, i.e. £100 × 0.9091 = £90.91. To check: take the £90.91 and add the year's interest, i.e. £90.91 × 10% = £9.091 + £90.91 = £100.00. You will not have to calculate discount factors: these are readily available in tables. One is included in Appendix 2 to this book.

To check that you understand the point about discounting, turn to Appendix 2. Look along the top line for the appropriate rate of interest: in our case it is 10%. Work down the 10% column until you come to the line opposite the year (shown in the left-hand column) in which the cash would be received. In our example, the cash is going to be received in one year's time, so it is not necessary to go further than the first line. The present value of £1 receivable in a year's time is, therefore, £0.9091, or £90.91 if £100 is to be received in a year's time.

In order to confirm that you follow the principle behind discounting, try the following example. Assuming a rate of interest of 15% per annum, what is the present value of £200 receivable in two years' time? Consult Appendix 2. The answer is £151.22 (£200 × 0.7561). You can check this as follows:

	£
At the beginning of Year 1 (as calculated)	151.22
At the end of Year 1, add 15% (£151.22 × 15%)	22.69*
At the beginning of Year 2	173.91
At the end of Year 2, add 15% (£173.91 × 15%)	26.09
Total	200.00

* This should really be 22.68. The discount table used in Appendix 2 only goes to four places of decimals and so some rounding is usually necessary.

Do you feel reasonably confident that you now know what is meant by the net present value of future net cash flows and what is involved in discounting? If so, we can move on to examine how discounting can be applied to the payback method (see Exhibit 19.2).

Exhibit 19.2 The discounted payback method

Newland City Council has investigated the possibility of investing in a new project, and the following information has been obtained:

	£000	£000
Total cost of project		500
Expected net cash flows:		
Year 1	20	
2	50	
3	100	
4	200	
5	300	
6	30	700
Net return		200

Required:
Assuming a rate of interest of 8%, calculate the project's overall return using the following methods:
(a) payback; and
(b) discounted payback.

Answer to Exhibit 19.2

(a) *Payback method*

Year	Net cash flow	Cumulative net cash flow
	£000	£000
0	(500)	(500)
1	20	(480)
2	50	(430)
3	100	(330)
4	200	(130)
5	300	170
6	30	200

Calculation:
By the end of the fifth year, the original investment of £500 000 will have been covered. Assuming that the net cash flows accrue evenly throughout the year, therefore, the payback period is about 4 years 5 months. After 4 years the total cash flows received = £370 000 (£20 000 + 50 000 + 100 000 + 200 000). The £130 000 still necessary to equal the original cost of the investment (£500 000 – 370 000) will be met part way through Year 5, i.e. (£130 000 ÷ 300 000) × 12 months = 5.2 months. The payback period is, therefore, about 4 years and 5 months (41 months)

(b) *Discounted payback*

Year	Net cash flow	Discount factors	Present value at 8% [Column (2) × Column (3)]	Cumulative present value
(1)	(2)	(3)	(4)	(5)
	£000		£000	£000
0	(500)	1.0	(500)	(500)
1	20	0.9259	19	(481)
2	50	0.8573	43	(438)
3	100	0.7938	79	(359)
4	200	0.7350	147	(212)
5	300	0.6860	206	(6)
6	30	0.6302	19	13

Calculation:
Using the discounted payback method, the project would recover all of its original cost during Year 6. Assuming that the net cash flows accrue evenly, this would be during the fourth month because (£6000 ÷ 19 000) × 12 months = 3.8 months. Hence the discounted payback period is about 5 years 4 months (64 months).

The discounted payback method has the following advantages:

1 It is relatively easy to understand.
2 It is not too difficult to compute.
3 It focuses on the cash recovery of an investment.
4 It allows for the fact that cash received now may be worth more than cash receivable in the future.
5 It takes into account more of the net cash flows, since the discounted payback period is always longer than under the simple payback method.
6 It enables a clear-cut decision to be taken, since a project is acceptable if the discounted net cash flow throughout its life exceeds the cost of the original investment.

However, like the simple payback method, it has some disadvantages. These are as follows:

1 It is sometimes difficult to estimate the amount and timing of instalments due to be paid on the original investment.
2 It is difficult to estimate the amount and timing of future net cash receipts and other payments.
3 It is not easy to determine an appropriate rate of interest.
4 Net cash flows received after the payback period are ignored.

Irrespective of these disadvantages, the discounted payback method can be usefully and readily adopted by those entities that do not employ staff specially trained in capital investment appraisal techniques.

Accounting rate of return

The *accounting rate of return* (ARR) method attempts to compare the *profit* of a project with the capital invested in it. It is usually expressed as a percentage, i.e.:

$$\text{ARR} = \frac{\text{Profit}}{\text{Capital employed}} \times 100\%$$

Two important problems arise from this definiton. These may be summarized as follows:

1 **The definition of profit**. Normally, the average annual net profit earned by a project would be used. However, as was explained in earlier chapters, accounting profit can be subject to a number of different assumptions and distortions (e.g. depreciation, taxation and inflation), and so it is relatively easy to arrive at different profit levels depending upon the accounting policies adopted. The most common definition is to take profit before interest and taxation. The profit included in the equation would then be a simple average of the profit that the project earns over its entire life.
2 **The definition of capital employed**. The capital employed could be either the initial capital employed in the project or the average capital employed over its life.

Thus, depending upon the definitions adopted, the ARR may be calculated in one of two ways, as follows:

1 Using the original capital employed:

$$\text{ARR} = \frac{\text{Average annual net profit before interest and taxation}}{\text{Initial capital employed on the project}} \times 100\%$$

2 Using the average capital employed:

$$\text{ARR} = \frac{\text{Average annual net profit before interest and taxation}}{\text{Average annual capital employed on the project}^*} \times 100\%$$

$$^* \frac{\text{Initial capital employed} + \text{Residual value}}{2}$$

The two methods are illustrated in Exhibit 19.3.

Exhibit 19.3 The accounting rate of return method

Bridge Limited is considering investing in a new project, the details of which are as follows:

	£000	£000
Project life	5 years	
Project cost		50
Estimated net profit:		
Year 1	12	
2	18	
3	30	
4	25	
5	5	
Total net profit	90	

The estimated residual value of the project at the end of Year 5 is £10 000.

Required:
Calculate the accounting rate of return of the proposed new project, using the two methods described above.

Answer to Exhibit 19.3

The accounting rate of return would be calculated as follows:
(a) Using the initial capital employed:

$$\frac{\text{Average annual net profits}}{\text{Cost of the investment}} \times 100\%$$

Average annual net profits = £18 000 (£90 000/5)

$$\therefore \text{ Accounting rate of return} = \frac{£18\,000}{50\,000} \times 100\% = \underline{\underline{36\%}}$$

(b) Using the average capital employed:

$$\frac{\text{Average annual net profits}}{\text{Average capital employed}} \times 100\%$$

$$= \frac{£18\,000}{\frac{1}{2}\,(£50\,000 + 10\,000)} \times 100\% = \underline{\underline{60\%}}$$

Like the payback and discounted payback methods, the accounting rate of return method has several advantages and disadvantages. These are as follows:

Advantages
1 The method is compatible with a similar accounting ratio used in financial accounting.
2 It is relatively easy to understand.
3 It is not difficult to compute.
4 It draws attention to the notion of overall profit.

Disadvantages
1 Net profit can be subject to different definitions, e.g. it can mean net profit before or after allowing for depreciation on the project.
2 It is not always clear whether the original cost of the investment should be used, or whether it is more appropriate to substitute an average for the amount of capital invested in the project.
3 The use of a residual value in calculating the average amount of capital employed means that the higher the residual value, the lower the ARR. For example, with no residual value, the ARR on a project costing £100000 and an average net profit of £50000 would be 100%, i.e.:

$$\frac{£50\,000}{\frac{1}{2} \times (100\,000 + 0)} \times 100 = 100\%$$

With a residual value of (say) £10000, the ARR would be 90.9%, i.e.:

$$\frac{£50\,000}{\frac{1}{2} \times (100\,000 + 10\,000)} \times 100 = 90.9\%$$

The estimation of residual values is very difficult, and it can make all the difference between one project and another.
4 The method gives no guidance on what is an acceptable rate of return.
5 The benefit of earning a high proportion of the total profit in the early years of the project is not allowed for.
6 The method does not take into account the time value of money.

Notwithstanding these disadvantages, the ARR method may be suitable where very similar short-term projects are being considered.

Net present value

One of the main disadvantages of using the payback and ARR methods in CI appraisal is that both methods ignore the time value of money. This concept has already been examined when we were dealing with the discounted payback method. There are two other methods that also adopt this concept: the net present value method, and the internal rate of return method. In this subsection, the net present value (NPV) method is examined.

The NPV method recognizes that cash received today is preferable to cash receivable sometime in the future. There is more risk in having to wait for future cash receipts and, while a smaller sum may be obtained now, at least it is available for other purposes. For example, it can be invested, and the subsequent rate of return may then compensate for the smaller amount received now (or at least be equal to it).

As was seen earlier in the chapter, £91 received now (assuming a rate of interest of 10%) is just as beneficial as receiving £100 in a year's time. This is also the principle behind the NPV method of CI appraisal. Basically, it involves taking the following steps:

1 calculate the annual net cash flows expected to arise from the project;
2 select an appropriate rate of interest, or required rate of return;
3 obtain the discount factors appropriate to the chosen rate of interest or rate of return;
4 multiply the annual net cash flow by the appropriate discount factors;
5 add together the present values for each of the net cash flows;
6 compare the total net present value with the initial outlay;
7 accept the project if the total NPV is positive.

This procedure is outlined in Exhibit 19.4.

Exhibit 19.4 The net present value method

Rage Limited is considering two capital investment projects. The details are outlined as follows:

Project	1	2
Estimated life	3 years	5 years
Commencement date	1.1.01	1.1.01
	£000	£000
Project cost at 1.01.01	100	100
Estimated net cash flows:		
Year to: 31.12.01	20	10
31.12.02	80	40
31.12.03	40	40
31.12.04	–	40
31.12.05	–	20
	140	150

The company expects a rate of return of 10% per annum on its capital employed.

Required:
Using the net present value method of project appraisal, assess which project would be more profitable.

Answer to Exhibit 19.4

Rage Ltd

Project appraisal:

Year	Net cash flow	Project 1 Discount factor	Present value	Net cash flow	Project 2 Discount factor	Present value
(1)	(2)	(3)	(4)	(5)	(6)	(7)
	£	10%	£	£	10%	£
31.12.01	20 000	0.9091	18 182	10 000	0.9091	9 091
31.12.02	80 000	0.8264	66 112	40 000	0.8264	33 056
31.12.03	40 000	0.7513	30 052	40 000	0.7513	30 052
31.12.04	–	–	–	40 000	0.6830	27 320
31.12.05	–	–	–	20 000	0.6209	12 418
Total present value			114 346			111 937
Less: Initial cost			100 000			100 000
Net present value			14 346			11 937

Tutorial notes

1 The net cash flows and the discount factor of 10% (i.e. the rate of return) were given in the question.
2 The discount factors may be obtained from the discount table shown in Appendix 2.
3 Column (4) has been calculated by multiplying column (2) by column (3).
4 Column (7) has been calculated by multiplying column (5) by column 6.

Both projects have a positive NPV, but project 1 will probably be chosen in preference to project 2 because it has a higher NPV, even though its total net cash flow of £140 000 is less than the total net cash flow of £150 000 for project 2.

The advantages and disadvantages of the NPV method are as follows:

Advantages
1 The use of net cash flows emphasizes the importance of liquidity.
2 Different accounting policies are not relevant as they do not affect the calculation of the net cash flows.
3 The time value of money is taken into account.
4 It is easy to compare the NPV of different projects and to reject projects that do not have an acceptable NPV.

Disadvantages
1 Some difficulties may be incurred in estimating the initial cost of the project and the time periods in which instalments must be paid back (although this is a common problem in CI appraisal).
2 It is difficult to estimate accurately the net cash flow for each year of the project's life (a difficulty that is again common to most other methods of project appraisal).

3 It is not easy to select an appropriate rate of interest. The rate of interest is sometimes referred to as the *cost of capital*, i.e. the cost of financing an investment. One rate that could be chosen is that rate which the company could earn if it decided to invest the funds outside the business (the external rate of interest). Alternatively, an internal rate of interest could be chosen. This rate would be based on an estimate of what return the company expects to earn on its existing investments. In the long run, if its internal rate of return is lower than the external rate, then it would appear more profitable to liquidate the company and invest the funds elsewhere. A local authority, however, may not have the same difficulty, because it would probably use a rate of interest that is set by central government.

NPV is considered to be a highly acceptable method of CI appraisal. It takes into account the timing of the net cash flows, the project's profitability, and the return of the original investment. However, an entity would not necessarily accept a project just because it had an acceptable NPV, because there are many non-financial factors that must be allowed for. Furthermore, other less profitable projects (or even projects with a negative NPV) may go ahead, perhaps because they are concerned with employee safety or welfare.

Internal rate of return

An alternative method of investment appraisal based on discounted net cash flow is known as the *internal rate of return* (IRR). This method is very similar to the NPV method. However, instead of discounting the expected net cash flows by a predetermined rate of return, the IRR method seeks to answer the following question:

What rate of return would be required in order to ensure that the total NPV equals the total initial cost?

In theory, a rate of return that was lower than the entity's required rate of return would be rejected. In practice, however, the IRR would only be one factor to be taken into account in deciding whether to go ahead with the project. The method is illustrated in Exhibit 19.5.

Exhibit 19.5 The internal rate of return method

Bruce Limited is considering whether to invest £50 000 in a new project. The project's expected net cash flows would be as follows:

Year	£000
1	7
2	25
3	30
4	5

Required:
Calculate the internal rate of return for the proposed new project.

Answer to Exhibit 19.5

Bruce Ltd

Calculation of the internal rate of return:

Step 1: Select two discount factors
The first step is to select two discount factors, and then calculate the net present value of the project using both factors. The two factors usually have to be chosen quite arbitrarily, although they should preferably cover a narrow range. One of the factors should produce a *positive* net present value (NPV), and the other factor a *negative* NPV. As far as this question is concerned, factors of 10% and 15% will be chosen to illustrate the method. In practice, you may have to try various factors before you come across two that are suitable for giving a positive and a negative result.

Year	Net cash flow	Discount factors		Present value	
(1)	(2)	(3)	(4)	(5)	(6)
		10%	15%	10%	15%
	£			£	£
1	7 000	0.9091	0.8696	6 364	6 087
2	25 000	0.8264	0.7561	20 660	18 903
3	30 000	0.7513	0.6575	22 539	19 725
4	5 000	0.6830	0.5718	3 415	2 859
Total present values				52 978	47 574
Initial cost				50 000	50 000
Net present value				2 978	(2 426)

Tutorial Notes

1 Column (2) has been obtained from the question.
2 Column (3) is based on the arbitary selection of two interest rates of 10% and 15% respectively. The discount factors may be found in Appendix 2.
3 Column (5) has been calculated by multiplying column (2) by column (3).
4 Column (6) has been calculated by multiplying column (2) by column (4).

The project is expected to cost £50 000. If the company expects a rate of return of 10%, the project will be accepted, because the NPV is positive. However, if the required rate of return is 15% it will not be accepted, because its NPV is negative. The maximum rate of return that will ensure a *positive* rate of return must, therefore, lie somewhere between 10% and 15%, so the next step is to calculate the rate of return at which the project would just pay for itself.

Step 2: Calculate the specific break-even rate of return
To do this, it is necessary to interpolate between the rates used in Step 1. This can be done by using the following formula:

$$\text{IRR} = \text{Positive rate} + \left[\frac{\text{Positive NPV}}{\text{Positive NPV} + \text{Negative NPV*}} \times \text{Range of rates} \right]$$

*Ignore the negative sign and add the positive NPV to the negative NPV.

Thus in our example:

$$\text{IRR} = 10\% + \left[\frac{2978}{(2978 + 2426)} \times (15\% - 10\%) \right]$$

$$= 10\% + (0.5511 \times 5\%)$$

$$= 10\% + 2.76\%$$

$$= \underline{\underline{12.76\%}}$$

The project will be profitable provided that the company does not require a rate of return in excess of about 13%. Note that the method of calculation used above does not give the precise rate of return (because the formula is only an approximation), but it is adequate enough for decision-making purposes.

Exhibit 19.5 demonstrates that the IRR method is similar to the NPV method: first, the initial cost of the project has to be estimated, as well as the future net cash flows arising from the project; and, second, the net cash flows are then discounted to their net present value using discount tables.

The main difference between the two methods is that the IRR method requires a rate of return to be estimated in order to give an NPV equal to the initial cost of the investment. The main difficulty arises in deciding which two rates of return to use so that one will give a positive NPV and the other will give a negative NPV. The range between the two rates should be as narrow as possible. You will find that if you use a trial-and-error method, you may have to try many times before you arrive at two suitable rates!

The advantages and disadvantages of the IRR method may be summarized as follows:

Advantages
1 Emphasis is placed on liquidity.
2 Attention is given to the timing of net cash flows.
3 An appropriate rate of return does not have to be calculated.
4 The method gives a clear percentage return on an investment.

Disadvantages
1 It is not easy to understand.
2 It is difficult to determine which two suitable rates to adopt unless a computer is used.
3 The method gives only an approximate rate of return.
4 In complex CI situations, the method can give some misleading results – for example, where there are negative net cash flows in subsequent years and where there are mutually exclusive projects.

As a non-accountant, you do not need to be too worried about the details of such rather technical considerations. All you need to know is that, in practice, the IRR method has to be used with some caution.

Net cash flows

Decision making normally involves dealing with future events, and CI appraisal is no exception. Irrespective of the particular method adopted, a crucial stage in CI appraisal is the estimation and timing of *future* net cash flows.

It is not always easy to estimate how much a project will cost, how much cash it will earn over its lifetime, and the precise periods in which the cash will be received. As inflation and taxation changes cause particular difficulties, we will deal with each of them in some detail.

Inflation

As we have seen, NPV revolves round the concept that £1 receivable now is not the same as £1 receivable in 12 months' time. Cash that is in hand now can be invested. Assume that we have the choice between receiving (say) £0.90 now and £1 in 12 months' time. We may be prepared to accept £0.90 now if we can invest it for 12 months at a rate of interest of at least 10%. However, £1 receivable in 12 months' time may not be worth as much as £1 now because the purchasing power of the currency may fall. We need to allow for such changes in estimating future net cash flows, i.e. inflation (and *deflation*) should be taken into account.

In order to allow for changing prices, future net cash flows should be put on the same *price base* so that a fair comparison can be made between the cash received and paid in different time periods. In CI appraisal this can be done in one of two ways:

1 *Indexing*. Future net cash flows may be indexed. For example, assume that the net cash flow arising from a particular project will be £100 in Year 1, £150 in Year 2 and £200 in Year 3. The relevant current price index at the beginning of Year 1 is 100 but the index is expected to rise to an average level of 120 for Year 1, 140 for Year 2 and 175 for Year 3. In order to compare the net cash flows over the next three years more fairly, they need to be put on the same price base. If they are indexed, Year 1's net cash flow becomes £83 [(£100 × 100) ÷ 120]; Year 2's net cash flow becomes £107 [(£150 × 100) ÷ 140]; and Year 3's net cash flow becomes £114 [(£200 × 100) ÷ 175]. The adjusted future net cash flows of £83, £107 and £114 for Years 1, 2 and 3 respectively will then be incorporated into an NPV exercise and discounted at the entity's cost of capital.

2 *Adjusting the rate of return*. Instead of indexing, we could select a higher rate of return. The easiest approach would be to add the expected rate of inflation to the entity's cost of capital. Thus with inflation at a rate of 5% per annum and a required rate of return of 10%, £100 receivable in 12 months' time would be discounted at a rate of return of 15%, i.e. £86.96 [(£100 × 100) ÷ 115].

Taxation

Corporation tax is based on the *accounting profit* for the year. In order to calculate the amount of *tax payable* for the year, the accounting profit is adjusted for those items that are not allowable against tax, e.g. depreciation, as well as for some tax allowances that are not included in the calculation of accounting profit. Capital allowances, for example, are a tax allowance given when fixed assets are purchased; in essence, they are the equivalent of a depreciation allowance. Sometimes up to 100% capital allowances are given, so that the entire cost of purchase can be deducted from the profit in the year that a fixed asset was purchased. This means that in the year that a fixed asset is purchased, other things being equal the amount of corporation tax will be low, although in subsequent years it can be expected to be higher.

Thus, in estimating future net cash flows, it is necessary to estimate what changes are likely to take place in the taxation system, what allowances will be available, what effect any changes will have on the amount of corporation tax payable, and in what periods tax will have to be paid. Needless to say, the forecasting of such events is enormously difficult!

Selecting a method

We have kept our description of CI techniques deliberately simple. As a non-accountant you probably would not have to decide what appraisal technique to adopt and it is highly unlikely that you would have to do the detailed calculations for yourself; your accountant would probably present you with a summary of his calculations and you would then be expected to come to a decision. In doing so, you would probably find it easier if you knew what CI appraisal method had been adopted and what data had been included in the calculations. A knowledge of the various appraisal methods and their respective advantages and disadvantages should enable you to arrive at a particular decision with a great deal more confidence. Which CI appraisal method is the most appropriate?

We consider it important that the time value of money is taken into account in a CI appraisal since the profitability of a future project may be grossly optimistic if such a concept is ignored. The discounted payback method, the net present value method and the internal rate of return method, therefore, are all strong possibilities.

The internal rate of return method involves some complex calculations, although the overall result is relatively easy to understand; none the less, it may be a little too sophisticated for most entities. The discounted payback method is simple to understand and intuitively appealing. Its main disadvantage, however, is that net cash flow received after the payback period may be ignored. Almost by default, therefore, the net present value method would appear to be the most favoured method. The main difficulty with the NPV method is the selection of a suitable rate of return for a particular project. Thus great care needs to be taken before accepting or rejecting a project based on the NPV method because it is highly dependent on the arbitrary determination of a specified rate of return.

Sources of finance

Once a decision has been taken to invest in a particular project, it is then necessary to search out a suitable method of financing it. There are a considerable number of available sources, although they vary depending upon what type of entity is involved. Central and local government, for example, are heavily dependent upon current tax receipts for financing capital investment projects, while charities rely on loans and grants. In this section, we will concentrate on the sources of finance available to limited liability companies.

The sources of finance available to companies depend upon the time period involved. For convenience, we will break our discussion down into (a) the short-term; (b) the medium-term; and (c) the long-term.

Sources of short-term finance

There are five major sources of short-term finance. They are as follows.

Trade credit   Trade credit is a form of financing common in all companies (and all other entities). An entity purchases goods and services from suppliers and agrees to pay for them some days or weeks after they have been delivered. This method is so common that sometimes discounts are given for prompt payment. By delaying the payment of creditors, the entity's immediate cash needs are less strained and it may be able to finance projects that otherwise could not be considered. However, it is clearly only a temporary method of financing projects (particularly long-term ones); the entity is also highly vulnerable to pressure from its creditors. Note that this method often operates in tandem with the demand to debtors for prompt settlement of their account.

Bank overdrafts   Bank overdrafts are a form of loan where the bank's customer is allowed to draw out more from the bank than has been deposited. An entity's overdraft may have to be secured by a *floating charge*. This means that the bank has a general claim on any of the entity's assets if the entity cannot repay the overdraft. There is usually an upper limit, the amount overdrawn can usually be called in at any time, and the interest charge may be high. The main advantages of an overdraft are that it is flexible and that interest is normally only charged on the outstanding balance on a daily basis.

Factoring   Factoring relates to an entity's debtors. There are two types of factoring: recourse factoring, where an entity obtains a loan based on the amount of its debtor balances; and non-recourse factoring, where the debtor balances are sold to a factor and the factor then takes responsibility for dealing with them. Factoring is a convenient way of obtaining ready cash, but either the interest rate on the loan or the discount on the invoices may be high.

Bills of exchange A bill of exchange is simply an invoice that has been endorsed (i.e. accepted) by a merchant bank. It can then be sold by the legal holder to obtain immediate finance. The interest charged depends upon the creditworthiness of the parties involved; clearly, if an entity has a poor reputation, it will expect to pay more interest.

Commercial paper Commercial paper is a form of short-term borrowing used by large listed companies. It is a bearer document, i.e. a person to whom the document is payable without naming that person. The minimum amount permitted is £100 000. This form of borrowing, therefore, is not appropriate for very many entities.

Sources of medium-term finance

There are four types of medium-term finance that should be noted.

Bank loans Banks may be prepared to loan a fixed amount to a customer over the medium- to long-term period. The loan may be secured on the company's assets and the interest charge may be variable. Regular repayments of both the capital and the interest will be expected. Bank loans are a common form of financing but the restrictions often placed on the borrower may be particularly demanding.

Credit sales Credit sales are a form of borrowing in which the purchaser agrees to pay for goods (and services) provided on an instalment basis over an agreed period of time. Once the agreement has been signed, the legal ownership of the goods is passed to the purchaser and the seller cannot reclaim them. Sometimes, very generous terms can be arranged, e.g. no payment may be necessary for at least 12 months; it is possible, however, that the basic cost of the goods may be far higher than other suppliers are charging.

Hire purchase Hire purchase (HP) is similar to credit sales except that the seller remains the legal owner of the goods until all payments due have been completed. An immediate deposit may be necessary, followed by a series of regular instalments. Once the goods have been paid for, the ownership passes to the purchaser. HP is usually an expensive method of financing the purchase of fixed assets.

Leasing Leasing is a form of renting. A fixed asset (such as a car or a printing press) remains legally in the ownership of the lessor. In the case of some leases, the asset may never actually be returned; in effect, the lessee becomes the *de facto* owner. Leasing can be expensive, although if the lessor passes on what can sometimes be some very generous tax allowances, it can be a reasonably economic method of financing projects.

Sources of long-term finance

Long-term finance can generally be obtained from the following three sources.

Debentures

Debentures are formal long-term loans made to a company; they may be for a certain period or open-ended. Debentures are usually secured on all or some of an entity's assets. Interest is payable, but because it is allowable against corporation tax, debentures can be an economic method of financing specific projects.

Other types of loans

Besides debentures, there are other types of loans. *Loan capital*, for example is a form of borrowing in which investors are paid a regular amount of interest and their capital is eventually repaid. The investors are creditors of the entity but they have no voting rights. *Unsecured loan stock* is similar to debenture stock except that there is no security for the loan. The interest rate tends to be higher than that on debenture stock because of the greater risk. *Convertible unsecured loan stock* gives stock holders the right to convert their stock into ordinary shares at specified dates. *Eurobond loan capital* can be obtained by borrowing overseas in the 'Euro' market. The loans are usually unsecured and they are redeemed at their face value on a certain date. Interest is normally paid annually; the rate depends partly on the size of the loan and partly on the particular issuer.

Shares

Expansion of the company could be financed by increasing the number of ordinary shares available, either on the open market or to existing shareholders in the form of a *rights issue*. An increase in an entity's ordinary share capital dilutes the holding of existing shareholders and all shareholders will expect to receive increasing amounts of dividend. Alternately, new or additional preference shares could be offered; preference shareholders would have an automatic right to a certain percentage level of dividend, and so the issue of preference shares limits the amount of dividend available to ordinary shareholders.

| Conclusion

CI appraisal is a complex and time-consuming exercise. It is not possible to be totally accurate in determining the viability of individual projects but a reasoned comparison can be made between them.

Managers tend to be very enthusiastic about their own sphere of responsibility. Thus a marketing manager may be sure that additional sales will be possible, a production director may be certain that a new machine will pay for itself quickly, and the data processing manager may be convinced that a new high-powered computer is essential.

In helping management to choose between such competing projects, the accountant's role is to try to assess their costs and to compare them with the possible benefits. Once a choice has been made, he then has to ensure that the necessary finance will be available for them. CI appraisal should not be used as a means of blocking new projects. It is no different from all the other accounting techniques, for it is meant to provide additional guidance to management and, ultimately, it is the responsibility of management to ensure that other factors are taken into account.

1 Capital investment appraisal forms part of the budgeting process.

2 There are five main methods of determining the viability of a project:
   (a) payback;
   (b) discounted payback;
   (c) accounting rate of return;
   (d) net present value;
   (e) internal rate of return.

3 All the methods listed in item 2 above have their advantages and disadvantages, but the recommended methods are discounted payback and net present value.

4 Capital expenditure may be financed by a variety of sources. Sources of short-term finance for entities include trade credit, bank overdrafts, factoring, bills of exchange and commercial paper. Medium-term sources include bank loans, credit sales, hire purchase, and leasing. Long-term sources include debentures and other types of loans, and share issues.

Check your learning

1 Insert the missing word or words in each of the following statements:
   (a) The evaluation of costs and benefits of proposed investments in specific fixed assets is known as _____ _____ _____.
   (b) The _____ of _____ is the cost of financing an investment, expressed as a percentage rate.
   (c) _____ _____ _____ refers to the discounting of the net cash flows of a capital project to ascertain present value.

2 List five methods used in capital investment appraisal.

3 Identify six main sources of finance available to a limited liability company in financing a capital investment.

[*The answers to these questions may be found at the back of the book.*]

Group discussion questions

19.1 'In capital expenditure appraisal, management cannot cope with any technique that is more advanced than payback.' How far do you think that this assertion is likely to be true?

19.2 'All capital expenditure techniques are irrelevant because (a) they cannot estimate accurately future cash flows, and (b) it is difficult to select an appropriate discount rate.' Discuss.

19.3 Do any of the traditional capital investment appraisal techniques help in determining social and welfare capital expenditure proposals?

19.4 'We can all dream up new capital expenditure proposals', asserted the Managing Director, 'but where is the money coming from?' How might the proposals be financed?

Practice questions

[Note: The questions marked with an asterisk have answers at the back of the book.]

19.5* Buchan Enterprises is considering investing in a new machine. The machine will be purchased on 1 January in Year 1 at a cost of £50 000. It is estimated that it would last for 5 years, and it will then be sold at the end of the year for £2000 in cash. The respective net cash flows estimated to be received by the company as a result of purchasing the machine during each year of its life are as follows:

Year	£	
1	8 000	(excluding the initial cost)
2	16 000	
3	40 000	
4	45 000	
5	35 000	(exclusive of the project's sale proceeds)

The company's cost of capital is 12%.

Required:
Calculate (a) the payback period for the project; and (b) its discounted payback period.

19.6* Lender Limited is considering investing in a new project. It is estimated that it will cost £100 000 to implement, and that the expected net profit after tax will be as follows:

Year	£
1	18 000
2	47 000
3	65 000
4	65 000
5	30 000

No residual value is expected.

Required:
Calculate the accounting rate of return of the proposed project.

19.7* The following net cash flows relate to Lockhart Limited in connection with a certain project that has an initial cost of £2 500 000:

Year	Net cash flow	
	£000	
1	800	(excluding the initial cost)
2	850	
3	830	
4	1 200	
5	700	

The company's required rate of return is 15%.

Required:
Calculate the net present value of the project.

19.8 Moffat District Council has calculated the following net cash flows for a proposed project costing £1 450 000:

Year	Net cash flow	
	£000	
1	230	(excluding the initial cost)
2	370	
3	600	
4	420	
5	110	

Required:
Calculate the internal rate of return generated by the project.

19.9 Prospect Limited is considering investing in some new plant. The plant would cost £1 000 000 to implement. It would last five years and it would then be sold for £50 000. The relevant profit and loss accounts for each year during the life of the project are as follows:

Year to 31 March	2001	2002	2003	2004	2005
	£000	£000	£000	£000	£000
Sales	2 000	2 400	2 800	2 900	2 000
Less: Cost of goods sold					
Opening stock	–	200	300	550	350
Purchases	1 600	1 790	2 220	1 960	1 110
	1 600	1 990	2 520	2 510	1 460
Less: Closing stock	200	300	550	350	50
	1 400	1 690	1 970	2 160	1 410
Gross profit	600	710	830	740	590
Less: Expenses	210	220	240	250	300
Depreciation	190	190	190	190	190
	400	410	430	440	490
Net profit	200	300	400	300	100
Taxation	40	70	100	100	10
Retained profits	160	230	300	200	90

Additional information:

1   All sales are made and all purchases are obtained on credit terms.

2   Outstanding trade debtors and trade creditors at the end of each year are expected
    to be as follows:

Year	Trade debtors	Trade creditors
	£000	£000
2001	200	250
2002	240	270
2003	300	330
2004	320	300
2005	400	150

3   Expenses would all be paid in cash during each year in question.

4   Taxation would be paid on 1 January following each year end.

5   Half the plant would be paid for in cash on 1 April 2000, and the remaining half
    (also in cash) on 1 January 2001. The resale value of £50 000 will be received in cash
    on 31 March 2006.

Required:

Calculate the annual net cash flow arising from the purchase of this new plant.

19.10   Nicol Limited is considering investing in a new machine. The machine would cost
        £500 000. It would have a life of five years and a nil residual value. The company uses
        the straight-line method of depreciation.

        It is expected that the machine will earn the following extra profits for the company
        during its expected life:

Year	Profits
	£000
1	200
2	120
3	120
4	100
5	60

The above profits also represent the extra net cash flows expected to be generated by
the machine (i.e. they exclude the machine's initial cost and the annual depreciation
charge). The company's cost of capital is 18%.

Required:

(a) Calculate:
     (i)   the machine's payback period; and
     (ii) its net present value.

(b) Advise management as to whether the new machine should be purchased.

19.11 Hewie Limited has some capital available for investment and is considering two projects, only one of which can be financed. The details are as follows:

	Project	
	(1)	(2)
Expected life (years)	4	3
	£000	£000
Initial cost	600	500
Expected net cash flows (excluding the initial cost)		
Year		
1	10	250
2	200	250
3	400	50
4	50	–
Residual value	Nil	Nil

Required:
Advise management on which project to accept.

19.12 Marsh Limited has investigated the possibility of investing in a new machine. The following data have been extracted from the report relating to the project:

Cost of machine on 1 January 2006: £500 000.
Life: 4 years to 31 December 2009.
Estimated scrap value: Nil.
Depreciation method: Straight-line.

Year	Accounting profit after tax	Net cash flows	
	£000	£000	
2006	100	50	(excluding the initial cost)
2007	250	200	
2008	250	225	
2009	200	225	
2010	–	100	

The company's required rate of return is 15%.

Required:
Calculate the return the machine would make using the following investment appraisal methods:
1 payback;
2 accounting rate of return;
3 net present value; and
4 internal rate of return.

Contemporary issues in management accounting

The new edition of the Chartered Institute of Management Accountants' *Official Terminology* reflects the developments taking place in management accounting practice

Understanding the language of the profession

The changing face of management accounting

In the five years since the previous revision of the Official Terminology, the role of the management accountant has changed considerably. Moving away from the establishment, analysis and evaluation of financial plans and budgets, management accounting's emerging role is now more dynamic, focusing on the strategic and emphasising both financial and non-financial aspects. Today's management accountant needs to be forward-looking to meet the needs of business in the 21st century and requires a broad range of business skills and knowledge.

The key areas of activity for the 'new' management accountant include performance management, information management, corporate governance, supply chain management and financial management. Management accountants are also being called on to employ 'soft skills' and contribute to areas traditionally outside their remit in areas such as human resource management.

Management Accounting, April 2000. Reprinted with permission.

In Chapters 13 to 19 we have concentrated on examining the more conventional techniques used in management accounting. In this chapter, we outline some recent developments taking place in management accounting practice. Unless you work for a large organization, however, it is unlikely that you will have yet come across them. Even traditional management accounting has been particularly slow to develop in small- and medium-sized entities, and it would be surprising if the newer techniques had begun to take root in such entities.

Learning objectives

By the end of this chapter, you should be able to:

- outline the historical development of management accounting;

- explain why changes in the commercial and industrial environment have affected traditional management accounting practices;

- consider the usefulness of activity based costing, activity based management, backflush costing, life cycle costing, strategic management accounting, target costing and throughput accounting.

Introduction

Most of the traditional management accounting techniques outlined in previous chapters are used by profit-making and not-for-profit entities in both the public and private sectors. The techniques were developed many years ago at a time when society was very different from what it is now. Manufacturing industry is much less significant than it used to be (particularly in Britain and the United States) and production methods have changed considerably. The service sector is of much great significance and there is now more focus on governmental activities. Perhaps the greatest change has been the increasing automation of economic activity and the electronic revolution.

While considerable changes have taken place in the commercial and industrial life of Britain, particularly since the end of the First World War in 1918, management accounting practices have generally failed to reflect those changes. Indeed, it is only in the last 20 years or so that the traditional techniques have been questioned and new developments have been put forward. It is fitting, therefore, that in the last chapter of this book we examine the historical development of management accounting in a rapidly changing world and the possible improvements that could be made to improve it.

In the next section, we examine briefly the development of management accounting. This section is then followed by a review of the more significant changes that have evolved in recent years.

Historical development

In this section we provide a brief review of the historical development of management accounting. The main aim of the section is to provide a framework for the main part of the chapter, which examines some of the emerging issues in management accounting. You will find it easier to understand how these issues have come about if you are familiar with the reasons why management accounting practices are only just beginning to change.

The section is divided into three subsections. In the first subsection, we examine the history of management accounting up to 1980. The second subsection covers the period from 1980 to the present day. The third subsection speculates about the long-term future of management accounting.

Before 1980

Management accounting, as we know it today, only began to develop as a separate branch of accounting in the 19th century. Following the Industrial Revolution in the 18th and early 19th centuries, Britain grew rapidly as an industrial nation. By about 1840 it had become apparent that sufficient finance to support the new industries could not be supplied from private sources without at least the guarantee of 'limited liability'. Hence the recognition in law of such a concept and the growth of limited liability companies.

Compared with the pre-industrial era, such entities were often large and complex and the owners were usually not in a position to manage them. Hence they had to employ someone to do it for them, and this led to the advent of professional managers. The managers soon found that they could not plan and control a developing company merely by personal observation and the consultation of some fairly rudimentary annual accounts. As a result, *management accounting* began to develop as a separate branch of accounting.

Progress, however, was slow. The main requirements of the *industrial* accountant (as he was then called) was to provide more detailed information for management much more frequently than was required for financial accounting purposes. The main requirements of *financial* accounting were to provide information for stock control, for pricing and for product costing. The compilation of product costs, however, was rudimentary and the treatment of overheads was somewhat simplistic.

The United States of America underwent its own industrial revolution in the second half of the 19th century, and management accounting practices rapidly developed to help support its industrial development. By the beginning of the 20th century most of the management accounting practices that we have incorporated in this book (e.g. absorption costing, budgetary control and standard costing) were already used by many American companies. Information about them gradually became known in Britain, and by 1925 some of the larger British, companies had begun to adopt them.

After 1925, there were very few developments in management accounting practices (either in the United States or Britain) until about 1980 – with, two notable exceptions: contribution analysis, and the use of discounting techniques in capital investment appraisal.

From 1980 to the present day

It is quite remarkable that over a period of some 55 years (from 1925 to 1980) management accounting practices remained stagnant. This might indicate that either the practices were able to accommodate the momentous changes that took place in the industrial and political world during that period, or that management accounting practitioners were short of ideas.

None the less, by about 1980 (the date is somewhat arbitrary), it had become apparent that *some* change was necessary. The main impetus came from the developments taking place in Japan. Prior to the Second World War (1939 to 1945), Japan had been a relatively unknown and somewhat backward country. The impact of the war required it to be almost completely rebuilt and modernized without having the benefit of many indigenous raw materials. Japan's leaders realized that the country could only survive if it sold high-quality low- cost products to the rest of the world. She had to start from an almost zero industrial base, but progress was helped by the close family traditions of Japanese culture and society. It took some time but eventually Japan was able to introduce the most modern practices into its industrial life.

These practices enabled the Japanese to be flexible in offering high-quality and reliable competitive products to its customers and to make sure that they were delivered on time. A detailed discussion of the managerial philosophy and various production techniques used by the Japanese is beyond this book, but you should note the following development pioneered in Japan:

1 *Advanced manufacturing technology (AMT)*. AMT production incorporates highly automated and highly computerized methods of design and operation. It enables machines to be easily and cheaply adapted for short production runs, thereby enabling the specific requirements of individuals to be met.

2 *Just-in-time (JIT) production*. Traditional plant and machinery was often time-consuming and expensive to convert if it needed to be switched from one product to another; once the plant and machinery was set up, therefore, long production runs were the norm. This meant that goods were often manufactured for stock (resulting in heavy storage and finance costs). By contrast, AMT (see item 1) leads to an overall JIT philosophy in which an attempt is made to manufacture goods only when they have been specifically ordered by a customer. The JIT approach has implications for management accountants. As goods are only manufactured when ordered, raw materials and components are similarly purchased only when they are required for a particular order. Hence no stock pricing problem arises and stock control becomes less of an issue since stock levels will, by definition, be kept to a minimum.

3 *Total quality management (TQM)*. Another approach that the Japanese have incorporated into their production methods is TQM. The basic concept of TQM reflects two concepts:

   (a) *Getting it right the first time*. Whatever task is being undertaken, it should be done correctly the first time that it is attempted. This means that there should then be savings on internal failure costs, e.g. no wastage, reworking, re-inspections, downgrading or discounted prices. There will also be savings on external costs, such as repairs, handling, legal expenses, lost sales and warranties. There could, however, be additional preventive costs – for example, planning, training and operating the system – as well as appraisal costs, such as administration, audit and inspection.

(b) *The quality of the output should reflect its specification.* In this context, the concept of 'quality' should not be confused with the feeling of 'luxury'. A small mass-produced car, for example, may be regarded as a quality product (because its performance meets its specification) in exactly the same way that we equate a luxury car (such as a Rolls-Royce) with quality.

TQM is a technique that involves all employees in an entity, irrespective of whether they are the chairman or a part-time caretaker. Thus accountants will also be involved in adopting a TQM approach in their work. However, management accountants may have some additional responsibilities towards collecting and reporting on appraisal, prevention and internal/external failure costs. Considering that TQM involves collecting and distributing a great deal of information, it is rather curious that management accountants have not been heavily involved in the implementation and operation of a TQM system – especially as, in the past, they have tended to get involved in everything! We do not have much evidence yet to indicate to what extent traditional management accounting practices have changed as a result of operating in a TQM environment, but it is possible that it could pose a threat to some traditional management accounting practices.

The industrial changes that had taken place in Japan were observed by other countries (especially the United States) and the new developments have gradually been adopted by many of them. The changes to industrial production methods has meant that many traditional management accounting techniques have either become less useful or less relevant. Thus, as in Japan, new techniques have had to be devised. We will consider some of them later in this chapter.

The future

Before we consider future developments in management accounting, i.e. those beyond the next 10–15 years, it would be useful to summarize the economic environment in which Britain (and other former industrialized nations) have found themselves in recent years:

1 *Decline of manufacturing industry.* Traditional extractive and heavy manufacturing industries (such as coal mining, iron and steel, shipbuilding and indigenous car manufacturing) is now much less important, and in some cases non-existent. Those manufacturing industries that do still exist are much less labour-intensive than they used to be and labour costs themselves can no longer be regarded as a variable cost.

2 *Growth of service industries.* There has been a growth of service industries such as finance services, entertainment, information supply and tourism.

Service industries do not generally employ the thousands of employees that manufacturing industries used to employ. The service sector now forms a major part of the economy.

3 *Automation and computerization.* Production processes and the administrative back-up is now intensively automated and computerized.

These trends are likely to continue into the future. The implications for management accounting are as follows:

● The collection, recording, extraction and summary of data for information purposes will be performed electronically. This function will no longer be serviced by a large army of management accountants.
● As JIT procedures become dominant, stock control, materials pricing and stock valuation will become relatively insignificant tasks.
● Product costing involving the use of more sophisticated overhead absorption techniques will still be important. However, it will become a relatively routine task as the data will be processed by computer.
● Budgeting and budgetary control will also become much more computerized. They will also be capable of being subject to a variety of different possible outcomes.
● Standard costing is likely to become less significant in a TQM environment. If it survives, it will be possible to produce different standard costs for a variety of different outcomes.
● The management accountant for an entity will become more of a general manager specializing in the financial implications of decision making, and he or she will use a wide variety of internal and external data.
● The management accountant will need to be able to develop and incorporate new techniques in order to cope with a commercial and industrial world that will be subject to rapid change.

It follows from the above that, as a non-accountant working in the future in a large organization, you are likely to meet a very different type of management accountant from the one that you are familiar with today. Tomorrow's management accountant will be much more of a team player, less bound to arithmetical recording of past events and more involved in taking highly informed decisions about future events. However, this is likely to be some time in the future. What of the present? We turn now to some developments in management accounting that have received some attention during the last 20 years or so.

Activity based costing

In Chapter 14 we explained how product costs may be calculated. The procedure involved identifying the *direct costs* of a product and then adding (or absorbing) a proportion of the *indirect costs* (i.e. the overheads) to the total of the direct costs.

Overheads are normally absorbed into product costs on the basis of either *direct labour hours* or *machine hours*. The production overhead charge for a particular cost centre is calculated by dividing the total production overhead by the total direct labour hours (or machine hours) worked in that centre. As far as a particular unit is concerned, the direct labour hours (or machine hours) worked on that unit will then be determined and multiplied by the absorption rate. Thus the total production cost of a particular unit will be made up of the direct costs plus a share of the production overheads. A *total unit cost* may then be calculated by applying a percentage addition to the total product cost in order to allow for non-manufacturing overheads.

Product costing has been conducted along the above lines for most of the 20th century. However, it was only in the 1980s that it began to be apparent that the traditional method of absorbing overhead was inappropriate in an advanced manufacturing environment. As the traditional method involves calculating the total cost of overheads in a particular cost centre and charging them out to particular units on a time basis, the total cost is *averaged* among those units that flow through that particular cost centre. The assumption behind this procedure is that the more time that a unit spends in production, the more overhead it will incur. Such an assumption means, of course, that no distinction is made between fixed and variable overhead; it also means that, irrespective of whether a particular unit causes a certain cost to arise in a cost centre, it is still charged with a proportion of that cost.

We will use an example to illustrate this point. The details are contained in Exhibit 20.1.

Exhibit 20.1 Overhead absorption: the unfairness of the traditional approach

In Jasmine Ltd's Production Cost Centre 1, two units are produced: Unit A and Unit B, the total overhead cost being £1000. This is made up of two costs: (1) machine set-up costs of £800; and (2) inspection costs of £200. Overhead is absorbed on the basis of direct labour hours. The total direct labour hours (DLH) amount to 200. Unit A requires 150 DLH and Unit B 50 DLH.

The machinery for Unit A only needs to be set up once, whereas Unit B requires nine set-ups. Unit A and Unit B both require two inspections each.

Required:
Calculate the total overhead to be charged to Unit A and to Unit B using: (a) the traditional method of absorbing overhead; and (b) a fairer method based on set-up and inspection costs.

Answer to Exhibit 20.1

(a) The traditional method

The absorption rate is £5 (£1000 total overhead ÷ 200 direct labour hours). As Unit A has 150 direct labour hours spent on it, it will absorb £750 (150 DLH × £5) of overhead. Unit B has 50 direct labour hours spent on it; it will, therefore, absorb £250 of overhead (50 DLH × £5).

(b) A fairer method

Each set-up costs £80 [£800 ÷ 10 (1 set-up for A + 9 set-ups for B)] and each inspection costs £50 [£200 ÷ 4 (2 inspections for A + 2 inspections for B)]. The total overhead charged to Unit A, therefore, would be £180: £80 for set-up costs (one set-up × £80) plus £100 inspection costs (2 inspections × £50). Unit B would be charged a total of £820: £720 of set-up costs (9 set-ups × £80) and £100 inspection costs (2 inspections × £50). The fairer method illustrated here is known as *activity based costing* (ABC).

(c) A companion

The table below compares the two approaches to overhead absorption:

JASMINE LIMITED

Product	Overhead absorbed on a traditional basis	Overhead absorbed on an activity basis
	£	£
A	750	180
B	250	820
Total	1 000	1 000

The simple example in Exhibit 20.1 illustrates the potential unfairness of the traditional method of absorbing overhead. As the method *averages* the total cost among particular units, those units that do not benefit from a particular activity bear a disproportionate amount of the total cost. In the above example, Unit A should only be charged £180 of overhead (compared with £750 under the traditional method), whereas Unit B should be charged £820 (compared with £250 under the traditional method).

It follows that if the eventual selling price is based on cost, the traditional method would grossly inflate Unit A's selling price and deflate Unit B's selling price. Unit A's selling price would probably be highly uncompetitive and only a few units might be sold. Unit B's selling price would probably be highly competitive. Thus a great many units of Unit B might be sold, but the total sales revenue may not be sufficient to recover all of the overhead costs.

In order to illustrate the principles behind ABC, we have made reference to just one cost centre. However, in practice, overheads for the whole of the entity (including both manufacturing and non-manufacturing overheads) would be dealt with collectively. They would then be allocated to *cost pools*, i.e. similar areas of activity. It is estimated that even in the largest entities, a total of about 30 cost pools is the maximum number that it is practicable to handle. This means that some costs may be allocated to a cost pool where there is only a distance relationship between some of the costs. In other words, like the traditional method of absorbing overheads, ABC also involves some averaging of costs.

Once the overheads have all been allocated to an appropriate cost pool, a *cost driver* for each pool is selected. A cost driver is the main cause of the costs attached to that pool. Once again, some approximation is necessary because some costs collected in that pool may only have a loose connection with the selected driver. By dividing the total cost in a particular cost pool by the cost driver, an overhead cost per driver can be calculated. For example, suppose the total overhead cost collected in a particular cost pool totalled £1000 and the costs in that pool were driven by the number of material requisitions (say 200), the cost driver rate would be £5 per material requisition (£1000 cost ÷ 200 material requisitions).

The final stage is to charge an appropriate amount of overhead to each unit benefiting from the service provided by the various cost pools. Thus if a particular unit required 10 material requisitions and the cost driver rate was £5 per material requisition, it would be charged £50 (£5 per material requisition × 10 requisitions). Of course, it may benefit from the services provided by a number of other cost pools, in which case it would collect a share of overhead from each of them as well.

The above procedures may be a little difficult to follow, so read it again before working your way through Exhibit 20.2. The exhibit illustrates the main steps involved in ABC.

Exhibit 20.2 Activity based costing (ABC)

Shish Limited has recently introduced an activity based costing (ABC) system. The following details relate to the month of March 2003.

1 Four cost pools have been identified: (1) Parts; (2) Maintenance; (3) Stores; and (4) Administration.

2 The cost drivers that were identified with each cost pool are: (1) total number of parts; (2) maintenance hours; (3) number of material requisitions; and (4) number of employees.

3 Costs and activities during March 2003 were:

Cost pool	Total overhead	Activity	Quantity
	£000		
Parts	10 000	Number of parts	500
Maintenance	18 000	Number of maintenance hours	600
Stores	10 000	Number of material requisitions	20
Administration	2 000	Number of employees	40

4 500 units of Product X3 were produced. Each unit of X3 required 100 parts and 200 maintenance hours; 6 material requisitions were made and 10 employees worked on the units.

Required:

Using activity based costing, calculate the total amount of overhead absorbed by each unit of Product X3.

Answer to Exhibit 20.2

Shish Ltd

Cost pool	Overhead cost	Cost driver	Cost driver rate	Usage by Product X3	Overhead cost charged to Product X3
(1)	(2)	(3)	(4)	(5)	(6)
	£000		£		£
Parts	10 000	500 parts	20	100 parts	2 000
Maintenance	18 000	600 hours	30	200 hours	6 000
Stores	10 000	20 requisitions	500	6 requisitions	3 000
Administration	2 000	40 employees	50	10 employees	500
TOTAL					11 500

Tutorial notes

1 Column (4) has been obtained by dividing the data in Column (2) by the data in Column (3).
2 The data in Column (6) has been obtained by multiplying the data in Column (4) by the data in Column (5).
3 The total amount of £11 500 shown in Column (6) is the total amount of overhead to be absorbed by Product X3.

Solution: The total amount of overhead to be absorbed by each unit of Product X3 will be £23 (£11 500 ÷ 500 units).

ABC is an attempt to absorb overhead into product costs on a basis that relates more closely to the overhead generated by particular activities. Its proponents claim that it is particularly suited to modern manufacturing circumstances because the more that a particular unit causes an increase in activity, the more overhead that particular unit is charged. By contrast, in traditional overhead absorption, total production overhead in any production cost centre is charged by using just one activity rate, which may not be closely related to the overhead generated by particular units.

In principle, there is no significant difference between ABC and traditional overhead absorption. ABC looks for a closer relationship between individual overhead costs and the cause of such costs, while the traditional method adopts a more general approach. However, ABC has another advantage: no distinction is made between manufacturing overhead and non-manufacturing overhead. Thus it avoids the problem inherent in total overhead absorption of finding a meaningful relationship between non-manufacturing overheads and manufacturing activity.

Backflush costing

The advent of just-in-time (JIT) systems has meant that the traditional method of recording costs can be simplified. A JIT system does not require us to record (or to track) the progress of a unit in production from the time that it commences its production run until the time that it is eventually sold. This is because units are only manufactured when they are ordered by a customer: they are not manufactured for stock that might or might not be sold. Consequently, a unit manufactured specifically for a customer should flow speedily through the production process, thereby avoiding the need for recording what is happening to it at every stage of its manufacture.

This simplified form of costing is known as *backflush costing* (or *backflush accounting*). The term arises because entries are only made in the books of account when a unit has completed its production process. When this has occurred, the costs are traced (or flushed) back. In practice, the budgeted or standard cost of the unit is more likely to be adopted rather than the actual cost.

The cost book-keeping is much simpler because fewer entries are made in the books of account and no work-in-progress accounts are kept. There is a danger, of course, that there could be a lack of control over the units as they pass through production because there will be no documentary record of their progress. This is especially the case if the production process for certain units is particularly lengthy or where there are unforeseen delays.

A further problem arises: *at what stage should a record be made in the books of account?* There are three possible stages. These stages are known as trigger points and they are as follows.

1 *When the units have been completed.* This is the purest and possibly the simplest form of backflush costing. No entries are made in the books of account until the units are transferred to the finished goods store. At that point the budgeted or standard cost of the units will be traced and the appropriate entries made in the relevant accounts. These are primarily the stores ledger account (for direct materials), the conversion cost account (direct labour and overheads), and the cost of goods sold account.

2 *When raw materials are purchased and the units have been completed.* In effect, this method uses two trigger points. An entry is made when raw materials are purchased specifically to complete the order (remember this would normally be the case with a JIT system). The entries in the conversion cost account and the cost of goods sold account would only be made when the units have been completed.

3 *When raw materials are purchased and the units have been sold.* This method also has two trigger points. The first is when raw materials are purchased specifically to complete an order. Unlike the previous method, the second stage only takes place when the units have been sold. Thus there could be a long delay in recording the details in the conversion cost account and the cost of goods sold account if, for some reason, the goods are not immediately sold.

Backflush costing might be viewed of relevance only to management accountants, since other managers will not want to become involved in detailed book-keeping procedures. However, this is not entirely the case, because the techniques might result in less control over an entity's resources. This will be of concern to all managers, particularly if the responsibility for any inefficiencies can be traced directly to them.

Life cycle costing

Life cycle costing is a relatively new form of cost accounting. The idea is to capture the total costs and revenues of a product over its entire lifetime. Indeed, the system is sometimes referred to as *'cradle to grave' costing*, albeit strictly speaking some costs may arise even before the cradle stage! Although life cycle costing is practised by many large companies (especially vehicle manufacturers), it still needs considerable development before it becomes more commonly used.

The lifetime of some products may range from just a few week or months (e.g. designer clothes) while others may last several generations (e.g. an aircraft). Irrespective of their lifespan, however, most products go through several stages. The main ones can be summarized as follows:

1 *Design*. This stage includes the period during which an idea for a new product is conceived, worked on, planned, designed and developed.
2 *Prototype*. At this stage a trial product has been produced and it is being tested.
3 *Development*. After assessing the test results, the product is further refined and prepared for going into production.
4 *Manufacturing*. The product is now in production. Depending upon the type of product, it may well continue to be manufactured for very many years.
5 *Disposal*. Eventually, the demand for the product declines to such an extent that it is taken out of production. There may then be a cost of disposing of it and of its production facilities (such as oil rigs and nuclear power plants).

Life cycle costing was developed by the American defence industry during the early 1960s. It was realized that traditional costing methods could be somewhat misleading when the profitability of various projects were being assessed. Traditional accounting methods would require design, prototype, development and disposal costs to be written off in the period in which they were incurred. The main interest would focus on the control of costs while the product was in its manufacturing stage.

Consequently, it is unusual to give as much attention to all of the costs of a project from the time that it is first conceived until the time that it is finally abandoned. This means that the overall total cost is not always closely correlated with the overall total revenues. In other word, the lifetime profitability of a project tends to be ignored, especially if it gets beyond its development stage.

As up to 90 per cent of the costs of a project could be incurred at the design stage, merely by agreeing to consider a particular project, entities have already committed themselves to considerable expenditure. This clearly has considerable resource implications within an entity. Thus it has became apparent that managers need to pay at least as much attention to the design and disposal stages as they do to the manufacturing stage.

The consequences for management accounting are that information for management should no longer be prepared on the basis of data being neatly packaged into calendar-year compartments. Instead, attempts need to be made to cost products on a much longer-term basis. Life cycle costing should, therefore, be of considerable benefit to non-accounting managers because it will enable them to assess more accurately the profitability of a particular project over its entire life.

Strategic management accounting

Strategic management accounting (SMA) has begun to develop as a separate branch of management accounting during the last 20 years but, as with life cycle costing, it is not yet well developed. SMA supports the move to a more strategic approach to managerial decisions.

The objective of SMA is to supply information to management for strategic decision-making purposes, incorporating both internal and external data of both a financial and non-financial nature. Thus in order to support a particular decision or a proposal of a long-term nature, a management accountant would not restrict the data collected either to that available within the entity or to that primarily related to costs and revenues. The external information would include financial and non-financial data relating to the entity's competitors because their long-term plans are likely to have a significant impact on what the entity itself proposes to do.

The procedures available for external data collection are extremely speculative. Indeed, they cannot be anything else because obviously the entity's competitors would wish to keep their plans as confidential as possible. However, information should be available from such published sources as annual reports and accounts, trade circulars, press releases, and newspaper and journal articles. It has also been suggested that several rather unorthodox sources may be available, such as information that might be provided by former employees of competitor companies or from visiting suppliers' representatives. In other words, management accountants may need to undertake a certain amount of detective work in order to obtain the data that they need!

In taking on this role, the main aim of the management accountants would be to compile competitors' plans in the form of financial statements similar to those of their own entity. The strategic planning team should then be able to make comparisons between sets of internal and external financial statements (including non-financial data) and, if need be, adjust their own strategic plan.

SMA should be of considerable assistance to the strategic planning team and it has the potential to be of considerable importance and relevance to non-accountants.

Target costing

Target costing is a cost-reduction technique. A target cost is established by subtracting the difference between the perceived or expected selling price of a product and the entity's desired profit margin. Suppose, for example, that a company is launching a new product on the market and expects to be able to sell it at £10 per unit. The company's desired profit margin is given as 10 per cent (i.e. £1 per unit), and so the cost per unit must be no more than £9 (£10 – £1). The target cost is usually set very tightly so that everyone throughout the entity has to search rigorously for economies.

In order to meet the target, the design of the product, the production process and the selling and distribution arrangements may all have to be carefully determined and re-examined. Hence the implementation of a target costing system can act as a considerable incentive to search for more efficient ways of manufacturing and selling the product. It is also very much part of a TQM environment.

Target costing is not a specific management accounting technique. Management accountants may be responsible for collecting the required data and submitting information to management. However, the application of target costing is the responsibility of management generally. In particular, use will be made of scientific principles and methods such as *value engineering*, a discipline that searches for the minimization of product and service costs without sacrificing quality and reliability.

Target costing is of considerable significance to those non-accountants who work in advanced manufacturing technology companies, although there is no reason why the principles cannot be applied in all types of entities.

Throughput accounting

Throughput accounting (or *throughput costing*) is an American concept that has been developed during the last 20 years. It grew out of a theory known as the *theory of constraints* (TOC). The theory suggests that all entities have some constraint that inhibits their growth. However, most companies experience some form of bottleneck (i.e. a situation that constrains activity). Thus there must be some limit on how big they grow. The aim of management, therefore, must be to seek out the bottlenecks and to eliminate them.

Suppose, for example, that Machine A produces units that are then transferred to Machine B. Machine A manufactures 100 units per hour, but B can only cope with 50 units an hour. If A continues to produce 100 units per hour, large stocks of units will be built up until such time that B can cope with all that A produces.

Management must seek to remove the bottleneck at Machine B. In the meantime, Machine A must limit its output to 50 units per hour. This is a highly radical approach and one that is quite contrary to traditional practice. It means that staff working on Machine A will become unemployed (or 'idle' as it is often termed) once they have produced 50 units in any particular hour. No manager likes to see his staff hanging around doing no work! However, if employees on Machine A go on producing units that Machine B cannot cope with, stocks will continue to be built up and extra storage space will be needed for them, thereby leading to extra costs. Once the bottleneck at Machine B is eliminated, Machine A can increase its output to match Machine B's output level. Thus a particular bottleneck should only exist in the short term, although new ones are always likely to occur.

The elimination of bottlenecks means that more and more materials can be processed without being held up. The more material that is processed and the more that can be sold, the more profitable an entity becomes (if it has got its costings right). Thus the main aim of the production team should be to increase the *throughput* of materials. Hence they will need some information about the relationship between sales and the turnover of materials. This need has given rise to the development of throughput accounting.

Throughput accounting is still at an early stage of development. At its simplest, it involves presenting a report to management emphasizing the *throughput contribution*. The throughput contribution is the difference between the sales revenue for a particular period less the direct material cost of those sales. All other costs are treated as fixed period costs and these are deducted from the throughput contribution to arrive at profit. Table 20.1 presents an example of a simple throughput accounting statement.

Table 20.1 A throughput accounting statement

	£
Sales revenue	10 000
Less: direct variable materials	6 000
Throughput contribution	4 000
Other costs	2 000
Profit	2 000

As can be seen from Table 20.1, a throughput accounting statement is very similar to a marginal cost statement. The main difference is that it only includes direct materials as a variable cost in arriving at contribution, whereas a marginal cost statement includes other direct costs. It thus emphasizes the need to process more and more direct materials at a faster and faster rate.

A throughput accounting approach has some relevance for non-accountants. It emphasizes (1) the need to eliminate bottlenecks and constraints on activity; (2) the importance of maximizing the amount of direct materials turned into finished goods sales; and (3) the control of other costs. There is, however, a danger that attention will be concentrated on increasing the throughput contribution and less attention given to the control of other costs (which could be substantial). While the maximization of the throughput contribution may be acceptable in the short term, the long-term goal must be to ensure that the company earns sufficient revenue to cover all its costs and to make a profit.

Conclusion

In the first part of this chapter we explained that by 1925 most management accounting techniques used today were already well established. Between 1925 and 1980 very few new management accounting techniques were developed. From about 1980 onwards, however, many developments began to take place, although it is only the larger and more internationally oriented companies that have introduced them. None the less the academic and professional literature regularly contains articles outlining new ideas for developing management accounting practices. It would be surprising if at least some of these did not become relevant in the 21st century.

It will take time before these ideas become established. In the meantime, some of the new techniques that have been introduced in recent years were outlined in the second part of the chapter. Activity based costing (ABC) appears to have become generally accepted, although this does not necessarily mean that it is widely practised. Other relatively new techniques that were discussed include backflush costing, life cycle costing, strategic management accounting, target costing and throughput accounting.

All of these techniques have their uses, especially in large manufacturing companies. Backflush costing is perhaps of particular relevance to management accountants and it probably does not have quite the same relevance for non-accountants. None the less, the absence of detailed records could mean that there is a possible loss of control over resources, and that is a matter that should be of concern to all managers.

Life cycle costing is of great relevance and importance to those companies where the design and disposal costs are of major importance. Strategic management accounting is likely to develop as a major branch of management accounting because it supports the move to a more strategic approach to management.

Target costing requires significant technical back-up, and it probably can only be operated successfully in large companies. Even so, the idea is of relevance in all entities that are interested in scientific methods of cost reduction.

Throughput accounting reflects a novel approach to operating a factory. Its application is contrary to the approach conventionally adopted by management in ensuring that employees are kept busy all the time. A manager has to be extremely self-assured to accept that some employees should be 'idle' because of a bottleneck elsewhere within the system. The basic idea is sound, however, and it deserves to be taken more seriously.

As for the future, in a brief sentence, it is doubtful whether management accounting practices will remain as static in the 21st century as they were throughout most of the 20th century.

Key points

1 Management accounting developed as a main branch of accounting towards the end of the 19th century.

2 By 1925 most management accounting techniques used today were in place and there was little further development until about 1980.

3 The decline of old industries in the western world and the emergence of new economies in the Far East (particularly Japan), the introduction of new management philosophies (such as total quality management and just-in-time procedures), and new technologically based industries have together necessitated the development of more relevant management accounting techniques.

4 Recent developments in management accounting practices that have found favour and that reflect the changes taking place in the commercial and industrial world include activity based costing, backflush costing, life cycle costing, strategic management accounting, target costing and throughput accounting.

Check your learning

1 What do the following initials mean:
   (a) ABC
   (b) JIT
   (c) SMA
   (d) TA
   (e) TQM.

2 What is a cost pool?

3 Give an example of a cost driver.

4 State whether each of the following assertions is largely either true or false:
   (a) Backflush costing may result in a lack of management control.   True/False
   (b) Life cycle costing does not follow the periodicity rule.   True/False
   (c) SMA incorporates external data into an entity's reporting system.   True/False
   (d) The main aim of target costing is to set a selling price.   True/False
   (e) Throughput contribution = sales revenue less all direct costs.   True/False

[*The answers to these questions may be found at the back of the book.*]

Group discussion questions

20.1 'Activity based costing is just a fad and a fashion.' Discuss.

20.2 Do you think that backflush costing has any relevance for non-accountants?

20.3 'Ugh!' snorted the Chairman when confronting the Chief Accountant. 'Strategic management accounting is another of those techniques dreamed up by you and your mates to keep you all in jobs.' Could the Chairman have a point?

Practice questions

20.4 Assess the usefulness of activity based costing (ABC) in managerial decision making.

20.5 How far does a just-in-time (JIT) production system avoid the materials pricing problem?

20.6 Giving you reasons, explain which one of the following management accounting techniques is likely to be the most useful to a non-accounting manager: backflush costing, life cycle costing, strategic management accounting, target costing and throughput accounting.

Further reading

This book contains sufficient material for most first-year modules in accounting for non-accounting students. Some students may require additional information, however, and it may be necessary for them to consult other books when attempting exercises set by their tutors.

There are many very good accounting books available for *accounting* students, but they usually go into considerable technical detail. *Non-accounting* students must use them with caution, otherwise they will find themselves completely lost. In any case, non-accounting students do not need to process vast amounts of highly technical data. It is sufficient for their purpose if they have an understanding of where accounting information comes from, why it is prepared in that way, what it means, and what reliance can be placed on it.

Bearing these points in mind, the following books are worth considering:

Financial accounting

Elliott, B. and Elliott, J. (2000) *Financial Accounting and Reporting 2000–2001*, 5th edn, Financial Times/Prentice Hall, Harlow. This is an excellent textbook that is now into its fifth edition. It should be a very useful reference book for non-accounting students.

Holmes, G. and Sugden, A. (2000) *Interpreting Company Reports and Accounts*, 7th edn, Financial Times/Prentice Hall, Harlow. A well-established text that deals with company financial reporting in some detail.

Wood, F. (1999) *Business Accounting*, Volumes 1 and 2, 8th edn, Financial Times/Pitman Publishing, London (Volume 2, F. Wood and A. Sangster). Wood is the master accounting textbook writer. His books can be recommended with absolute confidence.

Management accounting

Arnold, J. and Turley, S (1996) *Accounting for Management Decisions*, 3rd edn, Prentice Hall, Hemel Hempstead. This book is aimed at first- and second-year undergraduate and professional courses. Non-accounting students should be able to follow it without too much difficulty.

Ashton, D., Hopper, T. and Scapen, R.W. (eds) (1995) *Issues in Management Accounting*, 2nd edn, Prentice-Hall Europe, Hemel Hempstead. This book will be useful for those students who are interested in current developments in management accounting. However, be warned! It is written in an academic style and some of the chapters are very hard going.

Drury, C. (2000) *Management and Cost Accounting*, 5th edn, Business Press Thomson Learning, London. This book has become the established British text on management accounting. It is a big book in every sense of the word. Non-accounting students should only use it for reference.

Wilson, R.M.S. and Chua, W.F. (1993) *Managerial Accounting – method and meaning*, 2nd edn, Business Press Thomson Learning, London. This book is another first- and second-year undergraduate text. It has much more of a behavioural approach than most other management accounting books. It is a bit heavy going, but it is useful to see how management accounting can be approached from a completely different angle.

Discount table

Present value of £1 received after *n* years discounted at *i*%

i *n*	1	2	3	4	5	6	7	8	9	10
1	0.9901	0.9804	0.9709	0.9615	0.9524	0.9434	0.9346	0.9259	0.9174	0.9091
2	0.9803	0.9612	0.9426	0.9246	0.9070	0.8900	0.8734	0.8573	0.8417	0.8264
3	0.9706	0.9423	0.9151	0.8890	0.8638	0.8396	0.8163	0.7938	0.7722	0.7513
4	0.9610	0.9238	0.8885	0.8548	0.8227	0.7921	0.7629	0.7350	0.7084	0.6830
5	0.9515	0.9057	0.8626	0.8219	0.7835	0.7473	0.7130	0.6806	0.6499	0.6209
6	0.9420	0.8880	0.8375	0.7903	0.7462	0.7050	0.6663	0.6302	0.5963	0.5645

i *n*	11	12	13	14	15	16	17	18	19	20
1	0.9009	0.8929	0.8850	0.8772	0.8696	0.8621	0.8547	0.8475	0.8403	0.8333
2	0.8116	0.7929	0.7831	0.7695	0.7561	0.7432	0.7305	0.7182	0.7062	0.6944
3	0.7312	0.7118	0.6931	0.6750	0.6575	0.6407	0.6244	0.6086	0.5934	0.5787
4	0.6587	0.6355	0.6133	0.5921	0.5718	0.5523	0.5337	0.5158	0.4987	0.4823
5	0.5935	0.5674	0.5428	0.5194	0.4972	0.4761	0.4561	0.4371	0.4190	0.4019
6	0.5346	0.5066	0.4803	0.4556	0.4323	0.4104	0.3910	0.3704	0.3521	0.3349

Answers to 'check your learning' questions

Chapter 1		
	1	(a) Account (b) Profit
	2	(a) Financial accounting (b) Management accounting
	3	(a) False (b) False
	4	(c) Management consultancy
	5	(b) Six
	6	(a) Sole (b) Act (c) Company

Chapter 2		
	1	(a) False (b) False (c) True
	2	Overstate; understate
	3	(a) Boundary (b) Measurement (c) Measurement (d) Ethical (e) Boundary (f) Ethical

Chapter 3

1 (a) Assets; capital; liabilities (b) Left; credit

2 (a) Cash; sales (b) Rent paid; bank (c) Wages; cash (d) Supplier; bank (e) Ford; sales

3 Debit   Credit
   (a) Suppliers   Cash
   (b) Office rent   Bank
   (c) Cash   Sales
   (d) Bank   Dividends received

4 The entries are on the wrong side

5 (a) No (b) Yes (c) No

Chapter 4

1 (a) False (b) False (c) False

2 The trading and profit and loss account stage; and the balance sheet stage

3 (a) Gross profit/(loss) (b) Net profit/(loss)

4 The vertical format

Chapter 5

1 (a) False (b) True (c) True

2 (a) Purchases (b) Net profit (c) Assets

3 £1000 [(£12 000 − 2000) ÷ 10]

4 (a) distinction between capital and revenue (b) Revenue recognition (c) Stock valuation (d) Depreciation calculations (e) Estimates for outstanding creditors. (Note also that the historic cost accounting concept is used for the preparation of conventional accounting statements; this concept is covered in Chapter 12.)

Chapter 6

1 (a) Nineteenth century (b) Public limited (c) Ordinary; preference (d) Long-term loan (or borrowing)

2 (a) Gross profit (b) Dividends (c) Current assets (d) Shareholders' funds (e) Retained profit for the year

3 (a) Current liabilities (b) Loans (c) Fixed assets (d) Share capital (e) Current assets

Chapter 7

1 (a) True (b) False (c) True (d) True (e) True

2 Direct materials; direct labour; indirect materials; indirect labour; opening work-in-progress; closing work-in-progress

3 Raw materials

4 (a) Income; expenditure; balance (b) Accumulated (c) Net profit/(loss); financial year (d) Central; local; quasi

Chapter 8

1 (a) False (b) False (c) True (d) False (e) True (f) False

2 (a) Eight (b) Down (c) Up (d) Net cash inflow

Chapter 9

1 (a) True (b) True (c) True

2 (a) 100 (b) Return on capital employed (c) Credit sales (d) Cost of goods sold (e) Ordinary dividends (f) Long-term loans

3 (a) High (b) Low (c) High (depends upon the business) (d) High (e) Neither

Chapter 10

1 Legislation; professional requirements; stock exchange requirements

2 Companies Act 1985

3 (a) Accounting Standards Committee (b) Statement of Standard Accounting Practice (c) Financial Reporting Council (d) Accounting Standards Board (e) Financial Reporting Standard

4 The true and fair view rule

Chapter 11

1 The accounts

2 Profit and loss account; balance sheet; cash flow statement; notes to the accounts

3 Auditors' report; directors' report; statement of total recognized gains and losses; statement of directors' responsibilities for the accounts; chairman's report

4 Chairman's report

Chapter 12

1 (a) False (b) False (c) True (d) False

2 (a) Historic cost accounting (b) Summary Financial Statement (c) Financial Reporting Standard for Smaller Enterprises (d) International Accounting Standards (e) Financial Accounting Standards Board

3 Corporate governance

4 None

Chapter 13

1 (a) External (b) Management (c) Effectively; efficiently (d) Control (e) Planning

2 None

3 Out-of-date; not sufficiently detailed

4 Planning; control; cost accounting; decision making; financial management; auditing

5 (a) False (b) False (c) False (d) False (e) False

Chapter 14

1 (a) Direct cost (b) Indirect; indirect; indirect (c) Raw materials (d) Wages (or salaries)

2 Budgeted (or standard)

3 Unit cost; first-in, first-out; continuous weighted average; standard cost

4 (a) True (b) True (c) True (d) False (e) True (f) False

5 Direct labour hours; direct labour cost; machine hours

Chapter 15

1 (a) Plan (b) Budgetary control (c) Flexible

2 (b) A year

3 Master budget

4 (a) Sales budget (b) Estimate of total expenditure

Chapter 16

1 A predetermined measurable quantity set in defined conditions

2 (a) Set up a unit responsible for implementing it (b) Select an appropriate standard costing period (c) Determine the type of standard to be adopted (d) Obtain the information necessary to calculate the standards

3 Efficiency; capacity; production volume

4 (a) Direct material total (b) Direct labour rate (c) Variable production overhead efficiency (d) Fixed production overhead capacity (e) Selling price

Chapter 17

1 (a) Fixed cost (b) Variable costs

2 (a) Variable cost of sales (b) Profit/(loss) (c) Contribution – fixed costs (d) Contribution per unit (e) Margin of safety (in sales value terms)

3 Limiting (or key) factor

Chapter 18

1 (a) Affected (b) Opportunity (c) Fixed (d) Relevant (e) Sunk

2 (a) When a part or the whole of an entity permanently ceases to exist
   (b) When a part of the whole of an entity is temporarily closed
   (c) Whether to manufacture a unit internally or purchase it from an external supplier
   (d) The price charged by an outside supplier
   (e) The price charged for the supply of goods from one segment within an entity to another segment within the same entity
   (f) An order that is not normally part of the entity's sales and one that is not likely to be repeated

3 (a) False (b) True (c) False (d) False (e) False (f) True

Chapter 19

1 (a) Capital investment appraisal (b) Cost; capital (c) Discounted cash flow

2 Payback; discounted payback; accounting rate of return; net present value; internal rate of return

3 Bank overdraft; bank loan; hire purchase; factoring; debenture loans; issue of shares

Chapter 20

1 (a) Activity based costing (b) Just-in-time (c) Strategic management accounting (d) Throughput accounting (e) Total quality management

2 A collection of costs identifiable with similar activities

3 Number of material requisitions

4 (a) True (b) True (c) True (d) False (e) False

Answers to practice questions

Chapter 1   1.4   Accountants collect a great deal of information about an entity's activities and then translate it into monetary terms – a language that everyone understands. The information that is collected can help non-accountants do their job more effectively because it provides them with better guidance upon which to take decisions. Any eventual decision is still theirs. Futhermore, all managers must be aware of the statutory accounting obligations to which their organization has to adhere if they are to avoid taking part in unlawful acts.

1.5   (1) To collect and store detailed information about an entity's activities. (2) To abstract and summarize information in the most effective way for the requirements of a specified user or group of users.

1.6   None. The preparation of management accounts is for the entity to decide if it believes that they serve a useful purpose.

1.8   Statutory obligations are contained in the Companies Act 1985. In addition, listed companies have to abide by certain Stock Exchange requirements, and qualified accountants are also bound by a great many mandatory professional requirements.

Chapter 2   2.4   Matching.
Historic cost.
Quantitative.
Periodicity.
Prudence.
Going-concern.

2.5   Relevance.
Entity.
Consistency.
Materiality.
Historic cost.
Realization.

2.6   Entity.
Objectivity.
Periodicity.
Prudence.
Dual aspect.
Realization.

Chapter 3 3.4 Adam's books of account:

Account

Debit	*Credit*
Cash	Capital
Purchases	Cash
Van	Cash
Rent	Cash
Cash	Sales
Office machinery	Cash

3.5 Brown's books of account:

Account

Debit	*Credit*
Bank	Cash
Cash	Sales
Purchases	Bank
Office expenses	Cash
Bank	Sales
Motor car	Bank

3.10 Ivan's ledger accounts:

Cash Account

		£			£
1.9.00	Capital	10 000	2.9.00	Bank	8 000
12.9.00	Cash	3 000	3.9.00	Purchases	1 000

Capital Account

		£			£
			1.9.00	Cash	10 000

Bank Account

		£			£
2.9.00	Cash	8 000	20.9.00	Roy	6 000
30.9.00	Norman	2 000			

Purchases Account

		£			£
3.9.00	Cash	1 000			
10.9.00	Roy	6 000			

Roy's Account

		£			£
20.9.00	Bank	6 000	10.9.00	Purchases	6 000

Sales Account

		£			£
			12.9.00	Cash	3 000
			15.9.00	Norman	4 000

Norman

		£			£
15.9.00	Sales	4 000	30.9.00	Bank	2 000

3.11 Jones's ledger accounts:

Bank Account

		£			£
1.10.01	Capital	20 000	10.10.01	Petty cash	1 000
			25.10.01	Lang	5 000
			29.10.01	Green	10 000

Capital Account

		£			£
			1.10.01	Bank	20 000

Van Account

		£		£
2.10.01	Lang	5 000		

Lang's Account

		£			£
25.10.01	Bank	5 000	2.10.01	Van	5 000

Purchases Account

		£		£
6.10.01	Green	15 000		
20.10.01	Cash	3 000		

Green's Account

		£			£
28.10.01	Discounts received	500	6.10.01	Purchases	15 000
29.10.01	Bank	10 000			

Petty Cash Account

		£			£
10.10.01	Bank	1 000	22.10.01	Miscellaneous expenses	500

Sales

		£			£
			14.10.01	Haddock	6 000
			18.10.01	Cash	5 000

Haddock

		£			£
14.10.01	Sales	6 000	20.10.01	Discounts allowed	600
			31.10.01	Cash	5 400

Cash Account

		£			£
18.10.01	Sales	5 000	20.10.01	Purchases	3 000
31.10.01	Haddock	5 400			

Miscellaneous Expenses

		£		£
22.10.01	Petty cash	500		

Discounts Received Account

		£			£
			28.10.01	Green	500

Discounts Allowed Account

		£		£
30.10.01	Haddock	600		

3.13 (a), (b) and (c) Pat's ledger accounts:

Cash Account

		£			£
1.12.03	Capital	10 000	24.12.03	Office expenses	5 000
29.12.03	Fog	4 000	31.12.03	Grass	6 000
29.12.03	Mist	6 000	31.12.03	Seed	8 000
			31.12.03	Balance c/d	1 000
		20 000			20 000
1.1.04	Balance b/d	1 000			

Capital Account

		£			£
			1.12.03	Cash	10 000

Purchases Account

		£			£
2.12.03	Grass	6 000			
2.12.03	Seed	7 000			
15.12.03	Grass	3 000			
15.12.03	Seed	4 000	31.12.03	Balance c/d	20 000
		20 000			20 000
1.01.04	Balance b/d	20 000			

Grass's Account

		£			£
12.12.03	Purchases returned	1 000	2.12.03	Purchases	6 000
31.12.03	Cash	6 000	15.12.03	Purchases	3 000
31.12.03	Balance c/d	2 000			
		9 000			9 000
			1.1.04	Balance b/d	2 000

Seed's Account

		£			£
12.12.03	Purchases returned	2 000	2.12.03	Purchases	7 000
31.12.03	Cash	8 000	15.12.03	Purchases	4 000
31.12.03	Balance c/d	1 000			
		11 000			11 000
			1.1.04	Balance b/d	1 000

Sales Account

		£			£
			10.12.03	Fog	3 000
			10.12.03	Mist	4 000
			20.12.03	Fog	2 000
31.12.03	Balance c/d	12 000	20.12.03	Mist	3 000
		12 000			12 000
			1.1.04	Balance b/d	12 000

Fog's Account

		£			£
10.12.03	Sales	3 000	29.12.03	Cash	4 000
20.12.03	Sales	2 000	31.12.03	Balance c/d	1 000
		5 000			5 000
1.1.04	Balance b/d	1 000			

Mist's Account

		£			£
10.12.03	Sales	4 000	29.12.03	Cash	6 000
20.12.03	Sales	3 000	31.12.03	Balance c/d	1 000
		7 000			7 000
1.1.04	Balance b/d	1 000			

Purchases Returned Account

		£			£
			12.12.03	Grass	1 000
31.12.03	Balance c/d	3 000	12.12.03	Seed	2 000
		3 000			3 000
			1.1.04	Balance b/d	3 000

Office Expenses Account

		£		£
24.12.03	Cash	5 000		

Tutorial note

It is unnecessary to balance off an account and bring down the balance if there is only a single entry in it.

3.13 (d) Pat's trial balance:

PAT
Trial Balance at 31 December 2003

	£ Dr	£ Cr
Cash	1 000	
Capital		10 000
Purchases	20 000	
Grass		2 000
Seed		1 000
Sales		12 000
Fog	1 000	
Mist	1 000	
Purchases returned		3 000
Office expenses	5 000	
	28 000	28 000

3.14 (a) Vale's books of account:

Bank Account

		£			£
1.1.03	Balance b/d	5 000	31.12.03	Dodd	29 000
31.12.03	Fish	45 000	31.12.03	Delivery van	12 000
31.12.03	Cash	3 000	31.12.03	Balance c/d	12 000
		53 000			53 000
1.1.04	Balance b/d	12 000			

Capital Account

		£			£
			1.1.03	Balance b/d	20 000

Cash Account

		£			£
1.1.03	Balance b/d	1 000	31.12.03	Purchases	15 000
31.12.03	Sales	20 000	31.12.03	Office expenses	9 000
31.12.03	Fish	7 000	31.12.03	Bank	3 000
			31.12.03	Balance c/d	1 000
		28 000			28 000
1.1.04	Balance b/d	1 000			

Dodd's Account

		£			£
31.12.03	Bank	29 000	1.1.03	Balance b/d	2 000
31.12.03	Balance c/d	3 000	31.12.03	Purchases	30 000
		32 000			32 000
			1.1.04	Balance b/d	3 000

Fish's Account

	£		£
1.1.03 Balance b/d	6 000	31.12.03 Bank	45 000
31.12.03 Sales	50 000	31.12.03 Cash	7 000
		31.12.03 Balance c/d	4 000
	56 000		56 000
1.1.04 Balance b/d	4 000		

Furniture Account

	£		£
1.1.03 Balance b/d	10 000		

Purchases Account

	£		£
31.12.03 Dodd	30 000		
31.12.03 Cash	15 000	31.12.03 Balance c/d	45 000
	45 000		45 000
1.1.04 Balance b/d	45 000		

Sales Account

	£		£
		31.12.03 Cash	20 000
31.12.03 Balance c/d	70 000	31.12.03 Fish	50 000
	70 000		70 000
		1.1.04 Balance b/d	70 000

Office Expenses Account

	£		£
31.12.03 Cash	9 000		

Delivery Van Account

	£		£
31.12.03 Bank	12 000		

3.14 (b) Vale's trial balance:

VALE
Trial balance at 31 December 2003

	Dr	Cr
	£	£
Bank	12 000	
Capital		20 000
Cash	1 000	
Dodd		3 000
Fish	4 000	
Furniture	10 000	
Purchases	45 000	
Sales		70 000
Office expenses	9 000	
Delivery van	12 000	
	93 000	93 000

Chapter 4   **4.4**   Ethel's accounts:

ETHEL
Trading, profit and loss account for the year to 31 January 2001

	£
Sales	35 000
Less: Purchases	20 000
Gross profit	15 000
Less: Expenses:	
Office expenses	11 000
Net profit	4 000

ETHEL
Balance sheet at 31 January 2001

Fixed assets	£	£
Premises		8 000
Current assets		
Debtors	6 000	
Cash	3 000	
	9 000	
Less: Current liabilities		
Creditors	3 000	6 000
		14 000
Financed by:		
Capital		
Balance at 1 February 2000		10 000
Net profit for the year		4 000
		14 000

4.5   Marion's accounts:

MARION
Trading, profit and loss account for the year to 28 February 2002

	£000	£000
Sales		400
Less: Purchases		200
Gross profit		200
Less: Expenses:		
Heat and light	10	
Miscellaneous expenses	25	
Wages and salaries	98	133
Net profit		67

MARION
Balance sheet at 28 February 2002

Fixed assets	£000	£000
Buildings		50
Current assets		
Debtors	30	
Bank	4	
Cash	2	
	36	
Less: Current liabilities		
Creditors	24	12
		62

MARION
Balance sheet at 28 February 2002

	£000	£000
Financed by:		
Capital		
Balance at 1 March 2001		50
Net profit for the year	67	
Less: Drawings	55	12
		62

Chapter 5   5.4   (a) Lathom's trading account:

LATHOM
Trading account for the year to 30 April 2004

	£	£
Sales		60 000
Less: Cost of goods sold:		
Opening stock	3 000	
Purchases	45 000	
	48 000	
Less: Closing stock	4 000	44 000
Gross profit		16 000

(b) The stock would be shown under current assets, normally as the first item.

5.6   Standish's accounts:

STANDISH
Trading, profit and loss account for the year to 31 May 2006

	£	£
Sales		79 000
Less: Cost of goods sold:		
Opening stock	7 000	
Purchases	52 000	
	59 000	
Less: Closing stock	12 000	47 000
Gross profit		32 000
Less: Expenses:		
Heating and lighting	1 500	
Miscellaneous	6 700	
Wages and salaries	17 800	26 000
Net profit		6 000

STANDISH
Balance sheet at 31 May 2006

	£	£
Fixed assets		
Furniture and fittings		8 000
Current assets		
Stock	12 000	
Debtors	6 000	
Cash	1 200	
	19 200	
Less: *Current liabilities*		
Creditors	4 300	14 900
		22 900
Financed by:		
Capital		
Balance at 1 June 2005		22 400
Net profit for the year	6 000	
Less: Drawings	5 500	500
		22 900

5.9 Pine's accounts:

PINE
Trading, profit and loss account for the year to 30 September 2002

	£	£
Sales		40 000
Less: Cost of goods sold:		
Purchases	21 000	
Less: Closing stock	3 000	18 000
Gross profit		22 000
Less: Expenses:		
Depreciation: furniture (15% × £8 000)	1 200	
General expenses	14 000	
Insurance (£2 000 − 200)	1 800	
Telephone (£1 500 + 500)	2 000	19 000
Net profit		3 000

PINE
Balance sheet at 30 September 2002

	£	£	£
Fixed assets			
Furniture			8 000
Less: Depreciation			1 200
			6 800
Current assets			
Stock		3 000	
Debtors		5 000	
Prepayments		200	
Cash		400	
	c/f	8 600	6 800

PINE
Balance sheet at 30 September 2002

	£	£	£
		b/f 8 600	6 800
Less: Current liabilities			
Creditors	5 900		
Accrual	500	6 400	2 200
			9 000
Financed by:			
Capital			
At 1 October 2001			6 000
Net profit for the year			3 000
			9 000

Chapter 6   6.4   Margo Ltd's accounts:

MARGO LIMITED
Profit and loss account for the year to 31 January 2001

	£000
Profit for the financial year	10
Tax on profit	3
Profit after tax	7
Proposed dividend (10p × £50)	5
Retained profit for the year	2

MARGO LIMITED
Balance sheet at 31 January 2001

	£000	£000	£000
Fixed assets			
Plant and equipment at cost			70
Less: Accumulated depreciation			25
			45
Current assets			
Stocks		17	
Trade debtors		20	
Cash at bank and in hand		5	
		42	
Less: Current liabilities			
Trade creditors	12		
Taxation	3		
Proposed dividend	5	20	22
			67

Capital and reserves	*Authorized*	*Issued and fully paid*
	£000	£000
Share capital (ordinary shares of £1 each)	75	50
Profit and loss account (£15 + 2)		17
		67

6.5   Harry Ltd's accounts:

HARRY LIMITED

Profit and loss account for the year to 28 February 2002

	£000	£000
Gross profit for the year		150
Administration expenses [£65 + (10% × £60)]	71	
Distribution costs	15	86
Profit for the year		64
Taxation		24
Profit after tax		40
Dividends: Ordinary proposed	20	
Preference paid	6	26
Retained profit for the year		14

HARRY LIMITED

Balance sheet at 28 February 2002

	£000	£000	£000
Fixed assets			
Furniture and equipment at cost			60
Less: Accumulated depreciation			42
			18
Current assets			
Stocks		130	
Trade debtors		135	
Cash at bank and in hand		10	
		275	
Less: Current liabilities			
Trade creditors	25		
Taxation	24		
Proposed dividend	20	69	206
			224

Capital and reserves	*Authorized, issued and fully paid* £000
Ordinary shares of £1 each	100
Cumulative 15% preference shares of £1 each	40
	140
Share premium account	20
Profit and loss account (£50 + 14)	64
	224

6.6 Jim Ltd's accounts:

JIM LIMITED
Trading and profit and loss account for the year to 31 March 2003

	£000	£000	£000
Sales			270
Less: Cost of goods sold:			
Opening stock		16	
Purchases		124	
		140	
Less: Closing stock		14	126
Gross profit			144
Less: Expenses:			
Advertising		3	
Depreciation: furniture and fittings (15% × £20)	3		
vehicles (25% × £40)	10	13	
Directors' fees		6	
Rent and rates		10	
Telephone and stationery		5	
Travelling		2	
Wages and salaries		24	63
Net profit			81
Corporation tax			25
Net profit after tax			56
Proposed dividend			28
Retained profit for the year			28

JIM LIMITED
Balance sheet at 31 March 2003

	Cost	Depreciation	Net book value
	£000	£000	£000
Fixed assets			
Vehicles	40	20	20
Furniture and fittings	20	12	8
	60	32	28
Current assets			
Stocks		14	
Debtors		118	
Bank		11	
		143	
Less: *Current liabilities*			
Creditors	12		
Taxation	25		
Proposed dividend	28	65	78
			106

	Authorized	*Issued and fully paid*
	£000	£000
Capital and reserves		
Ordinary shares of £1 each	100	70
Profit and loss account (£8 + 28)		36
		106

Chapter 7   7.4   Megg's accounts:

MEGG

Manufacturing account for the year to 31 January 2001

	£000	£000
Direct materials:		
Stock at 1 February 2000	10	
Purchases	34	
	44	
Less: Stock at 31 January 2001	12	
Materials consumed		32
Direct wages		65
Prime cost		97
Factory overhead expenses:		
Administration	27	
Heat and light	9	
Indirect wages	13	49
		146
Work-in-progress at 1 February 2000	17	
Less: Work-in-progress at 31 January 2001	14	3
Manufacturing cost of goods produced		149

7.5   Moor's accounts:

MOOR

Manufacturing account for the year to 28 February 2002

	£	£
Direct materials:		
Stock at 1 March 2001	13 000	
Purchases	127 500	
	140 500	
Less: Stock at 28 February 2002	15 500	125 000
Direct wages		50 000
Prime cost		175 000
Factory overheads		27 700
		202 700
Work-in-progress at 1 March 2001	8 400	
Less: Work-in-progress at 28 February 2002	6 300	2 100
Manufacturing cost of goods produced		204 800

Chapter 8   8.4   Dennis Ltd's accounts:

DENNIS LIMITED
Cash flow statement for the year ended 31 January 2002

	£000	£000
Net cash inflow from operating activities		4
Capital expenditure		
Payments to acquire tangible fixed assets		(100)
		(96)
Management of liquid resource and financing		
Issue of ordinary share capital		100
Increase in cash		4

Reconciliation of operating profit to net cash inflow from operating activities

	£000
Operating profit (£60 – 26)	34
Increase in stocks	(20)
Increase in debtors	(50)
Increase in creditors	40
Net cash inflow from operating activities	4

8.5   Frank Ltd's accounts:

FRANK LIMITED
Cash flow statement for the year ended 28 February 2002

	£000	£000
Net cash inflow from operating activities		70
Management of liquid resources and financing		
Issue of debenture loan		60
Purchase of investments		(100)
Increase in cash		30

Reconciliation of operating profit to net cash inflow from operating activities

	£000
Operating profit (£40 – 30)	10
Depreciation charges	20
Increase in stocks	(30)
Decrease in debtors	110
Decrease in creditors	(40)
Net cash inflow from operating activities	70

No details of debenture interest were given in the question.

Reconciliation of net cash flow to movement in net debt

	£000	£000
Increase in cash in the period	30	
Cash inflow from increase in debt	(60)	(30)
Net debt at 1.3.01		(20)
Net debt at 28.2.02		(50)

Analysis of changes in net debt

	At 1.3.01	Cash flows	At 28.2.02
	£000	£000	£000
Cash at bank	(20)	30	10
Debt due after 1 year	–	(60)	(60)
Total	(20)	(30)	(50)

Chapter 9   9.4   BETTY

Accounting ratios year to 31 January 2001:

1 Gross profit ratio:

$$\frac{\text{Gross profit}}{\text{Total sales revenue}} \times 100 = \frac{30}{100} \times 100 = \underline{\underline{30\%}}$$

2 Net profit ratio:

$$\frac{\text{Net profit}}{\text{Sales}} \times 100 = \frac{14}{100} \times 100 = \underline{\underline{14\%}}$$

3 Return on capital employed:

$$\frac{\text{Net profit}}{\text{Average capital}} \times 100 = \frac{14}{\frac{1}{2}(40 + 48)} \times 100 = \underline{\underline{31.8\%}}$$

$$or \quad \frac{\text{Net profit}}{\text{Capital}} \times 100 = \frac{14}{48} \times 100 = \underline{\underline{29.2\%}}$$

4 Current ratio:

$$\frac{\text{Current assets}}{\text{Current liabilities}} = \frac{25}{6} = \underline{\underline{4.2 \text{ to } 1}}$$

5 Acid test:

$$\frac{\text{Current assets} - \text{stock}}{\text{Current liabilities}} = \frac{25 - 10}{6} = \underline{\underline{2.5 \text{ to } 1}}$$

6 Stock turnover:

$$\frac{\text{Cost of goods sold}}{\text{Average stock}} = \frac{70}{\frac{1}{2}(15 + 10)} = \underline{\underline{5.6 \text{ times}}}$$

7 Debtor collection period:

$$\frac{\text{Trade debtors}}{\text{Credit sales}} \times 365 = \frac{12}{100} \times 365 = \underline{\underline{44 \text{ days}}} \text{ (rounded up)}$$

9.5   JAMES LIMITED

Accounting ratios year to 28 February 2002:

1 Return on capital employed:

$$\frac{\text{Net profit before taxation and dividends}}{\text{Average shareholders' funds}} \times 100 = \frac{90}{\frac{1}{2}(600 + 620)} \times 100 = \underline{\underline{14.8\%}}$$

$$or \quad \frac{\text{Net profit before taxation and dividends}}{\text{Shareholders' funds}} \times 100 = \frac{90}{620} \times 100 = \underline{\underline{14.5\%}}$$

2 Gross profit:

$$\frac{\text{Gross profit}}{\text{Sales}} \times 100 = \frac{600}{1200} \times 100 = \underline{\underline{50\%}}$$

3 Mark-up:

$$\frac{\text{Gross profit}}{\text{Cost of goods sold}} \times 100 = \frac{600}{600} \times 100 = \underline{\underline{100\%}}$$

4 Net profit:

$$\frac{\text{Net profit before taxation and dividends}}{\text{Sales}} \times 100 = \frac{90}{1200} \times 100 = \underline{\underline{7.5\%}}$$

5 Acid test:

$$\frac{\text{Current assets} - \text{stock}}{\text{Current liabilities}} = \frac{275 - 75}{240} = \underline{\underline{0.83 \text{ to } 1}}$$

6 Fixed assets turnover:

$$\frac{\text{Sales}}{\text{Fixed assets (NBV)}} = \frac{1200}{685} = \underline{\underline{1.75 \text{ times}}}$$

7 Debtor collection period:

$$\frac{\text{Trade debtors}}{\text{Credit sales}} \times 365 = \frac{200}{1200} \times 365 = \underline{\underline{61 \text{ days}}} \text{ (rounded up)}$$

8 Capital gearing:

$$\frac{\text{Long-term loans}}{\text{Shareholders' funds and long-term loans}} \times 100 = \frac{100}{720} \times 100 = \underline{\underline{13.9\%}}$$

Chapter 13

13.4 The main function of *accounting* is to collect quantifiable data, translate it into monetary terms, store the information, and extract and summarize it in a format convenient for those parties who require such information.

Financial accounting and management accounting are two important branches of accounting. The main difference between them is that financial accounting specializes in supplying information to parties *external* to an entity, such as shareholders or governmental departments. Management accounting information is mainly directed at the supply of information to parties *internal* to an entity, such as the entity's directors and managers.

13.5 A management accountant employed by a large manufacturing entity will be involved in the collecting and storing of data (largely, although not exclusively, of a financial nature) and the supply of information to management for planning, control and decision-making purposes. Increasingly, a management accountant is seen to be an integral member of an entity's management team responsible for advice on all financial matters.

Depending upon his or her seniority, the management accountant may be involved in some routine and basic duties such as the processing of data and the calculation of product costs and the valuation of stocks. At a more senior level, the role may be much more concerned with advising on the financial impact of a wide variety of managerial decisions, such as whether to close down a product line or determining the selling price of a new product.

Chapter 14   14.6 Charge to production

1   FIFO: £
     1000 units   @ £20 =   20 000
      250 units   @ £25 =   6 250
     Charge to production   26 250

2   Continuous weighted average:

Date	Units		Value
			£
1.1.01	1 000	@ £20	20 000
15.1.01	500	@ £25	12 500
	1 500		32 500

$$\text{Average} = \frac{£32\,500}{1\,500} = £21.67$$

Charge to production on 31.1.01 = 1 250 × £21.67 = £27 088

14.7 Value of closing stock

MATERIAL ST 2

	Stock	Units	Total stock value	Average unit price
			£	£
1.2.02	Opening	500	500	1.00
10.2.02	Receipts	200	220	
		700	720	1.03
12.2.02	Receipts	100	112	
		800	832	1.04
17.2.02	Issues	(400)	(416)	
25.2.02	Receipts	300	345	
		700	761	1.09
27.2.02	Issues	(250)	(273)	
28.0.02	Closing stock	450	488	

14.11 Scar Ltd's overhead

SCAR LIMITED
Overhead apportionment January 2001:

		Production Department		Service Department
		A	B	
		£000	£000	£000
Allocated expenses	c/f	65	35	50

		Production Department		Service Department
		A	B	
		£000	£000	£000
	b/f	65	35	50
Apportionment of service department's expenses in the ratio 60 : 40		30	20	(50)
Overhead to be charged		95	55	–

14.12 Bank Ltd's overhead:

BANK LIMITED
Assembly department – overhead absorption methods:
1 Specific units:

$$\frac{\text{Total cost centre overhead}}{\text{Number of units}} = \frac{£250\,000}{50\,000} = \underline{\underline{£5 \text{ per unit}}}$$

2 Direct materials:

$$\frac{\text{Total cost centre overhead}}{\text{Direct materials}} \times 100 = \frac{£250\,000}{500\,000} \times 100 = 50\%$$

Therefore 50% of £8 = $\underline{\underline{£4 \text{ per unit}}}$

3 Direct labour:

$$\frac{\text{Total cost centre overhead}}{\text{Direct labour}} \times 100 = \frac{£250\,000}{1\,000\,000} \times 100 = 25\%$$

Therefore 25% of £30 = $\underline{\underline{£7.50 \text{ per unit}}}$

4 Prime cost:

$$\frac{\text{Total cost centre overhead}}{\text{Prime cost}} \times 100 = \frac{£250\,000}{1\,530\,000} \times 100 = 16.34\%$$

Therefore 16.34% of £40 = $\underline{\underline{£6.54 \text{ per unit}}}$

5 Direct labour hours:

$$\frac{\text{Total cost centre overhead}}{\text{Direct labour hours}} = \frac{£250\,000}{100\,000} = £2.50 \text{ per direct labour hour}$$

Therefore £2.50 of 3.5 DLH = $\underline{\underline{£8.75 \text{ per unit}}}$

6 Machine hours:

$$\frac{\text{Total cost centre overhead}}{\text{Machine hours}} = \frac{£250\,000}{25\,000} = £10 \text{ per machine hour}$$

Therefore £10 of 0.75 = $\underline{\underline{£7.50 \text{ per unit}}}$

Chapter 15   15.5 Direct labour cost budget for Tom Ltd.

TOM LIMITED

1 *Direct materials usage budget:*

Month	30.4.04	31.5.04	30.6.04	31.7.04	31.8.04	30.9.04	*Six months to 30.9.04*
				Number of units			
Component:							
A6 (2 units for X)	280	560	1 400	760	600	480	4 080
B9 (3 units for X)	420	840	2 100	1 140	900	720	6 120

2 *Direct materials purchase budget:*

Component A6							
Material usage (as above)	280	560	1 400	760	600	480	4 080
Add: Desired closing stock	110	220	560	300	240	200	200
	390	780	1 960	1 060	840	680	4 280
Less: Opening stock	100	110	220	560	300	240	100
Purchases (units) ×	290	670	1 740	500	540	440	4 180
Price per unit =	£5	£5	£5	£5	£5	£5	£5
Total purchases	£1 450	£3 350	£8 700	£2 500	£2 700	£2 200	£20 900

Component B9							
Material usage (as above)	420	840	2 100	1 140	900	720	6 120
Add: Desired closing stock	250	630	340	300	200	180	180
	670	1 470	2 440	1 440	1 100	900	6 300
Less: Opening stock	200	250	630	340	300	200	200
Purchases (units)	470	1 220	1 810	1 100	800	700	6 100
Price per unit	£10	£10	£10	£10	£10	£10	£10
Total purchases	£4 700	£12 200	£18 100	£11 000	£8 000	£7 000	£61 000

15.6 Direct labour budget for Don Ltd.

DON LIMITED

Direct labour cost budget:

Grade:	30.6.05	31.7.05	31.8.05	*Three months to 31.8.05*
		Quarter		
Production (units) ×	600	700	650	1 950
Direct labour hours per unit =	3	3	3	3
Total direct labour hours	1 800	2 100	1 950	5 850
Budgeted rate per hour (£) ×	4	4	4	4
Production cost (£) =	7 200	8 400	7 800	23 400
Finishing (units)	600	700	650	1 950
Direct labour hours per unit ×	2	2	2	2
Total direct labour hours =	1 200	1 400	1 300	3 900
Budgeted rate per hour (£) ×	8	8	8	8
Finishing cost (£) =	9 600	11 200	10 400	31 200
Total budgeted direct labour cost (£)	16 800	19 600	18 200	54 600

Chapter 16   16.4   Variances for X Ltd

1   Direct materials total variance: £
    Actual price per unit × actual quantity = £12 × 6 units   72
    Less: Standard price per unit × standard quantity
            for actual production = £10 × 5 units   50
                                                                               22   (A)

2   Direct materials price variance:
    (Actual price – standard price) × actual quantity
    = (£12 – 10) × 6 units   £12   (A)

3   Direct materials usage variance:
    (Actual quantity – standard quantity) × standard
            price = (6 – 5 units) × £10   £10   (A)

16.6   Variances for Bruce Ltd

1   Direct labour total variance: £
    Actual hours × actual hourly rate = 1000 hrs × £6.50   6 500
    Less: Standard hours for actual production ×
            standard hourly rate = 900 hrs × £6.00   5 400
                                                                            £1 100   (A)

2   Direct labour rate variance:
    (Actual hourly – standard hourly rate)
            × actual hours = (£6.50 – 6.00) × 1000 hrs   £500   (A)

3   Direct labour efficiency variance:
    (Actual hours – standard hours for actual production)
            × standard hourly rate = (1000 hrs – 900) × £6.00   £600   (A)

16.8   Overhead variances for Anthea Ltd

1   Fixed production overhead total variance: £
    Actual fixed overhead   150 000
    Less: Standard hours of production × fixed
            production overhead absorption rate = (8000 hrs × £15)   120 000
                                                                           £30 000   (A)

2   Fixed production overhead expenditure variance:
    Actual fixed overhead – budgeted fixed overhead =
            (£150 000 – 135 000)   £15 000   (A)

3   Fixed production overhead volume variance:
    Budgeted fixed overhead – (standard hours of
            production × fixed production overhead
            absorption rate) = [£135 000 – (8000 × £15)]   £15 000   (A)

4   Fixed production overhead capacity variance:
    Budgeted fixed overhead – (actual hours worked
            × fixed production overhead absorption rate)
            = [£135 000 – (10 000 hrs × £15)]   £15 000   (F)

5   Fixed production overhead efficiency variance:
    Actual hours worked – standard hours of production
            × fixed production overhead absorption rate
            = [(10 000 hrs – 8000) × £15]   £30 000   (A)

16.9 Performance measures for Anthea Ltd

Performance measures:

1 Efficiency ratio:
$$\frac{\text{SHP}}{\text{Actual hours}} \times 100 = \frac{800}{10\,000} \times 100 = \underline{\underline{80\%}}$$

2 Capacity ratio:
$$\frac{\text{Actual hours}}{\text{Budgeted hours*}} \times 100 = \frac{10\,000}{9000} \times 100 = \underline{\underline{111.1\%}}$$

$$*\frac{135\,000}{15}$$

3 Production volume ratio:
$$\frac{\text{SHP}}{\text{Budgeted hours}} \times 100 = \frac{8000}{9000} \times 100 = \underline{\underline{88.9\%}}$$

16.12 Selling price variance for Milton Ltd

1 Selling price variance:
Actual quantity × (actual selling price per unit – budgeted selling price per unit) = [9000 units × (£11* – 10)] = £9000 (F)

$$*\frac{99\,000}{9000}$$

2 Sales volume profit variance:
(Actual quantity – budgeted quantity) × standard profit = (9000 units – 10 000) × £3   £3000 (A)

3 Sales variances = £9000 (F) + 3000 (A)   =   £6000 (F)

Chapter 17   17.4 Contribution analysis for Pole Ltd

POLE LIMITED
Marginal cost statement for the year to 31 January 2002

	£000	£000
Sales		450
Less: Variable costs:		
Direct materials	60	
Direct wages	26	
Administration expenses: variable (£7 + 4)	11	
Research and development expenditure:		
variable (£15 + 5)	20	
Selling and distribution expenditure:		
variable (£4 + 9)	13	
		130
	c/f	320

POLE LIMITED

Marginal cost statement for the year to 31 January 2002

	£000		£000
		b/f	320
Contribution			
Less: Fixed costs:			
Administration expenses (£30 + 16)	46		
Materials: indirect	5		
Production overhead	40		
Research and development expenditure (£60 + 5)	65		
Selling and distribution expenditure (£80 + 21)	101		
Wages: indirect	13		270
Profit			50

17.5 Break-even chart for Giles Ltd.

GILES LIMITED

(a) (i) *Break-even point*:

In value terms:

$$\frac{\text{Fixed costs} \times \text{sales}}{\text{Contribution}} = \frac{£150}{(500 - 300)} \times 500 = \underline{\underline{£375\,000}}$$

In units:

	£
Selling price per unit (£500 ÷ 50)	10
Less: Variable cost per unit (£300 ÷ 50)	6
Contribution per unit	4

$$\frac{\text{Fixed costs}}{\text{Contribution per unit}} = \frac{£150\,000}{4} = \underline{\underline{37\,500 \text{ units}}}$$

(ii) *Margin of safety*:

In value terms:

$$\frac{\text{Profit} \times \text{sales}}{\text{Contribution}} = \frac{£50\,000 \times 500}{200} = \underline{\underline{£125\,000}}$$

In units:

$$\frac{\text{Profit}}{\text{Contribution per unit}} = \frac{£50\,000}{4} = \underline{\underline{12\,500 \text{ units}}}$$

(b) *Break-even chart*:

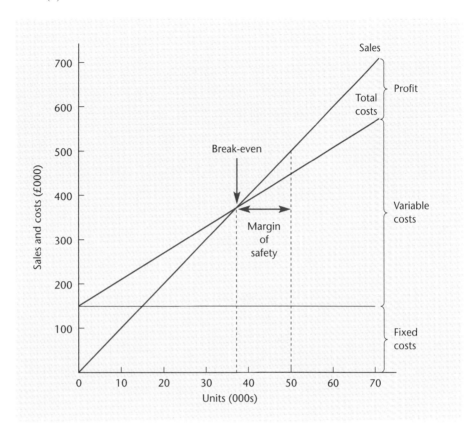

18.4 A special contract for Micro Ltd

Budgeted contribution per unit of limiting factor for the year:

$$\frac{£250\,000}{50\,000} = £5 \text{ per direct labour hour}$$

Contribution per unit of limiting factor for the special contract:

	£	£
Contract price		50 000
Less: Variable costs:		
Direct materials	10 000	
Direct labour	30 000	40 000
Contribution		10 000

Therefore contribution per unit of limiting factor:

$$\frac{£10\,000}{4000 \text{ DLH}} = £2.50 \text{ per direct labour hour}$$

Conclusion:
The special contract earns less contribution per unit of limiting factor than does the *average* of ordinary budgeted work. It may be profitable to accept the contract

if either it displaces less profitable work or surplus direct labour hours are available. A careful assessment should be undertaken to ascertain whether much more profitable work would be found than is the case with the contract if it will displace other more profitable contracts that could arise in the near future.

18.5 Contributions for Temple Ltd.

1 Calculation of the contribution per unit of limiting factor

(a) **Normal work**

	£
Sales	6 000
Direct materials (100 kilos)	700
Direct labour (200 hours)	3 000
Variable overhead	300
	4 000
Contribution	2 000

Contribution per unit of key factor:

$$\text{Direct materials: } \frac{£2000}{100 \text{ kilos}} = £20 \text{ per kilo}$$

$$\text{Direct labour: } \frac{£2000}{200 \text{ direct labour hours}} = £10 \text{ per direct labour hour}$$

(b) and (c) **Calculation of the contribution per unit of limiting factor for each of the proposed two new contracts:**

		CONTRACT 1	CONTRACT 2
		£000	£000
Contract price		1 000	2 100
Less: variable costs			
Direct materials		300	600
Direct labour		300	750
Variable overhead		100	250
		700	1 600
CONTRIBUTION		300	500

Contribution per unit of key factor:

		CONTRACT 1	CONTRACT 2
Direct materials		£300	£500
		50 kilos	100 kilos
	=	£6 per kilo	£5 per kilo
Direct labour		£300	£500
		10 DLH	25 DLH
	=	£30 per DLH	£20 per DLH

Summary of contribution per unit of limiting factor:

	Direct materials	Direct labour
	£	£
Normal work	20	10
Contract 1	6	5
Contract 2	30	20

2 Calculation of the total maximum contribution

Contract 1

If Contract 1 is accepted, it will earn a total contribution of £300 000. This will leave 150 000 kilos of direct material available for its normal work (200 000 kilos maximum available, less the 50 000 used on Contract 1). This means that 1 500 units of ordinary work could be undertaken (150 000 kilos divided by 100 kilos per unit).

However, Contract 1 will absorb 10 000 direct labour hours, leaving 90 000 DLH available (100 000 DLH less 10 000 DLH). As each unit of ordinary work uses 200 DLH, the maximum number of units that could be undertaken is 450 (90 000 DLH divided by 200 DLH). Thus the maximum number of units of ordinary work that could be undertaken if Contract 1 is accepted is 450 and NOT 1500 units if direct materials were the only limiting factor. As each unit makes a contribution of £2000, the total contribution would be £900 000 (450 units × £2000).

The total maximum contribution, if Contract 1 is accepted, is therefore, **£1 200 000** (£300 000 + 900 000).

Contract 2

If Contract 2 is accepted, only 100 000 kilos of direct materials will be available for ordinary work (200 000 kilos maximum available less 100 000 required for Contract 2). This means that only 1000 normal jobs could be undertaken (100 000 kilos divided by 100 kilos required per unit).

Contract 2 would absorb 25 000 direct labour hours, leaving 75 000 available for normal work (100 000 maximum DLH less the 25 000 DLH used by Contract 2). As each unit of normal work takes 200 hours, only 375 units could be made (75 000 DLH divided by 200 DLH per unit). Thus if this contract is accepted, 375 is the maximum number of normal jobs that could be undertaken. This would give a total contribution of £750 000 (375 units multiplied by £2000 of contribution per unit).

If Contract 2 is accepted, the total maximum contribution would be **£1 250 000**, i.e. Contract 2's contribution of £500 000 plus the contribution of £750 000 from the normal work.

The Decision

Accept Contract 2 because the maximum total contribution would be £1 250 000 compared with the £1 200 000 if Contract 1 was accepted.

Tutorial notes

1 The various cost relationships are assumed to remain unchanged at all levels of activity.
2 Fixed costs will not be affected irrespective of which contract is accepted.
3 The market for Temple's normal sales is assumed to be flexible.
4 Contract 2 will absorb one-half of the available direct materials and one-quarter of the available direct labour hours. Would the company want to commit such resources to work that may be uncertain and unreliable and that could have an adverse impact on its normal customers?

Chapter 19   19.5 Payback for Buchan Enterprises

(a) Payback period:

Year	Investment outlay £	Cash inflow £	Net cash flow £	Cumulative cash flow £
1	(50 000)	8 000	(42 000)	(42 000)
2	–	16 000	16 000	(26 000)
3	–	40 000	40 000	14 000
4	–	45 000	45 000	59 000
5	–	37 000	37 000	96 000

Net cash flow becomes positive in Year 3. Assuming the net cash flow accrues evenly, it becomes positive during August: $(26/40 \times 12) = 7.8$ months. Payback period therefore equals 2 years 7.8 months.

(b) Discounted payback period:

Year	Net cash flow £	Discount factor @ 12%	Discounted net cash flow £	Cumulative net cash flow £
0	(50 000)	1.0000	(50 000)	(50 000)
1	8 000	0.8929	7 143	(42 857)
2	16 000	0.7929	12 686	(30 171)
3	40 000	0.7118	28 472	(1 699)
4	45 000	0.6355	28 598	26 899
5	37 000	0.5674	20 994	47 893

Discounted net cash flow becomes positive in Year 4. Assuming the net cash flow accrues evenly throughout the year, it becomes positive in January $(1699/\ 28\ 598 \times 12 = 0.7)$. Discounted payback period therefore equals 4 years, 1 month. This value is in contrast with the payback method, where the net cash flow becomes positive in August of Year 3.

19.6 Lender Ltd's accounting rate of return

$$\text{Accounting rate of return (APR)} = \frac{\text{Average annual net profit after tax}}{\text{Cost of the investment}} \times 100\%$$

$$= \frac{\frac{1}{5}\ (£18\ 000 + 47\,000 + 65\,000 + 65\,000 + 30\,000)}{100\,000} \times 100\%$$

$$= \frac{45\,000}{100\,000} \times 100\%$$

$$= \underline{\underline{45\%}}$$

Note: Based on the average investment, the ARR

$$= \frac{£45\,000}{\frac{1}{2}\ (100\ 000 + 0)} \times 100\%$$

$$= \underline{\underline{90\%}}$$

19.7 Net present value for a Lockhart project

Net present value:

Year	Net cash flow £000	Discount factor @15%	Present value £000
1	800	0.8696	696
2	850	0.7561	643
3	830	0.6575	546
4	1 200	0.5718	686
5	700	0.4972	348
Total present value			2 919
Initial cost			2 500
Net present value			419

Index

Note: chapters are indicated by **bold** page references